P9-CQV-542

Growing Herbs
and Vegetables

TERRY AND MARK SILBER

Growing Herbs and Vegetables

FROM SEED TO HARVEST

Alfred A. Knopf NEW YORK 1999

This Is a Borzoi Book
Published by Alfred A. Knopf, Inc.

www.randomhouse.com

Library of Congress Cataloging-in-Publication Data
Silber, Mark.
Growing herbs and vegetables : from seed to harvest /
Terry and Mark Silber.—1st ed.
p.   cm.
Includes bibliographical references (p.   ) and index.
ISBN 0-394-57346-3 (alk. paper)
1. Herb gardening. 2. Vegetable gardening. 3. Herbs—Seeds.
4. Vegetables—Seeds.   I. Silber, Terry.   II. Title.
SB351.H5S54   1999
635—dc21   98-38189
CIP

Manufactured in the United States of America
First Edition

This book is dedicated to Aleksander and Cyla Silber
who have always managed to surround themselves
with a variety of exuberant plants.
Their ability to nurture life is evident
in everything that they grow.

Contents

Acknowledgments

WE WOULD LIKE to begin by expressing our appreciation for the people in our agricultural community. Many of our neighbors no longer farm as their ancestors did. Nonetheless, they are sympathetic toward horticultural endeavors and have always been encouraging of our efforts. As our gardens grew and as the farm became a more significant part of our lives in Maine, we have been supported by many other gardeners throughout the state. Visitors bring questions and advice. They come to purchase plants, and they also bring plants as gifts.

Members of the Cooperative Extension Agency have been very influential in our initial farming endeavors, most especially Charles Gould, an early and optimistic voice for gardening organically. We are also appreciative of the efforts of the Maine Organic Farmers and Gardeners Association for its work in support of agriculture and backyard gardening, and for the help offered by the organization's technical director, Dr. Eric Seidman.

The book has been a long time in the planning, and throughout that time we have called upon others in the agricultural community for information. Our thanks go to people at three Maine seed companies: Allen, Sterling, Lothrop; Johnny's Selected Seeds; and Pinetree Garden Seeds. We also appreciate the reading of our manuscript and useful comments by Dr. Lois Berg Stack, Professor of Horticulture at the University of Maine. State entomologists Richard Folsom and Dr. Clay Kirby were generous with information, as was Judy Grotenhuis at the National Seed Storage Laboratory at Fort Collins, Colorado.

Finally there are two people who deserve special thanks for their support all during this project. One is Cathy Lee, who has worked with us at Hedgehog Hill Farm for the past eighteen years. She has been a part of every aspect of the farm's development, in the greenhouses and in the gardens. She has carried much of the work load when writing was being done in the final stages of the book, always offering genuine support and interest in the project. And there is our editor, Jane Garrett, whose interest in the book allowed us to produce the kind of work we hope will be used by other people to benefit their gardening experiences. Jane, thank you for allowing us the time to shape this project into its final form. You are always patient and encouraging, and we have come to rely on you for the constructive responses that help us to do our best writing

Growing Herbs
and Vegetables

CHAPTER ONE

Getting Started

THE GARDENS AT Hedgehog Hill Farm are now home to more than five hundred species of plants. There are production areas for growing our annual supplies of vegetables, and special beds for the perennial food crops such as rhubarb and asparagus. There are production areas for annual crops of herbs, and gardens for dozens of varieties of flowering annuals that we use personally and commercially. The annuals are grown as bedding plants, for cut-flower gardens, and for ingredients to be used in potpourris. There are also thousands of plants, both annuals and perennials, planted for our dried-flower products. Then there are the sections of the gardens where we raise hundreds of species of perennials, some for selling, some for seed production, some for cutting fresh, and some to use in the various display beds located throughout the farm. Finally there is a growing area for fruit production and for a limited number of other nursery plants that are of interest ornamentally or commercially.

All of these gardens are our experimental station where we can observe plant performance, since we are constantly trying to grow and offer the best-quality plants we can for our location, for our personal gardens, and for our customers. It is a wonderful living laboratory where we can always justify trying more and more varieties. We have long given up on the notion of being reasonable in "keeping the numbers down." Neither of us can curb the other's enthusiasm for trying just one more new lavender or yet another variety of hot pepper.

Pots of Laurus nobilis, *or sweet bay, greet visitors to the farm when temperatures permit. During the winter months, these pots are brought into a greenhouse.*

When we look over the gardens in midsummer, we are greeted by acres of incredible diversity, texture, color, form, and literally hundreds of memories. There are the plants we received as gifts several decades ago. *Cimicifuga* came from Sandra; *Aconitum* came first from Glenn, misidentified as lupine, and then from Norm, correctly identified. Diego gave us one plant of *Filipendula rubra* 'Venusta' saying he knew we would like it. That one plant has spread to hundreds and is the source of all the cuttings we sell in our nursery. June mailed us a package of *Papaver rhoeas* seeds several years ago. Mollie gave us the breadseed poppy. Both poppies will probably still be self-seeding a generation from now.

The upper pasture, once used as a production garden for vegetables and perennial herbs, is now a grazing area for our three horses. They move along nibbling clover, timothy, and redtop, and pass over the volunteer plants of wild oregano, bee balm, chives, and tansy. One of our favorite natural gardens includes *Dicentra cucullaria* (small wild bleeding hearts or Dutchman's breeches) and *Matteuccia* (ostrich ferns, generous gifts from Jon).

Just outside the herb shop there is a very large tub planted with *Eucalyptus cinerea* which we have to prune back to size and haul inside the glass greenhouse every October. It was started from seeds we purchased from an Australian seed company many years ago. That purchase introduced us to a source for large numbers of eucalypts and made us aware there are hundreds of plants in that one genus. It's a genus of plants with incredible diversity in size and plant morphology.

It is winter as we write this section of the book. Our three old bay plants have also been hauled into the glass greenhouse. They live in wooden tubs requiring three people to lift them, and yet the tubs are already a bit too small for the ten-foot-tall plants. But more importantly, these luxurious old plants now have "offspring" that live on the farm. Two falls ago we noticed that the mature plants were setting buds. During their winter inside, the plant buds swelled and opened to reveal that we owned two males and a female bay. We did some hand-pollination, were assisted by insects living in the greenhouse, and by early spring of the following year we collected 150 plump, black, mature, seed-bearing fruits. Some of the seeds were planted immediately, some were stratified (stored in a moist cool environment) and the result was thirty healthy seedlings. It was a real thrill to witness and participate in the process.

All of this reminiscing is our way of reflecting on how far we have come from the neophyte gardeners who were literally led down the rows of our first kitchen garden by a couple of neighboring truck farmers. These neighbors guided us in how to hoe a furrow, drop seeds, thin plants, hill up rows of beans and corn, and even how to mature plants and save some of our seeds. It was a very rudimentary education, begun nearly thirty years ago. It was an education we have continued with real enthusiasm and one we hope will continue as long as we are here on the land.

Perhaps one of the most appealing aspects of gardening is the opportunity it provides all of us to teach ourselves at whatever pace we choose. For us, gardening has become an activity that constantly challenges us to observe more carefully, to rethink approaches, to read and discuss, to analyze, and, most of all, to always be delighted by discoveries. We remember clearly those early years when we couldn't keep any of the data straight. We tried to sort out what plants were annuals, what were biennials, what were perennials. Then we tried to figure out why some of the perennials didn't live very long and yet some had survived years of neglect when our homestead stood empty and abandoned before we purchased it.

It is probably accurate to say that we started our first garden with typical naïve enthusiasm. It is also important to add that our first teachers had us plant two acres as a kitchen garden and our initial yields were incredible. They were so incredible that we joined a farmers' market to get rid of some of our produce. At the same time we were still living in Boston, each of us involved in our urban careers. City people during weekdays, country people on the weekends, we lived this hectic mix for a full seven years.

At the end of those seven years, our gardens and the land in Maine won us over. Our first adventures with seeds and plants directed us into an area of physical and mental work so stimulating and satisfying that we packed our city belongings into a pickup truck twenty years ago and headed north to Sumner, Maine, where we have been farming full-time ever since.

But we digress. This reminiscing began as we thought of our initial attempts to grow plants and where the plants came from, where we bought and were given our first seeds. So let us begin this book with what we hope will be useful information on getting started.

Where to Find Seeds and Plants

THERE ARE BASICALLY two ways to purchase seeds and plant material. They may be bought locally, from a garden center, nursery, farmstand, farmers' market, even from seasonally designed sections of supermarkets and department and hardware stores. Seeds and plants may also be purchased through catalogues, which you have access to by mail, phone, fax, and through the Internet. Most gardeners will satisfy their need for plant material by shopping both locally and through the mail. Either method may fulfill your gardening needs, but before you decide where to shop, you need some very basic consumer guidance. Most importantly, you need to know what items are available and what varieties are most appropriate to your gardening interests and geographical area. Here are a few basic ideas that should give you ready access to that information.

Start your garden inquiries right next door or down the road, by asking for gardening information from your neighbors. If you are interested in gardening, then you have undoubtedly noticed where the best-looking gardens are located in your neighborhood. Or perhaps you drive by one or two splendid examples on your way to work. Don't be shy about stopping to ask a

ANY PHOTOGRAPH OF the production gardens at the farm will differ from year to year. Sometimes the cabbages are located in the middle of the acreage. Sometimes they are grown in the outside rows. The brilliant bands of color also tend to move around, as do the tea herbs, the cutting species, the vining crops, and the thousands of everlasting plants. We have sometimes had a bit of fun by interspersing our vegetables with different species of edible flowers or with culinary herbs. We have also paid attention to placing at the front of the garden those plants that need to be harvested frequently, perhaps even daily, locating plants like brussels sprouts or winter squashes at the far ends of the rows where they only need to be inspected from week to week and harvested at the end of the season.

The only thing that is consistent about the production gardens is that we try each year to relocate families of plants from one place to another and to design the garden so that there is biological and visual interest for those of us working in it and for visitors to the farm. We have often suggested to visiting gardeners that they introduce attractive vegetables into their annual flower beds or include annuals in the perennial borders. Sometimes this is received as an ordinary idea, meaning these gardeners have undoubtedly been doing just that for years. Sometimes the idea of mixing it up is received as a revolutionary notion. There are those gardeners who want a vegetable garden, an herb garden, a cutting garden, an annual border, a perennial garden, an alpine garden, a natural garden, and who knows whatever else, quite distinctly separated. To each his own. But we question if plants can and should be so strictly indexed and planted. Depending upon the reference works you use, some plants are classified as herbs in one and not another. Some annuals live over as perennials, or reseed with such vigor that they go on growing year after year in the same site. Some vegetables are so beautiful that they rival the visual appeal of the most desirable perennials.

Not only are there aesthetic arguments for interplanting different categories of plants, there is also strong evidence to suggest that the healthiest gardens are those with the greatest botanical diversity.

But perhaps the strongest argument of all is the need to make all of our garden spaces as stimulating as possible. We spend nearly seven days a week in our gardens, starting in March and April and continuing well into the fall when the last plants are set in for the winter, the bulbs are planted, and final seed collection takes place. It's a compelling reason to make our workplace as beautiful, as healthy, and as informative as possible.

The main production garden of herbs, vegetables, and flowers at Hedgehog Hill Farm.

few questions of experienced growers. For many of us, our gardens are an expression of one of our deepest passions, and we are usually more than willing to offer information and advice to anyone expressing a genuine interest. Start by making your questions specific enough to be answered. For example, ask where that grower buys seeds or plants, or what kind of tomatoes mature best in the area. If you find a willing mentor, you can proceed further by asking more general questions about suppliers, techniques, gardening problems. Chances are, in many cases you will be the happy recipient not only of good advice but of an occasional plant or package of favorite home-saved seeds.

If there are farmers' markets in your area, ask the growers to suggest varieties that work well for them. You will be surprised how responsive many of these growers will be, since you are asking them to talk about what they take pride in doing well. Local greenhouse growers and nurseries are also a good source of information. If they are successful, they have had to rely on repeat business; therefore they should be offering plants that are suited to the area climate. We will talk at length about evaluating greenhouse and nursery plants later in this chapter.

Next, find your local Cooperative Extension Agency and visit the offices to see what information is available. Usually these agencies will have some gardening pamphlets or regular mailings for which you can sign up. These agencies should also know about, and even be sponsoring, gardening workshops and programs. Such programs are often free or cost very little and are especially worthwhile for beginning gardeners, since the information will be specific to your region of the country. In addition, check out the adult education programs offered by area schools. Don't just rely on your local school district, but call for listings of adult education lectures and courses offered in neighboring towns.

Try to locate other area educational institutions for lectures and courses on gardening, including vocational schools, organic gardening organizations, community colleges, and state universities offering evening and weekend courses. On a number of occasions, we have given such classes in our own community and in communities as far away as thirty or forty miles. Programs can be one evening only, or last for several weeks; any of them will give you access to information and the opportunity to ask questions of experienced growers.

Take advantage of the periodicals and books at a good nearby library, bookstore, or newsstand, and look through as many magazines as you can find that deal with homes and gardens, country life, horticulture in general or specific areas of gardening, such as herb growing. Look at the issues of these magazines that come out late fall to midwinter, when seed companies and plant sellers are advertising their companies and offering copies of their mail-order catalogues. When we first came to our farm, we spent several days sending out postcards, coupons, and magazine bind-in cards requesting dozens of such gardening catalogues. Many seed and plant catalogues are free, and some cost anywhere from one to five dollars. (The cost is usually deducted from purchases made later.) These catalogues will be the best investment in time or money you can possibly make, because they will begin to show you how broad a selection you have in choosing seeds and plants. In your research, always look through local or regional magazines and send away for any seed or plant catalogues from companies in your area, as these companies usually specialize in plants that are best suited to your climate.

It is equally important to send away for catalogues from several of the largest nationally known companies. (They will be easily recognizable as you see their large full-color advertisements in one magazine after another.) These catalogues are often comprehensive gardening sources, with broad selections of seeds, plants, and gardening supplies. In addition, most of these catalogues will have lots of good photographic illustrations and cultural information and in all likelihood will turn out to be your best reference material. If you are interested in special types of gardens or plants, such as alpine plants, plants for naturalizing, or plants for water-saving gardens, then be on the lookout for companies that focus on these items.

If you are interested in obtaining seeds and plants of nonhybrid species, there are also companies and organizations that specialize in this area. Nonhybrid plants are also referred to as old-fashioned, heritage, heirloom, and open-pollinated species. Gardeners interested in propagating plants and saving seeds will want access to this information. See the box on page 251 in Chapter 7 about seed savers' exchanges.

In addition to the assortment of magazines that advertise seed and plant companies, there are many good regional and national publications with editorial material written especially for gardeners. The articles on seed companies and plant sources appear about the same time of year as the advertisements for mail-order catalogues. These articles are usually featured on the covers of the magazines and bear such titles as "The Best Seed Catalogues for This Year" or "Where to Find Perennials Through the Mail." These articles will often list and critique mail-order catalogues both big and small. When we say critique, we use the word rather casually, because many of these articles are only critiquing the catalogues themselves, as the writers have rarely visited the actual companies they are writing about. Instead, they have gathered dozens or hundreds of catalogues and read through their offerings, after which they select and distill a list of suggestions for readers. Nonetheless, these articles are very useful, as they have brought together information on the whereabouts of seedspeople and plantspeople and will list company names, addresses, and catalogue costs. Most importantly, these articles will provide information about interesting and unusual companies you might never have known about because these small specialized companies would not have the financial ability to advertise on a national level. Because these small specialized companies have limited budgets, they may charge a dollar or two for their catalogues. We have rarely regretted paying a nominal cost in return for the information obtained.

One of the most useful references for finding seeds and plants was first published several years ago by Barbara J. Barton, a reference librarian and avid gardener. The book, titled *Gardening by Mail* and now in its fifth edition, is an affordable paperback that lists thousands of seed companies, nurseries, garden supply and service companies, plant societies, and other horticultural reference works, primarily from the U.S. but also from around the world. Since its first publication in 1986, this book's format has been copied (usually less successfully) by a few other writers. You don't need to purchase a copy of your own; just get your library to stock it or make it available to you through interlibrary loan.

Finally, we highly recommend the newest tool you have for locating seed and plant sources and ever so much more information about gardening, and that is by using your computer and logging on to the Internet. Many seed companies have their catalogues posted as well as much additional information. You may view their offerings, read articles, order seeds and plants, and link up to other sites that are recommended. For the past five years, more and more plant and seed companies with printed catalogues once only available by mail have established Web sites and e-mail addresses. It is a trend that will most likely continue at an even more accelerated rate as companies large and small feel the competitive need to make themselves as visible and accessible as possible. Locating gardening sources on the Internet doesn't necessarily obviate wanting real tangible copies of catalogues in hand, but it will allow you to preview and edit which materials are appropriate to your needs. An hour or two of searching for plant sources on the Internet makes even the most rural gardeners feel very much in touch with what's available to them. The use of the Internet assists us most particularly in locating seed sources for more obscure or specialized plants. It makes purchasing internationally a much simpler task. It really explodes the possibilities for plantspeople, just as it has every other field of human activity. See the special section on page 10 about gardening sites on the Internet.

W E MENTION ALL of these sources for obtaining seeds and plants not to overwhelm you but to encourage you to gather before you a variety of sources so you can begin to evaluate where to shop, what to purchase, and how to spend your money wisely. Let us relay a brief anecdote to point out how important it is to get information before you spend your money. Not long ago, in doing some research for this book, we traveled around looking at many displays of seed packets in garden centers, general stores, and hardware stores, both locally owned and franchises. We also included stops at large national discount chains. In late winter the seed packets begin arriving in these stores, just at a time when

Antique seed catalogues from the nineteenth century include an 1891 edition of Eastman's Annual Seed Catalogue, from The Eastman Seed Company of East Sumner, Maine. The Eastman homestead is just down the road from our farm, reminding us that Sumner was once a lively agricultural community.

we are all tiring of snow and ice and yearning for the first signs of spring. Their colorful packages are so appealing that it is hard to resist impulse purchases. In fact, during one of our stops, we talked with a salesman who was setting up a seed display. As we looked over the selection, he asked us if we were interested in gardening, had we started anything from seeds, and then recommended a couple of varieties of flowers he had grown. We thanked him for his advice, but he was so enthusiastic about the packets he was arranging that he volunteered that he had been gardening for as long as he could remember, about twenty years or so, and was more interested in flowers than in vegetables, but grew both and preserved some of his own food. He had already spent more than sixty dollars that season on seed packages from his store's display, taking advantage of the specials that were being offered, and he was only partially through unpacking the latest shipment of seeds. None of this

information surprised us until, looking through the shipping cartons on his dolly, he mused, "I surely hope they sent some geranium seeds this year. Can't ever find any and I've always wanted to try growing my own."

Now here was a person who had been gardening for about twenty years and who did not know how to get seeds for plants beyond those offered locally. Geranium seeds are offered routinely by any number of well-known seed companies and are readily available, if he had only known about sending away for a catalogue. When we returned to the farm after that day's excursion, we took a quick look at only one very popular seed catalogue and found a two-page spread complete with full-color photographs, descriptions, and cultural information on how to grow some thirty varieties of geraniums from very reasonably priced seed.

If we reflected a bit more on this man's musing, we

SEARCHING FOR INFORMATION about gardening can be done easily by spending a few hours on the Internet, using a variety of search engines to locate special topics. There are entertaining and informative home pages set up by individuals, which often include excellent links to other related sites. There are hundreds of commercial sites with information on plants, tools, books, gardens, and nearly anything horticultural. A number of agricultural universities and educational research facilities also have sites that are valuable resources for information. It would be very easy to spend endless hours "surfing the Net" and gardening effortlessly in front of your computer screen. As you become more familiar with the sites and links available, you will undoubtedly begin to edit your time on the Internet by bookmarking special sites that provide useful and updated information specific to your gardening interests.

When we were assembling information on seed longevity for this book, we wanted to compare the data we had gathered over the years on storing our own garden seeds with information from the work of larger research facilities. One of the sites we found most helpful originated at the Texas A & M University information server. Included in an extensive list of horticultural topics was an entry on seeds, listing vegetable names, seed weights, germination temperatures, and seed longevity. Accessing these data allowed us to confirm many of our own findings.

We also use the Internet to locate unusual seeds that are not readily available from U.S. seed companies. It is often possible to make purchases of seeds, plants, and gardening supplies from commercially posted Web sites, both domestic and foreign. Alternatively, catalogues may be requested from these sites. There are no rules governing the size of the organizations that develop home pages or Internet sites, so it is possible to connect with a broad range of people and places. There are discussion sites for backyard gardeners as well as electronic tours of some of the world's major public gardens. Our own farm has a modest home page, so if you are interested in visiting Hedgehog Hill, all you need is our address: www.hedgehoghillfarm.com

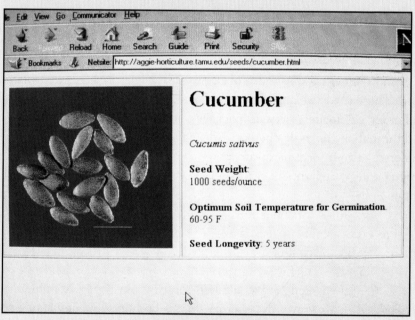

The Texas A & M site on the Internet is one of many good resources for agricultural information.

probably should not have been surprised, because we are routinely asked at our farm where a person can find seeds or plants for this or that. The question is not always from beginners, and not infrequently asked by other people with small businesses that resemble our own. Figuring out where to find things seems to have a lot of people stumped. Let us repeat, just go to the local library and spend a few hours. Look at their books and magazines. Use the library's computer and link up to the Internet. If you are not yet computer literate, ask the librarian for assistance. Even in our tiny town of a few hundred people, there are computers available in the community library and at the schools. It will open up the world of gardening to you. Remember that producing seeds and plants is a very big industry in this country, and there are literally thousands of sources of plant material readily accessible.

Assuming you have done a bit of research and have before you a number of seed and plant catalogues (either in hand or on the screen), you will then have to evaluate their offerings. It is important to know that seed companies are sellers of seed, not necessarily growers of seed. Some companies buy all of their seed and simply measure out and repackage varieties for resale. These seeds are marketed to customers through mail-order catalogues, or seed packages are distributed through a wholesale operation to small and large retailers like your local hardware store, general store, garden centers, department stores, and large discount centers.

There are also seed companies that own and operate large experimental seed acreage where they test plant varieties and conduct sophisticated work with plant production and hybridization. They may produce some of their seed, and in addition they will buy and package seeds grown by other producers both in this country and throughout the world. At the other end of the spectrum, there are also many small seed companies that consist of growers who raise most if not all of their own plants and process and harvest all the seed they sell.

If you are interested in how different seed and plant companies function, take the time to read the information these companies provide about themselves, usually found in the front of their catalogues or on their Web sites. Those companies that are most

closely involved with seed production and research will usually include that information. Some catalogues will tell you nothing at all about where the seeds and plants are produced. Take a moment to read what the companies tell you about themselves and also what they do not tell you about themselves. Some very down-home-looking companies may never plant, test, or do any on-site garden evaluations of the materials they sell, while the look of their catalogue would have you believe they are real hands-in-the-dirt farmers. Conversely, some companies with very slick glossy catalogues or Web sites may have good staffs of horticulturists who spend considerable time in the field testing and evaluating much of what they offer.

This information will become even more apparent as you read through the catalogue offerings. When companies describe how a species performed in its fields, how it survived a severe winter, how floriferous it was, how it stood up to early and late frosts, how it measured up to taste tests among staff members, you know there is some direct involvement in growing. We are going to make a broad generalization here, but it is based on our having purchased seeds and plant material from all over the world for the past twenty-five years. There is an absolute correlation between the quality of the seeds, plants, and company service and the company's direct involvement in active horticulture. This does not mean that there are not many reputable seed and plant companies who are only brokers of plant material and from whom you will be able to obtain first-rate merchandise. It is simply a statement of our personal preference in working with companies that are concerned with and involved in horticulture. We are applying this statement uniformly to large international companies and very small family-scale operations. It is an attitude we have developed after having worked with many companies and a considerable amount of plant material. We want there to be a person at the other end of the phone or someone willing to answer a letter of inquiry about the seeds and plants we are purchasing.

Whatever your own criteria for choosing where to purchase seeds and plants, here is a list of things you might want to keep in mind when evaluating seed and plant catalogues:

ಭ Is the information clearly organized with careful thought given to grouping plants in some logical order, and does the catalogue have a good index?

ಭ Is there a clear statement of the company's involvement in the business of producing the materials it sells, and a statement of responsibility for the things it is selling?

ಭ If the catalogue contains color photographs, are those photographs realistic? Despite the fact that most catalogues try to use the most productive and floriferous plants to represent their items, are those photographs then further doctored so the color is a bit too intense? If you have never seen a lilac bush with as many lilac blossoms looking so blue as the one in the catalogue, it is probably because no such specimen could exist.

ಭ When you read the plant descriptions, is the hyperbole a bit much? Admittedly, few catalogues will call a plant ordinary or acceptably productive, but when every other item is the most spectacular, the highest yielding, the biggest fruited, then all we can say is caveat emptor.

ಭ When catalogues offer plants, even if they list them by popular name, do they also include botanical names, including genus and species and variety information? With the exception of vegetables (a tomato is seldom confused with a cabbage), it is essential to know the genus and species of every plant you are buying. Otherwise there is no way of knowing what plant or seeds you are getting. The possibilities for confusion here are enormous. Furthermore, when it comes to buying vegetable seeds, you need to know what varieties are being offered, not simply that a tomato is a cherry type. There are cherry types that are appropriate for southern gardens, but not for northern growers, and vice versa.

ಭ Catalogues should always let you know how many seeds you are going to receive in a package, either by seed count or by weight. If weight is given, the company should let you know how many seeds of that given variety are contained in an ounce or pound, so you can calculate for yourself

what you are purchasing. This information may be included with each plant description or at the beginning of the catalogue itself, where general descriptions and purchasing instructions are found.

ಭ Many good seed and plant catalogues include guidelines for growing the materials they are selling. This information will vary greatly from one catalogue to another, but some catalogues are also excellent gardening reference works. You will find yourself saving and referring to these catalogues for general gardening information.

ಭ Reliable catalogues should give honest and accurate information about seed and plant performance in various parts of the country. That means telling whether the plant is an annual, biennial, or perennial and the many variations of that definition. For example, some perennials can only be grown as annuals in northern gardens, but the grower should be given that information, not simply told that the plant is a perennial. Many plants are in fact perennials, but could rarely survive in many parts of the country. It is always helpful if a catalogue includes a copy of the most recent version of the USDA (U.S. Department of Agriculture) list of gardening hardiness zones. This map will tell you, by number, what gardening zone you are in. See a copy of this map on pages 62–3, and further discussions on gardening zones in the next chapter. Good plant and seed catalogues should include hardiness information with each of the variety listings, so you will not try to grow plants in your Zone 4 garden that will flourish only in Zones 5 to 8. Catalogues should also give accurate dates for seed and plant development and maturity. This is listed in the number of days it will take the plant to mature either from seeding directly into the garden or from transplanting small seedlings into the garden. It is helpful to know the basic soil, moisture, and light requirements for plants, information that can be given succinctly in symbols and abbreviations.

ಭ You will need information about the germination rates of seeds. This sometimes appears in the catalogue copy but may only be stated on the seed

BOTANICAL LATIN IS essentially an international language for naming and describing plants. It has been developed over the past 250 years, its vocabulary enriched by words from Greek, Latin, and other languages, but accepted today as the one way botanists have, universally, for identifying and talking about plants.

Latin became the language of choice primarily because it derives from the language of the Roman writers about plants, most notably Pliny the Elder, who lived during the first century A.D. It survived because Latin remained the unchallenged language of learning among the peoples of Europe through the Middle Ages, the Renaissance, and into the eighteenth century. When Carl von Linné (Carolus Linnaeus) published his now famous works in the mid–eighteenth century, works that mark him as the founder of modern botanical nomenclature, he established a standard that is still in use throughout the scientific community. He did, however, modify the classical Latin of his education so that botanical Latin is an evolved and specialized language. The language has been enriched as centuries of scientists, explorers, and inquisitive gardeners have identified more plant species. Botanical Latin has also been expanded to explain the discoveries about plant life that were made possible by more sophisticated scientific instruments. When Pliny was writing about plants, he may have described what he saw by observing plant parts through a hand-held magnifying lens. Today's botanists have at their disposal electron microscopes, and yet researchers and taxonomists worldwide continue to communicate with one another through this common language.

It is, in fact, this "worldwide" connection that prompted us to begin to use botanical Latin in our own gardens. Part of our family emigrated from Poland and the Soviet Union. Several family members had training in botany and agronomy. When these family members visited the farm, we all had one language we could use to talk about the gardens. Furthermore, we have had people on our staff over the years from France, Japan, and Argentina. Once again, we had a common language for communicating about work; botanical Latin gave us a way of making certain that we were indeed talking about the same plants. Even if everyone on the staff was fluent with the English common names for plants, those names would vary greatly. Common plant names have no regulation, and what a gardener from Virginia calls bluebells may be a very different plant from the bluebells of northern Oregon. Or, for that matter, bluebells may be the common name of twenty or thirty different plants depending upon where and how you learned to identify the plants in your gardens.

A garden of sages when given true botanical names would be described, from front to back as Salvia officinalis *'Purpurascens',* Salvia officinalis *'Icterina', and* Salvia elegans. *Their common names are purple sage, golden variegated sage, and pineapple sage.*

ALL PLANTS THAT have been identified and accepted by the worldwide community of botanists have been scientifically classified according to a taxonomic system that places the plants into groupings. Their placement into these groupings is based on the plant's morphology (its form and structure), and more specifically, on the morphology of the reproductive parts. Our point here is not to go into the history of botany or of taxonomy but to say that for our purposes we try to teach ourselves the "international names" of the plants we have in our gardens. For most plants that simply means that we need to learn their binomial nomenclature, or the genus and species name of the plant. A parsley plant is named *Petroselinum crispum*. An eggplant is *Solanum melongena* var. *esculentum*. A white potato plant is *Solanum tuberosum*. A sweet potato plant is *Ipomoea batatas*. It is customary to capitalize the name of the genus and start the name of the species with a lower-case letter. Seed catalogues still tend to give us only the common names of vegetables, but recently we have noticed that the herb listings are often accompanied by their botanical names.

Seed or plant catalogues for annual and perennial flowers are gradually becoming more complete, their writers much more responsible, and we notice that

The showy bee balm, Monarda didyma, *was named after the Spanish botanist Dr. Nicholas Monardes, who wrote an herbal on American plants in the sixteenth century. The species name* didyma *means "in pairs," referring to the shapes of the flower petals.*

common and botanical names are often included. Companies that deal with nursery stock, shrubs and trees, seem to vary greatly, both those companies dealing with amateur gardeners and those who cater to professional growers. All of this can lead to tremendous confusion for everyone. We can know if we are talking about a specific plant only if we identify it by its botanical name.

Having made that plea for the common use of botanical names, we need to explain their usage a step further. Beyond the genus and species names for plants, there are variety and cultivar names that further distinguish one plant from another. So when dealing with certain vegetables, it is not enough to know that you are growing a tomato, *Lycopersicon lycopersicum*, you will also want to know that you are buying seeds or plants for a wonderful heirloom tomato known as Brandywine. Or you may want to grow a specific variety of mint, *Mentha spicata*, known as Kentucky Colonel. This plant would then be identified as *Mentha spicata* 'Kentucky Colonel'. When variety names are added to the botanical names, it is common for their identification to be noted in the language of the place of origin or plant development. This clarification is necessary when we are dealing with a genus of plants, mint being a prime example, that has many species and many varieties of the species. In some instances, the cultivation of a species results in so many different plants that taxonomists have developed botanical groups for identifying them. Plants of the genus *Brassica* are a primary example.

We will add what we hope is a reassuring note to all of this. When asked how we remember all those Latin names of plants, we always reply most sincerely: The names just pile up after a few years. We started with a few names, and since we talk about these "friends" all the time, the names simply stick in the brain, as if we were talking about real friends. Over the years, the list of names just keeps getting longer.

packages themselves. Some seed companies routinely test their seed for viability and, in so doing, are able to conclude what percentage of the seed should germinate successfully under favorable conditions. Germination percentages simply mean that for every hundred seeds planted under proper conditions a given percentage should germinate. The majority of popular vegetable, flower, and herb seeds offered for sale will have a relatively high germination rate, anywhere from 70 percent to 90 percent. When this information is given on the package, the date of testing should also be included. Some seeds retain their viability for many years, some for only a few. (See the charts at the end of Chapters 5 and 6 for a general guide on how long different vegetables and herb seeds can be safely stored.) There are some popular plants, however, whose seeds are known to have rather low germination rates, even when the seed is fresh; rosemary is one example that comes quickly to mind. The important point here is for you to have that information so you can purchase the appropriate amount of seed to meet your needs, or decide whether you want to try to grow such plants from seed at all.

❧ When seeds and plants are offered for many different varieties within a given species, how does one variety differ from the next? This is especially useful when you need to make choices based on such criteria as space, moisture, light, time for maintenance, and disease resistance. If you are planning to garden organically, you should be looking for plant varieties that demonstrate the greatest resistance to disease. If you are willing to use chemical pesticides, fungicides, and herbicides, you may want to choose from a different list of varieties.

❧ Gardeners need also to know if the seeds and plant material are hybrids or open-pollinated varieties. This is especially true for those of us who are interested in propagating our own plants.

❧ Catalogues should include information on whether or not the seeds come treated or untreated. Treated seeds are dusted or coated with one or another type of chemical fungicide to prevent disease. Without commenting here on whether or not to use chemically treated seeds, we only recommend that buyers know what they are purchasing.

🌿 Catalogues should let the buyer know if seeds are cleaned or still encased in various kinds of hulls or plant material. Cleaned seeds are usually easier to handle and germinate more readily.

🌿 Some catalogues offer seeds that are coated (to make seed size more uniform or to include a covering of fungicides) or pelleted (covered with a clay coating to make the seeds larger and easier to handle). This information should be included.

🌿 Pricing information is, of course, essential, and while it will be easy to understand any individual company's asking price, you may find yourself scratching your head when trying to understand why one seemingly reliable company charges one dollar for fifty seeds of sweet green basil while another well-known company charges two dollars for the exact same amount of the same variety. The word here is to do some comparison shopping. In any given season, we spend hundreds to thousands of dollars purchasing seeds and plants for our business, and if we did not take the time to shop around, we would spend hundreds more dollars than is necessary. While the proportions will be different for backyard gardeners, the savings may be just as important.

🌿 When purchasing plants through the mail, make certain you are clear as to what you are buying. A few companies offer plants for annual herbs, flowers, and vegetables. Annual plants are difficult to ship, but with appropriate packaging it can be well done. If you are buying annual plant material, you know that the seeds have been sown recently and the plants will be relatively young, probably small, and in an active stage of growth. A description of the plant size would be helpful. In other words, can you expect a seedling with only a set of true leaves, or a plant with a month or two of growth?

🌿 Many mail-order catalogues deal with perennial plants, and you need to be informed of the ages and sizes of the plants they are shipping.

"Perennial" simply means that the plant should live over from year to year in your garden. It does not mean that the plant will be sent to you at any specific age. There are perennial seedlings, perennial liners, pot-grown perennials, field-grown perennials, bare-root perennials. All of these could be plants of different size and maturity, and the prices could be very different. Perennials can be shipped while they are still dormant, they can be shipped bare-rooted, they can be shipped in pots and in active growth. Not all catalogues will tell you whether you are buying a first-year perennial seedling or a two-year-old perennial for the three dollars they are charging. Reputable companies should make this very clear in their copy. Take the time to read. While we have advised you to shop around for prices, if you receive a beautiful glossy plant catalogue offering you perennials (illustrated with lush full-color photographs) for unbelievably low prices, you may end up getting a seedling for that perennial, not the well-developed field-grown plant shown in the illustration. As plant buyers, we always write, call, or e-mail any company to get a full explanation about the sizes and ages of perennial plants we wish to purchase, if the catalogues are not absolutely explicit in their descriptions. We advise you to do the same if you have any questions.

All of this brings us back to the local hardware store with its racks of wonderful-looking seed packages. Many of these seeds are of first-rate quality, from companies that have conducted germination tests and packaged viable up-to-date material. The packages will have some if not all of the information that we have noted above. The variety of offerings will be limited compared to the varieties you can find from mail-order catalogues, and prices will vary considerably in comparison to purchasing through the mail. The important thing is that you view the locally sold seeds as but a sample of what is available to you and you read the seed packet information somewhat more critically. Having said all that, let us add that even after investing weeks of research and decision making each winter when we do our seed ordering, and even though we save a large percentage of our own seeds, it is hard to resist a rack of colorful seed packages. From the end of January until the beginning of May, we receive seeds and plants weekly in the mail from companies all over the world. Nonetheless, nearly every winter, when visiting the local farm-supply store, we find ourselves hanging around the seed displays and picking up a package or two of some very ordinary plants that we "overlooked" when ordering that year. Every gardener will recognize the impulse.

Buying Plants Locally

WHILE THE PURPOSE of this book is to motivate you and give you enough information to grow and propagate your own plants, we remember that you have to start somewhere. Our first vegetable gardens were planted with seedlings we purchased locally.

Our first perennial gardens were planted with purchased plants, plants donated by family and friends, and only a few things we ventured to grow from seed. Just as there are considerations to be made when purchasing seeds or plants directly or through mail-order catalogues, there are considerations to be made when purchasing live plant material directly. Here are a few points to keep in mind.

Anyone can buy and sell plants. The individual or business does not have to be involved in gardening. Flats of brightly colored seedlings, hanging baskets of petunias, and vegetable flats with pretty colored tags picturing large, delicious-looking tomatoes are sold everywhere. We expect to find them at greenhouses and nurseries, but now they are as likely to appear on racks outside the local supermarket, department store, or pharmacy. Remember that you will only know what you are buying if you can talk with the people who produced the plant material. And your

Worn-out garden clothes are stuffed with mulch hay and turned into whimsical scarecrows. These farmers do more relaxing than scaring.

JUST SOUND IT OUT

PERHAPS THE GREATEST impediment to learning the botanical names of plants is in having to say the name aloud to someone at a garden center or nursery. Our advice: don't agonize over the correct pronunciation, just sound it out as well as you are able. Chances are one of two things will happen: the person listening to you won't have any idea what you are talking about because he or she has never learned the real names of the plants, or the listener will pause for a split second and resound his or her own pronunciation silently, and then help you locate the plant you want.

If that's not reassuring enough because you want to be absolutely certain you don't make an embarrassing mistake, here's a wonderful piece of advice from a more lofty source. I am quoting from William Stearn's classic *Botanical Latin*, published originally in 1966 and now in its fourth edition. Professor Stearn's list of

A fragrant lavender garden at the farm. Lavandula, *the botanical genus for lavender, is so close to the English common name that it is easy to sound out.*

degrees, academic affiliations, learned societies, and publications numbering more than 350 should give his advice considerable weight. He writes: "Botanical Latin is essentially a written language, but the scientific names of plants often occur in speech. How they are pronounced really matters little provided they sound pleasant and are understood by all concerned. . . . People tend to pronounce Latin words by analogy with words of their own language."

As Stearn continues in his section on pronunciation, he talks about the differences between traditional English pronunciation used by gardeners and botanists and the academic pronunciation adopted by classical scholars. He gives further evidence of the lack of uniformity of pronunciation at international gatherings of scientists, scholars, and taxonomists. It's great reading, but we extracted for our own purposes, and for yours, the wonderful encouragement to sound pleasant and be understood.

This whole discussion reminds us of a rather uncomfortable encounter we witnessed one day in our herb shop. A couple of customers (each unknown to the other) were shopping, and there was casual talk about herb gardens. One woman asked a question about basil (pronounced with a long *a*). She was immediately greeted with a harrumph by the other woman, who declared it was next to vulgar to say the word that way. She insisted that basil have a short *a* and furthermore that the word "herb" be pronounced with an aspirate *h*. There are interesting linguistic histories to explain both pronunciations of both words. Which brings us back again to Stearn's sage advice.

eyes will not necessarily tell you the quality of the plants you are getting. Let us explain a bit further and indulge in a bit of oversimplification for the sake of making a point. The most vigorous plants are those that are grown consistently under conditions that will promote their continuous development. Plants that are being grown for resale may be subjected to any number of tricks to slow down or hasten their development so that they appear to be at the optimal size when it is time for them to go on sale. This is done by altering temperatures, water, light, fertilizers, and growth hormones. In some cases, manipulating plant development will not adversely affect the ultimate look or performance of the plant. In some cases, manipulating plant development will not be obvious in the plant's appearance, but it will affect the ultimate performance, and this is especially true when it comes to vegetables. Stressed vegetables may have significantly lower yields. Furthermore, perfectly healthy and vigorous-looking plants may or may not be varieties that will produce in your area. Inexperienced growers need to rely on responsible plantspeople to offer quality plants and varieties appropriate to local gardens.

When purchasing plants, talk to the growers or to informed salespeople who can get for you whatever information you may need about the plants' production. This goes for seedling flats of common annuals and vegetables, and it goes as well for larger, more expensive purchases like field-grown perennials, shrubs, and trees. It does not mean that the seller has to grow all of the stock for the information to be reliable. It does mean that the seller has to be responsible for the material and for having information about the material, its production and growing requirements.

In order to know if plants are suitable for your gardens, you need some of the same basic information as that printed in mail-order catalogues. This includes complete plant names, including botanical identification and variety names. It includes cultural requirements such as days to maturity for annuals, hardiness for perennials, soil, light, water, and winter care requirements. Any additional information about ongoing care is helpful. Some of this information should come on plant tags, but all of it should be available from the people handling the plant material. If an individual salesperson does not have this information, he or she should be willing to direct you to sources. Conversely, be wary of plant sellers who are quick to answer "Yes, yes, yes" to all of your questions in an effort to sell you the plant without really helping you figure out if that plant will perform well in your given location.

We recall a very enlightening day of shopping for shrubbery. We were looking for a particular species of flowering dogwood, an uncommon and uncommonly beautiful variety and one we had developed a particular fondness for, based on our having seen it in a number of books on shrubbery. We located a good plant nursery near the coast of Maine, in a zone one number higher than our own farm climate. The owner of the nursery had no way of knowing who we were, but could tell by our questions that we were already determined to have that species in our garden and that we knew very little about flowering shrubs. His approach to selling was to ask us a number of questions about the site where the plants were to be grown. Having done this, he told us that the variety we wanted would probably not survive at our farm. When we asked him if it would survive if we planted it in a protected location and gave it some extra winter protection, his answer was the same. He doubted that the plant would make it. To his credit, he had to talk us out of buying something. You may not often run into plantspeople of such integrity, but good plantspeople do care about the things they have worked to produce. You will hear it in their voices, in the quality of their information, and in their concern about their inventory. Enough said. You will find this out for yourself as you shop around. Readers will recognize our own particular bias in the writing, when we tell you to look for greenhouses, nurseries, and garden centers that have informed gardeners. It is the bias of a couple of professional growers, but at the same time we are still buyers of plants and seeds.

THE ADVICE we offer you to inform yourself when starting out is meant to give you the greatest possible opportunity for successful gardening. Your very first attempts at gardening should be joyful and successful. We have only to listen to visitors to our farm to know that many gardening efforts are met with frustration and disappointment. Often the reasons boil down to the fact that gardeners were simply trying to grow seeds or plants that were not appropriate to their particular gardening conditions. You won't always be able to do much about the weather or the woodchucks, but you can do something about choosing what seeds to plant and what plants to purchase. Bear with one last anecdote to underscore this point. As truck farmers, we chose to grow sweet green bell peppers as one of our cash crops. It took us a few seasons to find the varieties of peppers that would flower and fruit consistently in a climate that often is marked by cool and wet weather in late spring and early summer. We found two such varieties and in a given season would plant as many as three thousand plants. These are the varieties of pepper seedlings that we offer to our customers to this day. A few years ago, a longtime Maine gardener took a look at our flats of bell peppers and said that she had tried for years to raise peppers in her gardens, and they simply would not grow in Maine. We challenged her to try this variety and practically guaranteed her that she would be successful. Midsummer, the woman called us on the phone, and in a good-humored way she complained that she had so many peppers she didn't know what she was going to do with them. Let all gardeners have such complaints. But the real caveat follows: We still see seed packages for bell peppers sold in stores throughout the state for varieties we know have very little chance of performing well in our gardens. California Wonders are, by their name and by their reputation, meant for other parts of the country.

When pulling together information for this chapter, we gave much thought to the notion of having an appendix at the back of the book listing a few or even an exhaustive number of seed and plant companies. Our decision has been not to give you a list but instead to offer the information in this chapter as guidance for you to gather your own sources. Any list of companies is outdated the moment it is compiled. Large seed companies, even those that have existed for more than a hundred years, are now being bought and sold and in some cases taken over by nonagricultural conglomerates. Small independently owned companies appear and disappear, some lasting for years, some closing after a season. Names and addresses remain the same, names and addresses change. The constant here seems only to be change. The information you can gather by shopping locally, using current library publications, and searching on the Internet will be the most accurate and the most flexible.

A final thought in regard to the subject of searching for seeds and plants. The search is as much fun as the finding, regardless of whether you are trying to find seeds for a simple tasty cucumber or for an obscure perennial you saw pictured in an old herbal. Asking questions and doing a bit of reading will put you in contact with other gardeners, directly or indirectly. Our enthusiasm is infectious. Experienced gardeners know that some very strange force keeps them out in the field when the black flies are too thick for man or beast. Experienced gardeners recognize that the knees are a bit stiffer this season than the last, but it rarely stops them from kneeling in the cold mud if it's time to set out the cabbages. Experienced gardeners know that they have absolutely no more room in the perennial border when they "have" to add just a couple more plant varieties. As for new gardeners, well, they will most likely lose all perspective in a season or two, and if not, chances are they will move on to another hobby.

CHAPTER TWO

Seeding Indoors

A Seeding Calendar

ONCE YOU HAVE FINISHED making your seed purchases, you are ready to move on to the next stage of seeding indoors, but hold off just a while before opening any seed packages. There are important preparations that need to be made prior to seeding. All those tempting garden catalogues and seed packet displays appear in the mail and at garden centers weeks, if not months, before it would be prudent to start planting. We want to begin this chapter with the caveat that one of the most common mistakes made by new and even experienced gardeners is to start indoor seedlings too early.

The main reason for starting seeds indoors is to get a head start on the growing season, especially in areas of the country where the gardening season is short. However, getting a head start is only advantageous if plants are grown to just the right stage of development for transplanting into the garden when outdoor conditions are appropriate. There is nothing to be gained by having overly mature seedlings in your house, plants that were seeded so early that they are way beyond the best "setting out" stage when the weather has warmed and garden plots are prepared.

What every gardener needs to establish is a basic seeding schedule, calculated and laid out well before seeding begins. There is considerable variability in the time it takes different species of plants to germinate, mature to transplant stage, be grown on, be hardened off, and be set out into the garden. We recommend using whatever time you have midwinter to do some planning, studying, and note taking to determine what you plan to seed, how many plants you will want of each species, and when to start each variety.

IN ORDER TO establish a seeding calendar, it is necessary to understand a variety of conditions that affect a garden's climate. We will explain this by defining exactly where we garden. Our farm is located in the western foothills of Maine, in a gardening zone that has been identified by the USDA hardiness zone map as Zone 4B. A copy of the map is found on pages 62–3. Zones are determined by the average range of annual minimum temperatures. Knowing your gardening zone in these terms is a point of departure, but only that, because there are a number of other factors that will affect a garden site beyond the mere numerical definition of zone. It is necessary to gather even more specific data.

This information is most readily available by consulting gardening resources in your immediate area. The County Extension and Soil Conservation Agencies are two good sources, as are any workshops or courses offered by these agencies or colleges, universities, and adult education. But perhaps your best resources are even closer to home, and they are gardening neighbors. Anyone who has gardened for a few seasons has made some mental notes and gathered some practical wisdom about frost dates and other climatic factors that will be helpful. The closer you gather information to the actual gardening site, the better your chances will be of having that information be specific to your garden.

We use again as an example the climate of our particular farm. We are growing crops in fields at an elevation of about 600 feet, and the garden plots are located on the northwest side of a small mountain, now called Mount Oxford on the topographical maps, but formerly referred to as Hedgehog Hill, from which we took our farm name. Our soils are rather heavy clay soils that hold moisture well, but also tend, in some spots, to be a bit too moist for very early planting. On average, we do not have frosts after the middle of May and not before the end of September or very early into October.

If you walk a few thousand feet over the top of the mountain and onto the gardening plot of a neighbor, you come upon a garden with similar soil and similar frost dates. This nearby garden is ready for planting as much as a week earlier than our own, however, because the plot is located on the south side of the mountain, where winter snows melt earlier and the sun warms the soil more quickly. If you travel to the garden site of another neighbor only a couple of miles away, you encounter quite a different gardening climate. The elevation drops from 600 feet to 450 feet. Her soils are very sandy, and they not only dry quickly but they lose their moisture easily throughout the growing season. Moreover, she can expect a late May or early June frost at the start of the growing season, and a light damaging frost in August or the beginning of September. A killing frost typically arrives in her gardens one to three weeks before we are affected on our hill. A general zone map would have all three of the above garden plots defined as being in the same zone, while there is actually great variability from one plot to another. Each of these gardens would need a different calendar for planting outdoors and for starting seedlings inside.

It doesn't take long for new gardeners to gather basic information about conditions in their own gardens, and we urge you to assemble that information in the form of notes, diaries, or journals. Find a style of record keeping that is most comfortable, one that will encourage frequent entries. Once you have been able to establish outdoor planting times, you will be able to calculate and set up an accurate calendar for seeding indoors. These calculations are made by counting back from the outdoor planting dates, taking into account the following considerations.

Each variety of plant needs its own specific amount of time for the seed to germinate, for the plant to grow to transplant stage, and for the young transplanted seedling to grow into a large enough plant to go through the transition known as "hardening off" for planting outdoors. Determining that time is a matter of simple calculation. Seed catalogues will sometimes note this information with their plant descriptions. The information is often printed on seed packets. At the end of Chapters 5 and 6, there are complete tables for the plants discussed in this book. These tables will tell you that if a given variety of vegetable takes, for example, three to six days to germinate and four to five weeks to "grow on" (see Chapter 3) and approximately a week for hardening off, then you will need to seed that vegetable six or seven weeks before the last spring frost for your area.

Make a list of the plants you are going to seed and calculate a schedule for each plant. In so doing, you may well discover that you will be doing your indoor seeding over a period of several weeks. For example, we begin seeding our plants in late January or early February. The earliest varieties we work with are typically the slow-growing perennials and biennials such as lavender, parsley, thyme, leeks, onions, and celery. However, the majority of our annual vegetables and herbs are not seeded until much later. In early March we start eggplants and peppers, but wait until later in the month for tomatoes, and even later for members of the cabbage family. We don't begin to seed pots of cucumbers and melons until early to mid-May. There is nothing to be gained and in fact much to be lost by seeding plants too early.

The very best plants, those with the most vigor and potential for optimum flower and fruit production, are those plants that are seeded and grown to maturity in as even and unstressed a cycle as possible. Plants should not be held inside after they have reached the exact stage of maturity for going out into the garden. There are many ways to slow down or speed up the growth of young plants, by manipulating light, temperature, water, and the use of growth hormones, but all attempts to distort a natural growing cycle can adversely affect plant vigor. Common problems include leggy seedlings, young plants that bud or flower prematurely, stunting, discoloration of stems and leaves, and increased susceptibility to disease and predation.

Over the years, we have made a number of mistakes in having each and every variety of plant at just the right stage of readiness for transplanting into the garden. Some of the cabbage plants we grew in our first indoor seed flats were planted so early that they were ready to be set out long before the ground had even thawed. The plants had to be kept inside where they became leggy and anemic-looking. When the time came to harden them off, they were more easily damaged by sun and wind. Their thin, tender stems were more prone to mechanical damage when handled, and even more susceptible to being eaten by cutworms in the early spring soil. Younger, shorter cabbage plants with stocky, thicker stems and fewer young leaves always respond better to the hardening-off process and always transplant with less apparent stress. Once

SCARIFICATION

OCCASIONALLY A SEED CATALOGUE or package will suggest that certain seeds be scarified before planting. This is done to wear away some or most of the seed coat, so that water can penetrate the coat to initiate germination. Left to germinate naturally, such seeds might experience a number of natural conditions that would accomplish the same erosion of the seed coat, including freezing and thawing in the soil, ingestion by animals, forest fires, exposure to acidity in the soil, and a number of other factors. Since these conditions take place over a period of time in the wild, it helps explain why seeds germinate over such a long time range. To ensure germination at a given time, we intervene with a process of mechanical scarification right before planting. Techniques include nicking seed coats with a sharp knife, using sandpaper to scrape a part of the seed coat, and placing a few seeds with sand into a blender. On occasion, boiling water is poured over seeds to break down the seed coat. Simply follow whatever specific advice is given. If scarification is recommended and overlooked, you may have poor luck germinating the seeds.

in the garden, these same plants are more able to withstand temperature fluctuations, wind, heavy spring rains, and insect damage. They "size up" (grow) more quickly and are inevitably more productive. Timing is important, and it begins with seeding.

Plant Numbers

YOUR SEEDING PREPARATIONS should also include a calculation of how many plants you want to grow. If, for example, you want a dozen tomato plants of a single variety, then you need to check the seed packet or catalogue for the seed germination rate, the average percentage of seeds that can be relied upon to sprout. If the germination rate was given as 88 percent, you would need to plant only about fifteen seeds to end up with a dozen seedlings. That's a strictly mathematical calculation. Given that information, we would recommend planting about twenty seeds of the variety, because while 88 percent may well germinate, you will likely see differences even in the early performance of the seeds. There may be variability in speed of germination, growth rate, development of true leaves, and overall plant size. Planting a few extra seeds of a given variety will give you the opportunity to select the most vigorous young seedlings. You may also want a few extra as insurance against some unforeseeable mishap.

Conversely, we don't recommend planting very many more seeds than you will need to transplant, as reputable seed companies can be relied upon to give good germination rates and there is little point in wasting seeds or time or having to throw away perfectly good seedlings. Furthermore, we guarantee that it is nearly impossible to toss out healthy-looking little plants, and before you know it, you have modified your gardening plans in response to what is growing well, not to what you really want in your gardens.

In the process of setting up a seeding calendar, it is probably also good to evaluate just how much time and space you have indoors for growing seedlings and to limit yourself, at least for the first year, to a few plant varieties that are easy to grow. Information in Chapters 5 and 6 will be a guide to choosing the least demanding plants. Some of these include tomatoes, peppers, members of the cabbage family, basil, parsley, and

chives. You are almost guaranteed success with these varieties, and yet there is enough variability in their development that you will be able to gather considerable information from working with them, information that can later be applied to growing other species.

Setting Up a "Greenhouse" for Seeding

WE PURPOSEFULLY ENCLOSED the word greenhouse in quotation marks as our way of acknowledging that a grower's first indoor seeding area may or may not be a true greenhouse. Our own first "greenhouse" was located in an unused second floor bedroom of the farmhouse, with one small window that let in a bit of light and even less sun. It's great fun to think back on that adventure, as we had amazingly good luck with our attempts and those first successes played no small role in encouraging us to continue.

In those years, our farmhouse had no area suitable for starting plants, so we manufactured a table by nailing two-by-fours on end around a sheet of plywood, creating a large four-by-eight-foot tray. The tray was lined with a heavy plastic so it could hold water. We positioned a couple of household chairs under each end of this tray/table to serve as legs. Then seed flats were set into the tray, and we filled the trays with an inch or two of water, allowing the flats to soak up the water, wick fashion. Water was carried up to the second floor "greenhouse" bucket by bucket.

Our first seed flats consisted mostly of perennial flowers, including lupine and columbine. Since all of this happened more than twenty-five years ago, we can't now recall why we chose those particular plants. But we do recall our weekly schedule during those years. We were living half-time at the farm and the other half in Boston. From Friday evening until Tuesday morning we were in Maine, and early every Tuesday morning we got into our car and returned to our urban lives. That meant that our "greenhouse" was unattended for four days of each week. Not ideal, you are thinking, but we tell the story to point out that you can have some measured success with seeding your own plants under less than perfect conditions.

When we left for the city each week, we watered our seed flats and seedlings by filling the tray/table

COMMERCIALLY PREPARED SEEDS are presented in several ways. The majority of them are fully cleaned and dried. The seeds are natural in color, size, and shape. Nothing has been done beyond the cleaning to alter their appearance before packaging. There may, however, have been some processing to rid seeds of certain pathogens. These treatments may be done with hot water or chemical or biological agents, depending upon the pathogens involved. Such treatments are regulated by government agencies. They are not applied to all seeds, as there are some disease problems for which there are no known or approved seed treatments.

Some seeds, especially vegetable varieties, are packaged clean and dry but when we open the packages the seeds are highly colored with an obvious coating. We have witnessed coatings of bright pink, bright blue, and sometimes bluish green. These coatings are usually commercially applied fungicides that are added to prevent seeds from "damping off" either in the seed flats or in cool garden soils. (Damping off is a disease caused by soilborne fungi that results in seedlings rotting and collapsing at the soil line.)

There are a number of seed catalogues that offer pelleted seeds to their customers. Pelleted seeds are coated, usually with a claylike substance, to increase the size and shape of very small seeds, making them more easy to handle. The claylike coating breaks down in a moist environment, allowing the seed to germinate without interference. Pelleting is done mostly with inert material only to build up the size of the seeds, but coatings may also include fungicides and fertilizers.

If seeds have been "stratified" (stored in a moist, cold environment), they may be shipped in a couple of ways. We have received stratified seeds as they were stored, in moist peat moss inside plastic containers. We have also received stratified seeds dried and packaged in paper. This is done when the seeds have been cold stored and then removed from storage as they are shipped. However stratified seeds are received, it is recommended that they be seeded as soon after receipt as possible.

A few companies offer seeds embedded in a papery seed tape, for very fine seed. The seeds are evenly spaced in the tape, which is to be planted in the ground. The tape breaks down in the soil. We have never used any seed tapes; they strike us as expensive and an example of overpackaging. Small seeds may be a little more difficult to handle, but there is a certain pleasure in holding them during the seeding process.

Few seed companies send out seeds that are contained within their pods or fruit. Small, specialized companies may practice this on occasion. There may be some instances when mailing seeds within their fruit is advisable, but this would be the exception. Uncleaned seeds will come primarily from your own home-saved packages. The need to clean your own seeds, fully or partially, is discussed at length in Chapter 7.

From left to right: *cleaned carrot seeds, treated cucumber seeds, pelleted carrot seeds, stratified sweet cicely seeds, carrot seeds in tape, and woad seeds in pods.*

with gallons of water, hoping to keep the seed flats amply moist until Friday evening. During the early stages of seed germination, there was adequate, albeit rather uneven moisture. Our memories of returning to the farm every Friday evening and immediately running upstairs to check on our plants is as vivid as if it happened last week. The thrill of seeing the first signs of germinating seeds, the first cotyledons, the first true leaves is as constant today as it was back then. It matters not at all that we now have professional greenhouses and that we seed anywhere between three hundred and four hundred species of plants each season; we are still struck by the beauty of young seedlings growing.

As soon as the seed flats began to germinate, it became obvious that there wasn't adequate light for young plants to develop in the converted bedroom. We went to a salvage company and bought several used fluorescent light fixtures and suspended them over the table. We set the lights on a timer so they would work in our absence. And with this very primitive setup and total lack of experience, we managed to end up with a few respectable plants to set out into our first perennial border. Buoyed by that success we decided to continue growing more seedlings the next spring.

The following year we set up our "greenhouse" in much the same manner, but this time on the first floor of the farmhouse, nearer to a source of water, in a room with more windows, and over a floor register where we trapped heat from the furnace by draping the whole table with a piece of plastic and letting the plastic extend to the floor. We used the same lighting system, but substituted grow lights for regular fluorescent bulbs, and once again produced a few more perennials and some acceptable seedlings for cabbage, broccoli, and cauliflower.

Two years later we built our first glass greenhouse, on the east-southeast side of the farmhouse, and it is the place where we seed all our plants to this day. This greenhouse measures nine feet wide by thirty feet long, has homemade workbenches along each side and a worktable at one end. The space is small but efficient and it means we can do all our seeding from February until April in that one greenhouse before we move seed flats into the larger farm greenhouses for transplanting and growing on.

If you already have a greenhouse, either attached to the house or freestanding, give some thought to the physical layout of the space before using it for seeding. A greenhouse used as a conservatory or to grow houseplants functions differently from a greenhouse used for germinating seedlings. Here are some ideas on laying out a working greenhouse.

You will need a worktable or seeding area where seed packets, seed flats, and journals can be kept absolutely dry. If seeding is done in the same area where flats are to grow on, then separate the two areas somewhat so you can water seed flats easily during their growing-on stages without getting water on the seeding area.

Locate a seeding table, if possible, out of direct sunlight both for your own comfort and so that spread-out seed flats are not exposed to hot, drying sun. If this is not possible, try suspending a light curtain or shade cloth to protect the work area.

Make certain that any worktable and greenhouse benches are as level as possible. Chink table legs, if necessary, before filling benches with containers. This is not a trivial detail. When newly seeded flats or young seedlings are watered, the water quickly flows to the lowest corner of a table or an individual container, resulting in uneven watering.

Provide for storage areas in the greenhouse where supplies can be kept dry. That includes things such as planting containers, seeding mixtures, watering nozzles, watering cans, tubs or troughs for making seed mixtures, clipboards, paper, pencils, and the like. You don't want supplies to be constantly moist so that they will be damaged, corroded, or become perfect breeding places for insects, fungi, and disease.

Ideally, greenhouses should have some electricity that can be used for lighting, running appliances, and possibly heating mats. Be certain that the electrical outlets are supplied with ground fault interrupters, making them safer to use in an area where there is lots of water.

A good double work sink installed somewhere in the greenhouse would be helpful for washing out containers and tools, and even for soaking equipment. While these tasks can be done with hoses on the greenhouse floor, it would be easier, cleaner, and more efficient to have a work sink. Greenhouse work is messy, and whatever can be done to restrict tasks to well-designed areas will prove helpful.

An Indoor Growing Area

IF YOU DON'T HAVE a real greenhouse, it will be necessary to adapt some area in the house. Starting seeds inside necessitates setting up a working space with access to water, light, heat, and electricity and locating that space where you can create conditions that resemble as much as possible those of a real greenhouse. In addition to the requirements already noted, a greenhouse has more humidity than rooms in a typical household, especially during the winter months when the central heating is running.

Depending upon your plans, indoor seeding can be done in a space as small as a windowsill, or you could allocate a whole room to the setup. You can design simple but efficient homemade equipment for seeding areas, or you can invest in commercially built seeding shelves complete with supplemental lighting systems. Seeds can be sown in reused grocery containers or in purchased small seeding chambers with dome lids and internal heating coils. Garden centers and gardening catalogues are filled with seeding equipment and aids. Read the catalogues and look around at what is available commercially, but our advice to the beginner is to keep your first seeding area simple and personal and adapt your workspace as you recognize needs from experience.

We recommend that you set up a seeding area, whether it is in an existing greenhouse or inside the house, away from all other resident plants. Houseplants, no matter how healthy appearing, often host a variety of insects and diseases you don't want introduced into your seed flats. While a large jade plant may suffer a few mealybugs, little seedlings may not. Likewise for whiteflies, aphids, spider mites, scale, and a host of other things that are commonly found on ordinary houseplants. Keep the two areas separated.

Also be aware that an assortment of seed flats filled with soft, moist seeding soil is almost irresistible to house cats, regardless of how well behaved. There is no need to elaborate on how we discovered this. When

A very simple homemade setup can be placed near a good light source and adequate warmth for starting seedlings. The plastic drape helps keep humidity in the germinating area.

Found containers can be used just as successfully as store-bought ones for starting seeds. Just punch holes in the bottom for drainage.

it is time to set up seedlings in our own greenhouse, we install a screen door between it and the kitchen, and our cats sit looking out longingly at the hundreds of little dirt-filled boxes. It takes only a second for a cat to redistribute seeds from flat to flat. Moreover, cats seem to love young seedlings with particular fragrances, and seedlings are great to chew on in the early spring, when there is still nothing outdoors to taste other than last season's dried-up tufts of grass.

Depending upon how much space you will need, you can construct or buy a table for arranging seed flats and young plants. If at all possible, the table should be designed to allow the option of overhead or bottom watering. We will discuss the advantages of each method later in the chapter.

Choosing Containers

CONTAINERS FOR seeding plants are the easiest supplies to come by. They may be improvised from any variety of items lying around the house. There are a few simple guidelines when choosing seeding containers. They should be constructed of any inert material—pressed paper, pressed fiber, plastic, foam, or wood. The important thing is that they can be fitted with drainage holes in the bottom and that their proportions are suitable. Seeding trays need not and, in fact, should not be more than two to four inches deep. They should, of course, be flat bottomed for stability. They can be large enough to hold several rows of different varieties of seeds or a size to accommodate seeding a few seeds of one variety of plant or small enough to seed but a few seeds of a given species. This explanation is a case where a picture is worth a thousand words. See the illustration above, showing several ideas you can use.

Containers for seeding can also be purchased at garden centers or through catalogues. They include everything from shallow wooden trays to uniformly shaped plastic seed flats to peat containers, peat pellets, foam cells, and plastic plugs (multiple-celled containers). If you are doing extensive seeding and want the orderliness of uniform containers, then shallow plastic seed flats are probably the best choice. These can be reused from year to year and cleaned simply by washing them in hot water, soap, and a mild solution of bleach to disinfect them. We have also found good rectangular shallow plastic containers in the fish department of our supermarkets; these are usually available at a very nominal cost or sometimes for free. It is easy to punch holes in the bottoms and use them for seeding.

Years ago, when we were using reference books such as this one, we encountered the suggestion that empty egg cartons make good cavities for seeding. While a novel and thrifty idea, it turned out not to be a very good one. When seeding containers are too small, they dry out very quickly, and when seeds are beginning to germinate, it takes only a few hours of extreme dryness to kill a germinating seed. The containers we now use routinely measure 4½ inches wide by 6¼ inches long by 2½ inches deep. We restrict one species of plant to a seed flat. You may find that you prefer larger seed containers where you seed different species in "ribbon rows" (see photograph on page 35), but there is no right or wrong way. Experiment initially with a variety of methods and you will strike upon one that suits your needs, space, and the complexity of seeding being done.

Given as we are to solving gardening needs as easily as possible, we are inclined to offer one additional piece of advice. Make your first greenhouse or "greenhouse" as simple as possible. Don't be beguiled into spending too much money on outfits for this or that. There are many gardening supplies on the market and a number of supplies that will be helpful, but until you have some actual experience in planting a few seeds, it will be hard to evaluate what bells and whistles are really useful.

Seeding Mixtures

WHETHER YOU ARE GOING to purchase or make your own seeding mixture, let us point out from the outset that seeding mixtures and potting soils are two different things, and their use is not interchangeable. You should find both items available at your local gardening centers or through garden catalogues, but here is how they differ.

A seeding mixture is a blend of a variety of materials put together to create a medium that is light and porous, that will remain "friable" (easily crumbled) when wet, that will hold moisture well at the same time it allows oxygen to reach the plant roots. Seeding mixtures may or may not even contain any actual soil, and in fact most greenhouse growers today actually purchase manufactured soil-less mixtures for seeding and for growing plants.

Basic seeding mixtures are typically made up of combinations of finely milled peat moss, vermiculite, and perlite, in varying proportions depending upon the manufacturer. Recently we have seen mixtures that are made from composted bark and horticultural rock wool. Some manufacturers also include nutrients, wetting agents, limestone, and fungicides in their growing mixes. There is considerable variability in the manufactured products, but recently introduced labeling laws have made it necessary for manufacturers to identify ingredients on the packages, so you will be able to choose what you want and do not want in your mixture.

Potting soils are different from seeding mixtures in that they are usually made up of various combinations of some of the following ingredients: peat moss, vermiculite, perlite, pasteurized soil, compost, wetting agents, lime, and additional nutrients. They are heavier in weight and consistency than seeding mixtures and are meant to be used for potted plants.

After much experimentation with different mixtures and recipes, we have chosen to make up our own seeding mix, using two different recipes for two different circumstances. The first recipe is used for seeds that are sown into seed flats from which they will be transplanted to grow on; the majority of vegetable and herb seeds are treated this way. The second recipe is used for seeds that are sown directly into individual containers where they will be allowed to germinate and grow on without being transplanted. This practice is common with most members of the Cucurbitaceae family, such as cucumbers, melons, and squashes. It is also a method used for plants that resent being transplanted.

When choosing a seeding mixture for seeds that will be seeded and then transplanted, it is important to

THE COMPONENTS OF
SEEDING MIXTURES

SEEDING AND TRANSPLANTING mixtures, whether purchased or made at home, often consist of many of the same ingredients. Here is a brief description of the major components.

Peat moss is made up of decomposed bog plants. In areas where peat is mined, the depth of the bogs may represent hundreds of years of vegetative growth and decay. Peat moss is nearly sterile and slightly to very acidic. The level of acidity varies with the age, composition, and location of the area where the peat was collected. Peat moss is packaged for agricultural use in a number of ways. It usually comes ground and dried. Peat moss for seeding mixtures should be finely ground and as free of rough materials as possible. More coarse peat moss is used in building outdoor garden beds. Since peat moss has little nutritional value, it is used to build up the composition of soils or mixtures. It helps to keep soils friable, and it can absorb up to fifteen times its own weight in water. Concern about the harvesting of old bogs and the increasing use of peat moss has prompted research into finding alternative components for the greenhouse and agricultural community. Some of these include processed coconut fibers and peanut shells.

Perlite is volcanic glass that has been mined, pulverized, and then expanded by heating to produce grayish white granules that are used in a number of ways commercially. It has good insulating properties and is very lightweight. The granules are manufactured in various sizes, but medium and large granules are most often used in soil-less mixtures. Its primary function is to lighten the mixture and promote good aeration and soil drainage.

Vermiculite is also a naturally occurring rock, similar to what we commonly call mica. The rock is mined, crushed, and then expanded by heat into rough granules that are used agriculturally as well as for other commercial applications. Like perlite, it is graded into different sizes, and for seeding mixtures, the small fine grades are recommended. Like perlite and peat moss, vermiculite is nearly sterile and it has the ability to absorb water. It provides lightweight bulk for good aeration and drainage.

Pasteurized soil is used in this book to mean real garden soil that has been heated to a temperature of 140°F–160°F to rid the soil of weed seed and pathogens. We dig soil from our land and remove any top vegetative growth before treating the soil. Our explanation of pasteurized soil should not be confused with commercially prepared soils, as some of these do not contain any real soils, only mixtures of ingredients combined to resemble the look of soil. You will have to

A variety of containers filled to the right level for seeding are shown with the major components of seeding mixes. From left to right: *peat moss, perlite, vermiculite, compost, and soil.*

read labels to understand what is being sold for soil, as there is great variability from one product to another.

Pasteurized composts are also variable in their composition. We make our own compost from animal manures, leaves, grass clippings, leftover household foods, and other discarded organic matter that can be safely incorporated. Each gardener will have his or her own recipes and methods of making compost. When we refer to seeding mixtures that are homemade, we use our own compost. Since compost may contain pathogens, we pasteurize it for use in a growing-on mix, but use it without treatment in the outdoor garden. If composts are purchased, they will have many different ingredients in their makeup but are assumed to be disease free. As always, read labels to decide what you want to include in your soils.

Lime is a form of calcium carbonate, sold for agricultural use as a fine white powder. It may have differing amounts of magnesium carbonate. We use a high magnesium form called dolomitic lime for our soil mixtures and in our gardens. Lime without the added magnesium is sometimes referred to as agricultural lime. Plants need both magnesium and calcium in the soils, and some growers vary their use of agricultural and dolomitic lime to keep these two requirements in balance. The best way to evaluate what lime you need is to have soils tested periodically.

Individual growers and commercial manufacturers may incorporate other components into soil mixtures. These include various forms of plant fertilizers or soil amendments such as bonemeal, blood meal, fish meal, kelp meal, greensand, superphosphate, rock phosphate, and more. Some growers use sand as an ingredient to lighten the mixture and increase drainage. Each grower's recipe is derived from years of experimentation and results from finding what works best and what materials we feel comfortable using.

know that seeds will germinate perfectly well in a sterile soil-less mixture, since the seed contains all the food it needs to support germination and very early growth. We make this seeding mixture from a simple combination of peat moss, vermiculite, and perlite. All three ingredients are purchased in large containers. Peat moss for seeding should be very finely milled; vermiculite and perlite should also be small grained. When combining the three ingredients, we first break apart the compressed peat so that it is completely loosened and then measure two parts peat to one part perlite and one part vermiculite into a trough or large tub and stir the three together until they are completely mixed. When doing this, be certain to wear a face mask. Ingredients are dusty and should not be inhaled.

Once the ingredients are thoroughly combined, water is added slowly and blended in so that the whole mix is lightly moist but not soggy. Test the mixture with your hand; it should not clump together when pressed. Proper moisture in the seeding mixture is very important. If seeding mixtures are too dry, it is very hard to get them to absorb water. If they are properly moist, they will take up water readily, making it very easy to water newly seeded flats without disturbing any seeds.

Our second seeding mixture, for seeds to be sown and grown on in their original container, needs to have the same friable properties as the first, but it also needs to contain ingredients that will nourish the seedling for a longer period of time. Our recipe begins with the same three ingredients, two parts peat moss to one part each perlite and vermiculite, broken down and prepared as described above. In addition, this mixture includes one part pasteurized garden soil or pasteurized compost. All four ingredients are mixed together until well blended and moistened as described above. If you are purchasing pasteurized soils and composts to make your own mixtures, they should be weed free. If you are using your own soils and composts, as we do, they typically contain weed seeds and pathogens. Therefore we pasteurize our ingredients by heating them to about 160°F and letting them cool before mixing. We have used a couple of methods of pasteurizing, first in the kitchen oven, which works perfectly well if you can stand the mess and the earthy fragrances. When our needs for pasteurized soils grew to the extent that we were heating up bushels of garden soil, we moved the whole operation outdoors and set up an old maple sapping stove.

As home gardeners growing only a few hundred seedlings, we made our seeding mixes in a large plastic tub and blended the ingredients with an oversized spoon or garden trowel. As our business grew, we built a simple soil mixer by converting a discarded clothes dryer into a mixer. More recently we have built several simply constructed wooden troughs that stand on two-foot-tall legs. The ingredients for a growing medium are measured out into the troughs and everything is mixed with a trowel, hoe, or shovel. Using troughs has proved to be the easiest and most comfortable way to work. They are the right height so we don't need to bend uncomfortably, and it is easy to fill containers by simply dipping and scooping up the mixture. At the end of a day of seeding or transplanting, we cover any mixture in the trough to prevent it from drying out. Small amounts of leftover mixtures can also be stored in closed plastic bags or covered containers until needed.

There are a number of other options to using commercial soil mixtures or preparing your own. Some of these include peat pellets that expand in size when watered. There are artificial growing blocks, tools to make soil cubes, and devices to make paper pots for holding soils. Given what is available, we recommend simply buying a bag or two of prepared seeding mixture or the few ingredients that it takes to mix your own. If completely soil-less mixtures are used, with no components to fertilize young seedlings, then choices will have to be made about the nourishment of young plants at the time of transplanting. We will talk about this in the next chapter.

Seeding

NOW WITH THE physical space laid out, containers and seeding mixture on hand, and a seeding schedule worked out, you are ready to pull together the various seed packages and begin. Sort through the seed packets that are to be seeded on a given date and set them before you on the worktable. Count the number of varieties you will be seeding, decide what containers to use, and start the process by filling several containers with seeding mixture before you begin.

This will allow you to concentrate on seeding without having to go back and refill containers.

Fill the containers to the top with loose seeding mixture, smooth and level the top of the mixture, and then lightly tamp it down into the container so that it stands about a half inch from the top, but not much lower. The mixture should nearly fill the container so that when the seeds are germinating there will be optimal air circulation around the seedlings. At the same time, there needs to be a bit of space from the top of the soil level to the top of the seed flat so that you can water the flats without having water run off and out of the container, carrying with it mixture and perhaps some actual seeds. Use the same general procedure when filling individual seeding chambers, cells, or plugs.

Having filled a number of containers, isolate one container at a time so you will not confuse any newly seeded flat with ones that hold only the mixture. If this detailed advice sounds rather foolish, let us assure you that some seeds are so small they are difficult to see once distributed over the top of a seed flat. We have unintentionally double-seeded a container on more than one occasion. Look over the varieties you plan to seed in this session and begin with the plants that have the largest seeds. Good hand seeding demands a certain amount of dexterity, and practicing first with the largest seeds helps develop control and accuracy. You will be taking a small amount of some very small seeds and trying to distribute them evenly over a small surface area. It takes concentration and practice so that seeds are not spilled or clumped into one area of the container.

Open the seed packages, one variety at a time, preferably by cutting off a narrow part of the top of the package with sharp scissors. Crease the seed package and actually use it as a funnel to scatter the seeds over the top of the flat. If seed packages are pulled open and seeds are sprinkled over the glued flap, small seeds may adhere to the glued area. Likewise, if you tear rather than cut open the seed package, there are often rough paper fibers that can catch seeds, preventing them from flowing slowly and evenly out of the package.

As you become more familiar with handling seeds of different sizes, shapes, and textures, you will make distinctions in the precautions you need to take in the seeding process. Pepper seeds, for example, are so large, relatively speaking, that they may be emptied out into the palm of the hand and then actually placed one by one in a nearly perfect distribution over the top of the seed flat. That method would be difficult to use with the smaller seeds of basil and virtually impossible with the dustlike seeds of chamomile.

Begin seeding with the largest seeds you will plant in a given work session, crease the seed packet, tilt the packet ever so slowly, and try to sprinkle the seeds as evenly as possible over the top of the seed container. The number of seeds you want to seed in a given area is determined by the size of the seed and the size of the germinating seedling. As a general rule, the larger the seed, the more space it will need to germinate and grow in before it is ready for transplanting. Seed flats should hold as many seeds as they can support in early growth, but not so many that the flats will be too crowded. An ideally seeded flat would have each seed resting in its own tiny space next to but not touching any neighboring seeds. See the illustration and further information on page 36 as a guide for correct density in seed flats.

A folded piece of paper can be used to distribute seeds evenly into these ribbon rows.

Now, depending upon the variety of plant being seeded, it will be necessary to choose an appropriate planting depth. Some seeds will be sown and left on the top of the seeding mixture and only pressed into the surface without being covered; some will be sown on the top of the seeding mixture and covered very lightly with a dusting of additional mixture; some are totally covered after sowing; some are planted by pushing them down into the mixture so they are covered by a good half inch of mixture. Different seeds have different requirements for germinating: some need light, some need darkness, some are light neutral. Some seeds need more moisture than others to germinate. Some seeds will germinate in a couple of days, while others will not show any signs of life for a couple of weeks. For specific information on seeding and growing vegetables and herbs, refer to the specific

plants in the chapters that follow, as well as the seeding charts at the end of each of these chapters where you will find very specific guidelines for each species.

Once you have finished seeding one container, immediately label the container. Labels can be written before seeding begins or as the work is done. We like to use rigid plastic stakes for labeling, because they are easy to write on with a permanent marker or a lead pencil. Wooden labels are available, or there are adhesive labels that can be affixed to the side of a seed flat. Whatever form of label you choose, make certain that the writing won't fade or wash off. While it may be easy to recognize the difference between unlabeled tomato seedlings and parsley seedlings, there will be no way to distinguish two varieties of broccoli seedlings or two seeded containers of different varieties of sweet bell peppers if the labels are faded or misplaced.

In addition, we suggest that you think about what information to include on the label, beyond the obvious identification of plant species and variety. Here is what we write down: the date we seeded the container, the name of the plant, its variety, the seed source (either a company name or a notation that it was our own seed and from what year), and the number of flats seeded of that particular plant variety. Thus a typical tomato flat label might read: *3/12/98*,

Three seed flats with different seeding densities. The one on the top shows good, even seeding, while the container on the left is rather sparsely seeded and the container on the right is too thickly seeded.

TOMATO, *Brandywine, our 97, 4.* Home gardeners would want to record at least the first three pieces of data, but it may also be worthwhile noting the seed source, because you will be surprised how this helps in evaluating seed sources and seed longevity over a few seasons. Recording the number of flats that have been seeded of any one variety may not be necessary for the backyard gardener; we do this so that when it comes time to transplant, we know without going back to our printed journal that we have to gather perhaps two flats of sweet marjoram and fourteen flats of Ace peppers.

This brings us to the next bit of record keeping that we strongly recommend be done at the time of seeding. In a separate journal, gardening calendar, or diary, write down when, what, and how many containers or seeds you have seeded of each variety. You will be able to refer to the journal and add additional information about how long it took the seed flats to germinate, when flats were ready to be transplanted, the length of time it took for the plants to grow on to the hardening-off stage. The journals can and should be continued once plants are set outside, with entries on time of setting out, dates when different species blossomed, bore fruit, and any additional information that will make you more familiar with a plant's performance. While you may be shaking your head thinking you aren't really going to want to know all that about each plant, we assure you that your own record keeping, along with interesting observations and anecdotes, will become your most valuable gardening information. The note taking will teach you how to see, how to evaluate, and what to look for in all areas of gardening, and you will soon be extrapolating information from one area of growing to another. What's more, old gardening notes are just plain fun to go back to and read. They will trigger memories reminding you a few seasons down the road just how much progress you have made.

Continue seeding each variety, working with one at a time right through the labeling and record keeping. As flats are seeded and labeled, they may be set aside until the day's seeding has been completed. It is not necessary to water each flat as it is seeded.

When seeding is done, make certain that unused seeds are repackaged and tightly sealed. In many cases, well-packaged and well-stored seeds will retain their viability for at least a year, if not longer. Return any unused seeds to a dry, dark storage area for permanent storage. Never leave them in a humid greenhouse when they are not being used.

Watering Newly Seeded Containers

ONCE YOU ARE READY to water newly seeded containers, you have a choice of methods. Containers may be watered from the top with hoses or watering cans, or they may be watered from the bottom, allowing water to wick up into the soil mixture. Given the choice, we would always suggest that initial watering be done from the bottom. The process involves placing all the seed flats into a shallow tray, about two to four inches deep, and filling the tray with one to two inches of water. The seed flats will slowly absorb the water through the bottom drainage holes, and when the flats are fully moistened you will be able to see and feel moisture at the top of the seed flats. Depending upon the number of seed flats placed into the watering tray, this process can take anywhere from a few minutes to an hour or so. Here is what to watch for. Leave the seed containers in the watering tray until they are moist all the way from bottom to top, but remove them before the seeding mixture is too saturated. Water should not puddle on top of the seed flat.

The advantages of bottom watering are numerous. First, you can be certain that the flats are thoroughly

Bottom watering of flats can be done using plastic trays. Overhead watering means using hoses with a variety of watering nozzles, from misters to large flares. Choose nozzles that are appropriate to the size of the young plants.

watered. Second, you know that none of the seeds is disturbed or redistributed by the force of water from a watering can or hose. When we use the wick watering method, we use large old photographic trays that will accommodate as many as a dozen newly seeded flats. Any flat household containers can be substituted for watering, such as large baking pans or recycled plastic trays available from the fish and deli departments of many supermarkets. You don't need to have trays that will accommodate all the seed flats at one time. Water in stages if necessary.

While we recommend bottom watering for small-scale growers, admittedly we do so many seed flats in a given work session that we choose to water dozens of newly seeded flats all at the same time at the end of

hours of seeding. Since we have greenhouse benches, we arrange all the unwatered flats in a group and water with hoses. If you are lucky enough to have a greenhouse, you may also want to follow this practice.

When watering with a hose, always turn on the hose away from the flats or plants to be watered and adjust the water pressure before nozzles are aimed at the intended targets. A sudden blast of water aimed directly at a fine arrangement of seed and mixture can have disastrous results. Avoid creating any water craters in the middle of carefully seeded flats. It is frustrating and very time-consuming to try to recover tiny seeds from a soggy clump of seeding mixture and nearly impossible to reseed them evenly.

Start the watering process with the finest spray nozzle available, as any excessive force from an oversized nozzle can literally blow tiny seeds right off the top of a seed flat. Too much water or excessive water pressure can easily redistribute a careful seeding job, rearranging seeds all along one side or into a corner of the flat.

When top-watering with a hose or watering can, moisten the seed flats in a series of short stages, as it will take time for the flats to begin to absorb the water deep into the mixture. Don't allow excess water to build up on the surface of the container and puddle before it can percolate down into the soil. Spray the tops of all the seed flats evenly, waving the fine spray nozzle slowly back and forth over the tops of the flats. If the water is not being absorbed as quickly as it falls on the flats, stop watering for a few seconds and then resume, remembering to first aim the hose away from the flats.

Now that you can monitor how the water is being absorbed at a good even rate, continue watering the seed flats until they are thoroughly wet. That means wetting the flats all the way to the bottom of the containers, just the reverse of what is accomplished with wick watering. It is essential that flats contain moisture evenly from top to bottom. You will gather experience in recognizing a well-watered flat both by looking at the moisture on the surface of the soil and by lifting the flat so its weight tells you the difference between a flat that is only superficially moist and one that has moisture all the way to the drainage holes. Lift newly watered containers and actually look into the drainage holes to see if the growing medium is moist. We cannot underscore too strongly the importance of watering correctly for successful seed and plant growth. Correct moisture means a good balance of water and drainage and oxygen to root systems.

If you cannot use hoses or wick watering techniques for watering your seed flats and have to rely on hand-held watering devices such as watering cans or bottles, be certain they are outfitted with very fine nozzles. We would even recommend using a watering bottle with a fine misting nozzle to thoroughly dampen the surface of newly seeded flats before beginning to water with hand-held cans. It is very difficult to water slowly enough with a watering can to prevent puddling on the top of the seed flats. Once seeds have germinated and have some top growth, watering with hand-held devices will be easier; at this point, seeds will have a root and thus an anchor into the soil.

Watering is a messy undertaking, and you don't want to be doing it where you are trying not to moisten outside the areas of the seed flats. If you are trying to water an area thoroughly, that means you need to get moisture into every corner and along every edge of the containers. If this must be done in the middle of living space in the house, use a large piece of plastic that extends well beyond the area being watered, so that you won't be stingy with water at the outer perimeters of the seed flats. Or better still, place flats into a shower stall, bathtub, or stopped-up sink where there is no need to worry about messing up the floor around the containers.

Placing Seed Flats into Their Germinating Areas

WE HAVE SPOKEN about watering newly seeded flats as if they need to be watered in a location different from the place they will be left for germination,

A small glass greenhouse off the farmhouse kitchen is where we start all of our seeds for any given season. The thermostat, seen in the background, controls heat mats under all of the germinating seed flats.

because you may have to complete tasks in different areas if a real greenhouse is not available. In our own work areas, we seed on a worktable in the greenhouse and then move the seed flats directly onto the benches where they are watered and left to germinate.

When choosing a location to germinate seeds, it is best to find a growing area where you can control temperature, moisture, humidity, and light. The majority of vegetable and herb plants we discuss in this book will germinate best at temperatures between 65°F and 75°F. That uniformity of temperature may be maintained as air or ambient temperature, by controlling the temperature of a whole greenhouse, room, or section of a room. But that would often prove either very difficult or very costly, especially when you consider that many of us don't even keep our houses that warm around the clock. Germinating seeds will do just as well if the temperatures of the soils they are living in are kept at a required temperature, and controlling the temperature of soil in a group of seed flats is much more manageable and more economically feasible.

For this purpose, we use electric heat mats under all our germinating seed flats that require warm temperatures, enabling us to keep germinating flats at a constant temperature while the air temperatures in the whole greenhouse may fluctuate as much as twenty degrees around an ideal germinating temperature. In the middle of a sunny March day, our greenhouse may climb to 80°F or 85°F before we decide to vent it, and on a cold and windy March night, we may allow greenhouse temperatures to fall to 55°F before the furnaces go on. While warmer ambient air may heat the seed flats to temperatures warmer than 65°F, we do not want them to fall below a certain temperature. When ambient air temperatures cool, the heat mats keep flats from cooling down.

Heat mats or heat tapes are manufactured by many companies and come in a variety of styles. We suggest you examine samples at your local gardening centers or in any number of gardening catalogues. They are relatively inexpensive, when you consider them as an alternative to heating a whole room for germinating seeds, and, if well cared for, they will last for a number of seasons. While we are reluctant to recommend buying supplies that can be improvised at home, we feel that a small heat mat is perhaps an investment that will help you achieve some measure of success in growing seedlings indoors.

Heat mats and heat coils typically have thermostatic controls that allow you to place the seed flats on top of the mats and select a desired temperature. The mats we use at the farm require us to place a temperature-sensing probe into one seed flat; we appropriate an unseeded container for monitoring temperature and locate it among the seeded flats. If you use heat mats for growing several varieties of plants, it is necessary to choose a temperature that is an average optimum setting or to schedule the use of mats by grouping plants together that share similar temperature needs. For example, eggplant likes a very warm germinating medium, while broccoli likes germinating somewhat cooler. How do you choose the temperature setting? Heat mats are used primarily for germinating flats, and

once seeds have actually begun to germinate, the flats are relocated to another growing area. That means that each seed flat spends only a portion of its growing time on a heating device. If we review our seeding schedules, we are reminded that eggplant is seeded long before broccoli, meaning that the eggplant flats will have germinated and been moved off the heat mats when bottom heat, perhaps at a lower setting, is needed for the broccoli and cabbages.

Having made a recommendation for some sort of bottom heating devices, we remember clearly our first "greenhouse" and know that initially home gardeners often want to see just how well they can do something simply at first. Seeds of many, if not most, vegetables and herbs will germinate quite well under less than ideal temperatures. Ideal temperatures are arrived at for the sake of saying that seeds of a given species, with a given germination rate, say 88 percent, should germinate nearly 88 percent of the time in x number of days at a temperature of x degrees. It does not mean that you could not also get nearly the same germination under different conditions. What actually happens under different but acceptable conditions may simply be slower germination rates, uneven germination of seeds of one species over a longer germinating period, or something less than the calculated percentage of germination. Any of these variables may still provide you with satisfactory results.

When setting up your own growing areas, you are aiming to create acceptable conditions for germinating seeds. If you need a place to germinate seeds that is as close to 65°–75°F as constantly as possible and you don't want to purchase any heating devices, figure out where you can put together such a setup. One way we tried to do this in the early stages of growing was to arrange a tray of seed flats on legs over a heat register in the house. Some friends have told us of putting a few seed flats on the top of their refrigerator where there was warmth from the appliance motor. Other people have set up germinating tables near a woodstove, where the heat was good but the humidity very poor.

While we have focused on seeds that want heat for germination, as the majority of annual vegetables and herbs do, there are a number of species that need periods of warmer and cooler temperatures to fluctuate for germination. There are also species that need to be frozen, chilled, or chilled and warmed and rechilled before they will germinate. We refer you to specific plants in the book and to the tables for each of these plants located at the end of Chapters 5 and 6 for suggestions on germinating temperatures and other special needs. Also make use of the information printed on seed packages and in plant catalogues.

Light

In the description about seeding flats, we spoke of the planting-depth requirements of seeds in general. These depths are determined, at least in part, by consideration of a given seed's response to light for germination. Some seeds need light to break dormancy, to germinate. Examples that come quickly to mind are celery and lettuce. Some, like chervil, need darkness. Some seeds appear to be light neutral, meaning that given appropriate temperatures and moisture, they can germinate under a variety of light-related conditions. Refer to specific plants in this book, or to good seed catalogues and seed packets for this information. If information is not given about light requirements, it is usually because the plants are light neutral.

Whatever the light requirements of a particular variety, we never place our newly seeded flats into direct sunlight. Sunlight, even for seeds that need light, is just too harsh and too drying for seeds that are sitting on the surface or just beneath the surface of a seeding mixture. Sunlight will quickly rob the surface mixture of all its moisture and can quickly kill a tender germinating seed. If your beginning setup is a windowsill facing south, make certain you protect the germinating flats from sun with a sheer curtain or shade cloth. Better still, choose a windowsill with good light but no sun. We are making a distinction here between light for germinating seeds and sunlight you may very well want to take advantage of for the growing on of young seedlings.

When germinating seeds need darkness, their flats may be positioned under a bench or table or along with other containers on top of a table. Simply cover the top of these particular flats with a piece of heavy dark plastic or other lid during the daytime. We recommend that the cover be removed at night and replaced very early in the morning, because while you are trying to keep light away from the seeds, air circulation over the top of the flat is an important factor, as a deterrent against diseases and fungi that can destroy tender young seedlings.

Humidity

Humidity and moisture can be thought of as two separate but related requirements of germinating seeds and growing plants. We have discussed watering, but that specifically refers to the moisture content of the seeding mixture in the flat itself. Seed flats also do best in an environment that has adequate humidity. Real greenhouses are advantageous when it comes to keeping an environment humid. Our houses are a more difficult environment. They are typically very dry, most especially in the winter and early spring when heating systems are in use daily, precisely the same time indoor seeding takes place.

We attempted in our early indoor setups to re-create greenhouse humidity with simple makeshift plastic tents draped over the table/trays we set up. See the picture of a similar setup on page 29. The air inside the growing area is much more humid, and the seed flats do not dry out as quickly; even more importantly, it is easier to keep the flats uniformly moist, not just moist at the bottoms with the tops drying out quickly.

If you have spent any time in gardening centers or looking through catalogues that include manufactured germinating chambers, you have seen endless numbers of domed devices. Whether you purchase a covered chamber or create your own, the advantages of higher humidity will be apparent in successful germination. When we look at all the manufactured devices, we are struck by the ways in which manufacturers have chosen to photograph their products. You are indeed aiming to increase the humidity of areas when seeds are germinating, so an enclosed environment can be advantageous. But once the seeds have germinated, we like to take the seed flats out from under their tented areas where there is better light and most definitely better air circulation. We cannot imagine keeping a tomato plant with several sets of true leaves tightly enclosed in a little growing cell, with its dome just centimeters away from the top of the plant. Such advertisements are, perhaps, only a way to present the product in a more appealing way, but they are very misleading pieces of visual information. In the struggle to germinate seeds and produce healthy young seedlings, we are always weighing the conditions of heat, light, moisture, humidity, and air circulation to produce a healthy plant. We choose not to use chemical fungicides, herbicides, insecticides, and growth hormones, and so we are trying to set up environments that are most conducive to healthy growth. Small tightly enclosed individual cells are not suitable for young plants.

Air Circulation

AS SOON AS we begin to fill our greenhouse with newly seeded flats, we set up small fans that circulate air throughout the space. This prevents stagnant air from creating pockets of high humidity where bacteria and fungi can grow. Air circulation also lets the leaves of newly watered plants dry more quickly. Constantly wet leaves can also become a place for diseases to develop. We will discuss disease and insect problems more fully in the next chapter. For now, we want to introduce the idea that good air circulation, introduced early on in the growing cycle, is beneficial in creating a healthy environment.

The Watch Begins

SEEDING DONE, flats watered, growing area established, and you have set the growing cycle in motion. Watch everything, every day. Indulge yourself in the extra time it takes to closely observe what takes place in each and every seed container. Each container is a little environment where life will begin, or if looked at in a broader perspective, where life simply continues, since the ungerminated seeds were simply life suspended until the right conditions occurred.

We never get over the thrill of watching a seed begin to grow. Daily inspections reveal how different seeds begin to show change as they absorb moisture, as the seed cracks open ever so slightly, showing some little bit of light color before the actual radicle and cotyledon appear. Some seed flats will seem to go almost overnight from inactive-looking containers to ones with dozens of little organisms. Other flats will sprout one seed here and then another before they fill out with uniform germination. Some seeds will be so small and their initial growth so tiny as to be seen only on very close inspection. Other varieties will spring open with a cotyledon that seems all out of proportion to its origins.

Don't miss a thing. Take a few minutes whenever possible to add some written observations to your seeding journals. While you may never want to write a book about growing plants from seed, you never know where the record keeping can lead you.

CHAPTER THREE

Growing On

Germination

DURING THE PROCESS of germination, most seeds undergo a series of specific changes. Understanding these changes makes it easier to appreciate the kind of environment we need to set up and monitor. First there is the taking up of water by the seed, which is referred to as water imbibition. This is accompanied by an increase in the enzymatic activity of the seed, resulting in an increase in the seed's rate of metabolism. Increased moisture and metabolism initiate embryonic growth. That growth causes the seed coat to rupture, followed by the emergence of the seedling.

Depending upon the placement of the seeds in their seed flats, we are able to see various stages of development. Any seeds that are sown on or pressed into the surface of the seed flats, such as lettuce and basil, can be seen to enlarge within a matter of hours as they take in water. If surface-sown seeds have any appreciable size, we can watch not only the initial enlarging but also the distinct thin light-colored crack in the dark brown seed coat as it ruptures. Once the seed coat is broken, watch for the first visible growth in the form of a radicle, or the plant's primitive root. The radicle will extend down into the soil, forming the plant's primary root from which the secondary roots will develop.

The variability of shape, size, and color of cotyledons is evidenced by this arrangement of plants. From back row to front row, and left to right, they are: *buttercup squash, red sails lettuce, buttercrunch lettuce, and soybean; annual artemisia, delicata squash, green tomatillo, and luffa gourd; borage, cinnamon basil, dill, and German chamomile.*

Many of the seeds we plant are covered by a thin layer of soil so that their first visible growth is seen when the cotyledons begin to extend above the soil line. Cotyledons are the first seed leaves, usually quite dissimilar from the true leaves of the plants. Most of the vegetables and herbs discussed in this book have a pair of cotyledons, meaning that they are classified as dicotyledons. The small seed leaves appear, extend, and enlarge on the seedling stems days or even weeks before the true leaves begin to develop. Each of the drawings used to illustrate the plants discussed in Chapters 5 and 6 shows the shape and relative size of the plant's dicotyledons and the first set of true leaves. Use these illustrations to help you identify your own germinating seeds. From these drawings and from your own observations, you will begin to see what enormous variability there is early on in plant growth and plant morphology.

A few of the plants in this book, those belonging to the Liliaceae and Gramineae families, are classified as monocotyledons, because they have only one seed leaf in the embryo, and that seed leaf may not be apparent to the eye during germination. Therefore the drawings of plants such as asparagus, onion, and garlic chives show true leaves initially, as these are the leaves that are the first to emerge in the seed flats.

Watching for the first signs of growth also teaches us about a number of other characteristics of germinating seeds. Some seeds will germinate very rapidly, and in only a few days there will be evidence of growth, assuming temperatures are appropriately high. Lettuce, broccoli, cabbage, and chamomile behave this way, but in addition to their speed, they also germinate in a very uniform fashion. Once germination commences, their seed containers are evenly patterned by new growth. Some plants take as long as a week or two to show signs of growth, but once growth does begin, it will also take place evenly throughout the seed container. Peppers, eggplant, and celery are examples.

A number of species are slow to germinate even under optimum conditions. Parsley is known for this, to the extent that there is a whimsical old saying that the seed must "travel back and forth to the devil seven times before starting to grow." Regardless of how long the seeds take to germinate, once they start, they do so throughout the seed flat. Herbs such as rosemary and lavender germinate from seed in yet another way. There may well be several seeds that start to grow in a week's time, after which there will be days with no further activity. This uneven and irregular pattern can continue for several months in each seed flat.

We point out these differences in time and uniformity of germination so that you can expect various growth patterns in your seed containers. Use the charts at the end of Chapters 5 and 6 to help interpret your results. But remember that the charts are set up for controlled temperatures, proper light requirements, appropriate humidity, and high-quality seeds. Even if you duplicate all these optimum conditions, you are still apt to see some differences in your seed flats. Use the charts as a point of departure, but be certain to record your own data so you can begin to construct timetables that are unique to your growing conditions.

Thus far we have discussed the importance of water, temperature, humidity, and light for germination. In addition, germinating seeds and young seedlings are affected by air, or most critically by one of the components of air, and that is oxygen. Starting at germination, when respiration increases rapidly, a seed's ability to germinate is affected by the availability of oxygen. The porous soil mixture holding the seed is designed to allow oxygen to reach the seed, and later the roots of the young seedling.

When seeds are beginning to germinate, the most important thing to watch for is constant and accurate watering. Seed flats need to be checked each day. Once a seed has imbibed water and begun to grow, it cannot continue the process if it is allowed to dry out. We mist the tops of the seed flats every day or several times a day for the first few days after seeding. We also check to make certain that the flats are not drying from the bottom heat. A good way to test this is to pick up the container to check its weight and to examine the seeding mixture by looking into the bottom holes of the containers.

Follow the advice about watering seed flats with small nozzles and a gentle water pressure now and all during the early stages of plant growth. Accurate watering also implies avoiding overwatering. If you have set up seed flats in a domed seeding area, if the area is humid, if there are a series of dark, cloudy days when humidity is high, then it may be necessary to skip misting or watering. Overwatering can affect the availability of oxygen to the seeds and it can create seed flats that invite the growth of bacteria, fungi, and insects.

Early Growth

WHILE EXTRA HEAT may be beneficial to seed germination, it is often not necessary or even desirable for growing on. If we are using heat mats or a warm germinating location primarily to initiate germination, we need to relocate these flats when the time is appropriate. Here is how we evaluate when and where to move young seedlings.

Most of the vegetable and herb plants we discuss will germinate indoors over a period of three days to two weeks. You will be able to make a visual assessment of this growth by the presence of small green cotyledons covering the surface of the container. When about 80 percent of the seeds in any given flat have germinated, it is time to remove the flat from the heat mats and relocate it to an area for growing on. It is not necessary to wait until every single seed has germinated. In fact, it is important not to allow the flats to linger on the heat mat, because once growth has started, it will continue at a rapid rate. Any few seeds that have not germinated will most likely sprout in the next few days, whether or not the seed flat has bottom heat.

When setting up an area for germinated seed flats to develop, consider the temperature and light needs of the different species you are growing. Some may want more warmth, some more intense light. Take care to step the flats into place gradually, especially if you are relocating seedlings that were germinated in darkness. Never place seed flats from a sheltered germinating area immediately into a sunny location. Move the containers first to bright light, then filtered sun, and then to full sun over a period of a week.

Check the optimum conditions for your plants on the growing charts at the end of Chapters 5 and 6, and set up a growing-on area that accommodates the average requirements of the plants you are working with. Don't be overly concerned with the compromises you need to make in departing from ideal temperatures. This will almost always be necessary in a home. Be more concerned about light requirements, good humidity, and careful watering.

As young seedlings grow, there is an obvious increase in vegetative matter in each seed flat. When that vegetative matter increases in size, there are many more surfaces where water can land and moisture can build up. For this reason, it is important to evaluate how and when to water so you are maintaining as healthy an environment as possible. This means choosing to water plants not only when they are dry but on particular days and at particular times of day. All during the growing season, we check on the upcoming weather to gauge watering in our greenhouses.

Our first rule is to always water in the morning, so that we can wet the containers thoroughly and so that any water on the leaves of the plants will have ample time to dry out hours before the sun disappears and the temperatures drop. Plants allowed to sit overnight with wet leaves or overly moist soil are an invitation to disease and insects. If you are bottom watering, still choose the early morning, so that plants can absorb moisture and soil surfaces can dry out somewhat before the evening. If you notice that there have been a series of dark sunless days and water has not really been heavily used by the young plants, hold off watering as long as possible and let the plants grow a little on the dry side until the weather clears. All during the growing-on stages, we emphasize the need for good air circulation around the seed flats and transplanted containers. Air will remove excess moisture from the leaves and the top of the soils, a very effective hedge against disease.

Growing to Transplant Time

JUST AS THERE WAS considerable variability in the time it took different species of plants to germinate, there will continue to be variability in the time it

Light from the window alone would not be adequate for these young seedlings. But the addition of a simply constructed setup with grow lights keeps young plants from reaching for light and becoming leggy.

takes germinated seeds to size up and develop their first sets of true leaves. Consult the charts in this book for guidance, but watch and record the progress of your own tiny plants. Your notes will be valuable from year to year as you are establishing seeding and growing calendars.

Young seedlings grown in greenhouses are positioned in rather ideal light conditions and rarely need to be moved about until they are transplanted or prepared to go out into the garden. In a home growing area, it may be necessary to find the best light by moving seed containers from one window to another as the intensity of light changes. It may also be advisable to set up additional grow lights to extend the perceived day length for the young plants. The most obvious evidence of too little light will be seen if young plants are elongating and leaning decidedly toward the light. It is possible to correct for this slightly by turning seed flats from day to day, but if the light is simply not adequate, plants will correct the direction of leaning, but still stretch upward too rapidly, resulting in leggy, thin-stemmed plants. This can occur even in the very early stages of growth, before plants have begun to develop their true leaves. Leggy growth should be avoided anytime during the growing cycle. Remedies for this include setting up grow lights or postponing indoor seeding until there is a longer natural photoperiod, when seeds can be started indoors and then moved early on into an outdoor cold frame where light is appropriate.

GROWN ON THE SPOT

SOME PLANTS are sown directly into containers indoors and left to germinate and grow on without any transplanting. This is typically done with the "cucurbits," vining crops such as cucumbers, squashes, and melons, when gardeners want to get an early start on the season. We recommend using biodegradable containers for these plants so that the young seedlings can be put into the ground, container and all, resulting in absolutely no disturbance to the roots.

If any of these plants is started on heat mats, the plants will have to be moved into a sunny growing-on area, as would any other seedlings. But we like to start these crops in individual pots in a warm sunny spot in the greenhouse, in late April or early May. Since no transplanting will take place, seeds are started in a growing mixture containing some nutrition. Seeds are covered with about a half inch of mixture and watered well; germination takes place in just a few days. If seeds are germinated in bright sun, they adapt immediately to the light. Make certain they are always well watered and provided with good air circulation. This same direct seeding can be accomplished on a warm, sunny windowsill.

All of our caveats about waiting until the time is

These watermelon plants were seeded and grown in a fiber-based container that can be planted right into the garden.

right to start seeding indoors are very important with the cucurbits. Each of these vining crops cannot go out into the garden until the soils and temperatures have warmed. Furthermore, you want seedlings that have only a few true leaves when it is time to harden them off. Vining crops should never be vining when they are ready to be set out. This may cause them to flower too early and stunt the whole plant. If this happens to you, pinch off any early flowers on the plants either inside or in the garden, allowing plants to size up vegetatively before flowering and fruiting begin.

As the tiny seedlings are growing, you will see a number of changes in the plants beyond their size gain. Very soon after germination, plants begin to develop their own particular pigmentation and individualized leaf forms as the true leaves develop. These are the leaves that resemble the shape and form of the mature plant leaves, but in these early stages they are often, though not always, smaller in scale. There will be every shade of green imaginable in the seed flats, as well as nongreen leaves. Some leaves will be extremely light yellow-green. Some will be medium green and dull, others medium green and glossy. Some leaves will be green on the upper parts of the leaves and burgundy beneath. Some leaves will be hairy, mottled, smooth, veined. Leaves will begin to form with wonderfully different shapes and fragrances. If you are growing plants from seed for the first time, this may be the stage when you most appreciate the incredible diversity of plant morphology at a scale that can be readily examined.

Young seedlings are ready to be transplanted from their seed flats when the majority of the plants in a given flat have developed one or two sets of true leaves. We prefer to transplant when there is evidence of one set of true leaves, as this allows us to handle the plant when it is very young, ensuring the least amount of shock to the plant's top growth and root system. It is usually quite acceptable to transplant after a couple of sets of true leaves have formed, but we would advise waiting no longer than this stage. It is harder on plants to be transplanted later in their development, and it is important to remember that if seeds were sown in a soil-less medium, they will soon need more nutrition than what was available in the seed embryo. If seedlings are left too long in their original seed flats, you may begin to see stress from crowding and lack of nutrition. It will be evidenced by stretching, overall loss of color, yellowing of the cotyledons, and even some cotyledon and leaf drop.

If your response is anything like our own, it will not be necessary to urge you to transplant as early on as is most beneficial to the plants. Transplanting tiny seedlings is one of the most pleasurable activities in our greenhouses. We watch each seed flat with real anticipation. In our climate, we say that greenhouse work truly takes the curse off winter. As soon as we begin to handle all those beautiful young plants, it feels as if the gardening season has really begun.

Transplanting

CONTAINERS AND GROWING mixes need to be chosen once it comes time to transplant. Tiny seedlings may be planted into individual containers, or several plants can be grown in one container. The choice of a container is governed by the plant's rate of growth, its eventual size at setting-out time, and the ease with which it can be transplanted into the garden. You also have the choice between reusable and biodegradable containers.

Our first recommendation would be to transplant each seedling into its own individual container. This allows the plant to grow without competition for space, water, and light. It also allows you to isolate from the general growing area any plant that shows signs of disease or the presence of insects.

If your indoor growing space is limited, we would recommend, as a second choice, using containers for growing one species or variety of plant and spacing the individual plants far enough apart so they have ample light, root growth area, and moisture for the next few weeks of indoor growth. Another acceptable alternative to shared containers is the use of connected individual cells referred to as plugs. These come in many sizes and can be used successfully for a variety of plants. Plugs are designed in large tray sizes and in cell packs with six, eight, or ten cells connected together.

Another consideration when choosing containers is how difficult it may be to transplant a given plant from its container into the garden. Plants sharing a container will have to be separated as they are set out into the field. Plants in individual plugs or pots may be turned out of their container and set into the ground. Furthermore, if the individual containers are very lightweight and biodegradable, the whole plant can be set into the ground with the container and the container will simply break down into the soil during the growing season. Peat- or paper-based biodegradable containers are excellent for most herbs and vegetables and particularly well suited to growing vining crops such as cukes and melons, as there is little if any damage to the roots during planting outdoors.

If you are growing indoor plants for the first time, experiment with a number of suggestions and you will soon find methods that best suit the plants you are working with. See the photograph on page 30 showing various containers that are available. As with all the suggestions we have made to date, start simply with a modest investment in money and time and then edit and refine with the seasons.

Whatever your choice of containers, make certain they are absolutely clean. If they are new, they can be used without concern. If they are reused, they must be disinfected from season to season. Plastic and wooden containers should be washed thoroughly and dipped into a solution of water and bleach (about nine parts water to one part bleach) to kill any pathogens that may be present. We don't recommend reusing peat or fiber containers. It is best to break them up and till them into the garden as they are emptied during any growing season.

The same advice applies to seeding mixtures or transplanting mixtures. If they have been used, they should be discarded, not replanted with new seeds or plants. We simply till used mixtures into our gardens if they are not obviously affected with any fungal or bacterial growth. If we have had any disease problems with seed flats or container plants, we isolate the containers and the soils and incinerate them.

The growing-on mixture you use may be purchased or made at home from purchased ingredients. In the preceding chapter we discussed at length the ingredients of seeding mixtures. Now that seeds have reached the transplant stage, the young seedlings will need nourishment to support growth until being set out into the garden. Nourishment may be provided in a variety of ways. It may come entirely from the ingredients in the growing medium. It may be provided in part by the growing mixture and supplemented by additional fertilizers that are applied during watering. The nourishment may be applied entirely in the form of plant fertilizers added to the water, if the growing medium is a completely soil-less, nearly sterile mixture.

If you plan to purchase growing mixtures, there

TRANSPLANT AND REPLANT

THERE ARE SOME seeds that sprout very irregularly, even when all conditions are met for their germination. Examples are lavender, rosemary, asparagus, angelica, and bay. If you have seeded any one of these plants in a single seed flat, it may be time to transplant a portion of the seedlings when others are just beginning to germinate. When this happens, don't be overly concerned about handling very small ungerminated or partially germinated seeds during the work. Just pay attention to a few simple guidelines.

Don't let the seed flat dry out at all before separating the larger seedlings from the rest of the flat. Turn out the whole seed flat on a clean surface and disentangle the developed seedlings carefully for transplanting. Then refill a clean container with seeding mix, very well moistened, and distribute seeds and newly germinated seedlings on the top of the mixture, spacing them so they are not crowding one another. Cover everything with a thin layer of moist seeding mix and water well.

Baptisia seeds germinate over a long period of time. Many seedlings are ready to be transplanted while a few seeds have just begun to germinate.

Keep out of direct sunlight for a couple of days until the mixture of the flat has settled in around the replanted material. Then move back into the growing location that was used before some of the seedlings were transplanted. This may be done repeatedly without any harm to the slow growers.

When seed flats are ready to be transplanted, seedlings are removed in a block from the container and carefully separated.

While the plants are held by the top leaves, the roots are covered gently with soil mix at a level appropriate to the morphology of the plant.

in full on pages 31–4. The same procedures are followed for growing mixtures, but we add a small amount of dolomitic lime to adjust the pH. To a cubic foot of our homemade mixture we add about a handful of lime (two to three tablespoons). Once mixed, we fill each transplant container so it is nearly full. This growing-on mixture has a moderate amount of fertility, enough to support the transplanted seedlings for two to three weeks. If seedlings are grown inside for a longer period, it may be necessary to fertilize the young plants. This can be done with a commercial plant food or with a seaweed and fish emulsion solution. We have used both in response to the kinds of plants being grown and their different nutritional needs. The decision when and how often to apply additional fertilizers during the growing-on time is governed by watching the quality of plant growth and the pigmentation of the leaves. Yellowing and discoloration are often an indication of the need for increased nourishment.

Having chosen containers and growing mixtures, you are ready to begin the actual transplanting. We have talked repeatedly about the need for constant and careful watering of seed flats from the moment they are seeded. Now that it is time to transplant, hold off watering any flat on the day it is to be transplanted. You will find that recently watered seed flats are much more difficult to handle, as the seedlings will not separate easily if the soil is wet.

Set up an area for transplanting that is completely out of direct sun. Regardless of how rapidly the trans-

are many on the market. Read the labels carefully to interpret how they will sustain plant growth. Some have very little nutrition, some have slow-release fertilizers that will sustain seedling growth for several weeks without the need for additional plant food. There are growing mixtures that are made up entirely of organic components, including organic fertilizers. If you are just starting out or if you have a limited number of seedlings to transplant, the easiest approach may be to buy a bag or two of prepared growing mixture.

If you wish to mix your own mixture, we can recommend the recipe we use at the farm. It is made up of peat moss, vermiculite, perlite, pasteurized soil, or pasteurized compost and lime. Refer back to the section on mixing and wetting the ingredients explained

Seedlings here illustrate correct planting depths, which vary with the morphology of the plant. **From left to right:** *seedlings of angelica, anise hyssop, pepper, garlic chives, sage, lemon grass, and elecampane.*

planting is done, there will be a period of time when young plants are removed from their seed containers and their roots exposed to light and air. You do not want the roots to dry out any more than is necessary in the process.

Tiny seedlings are removed from their seed container and separated in a couple of ways. They can be "pricked out," that is, lifted gently out of the soil with the fingers or a small, sharp tool. This method works reasonably well when the seed containers are sparsely seeded or when the seedlings have been planted in ribbon rows. If the whole flat is uniformly seeded, however, we always gently tip the flat upside down, with one hand held under the block of plants and soil, so that the entire contents is removed from the container. Take care not to break or crush the seedling stems. We then place the block of soil and plants on the worktable and very gently work the individual seedlings apart from one another. If the seed containers are not overly wet, the plants will loosen one from another with ease and with imperceptible

damage to any of the tender roots. See the photos on page 50 for a demonstration of both transplanting methods.

Choose one species of plant to transplant at a time so that plants will not be confused with one another until they have been placed into their new containers and labeled. When separating plants or pricking them out of their original containers, do only a few seedlings at a time, plant them in their new container, and then continue to separate and plant until the seed container has been finished. Label the new containers with the same information that was on your original labels, plus the date of transplanting. At the end of a transplanting session, it is a good idea to add notes, observations, and any other data to the journals you are keeping.

When you are separating out seedlings for transplanting, there are several things to look for in evaluating the potential vigor of these young plants. This will help you choose the best of the transplants if you are going to keep only a percentage of the early crop of seedlings. It will also enable you to discard any

True leaves of every shape and size emerge in seed flats. Front row from left to right: *pennyroyal, garlic chives, catmint, parsley, winter savory.* Middle row: *lemon grass, sage, valerian, creeping thyme, sorrel.* Back row: *hyssop, lemon balm, bee balm, angelica, eucalyptus.*

THE USE OF COLD FRAMES

WHETHER YOU DECIDE to purchase a cold frame or make your own, here are a few ideas to help you evaluate their overall design and use.

Even with extensive greenhouses and ample outdoor garden space, we find that there is a certain period during the springtime when cold frames (or poly tunnels, see pages 84–5) are absolutely necessary. They provide a place where light is nearly as intense as the outdoors but where light can be somewhat shaded if full sun is too harsh. Cold frames are not very much different in temperature from the open garden, and yet it is possible to keep them from plunging below freezing with a little extra care. Cold frames can be opened to expose their contents to gentle wind and rain or partially opened to modify the impact of the outdoor elements. They are almost outdoors, but with a bit of protection possible.

We use our cold frames primarily for hardening off seedlings. By monitoring the temperatures, light intensity, water, and wind, we are able to get young plants ready for planting so they transition with very little stress. We have also used cold frames for direct seeding crops in the early spring or late summer. If they are used for growing, the soils must be prepared as well as for any garden plot.

We have designed and built many cold frames; some ideas have worked out better than others. When it comes to materials used, we strongly recommend cedar or any other rot-resistant wood that is available in your part of the country. That way the frame will have a long natural life without having to be treated with preservatives. While covers may be made from old windows, unless the windows are small and cased in aluminum, they may be too heavy to handle conveniently and safely. Furthermore, even glass encased in aluminum can break if dropped, moved around often, or accidentally blown about by strong winds. We have had all these experiences.

When possible, build the cold frame so that it goes together and comes apart easily, by designing the four sides so they can be assembled with nuts and bolts. Screws can be used, but each time you assemble and disassemble the frames, the holes will become more and more loose.

Think of designing the top of the cold frame so it can be vented by folding one part of the cover back over the other. That way you do not have to worry about anchoring one large lid to the frame for ventilation. There will be less likelihood of wind picking up the whole frame, ripping the cover off the frame, or loosening the cover enough so it falls back down on the frame. You can tell that all of these things have happened to make us evolve our designs and hence our suggestions. As an alternative to the sectioned cover, you could design a sliding top, with one half built slightly higher than the other, much like a sliding door that could be opened partially or totally. Give some consideration as to how to design a cover that stays securely on the frame but can be lifted off for full access. We have done this by having the hinged covers fit securely into a lip formed by the walls of the frame.

In order to make covers as lightweight as possible, given that we frame everything with wood, we use a rigid fiberglass. Plexiglas may be used, but it will scratch easily. Heavy plastic will work, but it will need to be replaced more often, will tear more easily, and will not be as pleasing visually. However covers are designed, they must be able to be opened manually or mechanically when the weather dictates. If you are always available to vent your frames, there are many solutions. If you are away from home during the day, you can attach thermostatically controlled hinges to covers that will automatically open when temperatures reach a certain level. Remember that plants can burn up in a closed cold frame very quickly. There are some days that may simply be too hot for very young plants even if the cold frames are fully vented. When this happens, we use a piece of shade cloth placed over the top of the frame. This dampens the intensity of the light just enough to reduce the stress of heat and light.

Give some thought to the overall size of any cold

frame. We all want as much growing space as possible, but at the same time it may be preferable to have a couple of small frames that can be set up and taken down easily and moved from site to site as the season and tasks demand. Frames that can be taken apart and stored inside when not in use will naturally last much longer than those exposed to weather year-round.

If you want to increase heat in the cold frame beyond what can be captured and held as a result of good snug construction, here are some further ideas. The old-fashioned method of making hot frames was done by digging down for a foot or two beneath ground level in the frame and lining the floor with fresh horse manure, then covering the warm decomposing manure with a thick layer of hay. The idea works well, but may not be manageable for many backyard gardeners. Today's solution for bottom heat is accomplished with the use of a heating cable, if the frame is set up near a source of electricity. Blankets may also be used to keep frames warmer at night. You could use actual old household blankets or improvise with pieces of canvas, heavy felt, or even sew covers out of lightweight water-resistant fabric.

We have designed a series of heat-assisted cold frames that use neither horse manure nor heating cables. The cold frame's back wall is either a shared wall of a building or has a window that matches the size of a home basement window. That way we take some of the heat from the adjacent building and blow it into the cold frame when the temperatures in the

This cold frame is used primarily to extend the season at the beginning of the year. Large tender perennial herbs are being moved from the greenhouse to the field. They will stay in this heat-assisted cold frame for several weeks before going into the open gardens.

cold frame fall too low. We have done this all along the front of one of our large greenhouses. There are window openings between the greenhouse and the frame, and small fans set on thermostats are placed in the openings. When the nighttime temperatures fall below a certain point, fans go on and circulate warm air from the greenhouse into the frame to keep temperatures at a safe level for whatever plants we have growing or hardening off. All parts of the cold frames on the front of the greenhouses can be disassembled in a short time and are stored in a dry shed when not in use.

If you are not certain that a cold frame will be of real use in your gardening work, consider trying a simple poly tunnel first. It may suffice as a season extender or motivate you to set up a more sturdy and permanent structure.

seedlings that are not worth being grown on. The first criterion for choice is size of seedlings in a group. Unless selecting for some specific characteristics, usually the work of plant hybridizers, it is safe to say that the largest, fastest-growing seedlings are the most desirable. Next, when you separate a given seedling out from the rest and can examine the roots, choose the plants with the most extensively developed root systems. You will often find that the roots of the young seedlings have developed significantly in relationship to the young top growth. This is particularly true with some young seedlings of the Labiatae family, plants such as thyme, lavender, rosemary, and winter savory. The existence of well-developed root systems is very important for all seedlings. Vigorous roots will take hold quickly in the transplanted containers and support rapid vegetative development. The opposite is also often true. On occasion you may separate out a series of young seedlings to discover that some roots are poorly formed. While these plants may grow after transplant, they will do so more slowly. Edit out such plants when possible.

Transplanting seedlings also requires some understanding of a seedling's basic morphology, so that the plants are put into their new containers at the best planting depth. As a general rule, seedlings can be transplanted up to the level of their cotyledons. Plants with upright stems may on occasion be planted a bit deeper, especially when trying to compensate for leggy seedlings. Plants that have crowns should never be transplanted any deeper in their new container than they were growing as seedlings. Most monocots are also transplanted to the same depth as they were growing in the seed flats. This explanation can be made ever so much clearer by referring to the photograph on page 50, where examples of different planting depths are shown.

We mentioned earlier that we would first recommend that each transplant be grown in its own individual container whenever possible for optimum growth. This is perhaps more important for the annual vegetable crops than for most herb plants, particularly the perennial herbs that do nicely when transplanted several to a flat. Their indoor growth for the first several weeks is rather slow, and they do not seem to suffer competition when grown in shared space. If you plan to transplant several plants into a shared container for growing on, you will have to make decisions about spacing. With most vegetables, we recommend that each transplant have at least four square inches of growing space, or an area that would be two inches in any direction between plants. This will allow each plant to develop a good root system and ample top growth during the time the plant has to remain indoors and in a shared container. Annual herbs such as basil and parsley should also be given the same amount of spacing when grown several to a container. Smaller perennial herbs may be spaced a bit closer without sacrificing their development.

There are a few simple rules to observe when handling seedlings. Some people like to transplant with fingers only. Some like to use small tools. Do what is most comfortable, but in either case pick up the young seedlings gently by their top leaves, not by their roots. Make a hole in the soil of the transplant container, and make it large enough so that all of the roots can be placed into the hole without squeezing them together. Holding the top of the seedling, let the roots fall gently into the hole and then bring the soil of the container in to the stem of the plant so that it is smooth and level with the surface of the remaining mixture. It is not necessary to press or pack the soil around the plant with any pressure. When the newly transplanted container is watered, the weight of the water will finish smoothing and compressing the soil.

Use common sense when deciding that it is time to stop transplanting and start watering newly transplanted seedlings. Plants have different tolerances for being handled. If you see any sign of wilting, transplant a few plants and water immediately. You do not want to stress the transplants in the slightest. Stress at this early stage of growth can significantly affect development.

Watering of newly transplanted seedlings can be done just as the watering of seed flats was done, using trays for bottom watering (usually preferable) or by top-watering with hoses and other watering devices. We refer you to the section on watering in Chapter 2 for techniques, amounts, and the few caveats that are included. One further reminder: The first watering after transplanting is of crucial importance. You have just removed an entire plant from its growing medium, disturbed its roots, and relocated it into a new container. Regardless of how carefully and success-

fully done, this interruption has, in some way, caused the plant to need to adjust to new circumstances. The temperature of the new container is perhaps different. The growing mixture and its moisture content are different. The roots have been rearranged from their naturally developed start. Make certain that water is made available to the young seedling so that roots and leaves never dry out. If you top-water, make certain the pressure of the water does not press any of the small seedlings into the soil of the container. Should this happen, carefully lift the top of the seedlings up off the soil.

Once transplanting has been done, it is advisable to locate new transplants to a spot where there will be no direct sun on the leaves for a day or two. Bright light is good, but keep the plants out of harsh sunlight, and when you reintroduce the young plants to a sunny growing-on location, check to see if they react well to the transition. You will observe quickly that some plants react more dramatically than others to being transplanted. Lettuce seedlings nearly always flop down after being handled even in the most careful fashion. They definitely need to be protected from sunlight. On the other hand, young pepper seedlings rarely show signs of stress during transplanting. Any rapid wilting of the leaves is an indication that the seedlings need some protection from full sunlight for a day or two longer. If we are transplanting seedlings during a long spell of sunny weather, we sometimes protect transplants by placing them on the floor under a table for a day or two, or we hang a shade cloth in front of the bench where they are growing. The shade cloth filters out about 40 percent of the sunlight and reduces any stress. In a matter of days, or with some plants even a week or two, we remove the shade cloth. Once acclimated to having been transplanted, most vegetable and herb seedlings grow happily in a sunny indoor location.

Ongoing Care

MAINTAINING YOUNG SEEDLINGS from transplant time until they are ready to go out into the garden usually involves a modest amount of daily care. The primary concerns are watering; making certain that seedlings have adequate light, nourishment, and appropriate temperatures; and monitoring for insects or disease. Remember also to allow space for plants to grow without crowding and to provide air circulation. All these requirements are essential for optimum growth.

It is important to add that seedlings can be transplanted inside more than once. If your plants develop more rapidly than you had expected or if slow spring warming necessitates your holding plants inside longer than you had planned, it may be advisable to transplant some seedlings a second time. The decision to do this would be based on the size of the plant in relationship to an individual container or to the apparent competition of several plants in a shared container. If you feel that a young plant has simply outgrown its space, you are probably right. Find a larger container and transplant a second time. This will stimulate more vigorous growth and give you stronger plants to harden off and set out when the time comes. Plants can be grown indoors for considerable periods of time so long as they have space, ample light, appropriate temperatures, water, and nutrition.

If you have chosen to use a soil-less growing medium that has fertilizers added to the mixture, there may be adequate nourishment for the seedlings until they are ready to be set out into the garden. If you have made up a mixture without any fertilizers or composts, seedlings will need to be fed during their growing-on time. Watch overall development and leaf color as an indication. We use fertilizers mixed in with the water and apply them in a very light concentration every week on the average. Plant foods come either in liquid or granular form and almost always have to be diluted before use. Don't start out by using commercially prepared plant foods at full strength. Very small seedlings could be injured by overfertilization. Whatever fertilizers you choose for young seedlings, read the instructions for mixing and make up the food only a quarter as strong as recommended. It is preferable to use weak solutions of plant food applied more frequently than full-strength solutions applied less often.

Diseases and Insects

IF YOU HAVE TAKEN every precaution to start your seedlings with clean containers and seeding mix-

WE START NUMEROUS plants from seed each spring. We also take a number of cuttings from established species, always from those that must be propagated vegetatively, but also from some that are simply as easy to start from cuttings as from seeds. Examples of plants that can be propagated either by seed or cuttings include standard rosemary, some thymes, some oregano, garden sage, common mint, lavender, and santolina. Stem cuttings are always used to propagate named varieties of herbs such as rosemaries, mints, and scented geraniums. They are also used to propagate perennial herbs that cannot be grown from seed, such as tarragon, sweet woodruff, lemon verbena, some thymes, myrtle, and tree germander.

Well-rooted cuttings from Greek oregano, sage, thyme, and rosemary are ready for potting. A full tray of newly cut rosemary stems will put out roots in a matter of weeks.

Cuttings can be started in several different media, including moist sand, vermiculite, peat moss, seeding mixture, and even plain water. We have experimented with a number of these and now use moist vermiculite almost exclusively. It is relatively inexpensive, so we use it only once for cuttings and then simply incorporate it into the compost pile. It is a clean, sterile medium, is lightweight, and holds moisture well. We start by filling a large four-inch-deep tray with vermiculite and then wetting it so it is saturated but firm enough to hold stems in place.

Cuttings are taken from plants when they have an abundance of soft growth, usually anytime from spring to early fall. If growth is woody, it may not set roots readily. Always choose the sturdiest stock for propagating and select healthy vigorous stems from any individual.

Stems of the plants to be propagated are cut with a sharp knife or stem cutters, making certain there are several leaf nodes on the cutting. Roots are usually produced near one of the nodes in the rooting medium. Remove any extra leaves from the bottom of the cutting so they do not rot in the vermiculite, and any buds or flowers so that they do not take strength from the rooting plant. Upright stems are placed into the wet vermiculite so that at least one if not more nodes are beneath the surface. If you are rooting low-

tures and have isolated them from other plants in the house, chances are you will have little problem with diseases and insects. But there are a few common problems that can occur when starting plants from seed, and these problems can be introduced with the seeds themselves, in the ingredients of the soil mixtures, and simply as airborne pathogens. Warmth and

good humidity, the very conditions that support seed germination, also invite the growth of some harmful fungi and bacteria.

The most widely experienced problem is known as "damping off." This condition can occur in flats as seeds are germinating and in flats of young seedlings. You will recognize it if you see the sudden collapse of

growing sprawling plants such as creeping thyme or Greek oregano, place the cutting into the vermiculite so that part of the plant is beneath the surface and several nodes are lying along the surface of the vermiculite. The roots will be sent out from the cuttings along the stem at the leaf nodes. During the rooting process, remove any yellow or wilted leaves from cuttings so they do not decompose in the tray. If you want to hasten the rooting process, try using a heating mat beneath the rooting tray.

Keep the cuttings out of direct sunlight while they are rooting. Make certain the rooting medium never dries out. Check the cuttings after a week's time by gently lifting a piece out of the medium, being very careful not to tear any newly forming roots. Depending upon the species being rooted, the time of year when the cutting was made, and the temperatures of the rooting medium, cuttings can root in as quickly as a week, or take as long as several months. There are some plants, such as bay, that can take considerably longer, but those are exceptions. Wait until cuttings have several well-developed roots before potting into individual containers. At transplant time, it will be easier to remove cuttings from the rooting tray if you first flood the tray with water so that there will be no need to exert pressure on the cuttings to lift them out of the vermiculite.

Newly potted cuttings should be protected for a week or two from bright sunlight. If you are planning to take the transplanted cuttings out into the garden, they must be treated just like any other young seedlings and put through a proper hardening off.

closely, you may catch this problem when only a few plants have been affected.

When confronted with any evidence of damping off, you should act quickly. First, remove the infected container from the area where other plants are seeded. With a spoon or similar tool, carefully remove the infected plants and a ring of healthy plants around the infected area. Stop watering the flat for as long as possible so that the top dries out. This will be a judgment call, as you are trying to dry up the fungus and at the same time keep healthy seedlings alive. Alternatively, you could try to relocate healthy seedlings into a newly filled seed flat, making certain that you don't take any plants close to the infected area. Keep any diseased flat away from the general growing area for several days, and water only when necessary. You may have arrested the growth of the fungus. When you are absolutely certain that the damping off has stopped, the seed flat can be returned to the general growing area. If the problem continues, the seed flat should be destroyed.

You need to be aware that our recommendations for dealing with diseases and insects are based on our personal gardening practices. We do not use chemical fungicides, nonorganic pesticides, or herbicides in our greenhouses or gardens. There are commercially prepared chemicals for dealing with any number of diseases and insects. We cannot make any recommendations for their use or comments about their effectiveness. Our methods for dealing with disease are using all the precautions of good hygiene, mechanical isolation, and editing out diseased plants whenever possible. If we feel the need for sprays to combat problems, we use a few organically approved remedies. See a list and explanation of types on page 92.

We have on occasion seen some molds on the soil surface of plant containers, usually when plants are more developed and almost always after a long stretch of cloudy weather. Our response to these problems is to cut back on watering as much as is possible, bottom-water if necessary, increase air circulation, and isolate any infected containers. In some cases we have removed healthy plants from seemingly contaminated soils and replanted them into new containers with fresh soil mixtures. These plants need to be kept isolated, monitored closely, watered sparingly from the bottom, and reintroduced to the general growing area

tiny seedlings right at the soil line. When examined closely, the stems appear to be pinched, sometimes discolored. The disease is caused by the presence of any of a number of fungi. The fungus attacks the plant stem, restricting the uptake of water, and the seedling dies. Once present in a seed flat, the disease can spread quickly. If you are monitoring the seed flats only after we are certain the problems are eliminated. We don't hesitate to dispose of contaminated plants that pose a threat to a general area.

Any common houseplant insects can find their way into a seeding area. The most common pests we have encountered on our young plants are whiteflies, fungus gnats, and aphids. Any of these insects can be devastating to young seedlings if allowed to go unchecked.

Whiteflies are very small, about $\frac{1}{32}$ inch long, but still very visible to the eye. They have two pairs of wings. These insects can go undetected if plants are not frequently examined or handled, as the flies live on the undersides of the leaves and move about primarily when the leaves are touched. Whiteflies are sucking insects and they leave a sticky secretion on leaves and stems that can become a growing surface for sooty black fungus. Populations of whiteflies can increase rapidly once present. Early detection and treatment are the most effective controls. First, move any affected plants and wash off the leaves with a mild soap and then rinse. If the infestation increases and repeated washing doesn't do the trick, there are several biological sprays effective against these insects. They include insecticidal soap, pyrethrum, and rotenone.

Fungus gnats, also known as mushroom flies, are about the same size as whiteflies, but the gnats are dark brown to black. Fungus gnats are our most troublesome pest in the greenhouse. They do not injure the top growth of the plants themselves, but instead lay their eggs in the dark, moist seed flats or seedling containers. In several days the eggs hatch into threadlike white maggots that feed in the soil, on the roots and lower leaves of young seedlings. Then they pupate, forming the next generation of adults. If there are larvae in a seed flat, you will begin to see an overall decline in the vigor of the young seedlings. If the larvae are not eliminated, the seedlings almost always weaken and die. Even when there is some damage to the seedlings, they show signs of stress and damage to the roots that will be visible during transplanting. If any gnats are seen in the growing area, use some measures to eradicate them. As a mechanical deterrent, we set up yellow monitoring cards to capture and indicate the presence of insects. These rigid plastic cards are coated with a sticky substance to attract and trap insects. In addition, there are several biological insecticides that can be used to water the flats. These insecticides act on the larval stage of the gnat. Fungus gnats breed regularly in manure and rotting vegetative matter and are commonly present in a number of gardening areas. They are attracted to dark, moist surfaces. They are easily brought inside with unpasteurized soils, composts, or manures. That is one reason to be very careful in keeping contaminated pots, used soils, and dirty tools away from indoor growing spaces. It is also a reason to be extra cautious about overwatering.

Aphids are probably already familiar to the backyard gardener. They are often seen on the new growth of trees, shrubs, and flowering ornamentals. While many outdoor plants can endure some aphid predation, an aphid infestation on young seedlings can not only severely injure plants but also infect plants with viral diseases. There are several species of aphids, varying in size from $\frac{1}{16}$ inch to $\frac{1}{8}$ inch long. They are pear-shaped insects ranging in color from white to pink, light green, dark green-gray, blue-black. Aphids are sucking insects that attach themselves to tender stems, leaves, and new growth, and they can weaken young seedlings very quickly. They are very visible to the eye. Monitor young plants and respond immediately to their presence, as they reproduce rapidly. In some instances they can be picked off plants if only a few are present. More often it is necessary to treat a whole plant. Washing in mild soap and rinsing will remove many insects. This can be done repeatedly if new insects appear. There are also effective insecticides such as insecticidal soap, pyrethrum, and rotenone.

Whatever methods you choose in dealing with diseases and insects indoors or in the outside garden, it is important to remember that every insecticide, fungicide, herbicide, either chemically based or biologically based, has the potential to be harmful. They may be used to target a specific problem but at the same time negatively affect beneficial insects or animals. We resort to the use of supposedly safe organically approved sprays only when we feel that all other methods have failed. We strongly recommend that you use caution in introducing any chemicals into your gardening. And always read all the information on the packages and bottles of sprays and repellents. Use gloves, protective clothing, and face masks when working with any sprays or dusts. Even if a product is natural, that does not ensure that it is nontoxic in every sense of the word. Any sprays can cause individual allergic reactions. Dusts can be irritating to the eyes, skin, and lungs. Carefully follow instructions for use. Don't use gardening chemicals or biological sprays as a preventive measure, but only when other precautions are not working. Also consider whether or not it might be worth sacrificing a plant or two in lieu of using sprays.

Hardening Off

WE USUALLY LIKE at least a week or two for transitioning our plants from their indoor growing area to their location in the garden. This transitioning is referred to as "hardening off." It is recommended that every plant grown inside be readied for this change of environment. During hardening off, the plants are subjected to a gradual change in temperature, a gradual exposure to direct sunlight, light wind, and even some gentle spring rain.

While hardening off is applied to every seedling, it cannot be applied at the same time or under the same conditions. Plants need to be evaluated in terms of their general hardiness before a schedule is made up for taking them outside. We start removing our most vigorous perennials from the greenhouses first. As soon as the plants have developed good top growth and the weather has moderated so that nights rarely fall below the freezing mark, we move our perennials out into protected cold frames (see pages 52–3) or poly tunnels (pages 84–5) where they are grown for the next several weeks before being removed from all protection. They are protected at first from exposure to full sun by covers or shade cloths that filter light. They are protected from strong winds by the covers that are opened and closed in accordance with the temperature and wind conditions. They are always protected overnight. After several days, covers are taken off during the daytime, exposing the plants to more direct sun and strong wind. Any shade-loving perennials are continuously protected from direct sun. If there is a gentle rain, we allow it to do the watering for us. If rains are very heavy, we protect young plants with the covers. In a matter of a week or two, there are obvious changes in the appearance of the plants. The stems usually stiffen. Leaves that were tender at first exposure to sun and wind become more hardy. Sometimes leaf pigmentation changes to a deeper shade. We like to plan on hardening our perennials off for anywhere from one to two weeks before they are to go out into the gardens. This results in plants that show minimal stress in response to being set out into the ground.

The next series of plants to be hardened off include the hardy annuals, plants like the cole crops, parsley, and coriander. We wait until nights do not drop much below the mid-forties before placing these plants into cold frames or poly tunnels. They are then sequenced in the same way as the perennials.

Plants that prefer warm weather and warm soils, like tomatoes and peppers, are not brought out into cold frames or poly tunnels until nighttime temperatures stay above 50°F. We like to expose these more tender plants to at least a week of hardening off. There is nothing to be gained by hurrying these plants into the ground before the weather has moderated and soils have warmed. They will continue to grow comfortably in the greenhouses and transplant without setback if conditions are favorable. On the other hand, they do need a transitioning period so their stems will stiffen and their leaves will withstand direct sun and wind and rain.

Some few plants must be kept inside until the out-

Onions, chives, garlic chives, and leeks benefit from having an early "haircut" just before transplanting. Use a sharp pair of scissors and trim the leaves about halfway back on the seedlings. This will stimulate the plants to grow larger, with sturdier lower growth, before the plants are set out into the garden.

MOST GARDENERS are familiar with the term "hardening off," referring to the process of transitioning seedlings and plants to go out into the garden. We have coined our own variation on this term for just the opposite plant transition. When plants are to be brought back into a greenhouse or house for the winter, some care needs to be given so that the change from one environment to another is accomplished with minimal stress to the plants. We refer to this care as "reverse hardening off," and here are a few suggestions.

Tender perennial herbs are potted up and left on the porch steps for a week or two before being brought inside for the winter months.

For plants that have been grown outside in containers, the transition is perhaps the easiest. Decide to bring the tender plants inside before the temperatures are too stressful. Many patio plants can survive very cold fall nights, but the longer they are subjected to cold stress, the more difficult it may be to reacclimatize to inside warm temperatures. Start the process by examining the plant for pests and wash off any visible whiteflies, scale, or other critters so you don't bring them inside to multiply. If possible, tip the plant out of its pot and examine the root system. If you see more roots than soil, consider a bit of root pruning and repotting to a larger container. Use potting soils liberally enriched with composted manure. Leave at least an inch of space from the top of the soil line to the top of the pot so that you have plenty of space to water. Plants can dry out quickly indoors.

If you plan to move plants from the outside to a room inside the house, try relocating the pot in stages. First, move the pot to a sheltered area right next to the house, then to a porch or cool room in the house, and finally to the room where the plant will spend the winter. Different plants have different requirements for light, heat, and water once inside, and for this information it is best to consult the literature on specific species. As a rule, however, it is correct to say that watering is one of the most important considerations. There is no hard-and-fast rule about the frequency of watering, as we all keep our homes at different temperatures, and the type of heat (hot air, baseboard, electric, wood heat) affects the humidity of each environment differently. Test the dryness of the soil of each plant by touch, feeling not only the surface but poking a finger an inch or so into the soil. When plants are watered, the water should penetrate to the base of the pot. Frequent superficial watering can damage or even kill some plants. As a general rule, it is better to water well and less frequently than to water superficially all the time.

Now a word about bringing plants indoors out of

the garden. If you are going to lift a plant out of the soil and repot for wintering inside, begin the process several weeks before a hard frost. Choose the most vigorous specimens, lift plants carefully out of the ground, trying to get all of the root system and at least some of the soil around it. Examine the size and shape of the roots so you choose a pot appropriate to the growing needs of the plant. Some roots reach deep, some spread along the top of the soil. Choose a container that is appropriately deep and wide and try to duplicate the arrangement of the roots when repotting. Place a layer of enriched potting soil in the bottom of the pot. Then pack the spaces around the roots and field soil with more enriched potting mixture. Position the plant at the same soil line as it was growing in the garden. Water well and bring the pot into a sheltered position, free from direct sun, wind, and cold temperatures.

Observe the plant for the next several days. If you have damaged numerous roots in the transplanting process, you may want to compensate by pruning a portion of the plant's top growth. Don't be timid about pruning back, to reduce stress, to reshape, or simply to reduce the size of the plant. If you observe no wilting or other signs of stress, such as sudden leaf drop, you may simply observe and water the pot as needed. After a week or so, follow the directions for container-grown plants outlined above, checking for insects, slowly relocating, and positioning to an inside location for winter maintenance.

While this explanation for reverse hardening off talks about plants in general, we have found it serves us well whether we are bringing in our huge old tubs of rosemary or potting up young first-year field-grown herbs. This gradual-stepped program of bringing plants inside has allowed us to winter-grow many species with considerable success.

door temperatures are truly mild. They include tender annuals like eggplant, melons, basil, and sesame. Tender annuals can be damaged by exposure to cold temperatures and soils to the point that their production is significantly reduced. There is no point in rushing to harden off these plants ahead of schedule.

If you are going to transition your seedlings without benefit of a cold frame or some improvised poly tunnel, think of what spaces you have available to step your plants out of the house and into the garden. Porches can be used, protected areas up against the foundation of a house, an area in a garage next to an open door. Watch the temperatures, light, and wind conditions and be prepared to move the plants in and out if necessary to protect them from conditions that damage the tender growth. Do take the time and make the effort to prepare young plants for a change of environment. Never think you can overlook the process of hardening off your seedlings. After all the time and work you have put into indoor seeding, transplanting, and growing on, it would be very foolish to hurry the trip into the outdoor garden. Plants that are moved too rapidly from indoors to outside invariably suffer some setback, making them more susceptible to damage from weather, disease, and insect predation.

If you are supplementing your own seedlings with any purchased young plants for your gardens, you can never assume that purchased plants have been put through a hardening-off period. Always inquire at a greenhouse or nursery center. The growers should be able to explain what has been done with the plants up until the time they went on sale. Very often, plants are sold directly out of the greenhouses where they were seeded and grown. They will need to be transitioned in the same manner as your own homegrown plants. If you purchase plants from a retail center where the is always best to assume that you need to harden them off. Purchased plants should be examined for overall health and insects before they are put into the same growing or hardening-off spaces with your own seedlings.

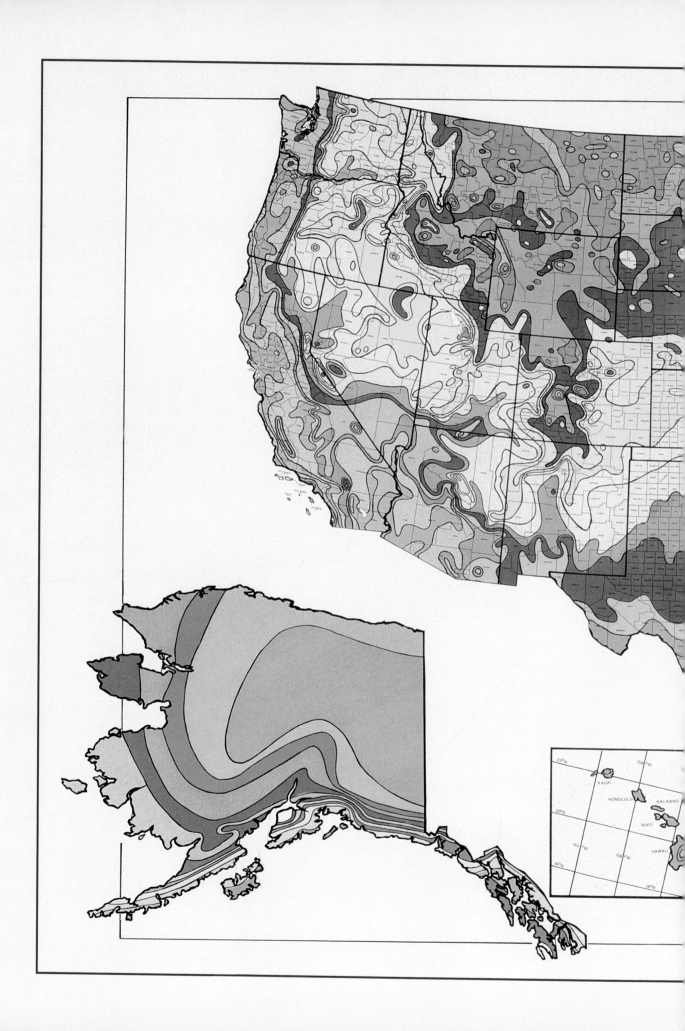

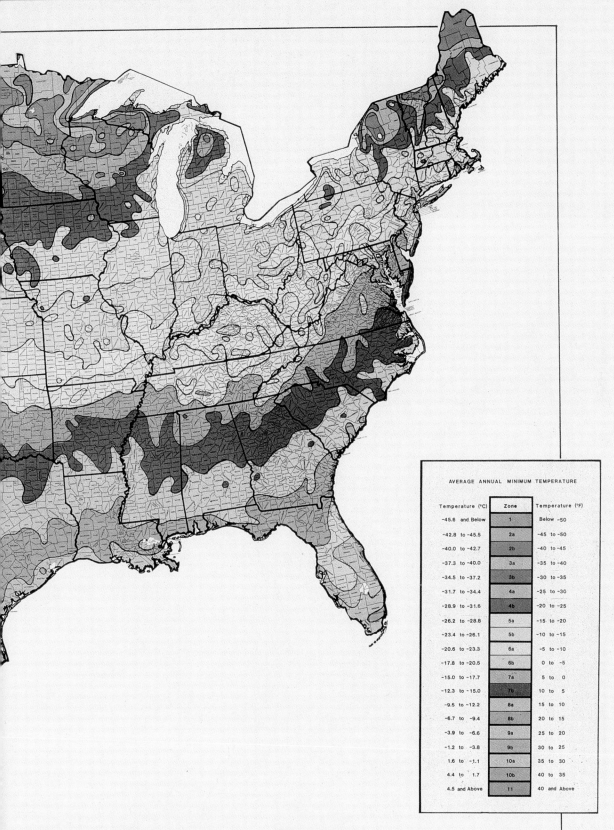

AVERAGE ANNUAL MINIMUM TEMPERATURE

Temperature (°C)	Zone	Temperature (°F)
-45.6 and Below	1	Below -50
-42.8 to -45.5	2a	-45 to -50
-40.0 to -42.7	2b	-40 to -45
-37.3 to -40.0	3a	-35 to -40
-34.5 to -37.2	3b	-30 to -35
-31.7 to -34.4	4a	-25 to -30
-28.9 to -31.6	4b	-20 to -25
-26.2 to -28.8	5a	-15 to -20
-23.4 to -26.1	5b	-10 to -15
-20.6 to -23.3	6a	-5 to -10
-17.8 to -20.5	6b	0 to -5
-15.0 to -17.7	7a	5 to 0
-12.3 to -15.0	7b	10 to 5
-9.5 to -12.2	8a	15 to 10
-6.7 to -9.4	8b	20 to 15
-3.9 to -6.6	9a	25 to 20
-1.2 to -3.8	9b	30 to 25
1.6 to -1.1	10a	35 to 30
4.4 to 1.7	10b	40 to 35
4.5 and Above	11	40 and Above

USDA Hardiness Zones

CHAPTER FOUR

In the Garden

THE ACTUAL WORK of planting is the easiest and most enjoyable part of establishing any garden. Planting is done after all the strenuous work has been accomplished, or at least it should take place then. On so many occasions, we hear gardeners leaving our greenhouses lamenting that they now have so much work ahead of them in setting out their plants. We, on the other hand, heave a sigh of relief when we have finished preparing our planting sites. Putting plants into the ground is a joy. It means that we have accomplished all the preliminary work of choosing a site, analyzing and preparing the soil of that site, and designing the methods we will use to establish rows, raised beds, or terraced areas. It means we have already shaped the contours of the land, added necessary soil amendments, applied any mulches, figured out a plant layout that will ensure good crop rotations from season to season. There are many factors to consider in preparing to plant, and the thoroughness of the preparation will have a significant impact on the success of every garden.

Choosing a Site

MOST OF US ESTABLISH our gardens on the land around our homes, starting as close as the ground around the foundations and venturing out from there to the spaces we call our yards, and if we are really fortunate, to the fields and pastures beyond. Regardless of the size or proximity of the garden to our homes, we need to start by analyzing the light and soil available in those spaces.

In gardening terms, the intensity of light is referred to as "full sun," "partial sun," "light shade," "filtered shade," "deep shade." The first term is the only one that is obvious. All the remaining are ambiguous, because the objects that cause the shade usually have an impact not only on the abundance of light but also on the kind of soil in the area and on the moisture of the soil. If a garden is not in full sun, it is necessary to analyze by what and how the light is blocked. If it is a building, the sun is typically blocked completely for a part of the day. Depending on the location of a garden near a building, it means that sun is available at different times during the day. It is sunny early in the east, latest on the west side, longest on the south side, and perhaps for a few hours at the beginning and end of the day on the north. Counted in hours, there may be sunlight for as many hours on the north side of the house as on another side, but that sun is available so early and so late in the day that it is less valuable to certain plants than fewer hours of midday light.

Filtered light and partial shade can also mean many different things. It is very easy to garden in sites that are located well away from the roots of big old trees, even when the canopy of those trees may filter some of the early-morning or late-afternoon light from the garden. It is very difficult to garden near the trunks of certain trees that filter sun for the same amount of time, but where tree roots constantly compete with plant roots for space and moisture. When plants are described as being suitable for shady gardens, it means that they can thrive in lower light but rarely in lower light combined with poor, dry, root-clogged soils.

Most vegetables and many herbs prefer to be grown in full sun, meaning that they should be provided with at least six to eight hours of sun in the middle of the day. This does not mean that they will perform well with a few hours of morning sun added to a few hours of late-day sun. Conversely, plants that

Gardens in full sun, like this one with purple basil, Amaranthus caudatus, *cleome, and annual dianthus, usually produce the brightest colors.*

Sweet cicely grows best in a garden of filtered sun. At the front corner of this small garden it receives just the right amount of sun and shade.

This shade garden exists beneath the canopy of large, old trees that compete with the plants for light and moisture.

are described as wanting partial shade are those that can tolerate some sun, but also need protection from long exposure to midday sun. If plants are described as needing full shade, it means they should always be protected from midday sun but can usually tolerate filtered sun very early and very late in the day. It is possible to choose one garden site to accommodate a variety of plant needs by modifying parts of a sunny garden with devices set up to create partial shade. These include pergolas, lathed areas, fences, and plants themselves.

Evaluating Soils

EVERY VEGETABLE we discuss in this book requires a good garden soil, with adequate organic matter and ample moisture. Many of the herbs grow best in the same soils, and a few are tolerant of somewhat poorer sites. If you are setting out a garden for the first time, it is essential that you understand something about the ground you are going to plant. You can begin to make simple assessments on your own. Take a shovel and dig a small hole into the earth to a depth of at least eighteen inches. You will see immediately the texture of the soil and the depth of the topsoil. That will begin to tell you something about the water-holding capacity of the garden site. It will not tell you anything about the pH level of the soil or about its composition in terms of organic matter and other micronutrients. Unless you have the abilities to evaluate your soils from previous gardening experience, the best thing to do at the outset is to get a good soil test. These are available through your local Cooperative Extension Office, Soil Conservation Agency, or some private companies. It involves sending or taking a soil sample for analysis. The analysis comes back in the form of a report and set of recommendations as to what you should add to the garden site to improve your soil. If you are gardening in several different sites, get soil samples from each of these sites. If your garden is very large, more than a quarter of an acre, take several samples from different areas of the site.

Regardless of what results you get back from your soil samples, don't feel you cannot garden on a given site just because it may need some work. All of our gardens need constant attention to soil building and

modification over the years. The work of building good soils will continue for all the years you are cultivating the spaces, in response to the fact that you will be working that land. Working sites always need to be replenished. As your gardening skills are honed, you will be able to assess more readily the requirements of good soils just from watching how plants perform, what weeds grow, how water percolates, and what diseases may be present.

Breaking Ground

NEW GARDEN SITES NEED to be prepared by breaking up top sod or other top growth, removing debris, roots, and large stones. We established our first garden in an old pasture that had been lying fallow for several decades. The first task was to remove some very small alders and three-foot-tall white pines that were beginning to take over the pasture. Then we plowed and harrowed the land, breaking up the sod and returning it to the soil. This meant we were gardening initially in rather rough land. After several seasons of plowing and harrowing, the texture of the soils became more porous because of the mechanical working of the soil, but also because of our applications of animal manures and composts each season. Backyard gardeners will most likely break the ground of their initial gardens by hand or with the use of small garden tillers.

If you must prepare the garden the same year you are planning to plant it, consider killing the top grass and weeds before tilling. This is done by covering the site for as long as a month with a large sheet of dark plastic or mat so that no light reaches the plants beneath. The combination of the heat and darkness will kill the top growth beneath the cover, making digging much easier. Alternatively, we have very carefully skimmed off the most superficial layer of sod and removed by hand the grass, weeds, and roots that were present. When doing this, don't discard any more soil than is absolutely necessary. Then to this grass-free area we add liberal amounts of composted manures, lime if indicated to correct the soil pH, and a bale or two of peat to lighten up the soil. We then dig and turn and mix all of the soil and additives to a depth of one to two feet. It is essential to prepare gar-

SOIL pH

THE SCALE THAT IS USED to describe the acidity or alkalinity of garden soils is called the pH scale. It is a logarithmic scale starting at 1 and ending at 14. Each number in the scale is ten times greater than the preceding number. A neutral soil has a pH of 7. The higher the number, the more alkaline the soil; the lower the number, the more acidic. A soil that measures 8 is moderately alkaline, whereas a reading of 9.5 would be considered intensely alkaline. Conversely, a soil pH of 5.5 would be called moderately acidic; a pH of 4 would be strongly acidic. Generally speaking, most herbaceous plants, trees, and shrubs prefer soils that are nearly neutral or just slightly below neutral, from 6 to 7. This is the range at which the most important plant nutrients are readily available to the plants. There are of course exceptions, some plants that definitely require an acidic or alkaline soil to grow well. There are even a few plants that are considered pH neutral, meaning they can grow in either acidic or alkaline soils.

It is very important to ascertain the pH of your garden soils, as both newly worked ground and well-used plots will have no predictable pH counts. Except in certain arid regions of the country, there is a tendency for soils to become increasingly acidic over time, rain being one of the most significant contributing factors.

You may send soil samples for evaluation to a number of state agencies, such as extension or soil conservation, or private testing laboratories that will test not only for pH but other soil characteristics. If you wish to perform your own pH tests, kits are sold at garden centers or through plant and garden catalogues. While usually not as accurate as laboratory tests, the kits are easy to use and will allow you to

Healthy, rich soils still need to have appropriate pH levels to grow the best-quality plants.

monitor the pH levels of your gardens from season to season.

Modifying soils to change their acidity or alkalinity is not at all difficult. Applications of lime (either agricultural or dolomitic) can be done in early spring or fall, but gardeners should follow directions for rates of application in accordance with recommendations from test results. It is not advisable to overlime soils at any time, but rather to correct soil acidity in stages. Overliming can have harmful effects on plants.

If soils need to be made more acidic, there are mulches that can be used on the top of the soils or incorporated into soils. They include oak leaf mold, composted bark, sawdust, and pine needles. When planting a new site, it is advisable to start with a reliable soil test. It is sound practice to monitor any garden soils every few years.

dening plots to some depth. In so doing, you are building up the organic matter in the soils, creating a friable soil where plant roots can develop readily and where oxygen is available to the plant roots. The soil amendments also help to create a soil that will accept water readily, have some moisture-retaining qualities, and still drain well enough.

An alternative to killing top growth, or "top skim-

ming," is a method called "double digging." This is done by removing the top several inches of sod, then digging out and reserving the next foot of soil. The top sods are placed into the bottom of the excavated site, grass downward, and then the removed soil is put back into the site along with the same amendments of manures, lime, and composts.

Some gardeners may prepare their sites with a

W E ARE NOT ALL BLESSED with naturally wonderful sites for vegetable and herb gardens. There are house lots that may be beautiful in and of themselves but not very conducive to gardening. Areas heavily planted in graceful old conifers usually offer up the double problem of shade and dry, thin, sandy soils. Many homes built near the shoreline of freshwater lakes are sitting on thin glacially formed soils barely covering extensive ledges. Newly constructed homes with evenly green grassy lawns may have almost no real soils beneath the thin layer of loam that was hauled in for seeding. If you have land that is difficult to cultivate, we recommend that you start small.

It is overwhelming to build garden sites over a vast area in a couple of seasons, but small plots can be worked intensively and reward the gardener with very respectable harvests. If soils are thin to nonexistent, consider building raised beds. We have done this right next to one building that we hadn't planned to use for gardening, so we did nothing to direct the earth moving at the time of construction. During the excavation work, heavy clay subsoil was scooped out and spread around the site. The land next to the foundation was

filled with sand for drainage, and when the work was finished we were left with soils that drained either too quickly or not at all.

It took us about fifteen years of building a series of raised beds to complete a complex but beautiful layout of gardens around this building. It is no exaggeration to say that initially we had to break up the ground surfaces with pickaxes. Then we made soils out of the clay that was mixed with woodland soil, copious amounts of animal manures, composts, peat moss, sand, and lime. Plot by plot, the space was completely transformed. Today, soils are friable and filled with organic matter. If added all together, these beds probably now cover a quarter of an acre.

Think small; start with one small plot. Dig down deep, enrich the soils yearly, mulch always, and sooner than you think you will begin to transform your sites. If you are trying to garden under large old trees, find a few spots as far as possible away from tree roots, construct a raised bed, and underline it with a heavy plastic to keep moisture in the bed and tree roots out. These beds may not allow you to grow vegetables that need full sun, but you may have some success with a few perennial herbs for culinary use and ornamentals that grow in shade.

If you have no sites with adequate sun for growing vegetables, consider having very small movable container gardens that can be positioned during different

It took several years to transform the front of the farm shop from a bare, unappealing site to its present state. The gardens were designed section by section, and eventually a large area was planted with perennial herbs, flowers, and shrubs.

times of the day to capture sunlight. Large barrels, buckets, or wooden crates can be equipped with casters so they can be rolled from one part of the lawn or one corner of a patio to another. A container may be planted with several vegetables and herbs at one time. Trellis a cherry tomato at one edge, plant a couple of heads of leafy lettuce along another, and let some Greek oregano or summer savory cascade over the edge. If the container is prepared with a good rich base of animal manure or compost with a fertile potting mixture, all you need to do is follow the sun and provide ample moisture.

hand-run tiller, or a tractor tiller. These break up the soils very well. They add nothing, however, to the quality of soils. Just because newly tilled soils look fluffy and ready to be planted doesn't mean they contain any of the nourishment that plants require. It also does not mean that the soils have a good balance of ingredients that will keep them from compacting after rain and foot traffic. Tilling only means breaking up, not preparing a site. Follow all the same suggestions for actual soil building as previously mentioned.

Ground Level

OUR FIRST GARDENING MENTORS taught us to plant our crops at ground level in thin ribbon rows, a technique that was fairly standard agricultural practice for farms of all sizes earlier in this century. That method meant that the largest portion of a garden was relegated to traffic paths, used all during the growing season for machinery or people. Large three- to four-foot walkways were cultivated to combat weeds up to the thin rows of cultivated crops. Once the garden was planted, the remainder of the summer was dedicated to hoeing and tilling and hilling the crops either by hand or with machines. It also meant that the garden was subjected constantly to the weight of machinery being driven over it, compacting the soils.

Our years of working the land have motivated us to evolve many different methods and techniques for planting. Except when planting trees, shrubs, and some fruiting crops, we rarely set out gardens in thin rows. We also don't plant our crops at ground level. Our current planting method has completely revised the proportions of growing space to work space. The farm's production gardens consist of slightly raised four-foot-wide rows running the length of the three-hundred-foot garden. Walkways are about two feet wide. A number of other specialty gardens are designed as two-

Our early gardens had narrow planted rows and large walkways.

foot-deep raised boxes of various dimensions. The entire box is planted, and all work is done by reaching in from the perimeters of these boxed gardens.

Slightly raised wide rows are not difficult to establish and prove to be an efficient way of assigning space in a garden. We prepare our garden in the spring, waiting until the ground has drained sufficiently but not become too dry. Our soils are rather heavy clay, and if we till the ground on schedule, make the raised rows and set out our mulches on time, we never water our gardens even in the driest of summers.

Once the ground has been tilled, we mark out the wide rows with the hillers on the tractor and spread manures and composts on the tops of the wide rows. The rows are then hilled up with the hilling disks, to a height of about four to five inches above walkway level. The tops of the rows are then raked as smooth as possible, during which time composted materials are incorporated into the soils. Immediately after the raking is done, a four-foot-wide black plastic mulch is drawn down the entire row, the edges are buried, and the walkway is then raked free of stones and any debris or impressions from the wheels of the tractor. We always make certain to do this work right after a rainy period, so that soils are amply moist beneath the black mulch. Areas of the garden that are to be used as nursery areas for direct seeding later crops are

Current gardens at the farm are planted on wide, raised beds with narrow, mulched walkways.

left until we are ready for them. Once the tilling, contouring, and mulching are done, we don't drive any machinery over the garden sites for the remainder of the summer. This helps considerably in keeping the soils from compacting.

As soon as the wide rows have been formed and mulched, we are ready to begin planting. Some plants are set out immediately, usually first-year perennial herbs and hardy vegetables. We wait for the soils to warm under the black mulches and for the springtime temperatures to moderate before doing any further planting. During the waiting period, the mulched rows are warming, but any weed seeds beneath them cannot develop in the darkness. A dark mulch can

warm the soils beneath them to temperatures as much as fifteen degrees warmer than bare soil. Some growers use clear plastic mulches on the tops of their rows, but this is mainly to warm the soil and keep moisture in. Clear mulches necessitate the use of herbicides, without which there would be rampant germination of weed seeds under every inch of clear plastic.

We use three types of mulches in the walkways between the raised planted rows. Our preference for walkways in vegetable and herb gardens is a mulch of paper and hay. Walkways should be very smooth and free of stones to start. Then we cover them with several layers of paper. Years ago we got bundles of used newspaper and unfolded sections to cover the ground. This was very labor intensive and sometimes difficult to manage if we needed to mulch on a day when there was any wind at all. We graduated from newspapers to rolls of unused printer's paper. This change not only proved easier but also had the advantage of keeping any printing inks out of the soils when the paper decomposed.

Unused rolls of paper are very easy to find from local printing companies that use web presses. Paper rolls are usually removed from printing presses with several inches of paper remaining on the rolls. Uncoated newspaper works best because the weight of the paper makes it easy to handle, and the paper contours readily to the land. Most printers in our area are

Making raised rows and spreading black plastic mulch.

In the Garden

Once rows are finished, plants and seeds are planted in holes made through the plastic.

out into. In addition, it means that with the entire surface of the garden under mulch, there is no evaporation of moisture from the soil, and during rains, water can percolate down in the walkways but never splash up off bare ground onto plant leaves or fruit. It takes us several weeks to lay out our entire production garden in this manner, but once it is done, we have very little maintenance for the remainder of the summer.

An alternative to the paper-and-hay mulch is our living-clover mulch. The raised rows are prepared in exactly the same way as described above. After the black plastic is secured, walkways are raked smooth and seeded with white Dutch clover, a low-growing perennial. It is important to seed the clover right away, or other weeds will get a start in the walkway and compete with the clover. Once seeded, make certain the walkway doesn't dry out completely for the next week or so that it takes for the clover to begin to sprout. And, of course, it will not be possible to walk in these areas until the clover has begun to develop, all of which takes about two to three weeks. Once growing, this vigorous living mulch provides a pleasing place to walk and work and a clean undergrowth for the leaves and vegetables in the garden. As the clover grows during the summer, it is usually necessary to mow the walkways several times to keep the growth from competing with the vegetables and herbs. This mowing causes the

more than willing to give or sell these roll ends at a very reasonable price.

We cover the garden walkways with two or three layers of this kind of paper, so that it will not break down immediately. The paper is then covered with a thick layer of mulch hay. The paper acts as a barrier to all the weed seed inherent in the hay. The weight of the hay keeps the paper in place. This mulch helps keep moisture in the soil and prevents weeds from growing all summer. It also creates a clean, comfortable walkway for people to use and for plants to extend

The garden is ready to be mulched between the rows.

clover to thicken and become an even more agreeable living carpet.

Both the paper-and-hay mulch and the clover mulch suppress weeds during the growing season. They are also beneficial to the garden when they are tilled back into the ground either at the end of the growing season or in the spring of the following year. If you take the time to inoculate your clover seed before sowing, you will have the extra advantage of adding even more nitrogen to the soils along with the organic matter from the decomposing mulches.

We have also used an inorganic mulch in some walkways, made from very heavy felt strips that were cut out of discarded paper-making blankets. This heavy felt allows water to pass through to the garden, it suppresses weed growth and keeps leaves and fruits clean in the abutting rows. It does not, however, add anything to the soil. This barrier mulch is used more as a time-saver for rows we establish late in the spring or simply don't get to when demands outweigh the hours in a workday.

Our raised-bed total-mulch program is used on a growing area that covers approximately two acres. It would be as successful and as efficient on a small back-yard garden. Raised rows can be easily made with hand tools. Dark-plastic, dark-fiber, or dark-paper mulches can be stretched out by hand. We have done this any number of times for isolated small plots. If your soils hold water well, you may not need any additional watering during the growing season. If your soils are sandy and dry out quickly, raised beds may be prepared and drip irrigation hoses can be placed throughout the garden before the mulches are installed.

A crew spreads paper and hay over the garden walkways.

Planting can take place after the walkways are mulched, and on overcast or rainy days when possible.

Garden Designs

WHETHER WE ARE setting out two acres or a small annual bed, we give considerable thought to the layout of every garden every season. Light and soil must be appropriate to the plants grown. But placement of the plants is very important. Different plants need different amounts of space to develop. Some can

The black plastic mulch on the planting rows both heats up the soil and keeps weeds from competing with the cultivated crops.

be trellised, some need to sprawl. Some produce more fruits and flowers if they are actually planted closer together. Others will have smaller fruit production in response to any slight crowding. The height of neighboring plants must be considered. Shading could negatively affect some plants while benefiting others.

We also give great thought to rotating our crops from year to year. If possible, never plant members of the same family in the same ground from one year to the next. Locate heavy feeders from one part of the garden to another. Notice if there are parts of the garden where soils dry out more quickly or where moisture is retained well into middle summer, and use these characteristics to your advantage during plant placement.

Think about ease of access to crops that will need to be weeded more often, picked frequently, or watered more than others and locate them accordingly. Our production gardens have very long wide rows. When we are harvesting vegetables, there are certain areas we visit daily to pick vegetables like cucumbers, summer squashes, and beans. Some vegetables such as winter squashes, potatoes, and brussels sprouts are not harvested until the end of the season. Herbs

such as basil and parsley are usually gathered daily for eating fresh, whereas some of the mints are harvested only on occasion for drying.

The overall beauty of our gardens is of utmost importance to us, and fortunately when we make many design decisions for garden layout, we are simultaneously making good decisions for healthy gardens. Initially we didn't think of gardens so openly. Like many first-time gardeners, we started by making strict separations between our vegetable, herb, annual, perennial, and flower beds. This isolation of kinds of plants was very limiting and became extremely boring. It is no exaggeration to say that we now mix everything up in an effort to rotate crops, find the best growing spots for species, and most of all create gardens that are so diverse and so beautiful that they keep us constantly interested.

We work in our gardens every day of the week from March until the time the snows arrive in November. The visual diversity we establish also means biological diversity. One season we may have our cutting annuals interspersed with the cole crops. The next season we may set out edible flowers with nonflowering vegetables. In our relatively small two-acre plot, there are anywhere from two hundred to four hundred different species of plants in a given season. We attribute much of our success in farming organically to the constant diversity of the plantings. While a backyard gardener

Weeding a fully mulched garden takes very little time.

A low-growing perennial clover is a good alternative to hay for mulching the walkways in our gardens.

may have fewer kinds of plants, it is still possible to combine many categories of plants into a small garden and move them around from year to year to maintain healthy plants and soils.

Setting Out Plants in Mulched Rows

ONCE A GARDEN DESIGN has been established, it is time to gather up the hardened-off seedlings and get them into the garden. Make certain you pay attention to the temperatures of the soil and the overall weather patterns. Don't rush to set out plants that need warm weather. There is no exact calendar for frost dates, only averages. Listen to weather reports and leave your tender seedlings in a protected area if conditions are not favorable. An unusually warm week in early spring may be followed by several nights of below-freezing temperatures. Many a customer has returned to our greenhouses to purchase seedlings for a second time because he or she hurried the planting. Be prudent.

If possible, pick an overcast day to plant. Even better, plant in the rain or before a spell of cloudy days. The brightest, sunniest days should be used for other tasks, as this weather may suit you best but it will be the hardest on young seedlings. If you must plant during a sunny spell, set out plants late in the afternoon so they have an overnight to adjust to the transition before a whole day of strong sun in the garden.

We set out our seedlings into the black plastic mulch by poking holes into the plastic with a long metal rod, carefully establishing a pattern to accommodate as many plants across the width of the row as possible. This sometimes results in spacing plants two or three abreast; with large plants, we stagger the pattern down the row. The charts at the end of chapters will help you determine outdoor spacing. Just before seedlings are placed into the ground, we water them very well so they have extra moisture for their first hours in the garden.

Planting depths will vary from plant to plant, but most seedlings will be set into the ground at the same depth as they were growing in their final containers. If

Squashes, onions, and holy basil grow alongside the production gardens, where vegetables, herbs, and flowers are intermingled throughout.

Cabbages for eating and globe amaranth for cutting and drying are neighbors in one section of the garden.

GROWING HERBS AND VEGETABLES

some plants have become leggy and they are not plants with crowns, they may be buried an inch or two deeper than they were in their pots. Placing plants slightly deeper will protect them from wind damage and allow additional roots to develop from the buried stems. Always be careful when handling seedlings so that the stems are not bent or damaged. Also make certain the planting hole is ample, so roots are not squashed. A dibble can be very useful for this. This hand-held tool will allow you to make a good planting hole without bruising your hands, especially useful in rocky soils. Once the plant is positioned in the hole, bring soil up around the stem, and firm the soil with your hands.

If you are planning to stake any plants, consider staking at the same time as planting. This means that you will be able to insert the stake close to the plant without touching any roots. By waiting a week or two, you may be damaging new root growth. Also consider using stakes for young seedlings that have some size to them at planting time, so that tall plants have support for the first several weeks of growth. Strong, gusty, early summer wind, alone or in combination with a heavy rain, can snap young stems that are supporting any amount of leafy top growth. Tie plants very loosely to the stakes with soft strips of cloth or very loose loops of large twine. Baling twine works very well. Pay attention to adding ties as the plants grow so that the tops don't fall over, possibly bending the stems beyond recovery.

You will notice that once you have made any holes in the black plastic mulch, wind can get in under the mulch and lift it slightly from the level of the ground. This is usually of no importance unless the seedlings you are setting out are very small or very low growing. If this is the case, you may want to weigh down the plastic right next to these plants with a few stones so that fluttering plastic doesn't catch plants and loosen their roots.

We almost always choose a cloudy spell for setting out seedlings, and our soils are amply moist. However,

if it is necessary to set out plants when the weather is sunny and dry for a spell, it may be necessary to water young transplants for several days after they are set out. Don't let them be stressed by dryness initially. Once they have had a chance to establish new roots they can endure more intense sun and wind.

Make certain you label plants in the garden with labels that will last throughout the summer for annual crops and for at least a year with perennial plants. We use one-foot-long plain wooden stakes and write the

Some crops, such as beets and carrots, are seeded directly into small holes made in the black plastic. Small greens are thinned out and eaten early, leaving a few beets in each hole to develop to full size for harvesting at the end of the season.

information on them with a permanent marker. These stakes remain legible and durable for a little longer than a year, but if the ink starts to fade, we simply rewrite any information needed while doing general gardening chores. Don't think you will remember your crops without labels, particularly if you are testing different varieties of plants that are similar in appearance. If you include planting dates on the labels, they will help in evaluating plant development. When time permits, transfer this information to any gardening journals you are keeping.

We also draw a general map of the entire garden so we can refer to the maps from season to season when figuring crop rotation. Keeping such maps for several seasons will be very helpful if you ever encounter diseases in a family of plants, meaning that you need to keep such crops away from parts of the garden for a few years. The ability to review old garden plans also allows us to revise and rethink design ideas that had merit as well as disadvantages.

Direct Seeding in Mulched Rows

MANY OF OUR VEGETABLES and a few of our herbs are seeded into the wide rows of black plastic mulch. It is not necessary to seed when it is cloudy and not advisable to do it when it is raining, simply because it's too cumbersome to keep seed packets dry and seeds from sticking together in the rain.

Greek oregano plants surround annual salpiglossis and a scented geranium in this ornamental garden that was planted through a bark mulch over landscape fabric. There will be no need for weeding or watering in this garden for the entire season.

Layouts and spacing requirements are followed with direct seeding just as for setting out plants. We make holes again with a long metal rod. If the holes need to be enlarged, we do it by enlarging the punctured hole with our fingers. Whenever possible, it is most convenient to punch a hole in the plastic and dig into the earth with the rod to the required planting depth. Such precision is not always possible, so it may be that the rod is used to establish the planting layout, and the actual planting depth is increased by hand or with a smaller tool, such as a dibble.

We don't plant more seeds in the ground than we want plants to germinate. Most vegetable and herb seeds have such a high germination rate that we prefer to seed this way and go back and spot-reseed when necessary. We rarely thin plants that are seeded directly into the mulched rows. Seeds are dropped into their spaces and covered to the depth required. Most plants will begin to germinate in the warm soils in a matter of days or with some slower-growing species within a week or two. Watch the newly seeded areas every day. Don't let the soils dry out. Since seeding is done early in the season, there are usually enough rainy days to keep soils adequately moist, but conditions may vary greatly in your gardens. It may be advisable to place a few heavy stones on the top of the plastic mulch in the newly seeded area to keep the plastic weighed firmly to the ground. On occasion we have seen a sudden strong gust pick up a section of plastic and tear it away from the row. It's very tedious to refit a mulch over young seedlings and seeded areas, and difficult to bury the edges of the plastic again once the garden is set out.

Planting on Open Ground

SOME GARDENERS MAY CHOOSE not to use black mulches and prefer instead to plant and seed into open ground. This can result in gardens that are as productive and as healthy, so long as a number of basic requirements are still met. Soils and light should be evaluated as described above. Raised rows may be made or rows can be defined at ground level.

There are certain crops we direct seed into open ground, and we try to choose garden sites that have

been worked to the point that they are as weed free as possible. We also want these sites to have very good amounts of organic matter and soils that hold their moisture. Without benefit of mulches, soils will have to be kept weed free through the use of tilling, hoeing, and hand weeding. That constant working of the soils causes them to dry out much more quickly than mulched soils.

Even when we are planting and seeding in open ground, we still make the rows wide and the walkways narrow. When plants and seeds are first set out, it will be very important to make certain they have ample moisture. Early and constant weeding should be done so that there is no competition for either space or water. Make certain that cultivation around young plants and shallow-rooted plants is done without disturbing roots.

Whenever possible, we add mulches to our open-ground gardens, but we do so later in the season. During planting time we want the soils to absorb as much warmth from the sun as is possible. The darkness of the soil itself causes it to absorb warmth. As plants develop and as the days of summer warm increasingly, we are then less concerned about soil warmth and more focused on the plants' need for moisture. Unless weeds are present in overwhelming numbers in any garden, they are mainly annoying because they look out of place. In fact, there are some weeds that act as good trap crops for insects that would otherwise be eating your cultivated crops. We don't mulch so much for weed control as we do to retain moisture. By late June, when plants have developed size, soils have warmed, and early summer rains are less frequent, we try to apply an organic summer mulch on open-ground gardens.

The most common summer mulch is either hay or straw, the difference being that the former includes the seed heads and the latter is seed free. Straw is almost always much more expensive, and we usually

Lettuce and tomatoes share space well. The lettuce will be harvested long before the tomatoes need to sprawl over the raised row.

In the Garden

have mulch hay readily available. The hay may be spread around the plants in the garden to a depth of two to four inches thick, or you can first cover the surface of the garden with several layers of paper and then cover the paper with hay. This way the paper acts as a barrier to weed seed, at least for the duration of the growing season.

In gardening zones where it would be beneficial to keep soils cooler from earlier on in the summer, an entire garden could be prepared, covered with paper

The kohlrabi leaves have been eaten by flea beetles, but the edible fruit is perfectly clean and needs no garden insecticides.

and hay, and then seeded and planted by making individual holes in the mulch through which to plant. In fact, we employ this practice, not because we have warm soils initially but because we occasionally have to wait until midsummer to set out some display gardens. Planting through a mulch is much easier to do than planting and then mulching up to the plants, only in that you are able to have a thicker, more evenly applied mulch when there are no stems to work around.

We have experimented with a number of other ground level gardens using varying mulching techniques. In every case, it is essential that the soil be very well prepared and amply moist before the mulch is put into place. If sites are at all dry, we will soak the

ground to a depth of several inches before applying any mulch. Weed-seed barriers include the use of paper, plastic, and landscape fabric. The last item is manufactured out of a number of different fibers to allow water and air to penetrate but also to suppress weed growth. It does discourage weeds from growing, but usually has been designed to be covered with a second mulch that will totally prevent light from reaching the soils beneath.

As a second-layer mulch, we have used straw, hay, grass clippings, pine needles, ground bark, and sawdust. Only straw and hay are chosen for our vegetable gardens, as they will be tilled into the soils without significantly altering the acidity of the soils. Grass clippings are acceptable for vegetable and herb gardens, but we simply don't have them in amounts that would be needed at our scale of gardening. A backyard gardener might find them useful in a small plot. Pine needles, bark, and sawdust are not used in the vegetable or herb beds as they would contribute too much acidity to the soils. We use these materials specifically for plants and shrubs such as heathers and blueberries that prefer acid soils.

Our strong penchant for mulching gardens whenever possible comes from evaluating many mulched and unmulched garden plots. If your climate permits and if you can match an appropriate mulching system to the site, you may find that the time it takes to mulch will be amply rewarded in hours saved having to weed and water.

Season Extenders

UNLESS YOU LIVE in a zone that allows gardening year-round, chances are you are always wishing for a little more growing time at either end of the season. There are simple devices for extending the growing season. We have already talked about poly tunnels and cold frames, both of which make early-spring and late-fall growing possible even in Maine. Other good ideas include individual plant cloches, which can be purchased or made from plastic milk bottles. There are plastic growing circles called "walls of water," which are water-filled devices that protect individual plants and increase the temperatures of the soil and air. There are slitted row covers similar to poly tunnels, but these row covers have slits cut in the plastic. When the temperatures are warm, the plastic droops and the slits open up; when the temperatures are cold, the fabric contracts and the slits remain nearly closed. Any of these temperature-altering protections can be used to your advantage, but they need to be monitored constantly. It takes only a few hours of hot midday sun to cook a plant left in an unvented cloche. The same disaster can happen in poly tunnels, cold frames, and slitted row covers if the weather turns unexpectedly warm and sunny.

Floating row covers are made from very lightweight spun fabric and can be placed on the top of young plants without hurting the plants. They increase temperatures beneath, offering some added protection from cold and wind. The fabric is so porous that water and air pass through it readily. It is not necessary to remove the covers even during warm, sunny days. They are also effective in protecting crops at the times in their growing cycles when they are most susceptible to insect damage. Conversely, row covers must be removed from crops that are reliant on insect pollination for production. Their use must be well timed in the early part of the growing season, but they are also helpful after fruiting has taken place to protect crops from predation and light early-fall frosts. We have used them extensively at the end of the season.

We have also used dark landscape fabric, not unlike white row covers in texture and weight. When tender crops are covered in the middle of the day, these dark covers warm up the air beneath; we have brought many frost-sensitive vegetables and herbs through below-freezing nights unharmed. These covers are then removed during sunny days and replaced as nighttime temperatures necessitate. They are preferable to the old-fashioned use of household blankets, not only for the obvious reasons but also because they do not absorb moisture and become so heavy that they break the plants they are protecting.

Most of these season extenders are affordable and, if well cared for, can be used for several seasons. Our advice is to experiment with a few devices before making any significant investment. Our other bias is to be creative with whatever materials you have on hand.

Ongoing Care

OUR FIELD WORK IS very demanding from early May until planting is completed in June. From then on, our time in the gardens is spent mainly observing and harvesting as needed. There is some ongoing care in the mulched gardens, but it is quite minimal compared to the early work. Tasks involve

When the first frosts threaten the gardens, we sometimes protect special areas with landscape fabric or floating row covers. The plants are covered before sunset and uncovered during the day for as long as the temperatures and our energy allow.

WHEN IT CAME TO designing poly tunnels, we could say that disaster was the mother of invention. A number of years ago, during a particularly heavy storm, one of our arched greenhouses collapsed under the weight of ice and snow. We were left with 150 feet of twisted and bent galvanized metal tubing and ripped greenhouse coverings beneath more than three feet of heavy wet snow. The cleanup was hastily done so we could erect another greenhouse to start the season. We threw out useless materials and made a junk pile

out of the metal. Since that time, we have cut and used three quarters of the pipe to build simple, effective poly tunnels, which are really mini versions of our arched greenhouses. The poly tunnels, however, are small enough to be built without using any ridge pieces, and they can be set up and taken down in a matter of minutes.

To anchor the poly tunnels to the ground, we cut two-foot-long pieces of galvanized pipe, flatten one end with a heavy sledgehammer, and drive the pipe into the ground. Supporting ground pieces are set up every three feet along each side of the tunnel. Then for the rounded arches that will support the cover, we use flexible 10-foot-long ¾-inch round PVC sched-

Flexible piping can be set up in a matter of minutes to form the arches of a poly tunnel. Once covered with plastic, you have a protective place for potted plants or for planting.

ule 40 pipes purchased from a hardware store at a very reasonable cost. The pipes are positioned into place by pushing one end into the galvanized footing and bending the pipe across the seven-foot tunnel and inserting the opposite end in the facing galvanized footing. Tunnels can be made as short or as long as space and needs demand.

Once the tunnel frame is set up, the covering is made from a skin of clear plastic that is at least four mil thick. The plastic covering can be anchored to the ground with any heavy objects such as boards, rocks, or buckets filled with water. We usually set these poly tunnels up and move them around constantly to meet the needs of our greenhouse and nursery business. If we were to set one up to be used in place over a longer period of time, we would make the effort to fasten the covering at least on one side of the tunnel in a more permanent manner. These poly tunnels are great season extenders at both ends of the summer. When days are sunny and cool or overcast, we usually only need open the covering on one end for cooling. During spring weather when days can be warm and nights quite cold, we may peel the covering off to one side during the day and close it up again for the evening.

This idea is kept quite simple for our purposes, but as mentioned previously, a home gardener could refine the design so that opening and closing were more simple and so that the whole unit was more neatly finished to fit into the design of a backyard. It would not be necessary to have metal piping for anchoring; instead one could use slightly larger diameter, heavier plastic pipe partially anchored in the ground. The poly tunnel is nothing but a variation on a cold frame. It has the advantages, however, of being lightweight and inexpensive, and it can be broken down in minutes and stored in a very small space until needed again.

weeding, watering, maintaining plant nourishment, and monitoring harmful insects, diseases, and animal predation.

It is no exaggeration to say that we spend no more than five to ten hours a summer weeding the large production garden. The only place weeds have an opportunity to sprout is in the planting or seeding holes we have made in the black plastic mulch. If the plants have any size at all at transplant time, they take up most of the planting hole and quickly shade whatever soil is exposed to sun around their stems. Transplants that are very small do allow some weed seed to germinate around them, but not to any great extent. Weeding the planted rows is done early, as soon as any weeds are visible. We usually do this with two people walking each side of one wide row so that almost every weed is spotted during the first weeding. Weeds are pulled with one hand while the cultivated plant is held firmly in place so that its roots are not disturbed in the slightest. We walk and inspect each row thoroughly the first time, usually managing to remove more than three quarters of the weeds that will be produced in the entire garden.

Naturally there will be some weeds overlooked and some more seeds to germinate before the plants have grown sufficiently large to suppress competition. The second weeding is done a week or two after the first, and usually it will be done by one person who is able to walk the rows rather quickly, stopping from place to place to pull weeds. After the first two deliberate weedings, we don't allocate time to weeding per se, but anyone who is working in the gardens for the remainder of the summer will do spot cleaning. If a few weeds or tenacious grasses go unnoticed and manage to get a good start next to a cultivated plant, we don't pull them out. Rather, we always carry pocket knives or shears when working, and the large weeds are carefully cut out at the root so they cannot regrow and so the roots of the plants we are cultivating are not disturbed.

Keeping our production gardens free of weeds was not always such an undemanding task. Our early gardens, with their unmulched narrow ribbon rows of crops, had to be cultivated weekly, hoed constantly, and weeded all summer. And regardless of how much maintenance time we spent, we almost always abandoned some parts of the garden that just got away from us. It's a complaint we hear often from visitors talking about their own sites.

Weeding production rows that are seeded in open ground takes a little more time, but our current practices are still a big improvement on our earlier methods. We hold off seeding on open ground until early or midsummer. During this time we either keep the open site blanketed or tilled to combat weeds until planting time. As soon as rows are seeded, we are able to mulch the walkways on either side. Since we always seed several parallel rows in a wide, long area, we have only the small alleys between the seeding to keep clean. This is done very thoroughly as early on as possible, when we can see the germinated plants that were sown and while weeds are very small. After this there is usually only one additional weeding done before the cultivated crops are large enough to suppress competition.

Any of our display gardens that are not permanently mulched are weeded thoroughly at the beginning of the season, just as soon as growth appears. Once cleaned, these gardens are top-dressed with well-composted manures to enrich the soils and feed the plants for the upcoming season. Spot cleaning is done throughout the summer, but the work is minimal. We do not clean our gardens at the end of the summer, but instead leave all the top growth to entangle fall leaves and build up a natural protective mulch for the winter. But before the gardens are covered with leaves, we try to make certain that any late summer weeds are removed. It is often this last weeding that gardeners tend to forget or simply not to take seriously. At the end of the gardening season we are sometimes tired of paying attention, and we let slide the tasks that are important for the next season. The last weeding is certainly such a task. The late-summer untended weeds are often precisely those with fully developed seed heads that will drop to earth, thus ensuring thousands of weeds the following spring. Our advice: forget about making your yard look neat in the fall and concentrate on getting the weed seeds out of the gardens.

Watering

WE HAVE TALKED at great length about not watering our gardens once they are set out and mulched. We have the advantage of gardening in an area where the soils are intrinsically heavy, and we have enriched them over the years with copious amounts of animal manures and composts. We have also spoken about the benefits of mulching to conserve water. But there will be many gardeners who will have to provide supplemental watering to their sites, if soils are very sandy or if there are periods of real dryness. Much attention has been paid recently to planning gardens that do not require much water, called "xeriscape" gardening. If you are working with ornamental gardens, it is worth finding plants that are suitable for dry soils. Most vegetables and many herbs, however, require adequate moisture.

If you must water your gardens, consider setting up a drip irrigation system with in-ground or ground-level hoses. These special hoses have small holes that allow water to be dripped slowly into the ground near the plant roots. They deliver water efficiently where it is needed. By comparison, top watering is very wasteful because so much of the moisture either evaporates or is taken up by the soils away from the plant roots. You might also consider setting up spot watering drip systems for the plants that need the most moisture. This can be done by setting a large container, with a few very small holes in the bottom, next to a plant. The container is filled with water that then drips slowly into the soil next to the plant roots. Consider also setting up water-collecting barrels at the downspouts of your buildings.

When you need to top-water gardens with hoses, there are also a few important things to consider. It is better to water well, so that the soil is thoroughly wet to a depth of several inches, than to water often and superficially. Frequent superficial watering is not only wasteful, it is actually harmful to many plants. Plant roots respond to dryness at the surface of the soil by sending down roots where they sense more moisture. Superficial watering rarely satisfies a plant's needs and may retard its root development into deeper, more constantly moist soil. You may keep a plant from drying out at the same time that you keep it from developing vigorously. Even when we are faced with an extended dry spell, we always evaluate any plant's ability to withstand a period of dryness by watching its vigor during the hottest part of the day. If there is no evidence of wilting, we simply don't water. If there is a slight bit of leaf wilting but the leaves quickly rebound

MANY VARIETIES OF HERBS are quite undemanding to grow. Once established in the garden, they exhibit very few disease problems, they are not attacked by many insects, and they are rarely eaten by wildlife. Even in the fall, when deer are looking for anything edible, they pass over nearly all the perennial herbs, including the mints, lavender, the artemisias, sages, oreganos, and thymes. When the large containers of rosemary, bay, lemon verbena, and myrtle are easily available for foraging animals, we have never seen any predation.

Herbs in the onion family do attract hungry animals, but at the same time they seem to repel aphids, not only from themselves but from any plants growing next to them in the garden. Out of all the annual culinary herbs, the only animal predation we witness is late summer feeding on parsley and occasionally on fennel and dill. Basils are left untouched whatever the season.

There is very little insect damage to herbs as well. Occasionally there are a few aphids on newly set out seedlings, but these pests don't last when there are other more appealing green growing things. All in all, the herbs are quite trouble free in the garden.

In addition, there are perennial herbs that will adapt nicely to drier soils. These include the artemisias, lavender, sage, rue, hyssop, santolina, tansy, wild oregano, comfrey, anise hyssop, and the thymes. The thymes are so flexible that they will grow in a wide variety of sites. At the far end of the production garden, we have some large old thyme plants that measure a couple of feet across, living in a fertile, moist soil in full sun. At the front of the garden, along a slate walkway, there are thyme plants, equally old, that were planted into thin, poor, sandy soil around the pieces of slate.

Most of the vegetables we discuss in the book require careful attention to their needs for proper soil, light, and moisture. Edible and ornamental herbs are a bit more forgiving.

Lavender and creeping thyme are dominant features in this perennial garden. They are hardy, reliable, and need little care.

at dusk, we hold off watering. If there is enough wilting for us to decide that watering is necessary, we wait until dusk and then water the soil around the plants heavily, as mentioned earlier to a depth of several inches. Never assume that water has percolated down adequately into the soil by making a visual assessment. Always dig down and turn over a section of soil to make certain you have done a thorough job.

Nutrition

DEPENDING UPON the composition of your soils, it may or may not be necessary to feed your plants during the summer. Furthermore, it may be necessary to supplement only a few of the vegetables or herbs you are growing. Supplemental feeding can be done in a number of ways. Since we have built up our soils over the past few decades, we rarely fertilize our gardens in the summer, except for occasional foliar feeding of the vegetables that are the heaviest feeders. On occasion we use a combination of seaweed and fish emulsion three or four times during the summer as an extra boost for plants when they are setting fruit.

If your gardens are mulched, foliar feeding is the easiest way to fertilize the plants. In addition, it is possible to feed and water plants with a homemade "manure tea." This is made by mixing a small amount of animal manure in the bottom of a bucket and filling the bucket with water. Let the whole thing stand for several days, stir occasionally, and then use the top "tea" as a plant food. Apply it through the holes of a black plastic mulch or around the base of a plant with an organic mulch. Manure teas could also be fed through a single container drip watering device as described earlier.

When we started to farm, we were taught to use commercially prepared fertilizers. These granular fertilizers come in bags of different weights, but usually contain three basic components, nitrogen, phosphorus, and potassium. When garden fertilizers have numbers on their labels, such as 5–10–5, or 10–10–10, these numbers refer to the relative percentages of the three basic ingredients, always in the same order, nitrogen first, then phosphorus, and last potassium. The components are sometimes abbreviated with the letters *N, P,* and *K*. We do not recommend using commercial fertilizers as a substitute for building garden soils. If you are starting with a rather poor garden site and feel you need to provide additional plant food for the first few gardening seasons, commercial plant food can be incorporated into the soils at planting time or used as a midseason boost by side dressing along the rows and working the food into the soil. Be aware that commercially prepared fertilizers will do nothing to improve the composition of your soil. They will feed the plants for that season, but not much else. Today we use only organic fertilizers in our gardens but acknowledge that any number of plant foods are available and effective in stimulating production. Whatever fertilizers you choose to use in your own gardens, make certain you read the labels and match the food to the crops being grown.

One of the plant foods you have readily available is compost. If you ever mow the lawn, rake up leaves, clean any organic debris from the yard, you are handling materials that can easily be composted. Any kitchen leftovers can be collected in a bucket and added to the compost pile. Our compost pile, located at the back door of the horse barn, is a huge dark brown mound that fluctuates in size from season to season. In addition to the animal manure and some shavings, we compost used greenhouse mixtures and leftover plants along with their biodegradable containers. We save kitchen leftovers, grass clippings, and the few leaves we ever rake. Most of our leaves are left to rot in the gardens where they collect naturally. We work different parts of the compost pile each year, using the oldest, richest, most decomposed areas first. If you are looking for a source of animal manure, try asking where pleasure horses are stabled. Unless the owners are maintaining their own pastures, they may be more than happy to have some place to get rid of the animal waste. Cow manure is a good garden fertilizer but harder to come by, as most farmers use it to replenish their own fields. If you have access to any other animal wastes such as sheep, goat, rabbit, or chicken, take advantage of it. Do not use pig manure on gardens, however, as pigs carry some pathogens that can infect human beings. All animal manures are best composted before being used. There are many books available on the art of composting; also try searching the Internet, and check to see what is available from your County Extension Office.

Insects

OUR GARDEN IS full of insects, just as it should be. They are some of the most interesting creatures on the farm, a testimony to the wonderfully complex small environment we are helping to create. Some insects are beautiful, some are annoying, some are beneficial, and some are harmful to the crops. But before we take any measures to eliminate insects, we need to know who's who. At the outset, buy yourself a good basic field guide so you will be able to identify the insects that buzz around you and your plants all during the growing season. It is important to be able to recognize them in every stage of growth, in egg masses, as nymphs, as larvae, as beetles, as caterpillars, in their winged forms, and even in their chrysalises. How many of us have smiled appreciatively over the much-mythologized ladybug but unknowingly crushed it in disgust during its less familiar larval stage? Out of the thousands of species of insects that inhabit our gardens, only a very small percentage are harmful to us or to our plants. Any random destruction of insects would be foolhardy. In the process we would be destroying pollinators, food for many other forms of life, and species that are essential in the delicately evolved ecosystem we live in.

Next we want to make a strong argument for learning to live with a few holes in the leaves of plants and with an acceptable level of insect predation. Early flea

BAN BUG ZAPPERS

THEY SEND OUT an eerie blue light into the evening darkness and an even more menacing sound as they electrically kill the insects that are lured to the light. But they do little to diminish the population of biting insects that people are trying to control so they can sit out in their yards on a summer evening. Electric bug lights, or bug zappers, are one of the most inappropriate inventions we can imagine. According to one of our state entomologists, there have been systematic studies showing that the lights have no effect on mosquito populations. Mosquitoes are attracted to carbon dioxide, not to light. Furthermore, black flies are diurnal and they too are not attracted to light.

If these lights are being purchased primarily to ward off biting insects, they are a waste of money—and worse. According to the same entomologist, the killing is wanton destruction of insect populations for no good reason. All that zapping is killing any number of rare moths along with equal numbers of harmless and even beneficial insects. It seems it is the sound of insects being killed that is consoling to the light owners, with little attention being paid to the potential harm done.

Gardeners need to do everything possible to keep

The beautiful night-flying luna moth is a frequent summer visitor to the farm.

their populations of insects alive and healthy. All insects play a vital part in the complex ecosystems of our yards. If you want to work in the garden at dusk or sit out on the deck, why not invest in a comfortable lightweight mesh shirt. These shirts come with hoods and face protection, elastic at the wrists, and a tie around the hips. They don't use any electricity, emit any light, and are perfectly quiet.

Garden friends include bees, spiders, praying mantises, lady bugs, and tiny toads.

If damage to the crops can be assessed as only aesthetic, we almost never respond. That would include watching and tolerating the presence of flea beetles, leafhoppers, some aphids, cabbage butterflies, slugs, earwigs, celery caterpillars, corn earworms and corn borers, and striped cucumber beetles. These insects are always in our vegetable gardens, but the populations vary greatly from year to year. When any of these insects is evidenced in unusually high numbers for a long period of time and we see damage to the young plants, we use a number of responses.

If possible, we will cover target crops with a floating row cover to prevent physical access to young plants. One of the added advantages of learning about all the life stages of different insects is that you will be able to select the times to shield crops from specific stages of insect predation. Insects have complex life cycles, and even with the most harmful of predators there are usually times in their cycle when they are the most destructive and times in the cycle when it is eas-

beetles do make holes in young plant leaves, but if they are not present in overwhelming numbers it may be worth remembering that we don't even eat the same leaves they do, at least not on crops like broccoli, cauliflower, cabbage, brussels sprouts, radishes, and tomatoes, to name only a few. We want our soils to be filled with earthworms, whose work and castings aerate and enrich the soils, so it would be very unwise to drench the soils in chemicals that eradicate them along with other soft-bodied soil dwellers.

Our gardens undergo a certain amount of insect damage each year, but rarely with the same problems at the same intensity from one season to the next. It would be costly, unwise, and ineffective to do any kind of preventive spraying even with the so-called acceptable sprays. Our first line of defense in dealing with insects is monitoring for their presence and knowing what insects can be endured in what proportions before we need to respond.

iest to combat their destructiveness. A good example of this is the Colorado potato beetle. In its beetle form, it is very easy to spot on plants and very easy to pick off mechanically. The egg clusters are also easy to see, as bright orange masses found on the undersides of leaves. They can be scraped off, or the whole leaf removed and destroyed. The hatched larvae of the potato beetles are the most difficult to see when they are very small, but they are also the most voracious eaters. Larvae can grow quickly as they consume the leaves of a young plant. The larval stage is also one of the easiest stages of the insect to treat with a relatively safe organic spray of *Bacillus thuringiensis* (see box on page 92). Knowing the life cycle of this one insect gives the gardener three different opportunities to respond to its presence.

While we tolerate a certain number of insects in the gardens, we also intervene and eliminate populations if necessary. We will pick off or hose off insect populations with soapy water when possible. If we use sprays, our arsenal of garden insecticides include wood ashes, insecticidal soaps, various varieties of *Bacillus*, rotenone, and pyrethrum. We resort to their use only when all else fails. Admittedly, there are some insects we do not tolerate in even small numbers, because experience has shown that once they appear in the garden, they usually explode in numbers and physically harm a plant or introduce diseases into the plants. We react quickly to the Colorado potato beetle as described above. We also hasten to respond to tarnish plant bugs, squash bugs, and Mexican bean beetles.

Garden insects will vary greatly from one part of the country to another. There is even considerable variation closely within a small region. Some neighbors have problems with Japanese beetles, partly due to the fact that they grow ornamentals that attract these insects. Some gardeners in sites much more suburban than ours experience more insect predation simply because there are fewer natural trap crops where insects can feed. Each gardener will have to assess the problems specific to his or her own site. We argue only for moderation in the use of insecticides and for the use of insecticides that are safe for humans as well as innocent bystanders.

A few of these bystanders are known as the beneficial insects. This means not only that they do no harm to our crops but that in many cases they prey on the insects we don't want in the gardens. The best-known beneficial insects in our climate are ladybugs, lacewings, praying mantises, syrphid flies, some ground beetles, dragonflies, spiders, and predacious mites. There are also a number of pollinating insects, most notably bees and wasps and hornets, some of which also act as predators on harmful insects by parasitizing them. The pollinators are more than useful; they are essential.

Since different regions of the country will have specific insect populations, it is helpful to use whatever resources we can that are specific to our areas. Ask for information from local extension and soil conservation offices on identifying and dealing with insects. Seek out any nearby organic gardening organizations as well. Then you can evolve your own considered response.

Plant Diseases

IF WE DECIDE to tolerate some insect predation, we must also accept the fact that insects can be vectors for diseases. Aphids secrete a sticky sap called honeydew that is a perfect environment for black sooty mold fungus. Cucumber beetles can transmit bacteria from plant to plant. In addition, there are a variety of soilborne diseases and airborne pathogens. Certain weather conditions can invite disease, such as a long, cloudy, humid, warm spell, following which some vegetables become covered with a powdery mildew. There are early blights and late blights, wilts and botrytis (gray mold). There are diseases that result from uneven periods of dryness and moisture.

Sound garden practices are the best defenses against plant diseases. Create healthy soils. Introduce only vigorous plants and clean seeds into the garden. When choosing seeds and plants, read the literature carefully and choose varieties of plants that show natural resistance to the diseases that most affect them. Keep plants as free from excessive stress as possible by providing ample water, air circulation, and adequate space for development. Use trellises to keep vines off the ground so there will be good air circulation and fruits will ripen away from the soil. Mulch under all ripening fruit so it doesn't come into contact with the soil.

IF AND WHEN YOU DECIDE to use any natural insecticides in your gardens, it's important to know what they are made of and what they are intended to do. Our list includes only what we have had experience with on our farm.

Wood Ashes—Ashes are collected from the kitchen woodstove and any of several wood furnaces used in the farmhouse and greenhouses. They are sprinkled on the leaves of crops that are eaten by soft-bodied insects. Ashes are corrosive and cause injury to the soft exoskeletons of insects, causing them to die from dehydration. They are effective for the larvae of cabbageworms on any of the cole crops, and they are useful to spread where slugs are likely to congregate. Wood ashes are also beneficial to the garden soil in moderate amounts. While they have no nitrogen and only trace amounts of phosphorus, they are high in potassium. Make certain you know what nutrients your soils need before applying wood ashes as a soil supplement. They cause soils to become more alkaline.

Rotenone—This plant-derived insecticide is made from the roots of certain tropical plants such as derris and cube. It is a stomach poison, toxic to both chewing and sucking insects, but it is also dangerous to cold-blooded animals such as frogs, fish, and snakes. It has a relatively short period of effectiveness so must be reapplied after rain. It should never be used indiscriminately, as it will kill beneficial insects as well as targeted pests. Rotenone is available as dust and wettable powder.

Pyrethrum—Another plant-based insecticide, pyrethrum is made from the dried inflorescence of *Chrysanthemum cinerarifolium,* a daisylike flower. It is toxic to some chewing and sucking insects and acts as a contact poison. It need not be ingested to be effective. It is available in liquid form. Whenever these insecticides are used, the gardener should wear protective gloves and a face mask and work so that wind does not blow the insecticides back on the user. While they are relatively innocuous to warm-blooded animals,

they may cause allergic reactions and should not be inhaled.

Bacillus thuringiensis—Often referred to as Bt, this bacterium is available under a number of trade names and in a number of varieties, each of which is capable of attacking different groups of insect hosts. Bt is a stomach poison that once ingested causes the insect to stop feeding and die. One of the chief advantages of any *Bacillus* is its effectiveness only on the targeted pests. Some of the better known are Bt var. *israelensis,* used against the fungus gnats. Bt var. *berliner* and var. *kurstaki* are used against cabbage loopers, cabbageworms, corn borers, and tomato hornworms—all members of the Lepidoptera (moth and butterfly) order. Bt var. *san diego* and subspecies *tenebrionis* are used against the Colorado potato beetle larvae. Bt var. *popilliae* is used to kill populations of Japanese beetle larvae (not considered very effective in cold areas such as Maine, where spores do not survive over the winter). Be certain you read any labels if choosing to use this insecticide, so you are purchasing the appropriate variety.

The larvae of the Colorado potato beetle are very destructive once present in large numbers. They are also easily controlled with a natural insecticide.

Be as vigilant as possible from the time you seed the plants until the time you harvest their fruits. Walk in the garden every day, even when there is no real work to do. Look at the plants, be aware of early signs of disease such as wilting, leaf curling, excessive insect predation, browning of leaf edges, any discoloration of leaves. Watch for any fungi or molds on any parts of the plants. Many times, if diseases are caught in the very early stages, a plant or two can be eliminated from the garden and the disease will be eradicated.

We battle diseases in our gardens almost entirely through our horticultural practices. In addition to the ideas already offered, it is essential to identify any diseases that occur on plants, either by using reference books or by having diseased specimens analyzed by plant pathologists. Once again, extension and soil conservation offices should be able to direct you. There are often newsletters mailed out from these offices that report on and describe common insect problems and plant diseases as they occur during any growing season. Some agricultural departments at state universities have laboratories where plant diseases can be identified if samples are mailed in.

Once a disease has been identified, plants should always be removed from the garden and disposed of by incineration when possible. Never throw infected plants off into the brush or place them on a compost pile. Be mindful of the fact that families of plants often are susceptible to the same diseases and that diseases can live over in soils for several years. Always rotate crops and keep related crops out of any diseased site for a minimum of three years. (Precise rotation times may vary from one disease to another.) Also be aware that there are some diseases that can live over in the soils for a decade or two, but these are less common and often specific to certain parts of the country. When such diseases are encountered, they need to be identified; susceptible crops are then kept from these sites for longer periods of time.

If you are handling any diseased plants, make certain you wash your hands and tools thoroughly before going on to other parts of the garden. Avoid harvesting plants during an extended rainy period if possible, except for small amounts of things to be consumed at the table. Picking in the rain has no effect on the fruits you are going to use, but diseases can easily be transmitted then, and in some cases these diseases will proliferate in wet vegetative matter more quickly than during sunny dry airy weather.

Animals in the Garden

ONE OF THE GREATEST pleasures of living in the country is the opportunity to observe wildlife any day of the year. We have deer, moose, bear, bobcats, raccoons, skunks, foxes, porcupines, woodchucks, coyotes, rabbits, rodents, birds, reptiles, and amphibians. We specifically don't have any canine pets so that the wildlife comes in close and often. This also means that we have chosen to try to accommodate their presence and at the same time protect important crops. The work we do to separate the raccoons from our corn is absurd. We plant and fence and plant and fence, and in a good year everyone eats well.

Porcupines are also indulged until one targets a favorite ornamental shade tree; then we relocate the creature to a woodland on the other side of the river. We've lost count of the number of trips with the Havahart trap in the back of the pickup. As for the woodchucks and the rabbits, there is so much to eat on the several hundred acres that they rarely end up in the garden. It's probably easier for us to tolerate these vegetarians because we are in our gardens from early morning until dusk every day of the week, so the animals stay away. A bear once made kindling wood out of a beehive that was left out in the garden too late in the fall. Moose walk through our fields several times a year, but the only damage they cause is directly under their big crushing feet. We will sacrifice a few plants any season to see these big graceful creatures.

Fortunately we never need be concerned about all the snakes and toads and frogs that inhabit the garden and the swampy area between the garden and the farmhouse. It is easy to appreciate how beneficial these creatures are in a region of the country where none of them is poisonous.

The biggest threat to our gardens is from several herd of deer that either live on the property or cross it daily on their way to water. There's a river bordering one part of our land and a pond very close to another boundary. Deer come early in the morning and just after dusk from the time the snows melt until the

Three strands of electric fencing positioned low to the ground around our corn discourages the raccoons from eating it before we do.

snow cover is too deep for them to successfully paw down to edible growth.

We use the following methods to try to keep them out of the production and display gardens. If the garden is very small, we fence all around the perimeter with six-foot-tall cedar posts and wire to the same height. While a deer could easily jump over a fence of this height, it has not yet happened, perhaps because we do this only on very small gardens and the inside feels too cramped. On the large production gardens we have surrounded the entire acreage with two strands of wire embedded in plastic ribbon; the wire is electrified with a fence charger. The charger is turned on whenever we are away from the garden. It only dissuades deer from entering, as they could easily jump over. Most of the time, however, they graze around the fence, where there is ample forage all during the spring, summer, and fall. Once we have planted cer-

tain crops that are particularly appealing, we spray them with a very smelly fish emulsion and seaweed, which repels the deer at the same time it feeds the plant. This will usually keep them out of the garden for a period of time, and if they wander back inside we repeat the spraying. We have tried deterrents such as hanging bags of human hair, bars of soap, and other repellents, but they worked less well. If we have important perennial crops we are planning to overwinter, we cover the plants in early fall with a protective landscape fabric or floating row cover. When natural forage is less available around the gardens, the deer are much more aggressive about jumping the fences. Deer are also repelled when we apply chicken manure to the gardens, but then so is everything and everybody else.

A neighbor claims she has kept deer away from her garden by using a spray made from beaten egg whites mixed with water and applied to the foliage of plants. Most sprayed-on repellents need to be reapplied after it rains. Many gardening catalogues and stores offer sprays, repellents, and mechanical devices to keep deer out of the garden. Since deer are becoming one of the main garden pests all over the country, there is increased attention being given to finding harmless repellents for gardeners to use. If we were working in a reasonably sized backyard garden, we would consider designing a pleasing and functional fencing system. The fence could double as trellising for a number of crops.

Harvesttime

HARVESTING HERBS and vegetables begins as early as May and continues into November, even in our climate. The earliest crops are rhubarb, sorrel, asparagus, and spring greens. Greens include the well-known cultivated kinds along with a mess or two of dandelion greens and fiddleheads. Fiddleheads are the young, tender, tightly curled fronds of the perennial ostrich fern, *Matteuccia struthiopteris*. There are optimum times for harvesting every edible plant, and specific information is given in Chapters 5 and 6. But one overall comment is worth making about harvesting vegetables from your own gardens. With the fruit right in your backyard, you have the advantage of picking just before eating and of picking the most tender young fruits of a number of vegetables.

There are several vegetables that, when picked young, are almost unrecognizable from their supermarket selves. They include summer squashes, cucumbers, eggplant, carrots, beets, new potatoes, peas, snap beans, radishes, kohlrabi, turnip, and the young greens of chard, kale, beets, and turnips. Don't wait for these crops to become large before starting to taste them.

Conversely, there are some vegetables in your own gardens that for the best flavor you should pick when they have ripened as long as possible on the plants. They include melons, tomatoes, tomatillos, and winter squashes. Sweet bell peppers, on the other hand, can be picked as soon as they are large enough, and they will be tasty and crunchy; the same varieties left on the plants until they mature to a bright red or chocolate brown will be deeply flavorful.

Sample your vegetables at different stages in their growth. It's one of the luxuries of growing your own food. Pick as you eat. Very little in the garden improves by sitting in the refrigerator, and there will be the entire winter for eating stored food. If you pick a little more than you eat right away, learn what vegetables should be kept in the pantry and what to put where it's cold. Leave the tomatoes on a kitchen shelf, and put the peas in the fridge.

Pick each of your herbs as you use them fresh, and if there are a few sprigs left over, recut stems and place the herbs in a glass of water for a day or so. If you don't use them fresh after that time, dry them for winter use. If you are harvesting herbs for storage, try to set up a schedule of harvesting all through the summer and early fall. Many herbs can be harvested a little at a time as soon as there is ample vegetative growth. Frequent harvesting is more manageable and beneficial to the plants, which will respond to repeated harvests by setting out new growth. The more you can accomplish during the summer, the better off

When frosts finally cover the annual production gardens, we leave the decaying plants to rot back into the soil and protect the topsoil until the following spring, when the ground is tilled and replanted.

ANTICIPATING GROWTH WHEN PLANTING PERENNIALS

WHEN DESIGNING GARDENS, we need to consider a number of factors, including soil and light requirements, plant heights, leaf and plant forms, flower colors, and periods of bloom. But perhaps one of the most important factors, much less discussed in gardening books, is knowing how plants behave and grow over a period of time. This information is essential when laying out any perennial herb gardens, so that we select plants that are compatible in a given space.

Knowing that an herb is a perennial tells us only a little about that plant. From that description we can expect the plant to reappear from its original rootstock from one season to the next, but we also need to know the plant's normal life expectancy. There are some short-lived perennials that are expected to perform for only three to four seasons and others that will be growing vigorously for decades. Anise hyssop is an example of the former, and baptisia an example of the latter. Anise hyssop lives for three to four seasons in our gardens, but appears to have a longer lifetime because it volunteers so freely, masking the fact that the original plants have been replaced by their progeny. Baptisia, on the other hand, continues to reappear from season to season, with the original plant simply enlarging at the base.

That brings us to the next major consideration in garden design, knowing how a plant sizes up over a

The showy, blue-blossomed baptisia plants and the brilliant red poppies share a garden. Both plants are slow to reach their mature size, but once they have, they can be counted on to perform as long-lived perennials.

period of several seasons. Presumably we set out a perennial garden with the hope that it will grow to maturity with some balance among the individual species in that garden. That means we must be able to anticipate the growing habits of each perennial in the mix. Let's look at some of the characteristics of a few popular herbs. Lavender increases in size gradually from one year to the next by developing more stems from the central part of the plant. It doesn't produce volunteers in the garden or invade its neighbors by underground root development. Creeping thyme also sizes up from the original central stem. It also can attach itself to surrounding ground by developing roots from leaf nodes that touch the earth. But more importantly, creeping thyme produces abundant volunteers in the garden from its seed, and these volunteers can take over a perennial bed in a few years if not weeded out.

Tarragon reproduces itself in our gardens, not by seed but through underground roots and stems that are produced from the main plant. The growth is moderately aggressive and can be held in check by some pruning, making tarragon a reasonable neighbor. Wild oregano, on the other hand, can quickly dominate a perennial herb garden by its abilities to spread through underground growth and abundant seed production. Many mints are simply so invasive with their vigorous underground runners that they must be confined to their own growing space and would be poor candidates for inclusion in a multispecies perennial herb garden.

When we are setting out any perennial bed, we always begin by assessing plant behavior, even before we consider the aesthetic principles of that garden. It is not enough to know that the pink blooms are pretty next to the light blue and soft yellows in early summer, if in a matter of a year or two, one of the plants in the mix may smother all the others or one of the key elements in the design needs to be replaced because it has lived out its expected lifetime. Learning how plants grow is as important as knowing that we like the way they look.

you will be when frosts have you running around the garden trying to save all the tender plants. When we leave too many things to be gathered and processed at the last minute, it means we don't harvest as much or as well as possible. It usually also means that some crops are left to sit in baskets and buckets before they are handled, so they are not at their absolute best before being processed.

Think of how plants behave and, if it is possible to stimulate productivity by picking off some of the fruit, make certain you do it, so that fruits don't overripen on the plants. This is effective with beans, peas, cucumbers, summer squashes, and any herbs that can be stimulated to set out leafy growth when the seeds or mature fruit are removed early in the growing cycle. Even if you don't want to eat any more summer squash, pick off developing fruit and compost it so that the plants continue to set flowers and young tender squash later in the summer when you have regained your appetite.

Watch for plants that can and should be harvested completely so you have access to the garden space for a second planting. Rather than leaving the garden peas to produce three or four more pods in midsummer, perhaps it would be better to harvest the entire young tender crop and have space for late summer greens. Regardless of how large our gardens, we usually expand the planting to use every inch, and welcome space for late crops.

Use your gardening journals all during the summer and particularly at harvesttime to note how plant varieties performed and how you might want to adjust numbers of plants in accordance with actual use for eating fresh and putting food by. As you experiment with new varieties of edible plants, your tastes will change. As you learn new ways to cook, dry, store, and process food, you will modify your gardens more than you might think. After a few years of gardening, you will really begin to know what plants suit you for eating fresh out of the garden and what plants are needed in greater quantity for making something special for the winter table. After thirty years we have in fact abandoned a number of vegetables we once grew for freezing and canning, and now only include them in the garden for harvesting fresh. Nonetheless, with only two of us living full-time at the farm, we still set out nearly fifty tomato plants. We've never found a marinara sauce to equal the one we simmer for several days on the kitchen woodstove before packaging it into freezer bags. When the harvest matches the plan, we are thawing out the last package just as we begin hauling in bushels of ripe Italian tomatoes for processing.

Fall Cleanup

AT THE END of the summer, gardens can look pretty tired. Plants have been harvested, and the remains are either dead or dying. Once a killing frost arrives, the browning is further hastened, until the whole plot becomes a graveyard of withered plants. It's probably this unappealing picture that prompts gardeners to get out the rakes and tillers and clean until the site is a neat, bare, smoothed-out rectangle ready for the next season. This may be good housekeeping, but if the work ends with the cleanup, it's not very good gardening. We suggest you either leave the garden alone after a frost or continue the work well beyond a thorough cleanup.

Unless there are diseased plants that need to be removed from a gardening site, every bit of top debris and organic mulch on a garden is potentially valuable food for the soils. We don't rake away any of the debris, and in fact we leave all of it in the gardens until the following spring. In the process, much of the top growth entangles falling leaves, and during the late fall, winter, and early spring, everything begins to decompose. By early spring, we are then able to add additional manures and composts to the gardens and till everything into the soil.

In some of our perennial gardens, the entangled leaves not only add organic matter to the soils but they also form a protective blanket for the cultivated plants. Whenever possible, we let the leaves remain in the gardens in the spring, top dressing if necessary; the perennials are quite successful in poking up through the top matter that continues to decompose all summer until the cycle repeats itself.

Soils that are left unprotected all during the fall, winter, and spring are subject to constant erosion from wind, rain, and melting snow. Every bit of topsoil

Buckwheat is a pretty and effective cover crop. Just as it flowers, it is ready to be tilled back into the soil.

is precious, and it's important to keep it in the garden sites. We are particularly aware of eroding soils when we watch spring rains carrying silt even from planted ground. The water flows downhill from our little mountain, then through a culvert to the woodland, then gullies are formed in the woodland that slopes precipitously to the river along the north boundary of the farm. Any unplanted ground gives up its soils even more readily.

If you must clean up the garden site in the fall, consider taking the cleanup beyond the bare-earth stage. You can protect your soil and improve it at the same time by the use of "cover crops," also referred to as "green manures." This may mean that you need to start your cleanup earlier than usual to allow cover crops to be seeded before the weather becomes too cool, but such planning is well worth it. Cover crops consist of a number of grasses and legumes that are used by gardeners as single crops or in combination to suppress weeds, build nitrogen in the soils, and add organic matter to the soils when they are tilled in.

Cover crops may be sown in late summer or early fall for winter protection, then the whole garden is tilled in the spring, usually two to three weeks before planting, so the newly tilled in matter can decompose. We have often used winter rye as a late-summer green manure. The rye is seeded in late August or early September in parts of the garden where we have finished harvesting. Some growth is seen in the fall before a hard frost, then growth recommences in the early spring. Tilling can be done before the rye forms seed heads or after. We usually wait until we are able to harvest the mature seed heads that we use for ornamental purposes before tilling in the stubble and preparing the land for cultivation.

It is not necessary to wait to plant cover crops until the whole garden is harvested and cleaned. It is possible to till and seed in the walkways of a late summer garden. Clovers and hairy vetch and grasses can germinate and begin their growth without adversely affecting late summer vegetables such as cole crops, potatoes, tomatoes, squashes, and corn.

Cover crops may be used to enrich whole gardens or sections of gardens by a series of plantings that start in the spring. You will not have these sections for annual vegetable or herb crops, but you will be building the soils for the ensuing year. Combinations of inoculated legumes grown along with grasses can greatly enrich soils, suppress weeds, and help to break up the ground to depths much greater than the tines of our tillers. Tillers reach only to a certain depth, and after several years of tilling, the soils can become compacted and form what is called "hardpan" just beneath tilled soil. In some soils, this hardpan is so dense that it blocks good drainage and prevents nutrients from reaching the upper levels of the soil. Whenever we allow a section of our production garden to rest for a year or two, we till the ground and then begin a program of soil building with green manures. We have used buckwheat, clovers of various kinds, and grasses. Many seed catalogues that specialize in seeds for vegetable and herb gardening also offer seeds and recommendations for green manure crops. Use this information in choosing crops that are best suited to your growing location, and ask for further advice from extension and soil conservation offices.

Fall Planting

SOME OF US never tire of planting, and once the last killing frosts have ended summer harvests, we still have the urge to get a head start on next year's gardens. Fall is a wonderful time to work in the gardens. The air is crisp, sometimes even very warm in the middle of the day. Perhaps best of all, there aren't any bugs, especially the dreadful black flies that are at their peak when planting must be done in the spring.

Garlic is always planted in the fall in our gardens. We usually rework a perennial bed or two now that there is more time. This fall we set out more than seven hundred flowering bulbs, taking advantage of the space in many new mint gardens we had designed earlier in the summer. Each of the beds contains a single mint that will be used to manufacture herbal teas. Each of the beds is underplanted with a different variety of daffodil. One of the wonderful things about fall planting is that you tend to forget it during the winter and then are delighted by the result after a long winter of snow and ice.

Fall is also a good time to direct seed any one of the herbs or vegetables you have noticed "volunteer" (reseed themselves) naturally in your spring gardens. This volunteering is an indication that the seeds win-

Fall is a good time to plant seeds that will germinate the following spring when the soils warm up. Plants from this open-ground nursery area will be transplanted into mulched gardens sometime in May or June.

ter over satisfactorily and germinate whenever the soils reach the appropriate temperatures. Rather than allowing chance to produce volunteers, we have made note of those crops we can start outdoors, late enough in the season so they do not germinate until the following spring. For us, that means seeding in an outdoor nursery bed sometime in October. It relieves us from always having to start certain plants in the greenhouse. Some of the herb crops include borage, chervil, caraway, chives, wild oregano, rue, tansy, catnip, hyssop, chamomile, anise hyssop, the bee balms, thyme, teasel, and valerian. Spinach and certain other early greens can be fall seeded even in Maine. Many tomato plants sprout in the spring from fruits that were left unharvested, suggesting that gardeners in warmer climates might have time to mature a number of fall-sown vegetables.

Late summer and early fall are good times to take advantage of poly tunnels and cold frames, especially for growing fresh salad greens. When located in protective sites, these small growing areas can be used to extend the gardening season well into the late fall in the Northeast, and year-round in warmer regions of the country.

Fall is a good time to wander through the gardens and make entries in your journals. It's the perfect time to reflect on what works and what doesn't. You now have the opportunity to revise sites for the next season without the pressure of spring chores. Summertime notes are often made in response to timely observations and for recording specific data. Once the garden is put to bed, musings can be more expansive.

CHAPTER FIVE

Vegetables

WE HAVE PLANTED a sizable vegetable garden on our Maine farm every year for the past twenty-nine summers. We couldn't imagine not growing a good portion of our own food. From late April until late October there is always something to be harvested fresh, even in this region with such a short growing season. Better still, we eat food from our own gardens a full twelve months of the year. There are the winter storage crops, such as potatoes, carrots, beets, squashes, and onions. We put by frozen and canned foods, including wonderful marinara sauces, leek and potato soup, pickled horseradish, spicy rhubarb sauce, brussels sprouts, broccoli, peas, sauerkraut, salsas, and pesto. Our pantry is filled with dried herbs for cooking and baking. There are canisters of dried tea herbs. We have jars of honey, jams and jellies, chutneys, and relishes made from our harvests.

It can truly be said that gardening feeds us in many ways, because in addition to the actual food that it provides, our gardens also nourish us with the pleasures of physical work and the rewards of learning as much as we are able to observe and absorb as stewards of the land.

In the following chapter, we will focus on the horticultural requirements of several dozen important vegetable crops. These crops are planted routinely in our gardens, and most of them are suitable to gardens throughout the country. The text with each entry reflects the

By midsummer, the vegetable garden can be as beautiful as any ornamental border, when crops for harvesting are interplanted with flowers and herbs.

experiences that we have had with these vegetables, a few anecdotes that might be amusing or instructive, and an occasional warning or bias that comes inevitably from years spent working with plants.

Since we have planted vegetable gardens both on open ground and using a total mulching system, we will talk about both methods. You may also want to experiment with different approaches. Some of the vegetables discussed are either seeded indoors or directly seeded into the garden; we will give information on both methods when appropriate. When talking about indoor seeding, we use the word "peat pot" to suggest a biodegradable container, which could be a peat pot, paper pot, peat pellet, or any other container that can be set into the ground. Also included with each entry is a simple line drawing of the vegetable in its seedling stage, showing the shape and relative sizes

of the plant cotyledons and first true leaves. We hope that these drawings will help you recognize your own germinating seedlings.

At the end of the chapter, there is a complete listing of all the vegetables discussed along with very specific information on the requirements for starting each plant from seed (pages 167–71). We have charted the information in one place so you can simply open up the book to that section when you are seeding, and use it as a guide for the work you are doing.

Vegetable sections are arranged alphabetically by common name. That is followed by the plant's botanical name and family identification. Whenever several vegetables are grouped under one heading, there is a cross-reference of each common name within the alphabetical order.

ASPARAGUS

Asparagus officinalis

LILIACEAE

WHILE MOST GARDENERS begin asparagus beds from purchased roots (known as crowns), it is very easy to grow this vegetable from seed; in fact, the tiny seedlings are so interesting and durable that the beginner is almost always successful. Asparagus seed is large enough to be handled easily either as clean purchased seed or as seed saved from the red berries of the flowering female asparagus plants. Seeds (or crushed seed berries) may be planted either indoors in the early spring or outdoors in late fall or as early in the spring as the seedbed can be prepared. We start most of our crops indoors, seeding flats in mid-February so that transplanted seedlings are ready to be set out into a first-year nursery bed in May. Greenhouse seeds are buried with ¼ inch of soil. If you are using your own dried seed pods, it is helpful to soak the lightly crushed berries for 24 hours before planting. Seedlings germinate in about 7–10 days, and seedlings develop into tiny ferns, which look exactly like the commonly known ornamental asparagus fern. The small seedlings are transplanted into individual pots, with roots planted at the same depth as they were growing in the seed flats. When transplants are set into the nursery bed in the spring (at a distance of about 6 inches) they are again planted at the same depth as in the pot for the first season of growth.

Asparagus seeds are sown into an outdoor nursery bed either in the fall or early spring. When planted 1½ inches deep, with seeds spaced 4–6 inches apart, there will be no need for thinning the first season. Since outdoor germination will take longer (about 2–3 weeks), a marker crop, such as radishes, will allow you to keep the row weeded and moist during germination. For the first year the seedlings are left to grow, mature, and die back naturally in the nursery bed, which should contain a good fertile friable soil and ample moisture.

In the spring of the second season, the year-old plants are ready to be transplanted into their permanent location. Asparagus is a perennial vegetable. Since you can plan on harvesting crops for at least 15–20 years from a well-maintained bed, it is very important to make careful plans as to where to locate this bed. Although many commercial beds are restored or replanted after a decade or two, asparagus plants can continue to produce for many decades if the conditions are favorable. Our first permanent asparagus bed was a series of two long trenched rows at one end of our annual garden—or what we thought was an end of the garden. Over the years we extended the size of the annual garden and "jumped over" the asparagus, which we had neglected to weed as carefully as we might have. Eventually we were battling an area of weeds that continually polluted the abutting rows of annual crops. We eventually abandoned this first planting in favor of a completely separate raised bed, contained by cedar logs, which we have located in an arrangement of other raised beds planted with ornamental and culinary perennials. In so doing, we have isolated the asparagus bed so that we can maintain it more carefully and continue to replenish it each season with composted manure. Asparagus beds also benefit from mulches of hay or grass clippings, which add organic matter to the soil and help conserve soil moisture. Asparagus plants are beautiful after the spears are left

to develop into graceful tall ferns that reach heights of 4–5 feet.

Whether you choose to establish your asparagus bed in rows or in a contained area, remember that asparagus is a heavy feeder and needs ample moisture throughout the season. Once the location has been chosen, the bed should be well dug, limed, enriched with compost, manures, and other soil amendments to produce a fertile soil with good drainage. When you have prepared the bed thoroughly, choose only the most vigorous year-old plants from your nursery for the permanent planting. One-year-old plants (or purchased crowns) are planted in a well-prepared soil, usually in a trench 8–18 inches deep, spacing the plants about 18 inches apart. Roots are covered with rich soil and pressed firmly into place. As the plants send out new growth that opens into fern-like leaves, the trench is filled in with rich composted soil until the whole trench is level with the ground. During the first season, the plants are allowed to develop and die back naturally, and the browned tops of the asparagus are cut back to a few inches above ground in the fall. The top growth of asparagus should never be cut back until it has died naturally, since it is the quality of this growth that determines the quality of the ensuing year's crop. The following spring the whole bed should be well top-dressed with manure and left to develop as it did the previous year. Then in the spring of the third year, top-dress very early and begin to harvest a few spears of asparagus from each plant. Harvest the young tender spears when they are about 4–8 inches tall, by inserting a sharp knife just below the soil surface and cutting carefully so as not to damage any other emerging growth. Don't cut more than you want to eat fresh or freeze immediately, because the texture and flavor are superb when the vegetable is very fresh. From the fourth season on (from seed, or the third from crown-planting), we harvest our plants for a period of several weeks each spring and early summer, then allow the plants to mature and die back naturally. Maintenance and upkeep continue as described. It is very important to keep the beds fertile and free of weeds.

Asparagus seeds produce male and female plants. Flowers are insect pollinated and the bright red berries will appear during late summer on the female plants. If you wish to save your own seed you will

EDIBLE FLOWERS

I F YOU HAVE an herb garden, you are already growing a number of tasty edible flowers. There are pink chive blossoms, royal blue borage flowers, the lavender flowers of anise hyssop, and the lavender blossoms themselves. Bee balm flowers are colorful and edible as are the blossoms of chamomile, garlic chives, sage, fennel, and dill.

Once you venture outside the culinary herb garden, be certain you know what you are picking. Calendula blossoms are pretty in salads as are all the flowers of the scented geraniums.

Violets are edible and they can be beautifully preserved by drying them in sugar (see page 223). The same is true of the tiny flowers of wax begonias. The blossoms of summer squash are very nice to use in tempura or to stuff and fry. If you try this delicacy, be certain you know the difference between the male and the female blossoms or you may end up with no fruits on your plants. See the photo and explanation on page 156.

Nasturtiums are tasty, and when sprinkled over the top of a green tossed salad, make it look very appetizing. The pods of these flowers can also be picked and eaten while they are still green, or they can be pickled. The young flowers of hemerocallis are tender and delicious when dipped in batter and fried, tempura-style.

Other edible blooms include roses, pinks (members of the genus *Dianthus*), and pineapple sage. Whenever fresh flowers are picked for food, be certain they have not been sprayed with any harmful insecticides. Pick the blossoms young, wash any garden dust from their petals, and remove any green stem or calyx, which can be bitter to the taste.

Since there are probably more poisonous flowers than edibles, be certain you know what you are picking. If you teach your youngsters to eat flowers in their salads, caution them against foraging on their own in the garden.

An entire garden can be designed for its edible flowers.

need both genders, but if you are only concerned about productivity, male plants produce more spears for harvesting. Seeds are produced in the red berries and should be allowed to mature on the plants. They are collected in the fall and sown directly into a prepared nursery bed, or dried and then stored until the following season.

Asparagus is a member of the lily family. It is native to Western Europe and Central Asia and has been under cultivation for more than two thousand years. Modern strains of the plant have been developed that are relatively disease resistant; both Mary Washington and Martha Washington are recommended varieties. Asparagus is well adapted to temperate regions. Although it takes some patience and diligence in its cultivation, fresh asparagus is one of the first spring vegetables and one of the most delicious. For a small family, 25 plants would provide enough food for eating fresh, but since the vegetable freezes so well, we like having closer to 50 plants.

BEANS

Glycine spp., *Phaseolus* spp.,
Vicia spp., *Vigna* spp.

LEGUMINOSAE

asparagus bean

THERE ARE SO MANY species and varieties and bean hybrids that one could devote an entire garden to their culture. To simplify the subject, it is helpful to think of beans by dividing them into three categories according to how they are eaten. There are the common string or snap beans which are grown for their young pods; these include varieties that are green, yellow, and purple; ones with mottled pods and speckled pods; pencil-thin beans; short podded beans; yard-long pods; and flattened pods. Most popular gardening catalogues offer a variety of these types, with differing times for maturation, and differing growth habits. The most common are bush beans and pole or climbing beans. All of these beans are meant to be picked when the pods are young, before the seeds have developed any size within the pods.

Next there is the category of beans that are grown for their developed fleshy but unripe seeds, such as horticultural (or shell) beans, lima beans, and fava beans. These beans are collected when the pods have plumped up; the beans are removed fresh from the pods. The third general cat-

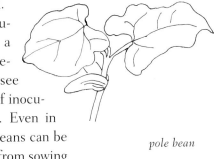

pencil pod bush bean

egory includes beans that are grown for their mature seeds, which are left to mature on the plant and then harvested and dried for storage. Well-known examples of this type include kidney beans, Jacob's cattle, pinto, soy, and soldier beans. Lists of favorites will vary greatly from one region of the country to another. The second and third category of beans may overlap somewhat as there are some varieties that may be shelled fresh as well as dried. Soy beans are a good example.

In all cases (and forgive us for paraphrasing), a bean is a bean is a bean. All beans are legumes, so there are some generalizations we can make when it comes to talking about growing them from seed. Assuming that you have chosen varieties that are suitable to the length of your growing season, and that you have a reasonably fertile garden plot with full sun and enough water, you should be able to produce successful bean crops from any of the categories described.

We like to inoculate our beans with a nitrogen fixing bacteria before planting (see further discussion of inoculants on page 109). Even in northern gardens, beans can be successfully grown from sowing the seeds directly into the garden. In all cases except for fava beans, which will be discussed separately, beans need a warm soil to germinate and there is nothing to be gained by seeding too early; the seed will not germinate evenly or vigorously unless the conditions are right. Even if you do have an early warm spell that you know to be unusual, don't be fooled into trying to hasten bean planting because any early growth will be killed by a late spring frost. We have on occasion started a few varieties of early snap beans by

pole bean

planting seeds in peat pots in the greenhouse a couple of weeks before the last frost. We transplant them into the garden when temperatures have warmed. Indoor germination at temperatures of 65°–70°F takes place in only 3–5 days. When the soil has warmed up outdoors, germination should take place in a week or two. Plants started indoors will mature only slightly earlier than those seeded directly, but there is also the enjoyment factor to be evaluated. Since there are so many plants that really do need to be started indoors, it is probably best to leave space and time for them and to go directly to the garden with your bean seeds.

lima bean

The most efficient use of garden space for bush type beans is a wide raised bed in which you can plant two parallel rows of beans. Bury the seed 1–2 inches deep, depending on soil moisture (the dryer the soil, the deeper the planting depth), and space beans 4–6 inches apart. Seed germination is usually so reliable that this spacing will eliminate the need for thinning and save on the use of seed as well. In the early years of farming, we seeded everything more thickly, and then thinned and hoed the crop into final shape. In so doing we spent more money on seed and more time on labor than was necessary. Careful sowing takes only a few more minutes with seed as large as bean seed, and the seedlings are left undisturbed to develop more speedily. If your planting is a bit crowded, it is best to thin because good air circulation is important, especially among plants that will mature over the hot humid periods of late summer. Crowded plants are more susceptible to attacks of fungus and mildew, which can severely damage or completely ruin a crop. When young plants are 3–6 inches tall and planted on open ground, shallow cultivation and weeding can be performed and soil brought up around the base of the stems, giving more support to the young plants. Bush beans (those that do not vine or climb) rarely need any support if you keep soil pulled firmly

purple pod royalty bean

around the stems of the plants. Once the plants develop good leaf growth, the leaves shade out most competing weeds, so little maintenance is needed after the first three or four weeks. Climbing or pole beans however do need some form of trellis, pole teepee, or wire support, and these structures should be put in place at planting time so you will not have to work around tender young seedlings or plants when they are most vulnerable to damage. Pole beans are often planted in hills, with 1–3 seeds in each hill and hills 18 inches apart. After germination, the seedlings are trained to climb. Climbing beans may also be planted along a string, wire, or wooden trellis. Beans are buried along one side of the trellis at distances of 4–8 inches apart and then trained to climb the supports. The well-known scarlet runner bean is an example of a climber that is used most often as an ornamental, but it is equally edible when harvested young.

In fact all string or snap beans should be harvested when the pods are on the young side; the texture and flavor are best at this stage. If you want a different variety of snap beans, choose varieties that mature over different periods of time and stagger your planting. If you don't, you will find yourself with

shell bean

all of your varieties coming into maturity at the same time. The warmer the soil and summer temperatures, the faster the beans will mature. A variety that is labeled to mature in "x" number of days and planted in early June may mature at the same time as that same variety planted a week or two later when day and nighttime temperature have risen. If you find yourself with too many fresh beans to consume and more than you want to freeze or can, you can keep the vines producing young beans for eating fresh by picking off the older pods. Seeds allowed to mature within the pod signal the plant to stop producing flowers and fruit. One additional caveat, and that is to harvest beans only when plants are dry. Harvesting beans that are laden with dew or wet from showers is not recommended because it can spread disease throughout the planting.

PLANTS OF THE FAMILY Leguminosae, commonly referred to as legumes, include vegetables such as peas, beans, soybeans, limas, favas, peanuts, and pasture crops such as clover, alfalfa, and hairy vetch. They also include such flowering plants as sweet peas, baptisia, and lupines. When growing any of these plants, it is advisable to first inoculate the seeds with a nitrogen-fixing bacteria. In so doing, you are increasing the plant's ability to fix nitrogen from the atmosphere to nourish itself and to enrich the soil. The process takes place when a group of bacteria of the genus Rhizobium live in symbiotic relationship on the roots of legumes. The plant roots feed the bacteria which in turn fix molecular nitrogen from the atmosphere and convert the nitrogen into a form that the plant can use. If the legumes are edible vegetable crops, the inoculant has the obvious advantage of promoting more vigorous and productive crops. If the legumes are used as cover crops, the inoculant stimulates more vigorous growth which in turn is used to replenish and enrich garden soils.

Legume inoculant is available from many garden centers and catalogues and is worth the cost and time to apply. It usually comes tightly sealed in a moisture-protected container. When you are ready to use it, simply spread out the seeds to be treated in a shallow tray or pan, spray them very lightly with water so the inoculant adheres, and then sprinkle the powdery inoculant to cover the seeds. Use an old spoon or stick to stir and turn the seed so it is completely coated. Plant the seeds as soon as they are treated and sprinkle

Soybeans are covered with inoculant before being planted.

any inoculant left in the bottom of the tray directly over the seeds in their row or holes before covering with soil.

There are different species of Rhizobium appropriate to different legumes, so read the description of the inoculant before purchasing. Also pay attention to the expiration dates on the inoculant. While seeds may be stored for one to several years successfully, the inoculant has a limited period of viability.

Legumes that have been treated with a nitrogen-fixing bacteria will have very characteristic nodules on their roots, which you can examine at the end of the season after harvest. We always recommend tilling unusable vegetative matter from members of the Leguminosae family into the garden to enhance the soil.

Cultural requirements for beans for shelling are the same as those for snap beans. Harvest these beans when the pods have plumped up and the seeds within are full but still young enough to be moist. As a rule these beans produce only one crop in a season, and there is not adequate time for the plants to set new flowers and pods after harvest has begun. Most shelled beans can be successfully frozen for winter eating. As we mentioned earlier, fava beans are an exception to the rule for cultivation. Fava beans need cool soil temperatures and should be planted in the spring when the soil can be worked so that plants develop during the cooler parts of the summer. Fava beans are well known to gardeners throughout Europe from England to the Middle East. They should be considered by many northern gardeners in this country, where the season is too short and too cool for growing lima beans successfully. We have tried repeatedly to grow limas; the results have been so uneven that we have abandoned them in favor of crops that are more reliable.

These yellow wax-bean plants produce perfect flowers that are almost always self-pollinating.

Plants are allowed to mature in the field where they are left until many of their leaves drop. Before a hard fall frost plants are pulled up completely by the roots, the roots are shaken clean or cut off, and the plants are placed in a cool dry place to finish drying. Keep an eye on the various types of dried beans in the field because they will mature at different periods. If you see that some varieties have done most of their drying in the field, *soy bean* be certain to harvest them and bring them inside before the pods actually split open and shed the beans on the ground. When the pods are totally dried, small quantities can be threshed by hand, in a sack or pail, or with a flail. The beans are then separated from the pieces of stem or leaves and stored in dry containers until you want them for cooking.

Beans, as a category of plants, are unusually diverse in their botanical and economic histories. Soy beans, for example, were cultivated for centuries before recorded history. The common garden snap beans were not even known in Europe until they were introduced there after the discovery of America. Prior to that time, Europeans grew and ate only broad beans. If we can make one final recommendation about growing beans, it would be to encourage you to try new varieties from season to season. There are so many kinds offered that you will be surprised at the differences in tastes and textures even from one common green bean to the next. Some varieties are more prolific, some have more eye appeal, some are better to eat fresh, and others are better for canning or freezing. It will take you many gardens before you exhaust the possibilities.

We have had, on the other hand, good success with dried beans. Although backyard gardeners may not want to include them regularly, they are such fun to grow, dry, thresh, and store that you should give them a try. Cultural requirements are similar to those for snap and shell beans, but it is important to pay attention to soil moisture as these beans mature over a long period of time and will be affected by extended dry periods from midsummer on. If your soils drain very rapidly and you are gardening on open ground, then a good mulch applied in early summer will help the soil conserve moisture. Like other beans, these varieties need a fertile but not overly rich garden soil. *soldier bean*

Saving your own bean seeds is very easy assuming you are growing non-hybrid varieties. Bean flowers are perfect (containing both male and female parts) and are self-pollinating. As they are usually pollinated before the flowers open, there is little insect cross-pollination, but if you want to be certain to have purity in the seed strains that you are saving, you can plant different varieties at least 100 feet apart. The clean threshed beans of the dried varieties are ready to be used for seeding. Seeds for the snap and shell varieties need to be matured on the plants before being harvested. Select a few vigorous plants from the kinds that you wish to collect, allow the plant to grow until the pods are fully mature and drying on the plant. Before a hard frost, harvest the whole plant and treat like dried beans. Make certain that all bean seeds are completely dried before they are stored, because they can easily mold and spoil if there is too much moisture left in them.

BEETS

Beta vulgaris

CHENOPODIACEAE

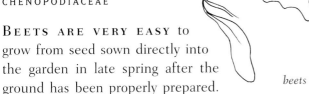

beets

BEETS ARE VERY EASY to grow from seed sown directly into the garden in late spring after the ground has been properly prepared. Beets like a fertile garden soil with adequate moisture and fairly high pH. Beets should not be grown in soil with too much nitrogen. Avoid using fresh stable manures because they will cause excessive top growth and forking or fibrous roots. We like to grow our crops on wide raised mulched beds with 2 or 3 rows in the bed. They may also be grown in open ground and mulched midsummer. If you examine beet seeds you will see that they are actually small irregularly shaped fruits that contain several seeds surrounded by a corky "pericarp." Soak the seed overnight before planting and don't seed rows too thickly, as each pericarp will produce several plants. Cover seed with ¼–½ inch of soil and tamp well. You might want to mark the rows with radishes. Germination time is 2–3 weeks, during which time the planting should be kept free of weeds and not be allowed to dry out. If you are planting on open ground, shallow cultivation is important so that roots are not disturbed. Small beet seedlings can be transplanted, but this is not a common practice. If beets are seeded too thickly, they need to be thinned out to 3–6 inches between plants, but this can be done in stages. Allow the small seedlings to develop enough so that the first thinnings are used for greens. The next thinning is done when the young greens are still tender and the beets are very small so that greens and beets are cooked together. Thinning accomplished, the final plants are left in place to develop into mature roots for harvesting. There are many varieties of beets: not only red round roots, but beets that are oval, cylindrical, white, and golden. Short season summer beets are excellent for eating fresh, but if you want beets for storage, read catalogue descriptions and choose varieties that have been developed for that purpose. Most summer varieties do not store well. Fall crops are pulled before a hard frost, tops are twisted or cut off an inch or two above the roots, and roots are stored in sand for the winter.

Given the reasonable price for beet seed, the average gardener will probably not want to go to the trouble of saving seed. Beets are biennials, which means that the roots need to be harvested, stored, and planted again the second season in any climate where they will not winter over. This process involves choosing about a half dozen top quality plants at the end of the season, pulling them and cutting off the top growth to approximately 2 inches from the root, and storing the roots in buckets of slightly moist sand in a cool root cellar where temperatures range from 40°–50°F. Storing roots at significantly lower temperatures may inhibit the roots from producing flowering plants. The following spring, roots are planted in the garden, with the crowns of each plant just below the soil surface about 2 feet apart. Seed stalks can grow several feet tall and you may want to stake them. The flowers are wind pollinated and will cross-pollinate readily with other members of the genus (which includes both beets and chard), so varieties need to be isolated from each other. When flowers have matured into seed pods and the pericarps turn brown, the stalks are collected and seeds are stripped by hand, dried completely, and stored.

sugar beets

IN THE CLASSIFICATION of living things, the category of family names immediately precedes the genus and species identifications. Family, in a botanical sense, is an assemblage or grouping of genera that are closely related to one another. That means that the genera tend to resemble one another in general appearance or in a number of more technical characteristics. There are more than 300 different families of seed-bearing or flowering plants that are recognized today by botanists and taxonomists. However a quick look at the several dozen garden vegetables discussed in this chapter shows that they are members of no more than 13 different families. One of the largest families in a typical vegetable garden is the Cruciferae family, commonly called the Mustard family. It includes broccoli, brussels sprouts, cabbages of all kinds, cauliflower, kale, kohlrabi, rutabaga, turnip, radishes, horseradish, and a large assortment of green leafy salad herbs or mustards.

Note the similarity in fruit shape among these members of the Cruciferae. From left to right: broccoli, arugula, Chinese cabbage, *and two varieties of wild mustard.*

The Leguminosae family is also well represented in the vegetable garden. Commonly known as the Pea family, it includes numerous varieties of peas, beans, many field and forage crops, and ornamental plants. The Leguminosae is second only to the Gramineae or Grass family as a food source for man and animals alike. In our cultivated gardens, corn is the best-known grass.

Even the most modest vegetable garden usually contains several genera of the Solanaceae or Nightshade family. Plants include tomatoes, peppers, potatoes, eggplant, and tomatillo. Tobacco is also a member. The Nightshade family is noted for plants that have poisonous as well as medicinal properties.

The Umbelliferae family includes a number of edible plants, referred to as either vegetables or herbs. Carrots, celery, parsnips, parsley, chervil, dill, and fennel are all members of this group, which is commonly referred to as the Carrot or Parsley family.

The Cucurbitaceae family, commonly called the Gourd family, contains many gardening favorites. These plants are some of the easiest vegetables to grow in ordinary garden soils with ample sun and warmth.

As the name suggests, the family includes cucumbers, melons, watermelons, squashes (both summer and winter), and gourds.

Other plant families represented in this chapter include Liliaceae (Lily family), Chenopodiaceae (Goosefoot family), Amaryllidaceae (Amaryllis family), Compositae, Malvaceae (Mallow family), Polygonaceae (Buckwheat family), and Tetragoniaceae (New Zealand Spinach family). With the exception of Tetragoniaceae, the other 6 families named are not necessarily less populated than ones described earlier. They simply have fewer genera of commonly grown vegetables. In fact one of the families to appear only twice in the vegetable chapter, Compositae, of which lettuce and chicory are members, is so large that it is broken down into 12 or 13 tribes representing about 950 different genera. This family is commonly called the Sunflower family.

We include this very brief taxonomic information to suggest that learning a bit about the relationships of plants can really be helpful in day-to-day gardening. When you are growing a number of plants, take the time to learn the genus and the family of the plant and you are on the way to being able to extrapolate information from one group of individuals to another. Not only do related plants have similar characteristics, they often have similar cultural requirements. They may share similar diseases and insect predators. Family members often have similar seed development characteristics that will be helpful to understand when it comes to collecting and saving your own garden seeds. By teaching ourselves how things are related, we are teaching ourselves how to see and interpret plant performance and behavior, or simply put, how to be better gardeners.

BROCCOLI

Brassica oleracea Botrytis Group

CRUCIFERAE

BROCCOLI SEED WILL germinate readily in a broad range of soil temperatures, making it a crop that can be started indoors, in cold frames, in an open outdoor nursery bed, or in place in a mulched garden row. We have used all methods successfully. For the earliest summer crops we sow seeds in flats inside, about 6–8 weeks before planting out. Cover seed with ⅛ inch of soil. Seed germinates in 3–7 days, and once transplanted, young broccoli plants should be grown in a cool greenhouse. This allows them to develop into short, sturdy, robust plants that are hardened off and transplanted into the garden in the spring. Young field transplants will tolerate light frosts, but not heavy spring freezes. Broccoli seeded directly into cold frames or outdoor seedbeds (at a depth of ½ inch) will germinate anywhere between 1–3 weeks, depending on the temperature variations. When directly seeded plants have well established leaf growth, they can be transplanted into the garden, spacing plants in a staggered row pattern 12–18 inches apart, depending on the varieties. Small early varieties that produce one main head for summer consumption require less growing room than the later varieties that first produce a large central head and then send out repeated side shoots. Broccoli seedlings should not have their growth checked by holding them too long in the seed flat, transplanted flat, or nursery bed, because stress can greatly affect the development of the main heading stalk. The plants will do well in an average garden soil with adequate moisture. Broccoli should be harvested when the buds of the central heads are fully developed but before the individual florets begin to soften and open into flower. Unharvested heads will flower quickly during the summer, so crops should be checked almost every day.

Broccoli (like its many relatives in the cabbage family) has as its wild ancestor a stout weedy perennial known as colewort, a plant still found on the coastal areas of Great Britain and southwestern Europe. Cabbage family plants are often referred to as the cole crops, from which comes the familiar coleslaw. True broccoli was grown by the Greeks and Romans and the genus name *brassica* is derived from the Celtic *bresic* for the coleworts. This little bit of plant history helps us understand some of the requirements for saving our own broccoli seeds. All of the brassicas will cross-pollinate readily, including wild brassicas like some mustards that may be growing around your gardens. Broccoli flowers are perfect but not self-pollinating; if you wish to save seed, you should isolate several vigorous plants of one non-hybrid. Fortunately for the seed saver however broccoli is one of the few annual brassicas, so plants will flower and produce seed in the same season. Selected plants are left unharvested so that the first heads go immediately into flower and seed production. The tall flowering stalks produce yellow flowers (which are insect pollinated) and then light brown elongated seed pods. Pods should be allowed to mature and dry on the plants. Collect pods before they split, finish drying, clean seed, and store.

BRUSSELS SPROUTS

Brassica oleracea Gemmifera Group

CRUCIFERAE

BRUSSELS SPROUTS ARE easy to grow from seed, and you can use the same instructions given for broccoli. Unlike broccoli, however, brussels sprouts need a longer season to develop good-sized, tasty, tight little sprouts along the main stem of each plant. We start our plants indoors mainly as a convenience, since we will need only 12–18 plants to give enough sprouts for eating fresh and freezing. Whether you seed indoors or outside (early in the season), it is especially important never to allow the young plants to dry out or stay too long in the early transplant stages. Uneven growth may result in inferior crops. Brussels sprouts will develop into tall bushy plants by midsummer; small buds or sprouts begin to

In late summer, the side leaves are removed from the brussels sprout plants, allowing space for the sprouts to size up.

appear between the bases of the leaf petioles, starting from the base of the stems and maturing upward. The best, tastiest, and tightest sprouts develop during cool weather. Once plants have begun to develop sprouts, it is helpful to remove the bottom leaves and stalks of the main stems to allow more room and light for sprout growth. In the late summer, we pinch off the top center growth of the plants so that energy will go into sizing-up the sprouts themselves. Sprouts can be harvested when they have size and firmness, usually starting in late August or early September in our gardens. Harvest by cutting or twisting off sprouts from the lower parts of several plants. At the end of the season, before a hard freeze, we pull the entire plant and hang it upside down in a cool root cellar. Although sprouts can be stored fresh for a few weeks, they do begin to deteriorate after that, so we like to freeze the remainder of the crop for a winter supply.

Like most other members of the genus *Brassica*, brussels sprouts are biennials and need two growing seasons to produce seeds. This means that plants have to be either wintered over outside (not feasible in our climate) or stored properly and replanted in the spring. For sheer lack of time and determination, we have attempted neither and rely upon seed companies for our supplies.

CABBAGE

Brassica oleracea
Capitata Group

CRUCIFERAE

SEEDING AND CULTURAL information for broccoli can be equally well applied to the growing of cabbage. It is worth noting however that cabbage will withstand heavier spring frosts than most other brassicas, and we have seen field transplants shake off the effects of nighttime temperatures as low as 20°F. The plants were injured but went on to produce respectable yields. Most good seed catalogues offer a broad variety of cabbages, all of which are easy to grow in ordinary garden soil, even heavy clay soils. Cabbages need adequate moisture, and like their relatives, prefer cooler summer soils. A good light colored mulch is beneficial. We plant our seedlings in the usual rows of black plastic early in the season, and as the weather warms, we pull some of the hay mulch from the walkways up over the black plastic to cool down the soils where cole crops are being grown. This gives us the advantage of having warm soils for early growth and cooler soils for growing on. If you want plants for summer salads, cooking, and storing, it is best to plant several varieties. Although summer cabbages (varieties that mature more quickly) can stand for some time in the field without being harvested, they are not very good to store, even if they have been seeded later so that they mature in the early fall. The long season varieties will produce heavier tighter heads and will hold up better in storage. We encourage you to experiment with a number of varieties before deciding what regulars you want to plant.

There are round, oval, blunt, and cylindrical shaped heads; light green, medium green, and purple varieties; and crinkled or savoyed leaf types. If you have very limited space and want cabbage principally for eating fresh, try growing a couple of short season varieties. Those specimens that are cut early in the season by severing the head and leaving the stalk intact will often have enough time to develop several small secondary heads per stalk. These small heads can be harvested in the early fall. They will not be as heavy or tightly headed as the original head but the flavor is equally good.

Brassicas should not be planted in the same site one season to the next because soilborne diseases can remain in the ground and destroy crops for several seasons. Good crop rotation is especially important with so many vegetables belonging to the same genus. If you do find diseased plants in your garden, pull and destroy them, but do not introduce them into the compost pile. When gardening space is at a premium, you might want to tuck a few cabbages in with your ornamental beds, as the cabbages are themselves so beautiful. We once designed a flower garden using purple cabbages with red and orange flowering annuals. It was beautiful all summer, and after the frosts had killed the annuals, we still had food to harvest.

If you end up with more summer cabbages than you consume before a hard frost, there is always the option of storing a few heads in the refrigerator for several weeks or making sauerkraut. Before the first hard freeze, we pull all of our storing heads, shake off excess dirt, and hang the heads in the root cellar. During the first weeks of storage, the outer leaves of the heads wither and dry, encasing the inner heads. The root cellar temperatures vary from 32°–40°F, and in these conditions, we are able to keep cabbage for the entire winter.

We purchase all our cabbage seed. Cabbage is a biennial and we are not willing to invest the time and labor in wintering over or storing and replanting one-year-old plants. If you do want to attempt to save your own seed, however, cabbage would prob-

savoy cabbage

W E ' R E N O T S L A V E S to the notion that everything homemade is better. In fact there are a number of food items (bagels for example) that we are quite happy to buy from a professional. But when it comes to sauerkraut, we have to hold out for the real thing made in our kitchen from our own garden cabbage. Not only can you vary the recipes and brines, you can also put up a year's supply without an inordinate amount of labor.

The process begins when your best large winter cabbages have reached full size in the field. We like to wait until early fall, long enough so that the heat of summer is past, but not so late that hard frosts have injured the outer layers of the cabbage plants.

Cut the heads, remove the outer loose leaves around the full hard dense heads, and shred the cabbage. We use either the handy home food processor or a single or double-blade wooden cabbage slicer. We slice all of the heads at one time, using usually about 15–20 heads for a small crock of kraut.

The real old-fashioned ceramic crocks are excellent, and if you haven't been fortunate enough to inherit some, you can still purchase stone crocks at many hardware stores. Make certain that the crock is scrubbed clean and rinsed well. Begin to fill the crock with a layer of shredded cabbage, each layer measuring 2–3 inches deep. After each layer, sprinkle the cabbage evenly with 3½ tablespoons of coarse salt for every 5 pounds of cabbage. Layer and salt until the container is two-thirds to three-quarters full.

Next you will need to tamp down the contents so that the salt and moisture in the cabbage mix to create a brine. The more you tamp down, the more brine will develop. Eventually you want the brine to cover the whole contents of the crock. We have read directions that caution you to tamp gently with a potato masher, but we have found that an old-fashioned wooden baseball bat (what we had on hand) when wielded gently on end was very persuasive.

Once this stage has been reached, cover the top of the cabbage with thoroughly washed grape leaves. The grape leaf cover is optional, but since we have a grape arbor on the farm, we like to use this step as the leaves help to keep the brine from developing molds. In turn, cover the leaves or the cabbage with several clean layers of cheesecloth. Place a large glass or pottery plate on top of the cloth and weigh down the plate with a heavy clean rock. What you are

A couple of old wooden shredding boards make the work go quickly.

doing is making certain that a layer of brine covers the cabbage.

Now the crock is ready to be stored in a convenient place where the fermentation process can begin. Room temperature is best, around 65°–70°F. Check the contents daily and pour off any discolored brine from the top. After 2–3 weeks, the kraut may be removed from the crock, packed in canning jars, pints or quarts, and processed in a water bath for about 30 minutes. If more brine is needed anytime during the fermentation process or for filling the canning jars to cover the cabbage, additional brine may be made by mixing 1½ tablespoons of salt to a quart of water.

One season we overscheduled ourselves and when it came time to can and process all the sauerkraut we had made, we simply couldn't find the time but still didn't want to lose the work we had already done. So we experimented with bagging and freezing the kraut. When we were ready to use it, we simply emptied the contents of the bags into a skillet of hot oil and fried onions and cooked the kraut as we would have normally, with generous amounts of caraway and bits of apple and carrot tossed in during the last 15 minutes of cooking. Some of the salt can be removed from the uncooked sauerkraut by rinsing the kraut repeatedly in a colander before cooking.

When our family was growing up in the Ukraine, they also made "pickled cabbage." The process was much the same as described above, but wooden barrels were used and the carrots and apples were put directly into the wooden barrels in layers with the cabbages. The whole mess was salted, fermented, and then stored in a deep pit for the winter.

ably be one of the easier of the biennial brassicas to manage successfully. We have in fact noticed a number of our leftover storage cabbages actually begin to send out second-year flowering shoots from the stored heads, sometime in very late winter or early spring. If you want to try to save your own seed, harvest several excellent mature specimens at the end of the first year by pulling the entire plants with roots. Trim off the loose outer leaves and store heads in a cool root cellar where humidity is high so that the roots never completely dry out. In the spring replant root and head so that head is nestled into the soil a few inches deeper than it would have grown originally. Some seed growers make a shallow cross slash in the top of the head from which the seed stalks will emerge. Remember that the stalks will be long and large, so seed plants should be spaced 2–3 feet apart. You may wish to stake the new growth. Like broccoli, the flowers of cabbage are perfect but cross-pollinating, so you need several heads. When elongated seed pods have turned brown and begun to dry, collect the entire stalks and gather seeds for final drying.

CARROTS

Daucus carota var. *sativus*

UMBELLIFERAE

FRESHLY HARVESTED carrots that are grown in good fertile garden soils with ample moisture have flavor and texture that are unequaled by any store-purchased varieties. And although we have longed for less heavy, less rocky soils than those at our old New England farm, we have never in our travels tasted carrots as crunchy or as sweet as those from our own gardens. Carrots are very easy to grow. We have used two methods of seeding directly into the garden: one on open ground and the other using black plastic. We will discuss both methods, noting the advantages of each.

When planting in open ground, carrots are sown directly into the garden when the soils have been thoroughly prepared and allowed to warm up to temperatures of at least 50°–60°F. Very early spring planting is not recommended for the following reasons. Germination in cold soils will be inhibited, but at the same time annual and perennial weed seeds will have a good start and make maintenance more difficult. Carrot seed is very small and the roots need a very deep friable soil, well prepared. Ideally the soils should be rock free but moisture retentive. Fresh stable manures are not used as this can promote hairiness and forking of the roots. Take the time to amend your soils for this one crop; it is worth the effort. Even in northern gardens, there is ample time to seed carrots after spinach or other early spring greens have been harvested. This means that you have the opportunity to cultivate or till the garden and destroy the first crop of summer weeds. Alternatively, here is a good trick for the carrot patch. Prepare the soils and cover the area desired with a piece of clear plastic or old storm windows, so the soil is warmed by the sun to stimulate rapid germination of weed seeds. In a week or two, remove the cover and till very lightly, killing any surface weed growth but not going too deep to dredge up another supply of weed seeds.

Our open-ground beds are prepared as follows: Soils are raised in rows about 3 feet wide, with 3–5 rows running parallel in a bed. The bed is raked until smooth, several narrow and shallow furrows are made in the bed, and the carrot seed is sown very carefully so that it is not too thick. We mix our carrot seed with very fine sand and/or radish seed so that we can handle it better and so that the radish marks the rows for early weeding. Some gardeners might want to consider pelleted seed to make the handling easier. Seeds are covered lightly and the soil is tamped well. If soils are dry at the time of seeding, water the entire area after tamping the soil. In addition we mark the position of the rows so that we can begin weeding between the rows even before any crop germination is visible. Never let the seed bed dry out as it will greatly affect germination. In a week or two, tiny seedlings will be visible. Weed the rows when the soil is moist or water lightly before weeding because it will help protect young carrot seedlings. If we have mentioned the word *weed* often, it is because weeds are the greatest threat to growing a successful carrot crop. Carrots do not compete well for space, water, or light.

Despite attempts to sow carefully, carrots may need thinning to a final stand of 2–4 inches apart. Begin thinning when you can utilize the small carrots; the little "fingerlings" are delicious fresh and they freeze well. Good summer maintenance is all that is needed for a healthy crop.

A few years ago we decided to make a serious attempt at growing carrots, directly seeded through a black plastic mulch. The process is very time consuming at the beginning, but our results more than compensated for the effort. Here's what we did. Prepare the bed just as you would for working on open ground. Cover the raised bed with a black plastic mulch as early in the season as you can. In so doing, moisture is captured beneath the plastic, the soils begin to warm, and darkness prevents germinating weeds from surviving. Sometime early summer, when time permits us a couple of hours to seed our carrots, we prepare the plastic row for planting. With a long, very thin metal rod, we make hundreds of tiny holes about 3 or 4 abreast at a spacing of 4–6 inches down the row. Then we reach in through each hole to smooth and level the soil since we need to seed carrots at soil level just beneath the plastic. We then actually count out 3–4 seeds (not using pelleted, which would help) and press them firmly into the soil of each hole. It is important to press the seeds in firmly since you do not want wind and rain to relocate them to germinate under the plastic. You are aiming to have the growing holes small (ours are about 2 inches in diameter) to prevent weeds from competing with carrots, but at the same time, you want the carrots to have light and space directly above. After seeding, we water lightly and make certain that the soil never dries out during the next week or two. The black mulch will help conserve moisture. During germination, there will be a few weeds, but we never spend more than a few minutes weeding carrots seeded this way, as compared to the hours in open ground plantings. Typically, 2–3 seeds will germinate and survive in each hole and we do not need to thin at all. If after a couple of weeks you notice any holes without carrot seedlings, there is plenty of time to reseed. After a month, the carrot tops are

ARROTS, LIKE MOST root vegetables, are best stored in a cool winter location. Root cellars are ideal for this purpose, assuming the cellar temperatures don't fall below freezing. Traditional root cellars also have dirt floors, ensuring good humidity levels for the crops. We have a well-designed root cellar at the farm and have experimented with several methods of keeping our carrots from late summer until the following spring.

Here's the most successful method we have found. Carrots are left in the ground usually until late September. We want to leave them there as long as possible, but not so long that hard frosts damage the tops of the roots. It is possible to extend their field time by covering the tops with hay or a protective fabric until the weather really turns cold.

When we're ready to harvest the whole crop, we choose a comfortably warm day in September or October, pull all of the carrots, and lay them out in the field to dry just long enough so that the excess dirt shakes easily off the roots. Drying should take no longer than an hour or so. Don't leave the roots in the sun and wind so long that they lose moisture.

Before packing the storage carrots, examine the harvest and sort out any small, misshapen, or broken roots. These may be washed, stored in a plastic bag in the refrigerator, and eaten first. These culls won't store as well as the larger perfectly formed roots, but they can be enjoyed soon after harvest.

For winter storage, we use five-gallon plastic buckets and a moderately coarse sand. Start by spreading a layer of slightly moist sand in the bottom of the bucket, arrange a layer of carrots so that roots are touching one another, but not crowded, then layer sand and carrots in this manner until the bucket is filled. Top off the bucket with sand.

Once this is done, we take all of the buckets into the root cellar where they are kept throughout the winter. When you want a supply for eating, simply remove layers of sand and carrots. If you want a supply for several days, remove carrots from the buckets, place them in a plastic bag and they will stay crisp for several weeks in the refrigerator, just as the store-bought carrots do.

We hasten to add that after all these years of farming, some of our enthusiasm for putting food by has diminished, as we find we can purchase winter vegetables that satisfy our needs. Our homegrown carrots, however, seem to us to be more flavorful than any we have found in the supermarkets. It is one crop that we continue to take seriously so that we always try to plant a full year's supply. That means that the two of us (and we regularly entertain friends) need about three bushels of carrots at harvesttime.

The sand layering method may also be used for storing beets, parsnips, radishes, and rutabagas.

Carrots are dried only slightly before tops are cut and the crop is stored in sand for the winter.

large enough to shade out any competition. We begin harvesting carrots, one at a time, from any individual hole, by mid to late summer. At the end of the season, we pull the entire harvest. To give you some idea of the time and the yield for this method, we estimate 4 hours of summer labor for 3 or 4 bushels of beautifully formed roots. (Time includes laying mulch, seeding, weeding, and harvesting.)

Carrots are available in endless varieties, from baby round types to thin long tapers. Choose varieties that are best suited to your soil type. We plant varieties that have broader shoulders, medium length, and blunt tapers. Gardeners with deeper, rock-free, sandier soils can enjoy the longer more slender varieties. If you want carrots for eating fresh and storing, pay attention to the maturity dates. You do not want to have short season varieties as winter keepers. Short season varieties left in the ground too long become oversized, woody, less flavorful, and they may split. We harvest our storage carrots early in the fall before a freeze and pack them in buckets of moist sand in the root cellar. At temperatures of 32°–40°F, they last all winter.

Carrots have been cultivated for at least two thousand years. They are native to Europe and the Mediterranean and were brought to this country in the early 1600s. They are a biennial and it is not difficult to carry them over for seed production a second year. Where winters are not too severe, they may be left in the ground. With a good mulch, they winter over in our gardens. Or you may choose a few select specimens, store them in moist sand in a cool root cellar, and replant the roots the following spring, placing them about a foot apart. Seed stalks are 2–6 feet tall, so you may want to stake them. Carrots are closely related to Queen Anne's lace and will cross-pollinate. Seed savers must keep these plants isolated from each other when they are in flower. You will see the resemblance when carrots flower and seed. Collect the seed heads when they have matured but before they begin to spill seed in the garden. Bring seed heads inside, finish drying, and hand rub to collect.

CAULIFLOWER

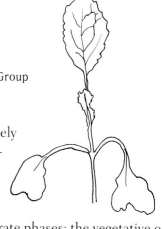

Brassica oleracea Botrytis Group

CRUCIFERAE

ALTHOUGH IT IS closely related to broccoli, cauliflower is not quite so easy to grow successfully. Cauliflower growth is divided into three separate phases: the vegetative or leafy stage, curd formation, and head development. Each of these phases must be accomplished successfully and without any check in growth, or the resulting heads may be anything from inferior to nonexistent. The plants are no more difficult to start from seed than broccoli, and in fact you can follow the same cultural directions. Remember that young cauliflower seedlings are a bit more sensitive to cold weather, so you should hold off seeding until you are certain that you will be able to transplant and set out in the field when plants are at the proper stages. In areas where summers are very warm, it is a good idea to time your seeding and transplanting so that cauliflower can develop and mature in the late summer and early fall. Plants subjected to the stress of extreme hot or cold temperatures, extreme dryness, or held too long in flats or untransplanted nursery beds often "button." You can recognize this if a small transplant forms a tiny center head, known as a button, before the plant has had time to develop its full size and mature leaf development. Any such plants should be discarded.

Cauliflower likes a good fertile garden soil with adequate moisture. Summer organic mulches keep soil temperatures cool and maintain soil moisture. During any period of growth, if there is an extended period of dryness you must make certain that this vegetable has ample water. There are a number of cauliflower varieties, and you should read your seed catalogues to decide what varieties best suit your region. When cauliflower reaches head development in the field (when the healthy leafy plant produces a small tight white curd about the size of a baseball), it

Purple-headed cauliflower needs no blanching while the heads develop.

is important to shield the growing white heads from direct intense sun. We do this by pulling together the large outer leaves of the plant and tying them with string or an elastic thus forming a living cloche over the heads. Some cauliflower varieties are described as self-blanching, which means the inner leaves of the plant curve in over the central heads. Although this does provide some sun protection, you may still want to watch the developing heads so that they are not allowed to discolor, a process that affects the vegetable's texture and flavor. While most cauliflower produces white heads, there are some purple-headed varieties (they turn green when cooked) that do not require any blanching. All of these caveats about growing cauliflower should in no way discourage you from including it in your gardens. In the twenty or so years that we have raised cauliflower, we have had success every season except for those uncommon Maine summers when the temperatures stayed in the eighties and nineties for several weeks at a time.

Southern gardeners usually grow this vegetable as a winter crop for just that reason.

Cauliflower is a biennial, and saving seeds is not a task for beginners—nor for us, either. It is difficult to winter over the plants in most regions and equally hard to store heads properly for replanting a second season. We purchase all of our seeds.

CHARD

Beta vulgaris Cicla Group

CHENOPODIACEAE

AS IS OBVIOUS by the botanical name, chard, also known as Swiss chard, is a type of beet, in fact the oldest type of beet. Records show that it was grown as long ago as 300 B.C., initially

THERE ARE A NUMBER of vegetables that are grown in full sun and then protected from exposure to sun, so that some or all of the edible parts are bleached before harvesting. This practice, called blanching, is done routinely with the heads of cauliflower so that the curds are not discolored before they are picked. In this case the blanching is a necessary part of the cultivation, since discoloration not only reduces the visual appeal of a head of cauliflower but also negatively affects the taste and texture of the vegetable. We blanch our cauliflower by simply pulling up the largest outside leaves and tying them over the heads with elastics or pieces of thick twine. If cauliflower is picked very small (just as the heads have formed), it is not usually necessary to blanch them, but if you want the heads to reach their full potential, give them some protection.

The centers or hearts of escarole and endive may be blanched in the same manner as cauliflower. Pull together the largest outer leaves and tie up around the centers for several days to 1 or 2 weeks. In the case of these two greens, blanching is optional, but when done, the heads have more tender, milder flavored hearts.

Some commercial growers blanch their crops of celery, asparagus, and leeks. In each case, the blanching is done to alter the color and the taste of the crop. Lighter colored stalks of celery and asparagus have more tender texture and their flavor is less intense. We have experimented with these two vegetables and allow them to develop in full sun because we like the tastes and textures of fully green fruit.

Leeks are also often blanched commercially so that the stems are white for a longer distance than

Cauliflower benefits from having its large leaves tied over the tops of the developing white curds.

they would be if left totally exposed to light. The longer white stems (or throats) give more edible leek than those plants that green up very close to the soil line. It also means that fewer outer leaves need to be removed to get to the white tender stems for eating fresh or cooking. We recommend blanching of leeks for the most usable amount of harvest.

In the case of celery, asparagus, and leeks, several simple methods can be used effectively for blanching. The first and easiest is hilling the base of the plants with soil. This is done when the plants are nearing maturity but enough before harvest so that the vegetables will have a few weeks to bleach out before harvest. Try experimenting with the time that it takes to blanch each vegetable to your own particular taste.

A second method of blanching is to use a straw or hay mulch around the lower parts of the crops. Mulches may be applied when the plants have developed size, but at least a few weeks before harvest.

An older but equally effective method of blanching vegetables is to use wide boards anchored upright along each side of the rows of vegetables to be blanched. These upright boards allow the sun to hit the tops of the crops while shielding their stems from light. If wood is used, store it from year to year, because wood (unless made of cedar or redwood) rots after a few seasons. We recommend that pressure-treated lumber *not* be used in the vegetable garden.

Blanching certainly alters the texture and flavor of crops; it will be up to individual gardeners to decide which vegetables are most suited to this process. Our only advice to beginners is to forget what you've read about the definition of elegant food. More or less chlorophyll and more or less crunchiness are not barometers of sophistication. Trust your taste buds.

for its root and later cultivated for its thick stalks and leaves. Chard is often overlooked, but we feel it is indispensable in the garden. It can be harvested from early summer until a hard fall frost. In northern gardens, it is one of the longest-producing greens. Like the garden beet, chard seeds are actually corky pericarps containing several seeds. Chard will grow in most garden soils with adequate moisture and full sun. Sow seeds directly into the garden in spring after the bed or raised mulched row is prepared, in ¼–½ inch of soil, and tamp well. The seeds may be presoaked to speed germination. They are large enough to be sown 4–8 inches apart, and young plants are thinned to 8–12 inches. Thin when the plants are large enough to make use of the thinnings. Once the plants have established some size, we begin to harvest by carefully removing the outer stalks from several plants. They will continue to size up from new center growth. The leaves are excellent in salads, can be cooked like spinach, and the fleshy stalks are excellent fresh or in stir-fry cooking. You will need only a few plants for use all summer and early fall, and we recommend trying white, red, and some of the multicolored varieties.

CHICORIES

Cichorium endivia. Endive
Cichorium endivia. Escarole
Cichorium intybus. Radicchio

COMPOSITAE

endive

ALL OF THE CHICORIES are grown as salad vegetables, and each has an unusual, slightly bitter flavor when eaten fresh. Seeds for any one of the crops may be sown indoors early in the spring so that seedlings are ready to be set out in the garden to size up before very hot weather arrives. Alternatively, chicories may be sown midsummer so that they mature in the garden before heavy fall frosts.

There are different varieties of radicchio. The most widely known are the small curled heads of burgundy with white ribs. There are also plants with green outer leaves and reddish inner rosettes. Radicchio are best used when young. The outermost leaves are the most bitter. Some prefer to discard these and use only the more tender, milder center growth. If the weather gets very warm and dry, the bitterness will increase in the plants, and so they are generally grown for early summer or late summer harvests.

escarole

Although the words *endive* and *escarole* are sometimes used interchangeably, they are distinctly different plants. Escarole is sometimes referred to as a broad-leafed endive. Plants develop into medium-sized heads of ruffled leaves that look a bit like loose-leaf lettuce. The flavor of escarole is mildly bitter. With both endive and escarole, harvesttime is governed somewhat by the regional climate. In very hot summers, pick the leaves when the plants are very young. In moderately warm summers, grow the plants to their full size before harvesting.

Endives have finely cut lacy leaves. When plants have grown to size, bring up and tie together the outer leaves, so the inner leaves are blanched before being eaten. If you have only tasted these greens from the supermarket, you are in for a treat.

Belgian endives (very light green, small, tight cylindrical heads eaten fresh or cooked), are a specific type of Witloof chicory. These little delicacies are grown in two stages.

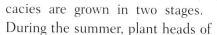
radicchio

During the summer, plant heads of Witloof chicory from seed in the garden as you would any of the other varieties. Allow the plants to develop to full size, and in the early fall, lift the entire plant, root and all. Cut the head above the crown and store the roots until ready for forcing. We use the root cellar for storage. When you are ready to grow the endives, trim some roots from the bottom to about 8–10 inches long. Insert the roots in deep buckets filled with moist sand. Place the buckets into a dark place where temperatures are about 60°F. In 3–4 weeks, the small Belgian endives or "chicons" will sprout from the top of each root. They are cut from the roots and used as salad greens or braised as a cooked vegetable.

CHINESE CABBAGE

Brassica rapa Pekinensis Group
   (for the heading types)
Brassica rapa Chinensis Group
   (for the nonheading types)

CRUCIFERAE

THE INCREASING POPULARITY of these cabbages is apparent by the increasing varieties being offered in seed catalogues all over the country. There is, however, some inconsistency in their placement in these catalogues and in the common names that are applied to the plants. We can simplify the confusion a bit by saying that Chinese cabbage is still the common name for the "heading" type of cabbage that we use fresh in salads, or cook as we would regular cabbage, by chopping both stems and leaves together. Another popular type of *Brassica rapa,* a nonheading variety, is usually referred to in the catalogues as pac choi, bok choi, or pak choi (different spellings for the same plant). Both leaves and stems are edible, but the plant is grown mainly for its stems or thick leafy petioles (white to light green in color) that are used as a summer vegetable in stir-fry cooking.

Both groups of plants are very easy to grow from seed, following the cultural requirements for broccoli. Although some gardening books say that these plants are difficult to transplant, we have never found this to be the case. However, plants should be transplanted when young and should not be allowed to languish in any stage before being set out in the field, or they are apt to bolt. In addition, read your seed catalogues carefully, because each variety is best suited for a particular season. This means that some varieties will perform well when young plants are exposed to cool spring or early summer nighttime temperatures, but others will not tolerate these low temperatures and will bolt in the early stages of growth.

pak choi

We start several varieties in

MANY YEARS AGO a thoughtful customer brought us a seed packet from her home in Provence. It was labeled "mesclun" and the woman praised its performance in her *potager,* the French word for "kitchen garden." The word *mesclun* is the French Provençal term for a "mixture of young tender greens." Today, mesclun is offered by nearly every well-known seed company. These seed packages contain several colorful and tasty varieties of leafy vegetables designed to be used primarily in salads. These include lettuces, chicories, arugulas, radicchios, various members of the mustard family, corn salad or mâche, dandelion, cresses, purslanes, Oriental greens, and occasional herb species such as broad-leaf parsley and chervil.

In spring when the ground can be worked, mesclun seed mixtures are usually sown directly into a well-prepared garden soil where the crops are to be grown and harvested. Crops are picked when

arugula

leaves are young, tender, and most pleasing in flavor. For a continuous supply, gardeners usually have several seedings throughout the summer. Many salad greens are also easily grown in a cool greenhouse during the winter months or in a cold frame in early spring or late fall.

That first gift of a mixed-seed package of greens was a novel introduction to some lesser known edible salad plants. We have since preferred however to grow individual and specific early greens for a number of reasons. We've experimented with many plants from the mustard family, finding those with the textures and tastes that we most enjoy. The same is true of various chicories, leaf lettuces, and different varieties of arugula (also referred to as rocket and roquette). It is also fair to say that we are somewhat biased against seed packages of mixtures (edible or ornamental). When we seed and cultivate a plant, we want to be able to study it, to

corn salad

learn about its growth requirements, appearance, vigor or lack thereof, its possible uses, its potential as a plant from which we can save seed, and in the case of edible plants, its texture and flavor. That being the case, we are inclined to choose a few specific new plants each season and to concentrate on those. Trying, selecting, adding, and eliminating salad herbs will be an ongoing project. It is also important to note that seed companies have been quick to respond to the growing interest in salad greens and it's very easy now to find individual seed packages for a wide variety of delicious plants.

Radicchio leaves are often included in mesclun mixes, providing a sharp accent to the flavors.

the greenhouse and transplant, harden off, and set out young plants in the garden in late May or early June, spacing them about 8–12 inches apart in a wide staggered row. If space is limited, interplant young cabbages with potatoes; you will be harvesting the cabbages before they are overshadowed by their companion crops. Alternatively, you may plant these cabbages in their own space, harvest them, and use the space for a short second-season crop. Developing plants like fertile soils, ample moisture, and cool soil temperatures, so a light summer mulch is helpful. Heading types of Chinese cabbage are usually harvested by cutting the whole plant off at the roots, whereas the pac choi types are harvested by carefully tearing off the outer larger stems, allowing the plants to continue to supply new growth from the center. Late summer and fall crops are best seeded directly into the garden and transplanted or thinned to proper spacing. Do this in areas of the garden where you have harvested early crops such as spinach or peas.

Chinese cabbages are annual members of the genus *Brassica,* meaning that they will produce seed the first season, and readily cross with other relatives, like flowering broccoli. If you want to save seed in a small backyard garden, do so with one species at a time because the flowers are insect-pollinated. Plants seeded and grown in the spring and early summer will have ample time to flower and produce elongated seed pods by the end of the summer. We have left unattended a number of bolted plants in the field only to find volunteer Chinese cabbages throughout the garden the following season. Seed keeps well for a long time.

CELERY

Apium graveolens
var. *dulce*

UMBELLIFERAE

CELERY, AS WE KNOW IT, was developed from a wild biennial, native to Europe. It is of recent cultivation, and was not very popular in this country until the beginning of this century. Now there are thousands of acres devoted to its production, principally in the South and the West Coast. Celery is not difficult to grow from seed, but it needs a bit of extra attention both in the seedling stage and in the field. Celery takes several months from seed to harvest, so we seed our flats in late January. The seed is very small, and must be handled carefully, so the flat is not seeded too thickly. Fill the seed flats with starting mixture almost to the top (for best air circulation) and cover the seed very lightly with fine vermiculite because the seeds need light for germination. Germination takes 2–3 weeks. Celery is susceptible to damping-off so you may want to water the flats from the bottom and thin out any crowded areas in the seed flat if you have overplanted. When the seedlings have developed a set of true leaves they are transplanted into individual pots or plant trays. When transplanting, it is important to bury the plants at the same depth as they grew originally, which may mean pressing the roots into place. The top growth will flop over for a few days until the roots take hold. Do not bury the crowns of the seedlings. Continue to grow the young plants at temperatures that do not drop below 55°F. Extended periods of cold temperatures at the early stages of growth may cause plants to become what are known as "seeders," which are plants that go to seed the first year resulting in vegetables that are fibrous and inedible. Also make certain that the plants never dry out.

When soils have warmed and there is no danger of frosts, young plants are set into the garden. We grow all of our celery on raised beds covered with black mulch, and space the plants 2 or 3 abreast about 12 inches apart. Celery does well in good rich soils with ample organic matter and constant moisture. If the plants are allowed to dry out for long periods of time, the celery will be very poor in quality. If celery is grown on open ground, a moisture-conserving mulch should be used. There are differing opinions about whether or not to blanch this crop to make the leaf stalks a pale green, like those purchased at the markets. We don't blanch our crops because we like the deep-green color and the accompanying pungent flavor, but you should experiment with each method. In order to blanch the plants, pull up the soil around them or shade the stalks with paper collars, straw mulch, or wide boards set alongside the rows to shield the light. Do this when the plants are nearly full grown and leave the covers in place for several weeks to allow the stems to pale.

Commercial growers harvest celery by cutting the entire plant, but you do not need to wait until the end of the summer to begin harvest. As soon as the plants have developed some size (by midsummer in our gardens) we harvest a few stalks from the outside of several plants. The plant continues to develop new center growth. Just before a hard frost, we cut all remaining plants, store a few heads in the refrigerator, chop and freeze stems for winter cooking, and cut and dry leaves for flavoring. Dried leaves retain their color and flavor for a year or two easily.

We do not save our own celery seed because this plant needs to be wintered over and set out again in the spring. Wintering over is tricky. If you want to try, harvest a few select plants by digging roots in a ball of soil and store the plants in a cool root cellar. In the spring, trim off the decayed top growth and replant the roots about 2 feet apart after danger of frost has passed. New growth is large and bushy with small white flowers appearing first at the top of the growth and then lower down on the plants. Allow the flower heads to mature on the plants, but watch so that the seeds do not begin to dry out and scatter. Cut the entire flower stalk and continue to dry seed inside over a sheet or other surface to catch drying seeds. Celery flowers are insect-pollinated, so if you are saving seeds of several types, they must be separated from each other.

CORN

Zea mays var. *rugosa*, Sweet Corn
Zea mays var. *indurata*,
    Ornamental Corn
Zea mays var. *praecox*, Popcorn

GRAMINEAE

CORN, LARGEST OF the cereal crops, is a tall annual grass that grows anywhere from 3 to 15 feet tall. It is America's contribution to the important food group of cereals and is thought to have originated in the wild state in tropical South America. Corn has been grown as far back as prehistoric times, and by the time America was discovered, it was growing all the way from the Great Lakes to Argentina and Chile. The corn that was shared by the Indians at the First Thanksgiving has undergone extensive changes initiated by plant breeders, so we now have a broad selection of varieties from which to choose. Corn is very easy to grow, assuming you have the space, a good fertile soil, and ample moisture.

The most common way to sow sweet corn is to direct seed it into rows or hills when the soil is warm, at least 60°–70°F. If soils are much cooler, seeds are likely to rot in the ground. Depending on soil moisture at the time of planting, cover seed with ½–3 inches of soil and tamp the earth over the seeds. In row planting, sow seeds every 2–6 inches and thin young plants to 12 inches apart. When planting in hills, sow 4–6 seeds every 18 inches and thin hills to 3 plants each. Corn is one of the few vegetables we continue to plant on open ground and mulch to conserve moisture after the hilling is done. Corn is best planted in blocks rather than rows so that there is good pollination. When plants are 6–8 inches tall, draw up soil around them for support. This hilling can be done several times during the season; side-dressing with a composted manure is beneficial mid-season. Corn needs constant moisture especially during the flower and fruit formation.

Each corn plant produces two kinds of flowers; the tassel on the top of the stem is the male flower (staminate), and the cob or ear contains the female flower (pistillate). Corn silks are actually long silky styles leading to the individual ovaries. Corn is wind-pollinated, and since pollination can take place over a considerable distance, it is important to isolate different varieties either by separating them or by timing the varieties so that they flower at different times. Since we have a relatively short growing season at our farm, we have experimented successfully with seeding some early corn in the greenhouse. This is done by sowing 3 seeds in individual peat or paper pots 2–3 weeks before the last spring frost, and then transplanting the young seedlings (pot and all) in the garden. With a little extra effort (and the use of transplants, cloches, or row covers), we have had very early harvests and been able to stagger several varieties in one season.

The old saying that goes "you should have the

cooking pot boiling before going out to pick the corn" refers to the fact that the sugars in corn quickly convert to starch and affect the flavor and texture of the vegetable. For older varieties (both open-pollinated and hybrids), that may be good advice, but recent breeding has produced sweet corn hybrids that are not only much sweeter than their ancestors but retain their sweetness longer after harvest. When you are selecting seed, you need to be aware of the following basic differences in corn varieties; reputable seed catalogues provide this information. There are good older varieties of open-pollinated corn, flavorful and useful to grow if you wish to save your own seed. You will find fewer of these varieties offered in the larger seed catalogues, so you may have to look for companies specializing in open-pollinated vegetable varieties. These varieties are sometimes referred to as old-fashioned types.

Varieties called normal sugary (su) or standard sweet corn include some open-pollinated types, but are more typically hybrids. They are bred for color, taste, and performance, and they come in yellows, bicolors, and whites. Many of these varieties have been on the market for years; when picked fresh, their taste is excellent, but they do not store well—that is, they become starchy. More recently developed sugary enhanced (se) varieties contain modified genes that increase sugar content and retard the conversion of sugar to starch after harvest. Growers can plant and harvest these varieties similarly.

Finally there are the super sweet or extra sweet varieties (sh) of corn that have been bred with a shrunken gene which produces an even sweeter corn with slower sugar-to-starch conversion after harvest, giving it greater shelf life. This last variety needs to be planted in a warm soil, at least 70°F or higher, and it needs to be isolated from other types because cross-pollination may result in kernels that are tough and starchy. Further breeding continues with all of these varieties, and there is some development of the sh types that are known as super sweet enhanced hybrids (eh), indicating that these particular super sweets will not need to be isolated at tasseling time from other sweet corns. This information is a basic guide to the broad range of options that exist in seed selection, but you should refer to your seed catalogues for guidance,

as breeding work is going on continually with this favorite vegetable.

Whatever varieties you choose to include in your gardens, notes for harvesting them remain the same. The silk on the ends of the cobs will turn a bit dry and the kernels on the tips of the ears plump up when the ears are ready to harvest. When we first pick any variety, we always peel back the husks from the very tips of a few ears to test for ripeness before picking. Experience will teach you to spot ripening ears and to test for maturity by feeling the fullness of the whole ear. We leave it to you to decide whether or not to have the cooking pot at a ready boil.

Cultural requirements for ornamental and popcorn are almost the same as for sweet corn. Both types need a longer season than many of the sweet corn varieties, and they can cross-pollinate with the sweet and with each other. If you wish to grow several types, you need either to have the space (as much as 1,000 feet is recommended between types) or to manage flowering times by successive planting. In our own gardens, we usually choose either sweet or ornamental corn in any given season. Ornamental and popcorn need to develop fully and begin drying on the plant. Once kernels are glossy and partially dry (but before a hard frost), the ears are picked and brought inside to cure. Ornamental corns, which are sometimes called Indian corn, have colorful kernels and are husked immediately after picking, by pulling the husks back and leaving them on the cob. They are then dried fully and used for decoration. Popcorn is also husked after harvest, either leaving the husks attached so that the cobs can be hung to dry, or removing the husks so that the kernels can dry before shucking.

Those of you wishing to save your own corn seed must begin by planting only the open-pollinated varieties. Varieties will cross-pollinate, so they must be isolated from one another. About 3–5 weeks after what would have been the eating stage of the corn (when the kernels have become firm), the ears are harvested, husked, and allowed to dry for a couple of weeks. Choose the fullest and best proportioned ears from your plants for seed. Dried cobs are shelled by twisting the cobs. Discard the smallest and least developed seeds.

AFTER YEARS OF making pickles out of every edible member of the Gourd Family, and after years of laboring over recipes that always took a number of hours or even days, it was a thrill to be shown how to make wonderful crisp pickles in just a few hours. Our teacher, a long-time member of the staff, came to Maine from a small village in northern Japan. We refer to this technique as Japanese Pickling.

> *1 large daikon radish, or*
> *2–3 medium-sized turnips, or*
> *2–3 medium-sized kohlrabi, or*
> *2–3 young, firm slicing cucumbers*
> *coarse canning salt*

MARINADE

> *½ cup high quality vinegar or herb vinegar (savory, garlic chive, or dill)*
> *1–3 tablespoons hot sauce (to individual taste)*
> *1 tablespoon soy sauce*
> *3 tablespoons finely minced fresh ginger root*
> *4 tablespoons honey*

Instructions: Pick whatever vegetable you wish to pickle fresh from the garden and scrub it clean. This way there is no need to peel it. If you must use purchased or stored vegetables, they should be peeled. With a sharp knife, slice the vegetables into very thin pieces, no thicker than ⅟₁₆ inch. If the pieces are very large in diameter, cut them in half.

Lay the slices loosely arranged on the top of a large

Make them in the morning and they are ready for eating at dinnertime.

cutting board and sprinkle them liberally with coarse canning salt. Turn pieces over a couple of times to coat both sides with salt. Lift one end of the cutting board slightly so that the opposite end of the board rests over a sink or other space where liquid can drain off the board naturally. Let the vegetable pieces absorb the salt for 30 minutes to 1 hour. During this time, water will drain out of the pieces.

Remove all the pieces into a large ceramic or stainless steel bowl or colander and rinse repeatedly, removing as much salt as possible each time.

Mix the marinade ingredients thoroughly in a clean ceramic or stainless steel bowl. Add the rinsed vegetables, stirring a couple of times to cover all pieces with the marinade. Place bowl in the refrigerator for 1–2 hours, or overnight. That's it. Pickles are crisp and tasty; store any not eaten at the first sitting in the refrigerator where they will keep for 1–2 weeks (actually improving in flavor).

CUCUMBER

Cucumis sativus

CUCURBITACEAE

CUCUMBERS ARE so easily grown from seed and take so little space in the garden that a few well-chosen plants will produce enough cucumbers both to eat fresh all season and to pickle. Cukes offered in the seed catalogues are separated into four categories: Pickling cucumbers are small fruited varieties, usually with white or black spines, that mature quite early and are grown for early eating and pickling. They are meant to be picked when young and small and are available in both vining and bush types. "Slicing" cukes (also available in vining and bush varieties) are grown primarily for eating fresh, although they are perfectly well suited to pickling if harvested when small. Oriental cukes are also slicing types but usually have a long vining habit and produce very long, slender, and sometimes curved, fruit. They can be picked when young or be allowed to develop to lengths of over a foot, remaining tender and sweet. All types are bred for growing in an open garden. They may be seeded directly into the garden or started indoors 2 or 3 weeks before the last spring frost and then transplanted into the garden. When seeding indoors, 2 or 3 seeds are covered with 1 inch of soil in a peat or paper container where they will germinate in 5–8 days in soils kept about 70°F. Continue to grow them in a warm place, harden off the plants, and set them in the garden when the weather is warm. Don't keep the cukes inside too long or they will begin to put out runners and will not transplant or develop as well. When setting the young transplants in the garden, bury the whole biodegradable container and take care not to damage the roots. Pots are buried so that the soil level is the same as it was in the starting pot. Transplants benefit from a cloche or row cover if the nights turn chilly.

Cucumbers that are sown directly into the garden may be sown either in rows or in hills, but only after the soil has warmed up to a temperature of 65°–70°F. Depending on the size of the plants, sow seeds every 2–6 inches and thin to 6 inches apart, or seed in hills with 2–3 seeds per hill and arrange hills 12–18 inches apart. Shallow cultivation is necessary. We prefer to grow our cukes on a black plastic mulch for earlier and more prolific yields. We also prefer to trellis all of our plants as we have found that they produce over a longer period, and the fruits are better in quality than those plants that are left to sprawl on the ground. Trellised plants are better pollinated (by insects) and the vines remain healthy because of continuous air circulation. Gardeners with very limited space may want to grow a tub or two of bush-type cucumbers, which will produce excellent fruits in a rich potting soil, with ample sun and moisture.

It is also important to note that pickling, slicing, and Oriental cucumbers may be open-pollinated or hybrid varieties; there are excellent choices in each category. Cucumbers will not cross-pollinate with melons or squashes, but they will cross-pollinate with each other. If you are saving seeds of particular varieties, you will need to isolate them by a distance of at least 200 feet. For purposes of eating or pickling, we simply sow several varieties in one small section of the garden. Many cucumber varieties are monoecious, that is, having both male and female blooms on the plants, but some of the popular hybrids are gynoecious, and it is important to note this when ordering seeds. Gynoecious plants have only female flowers and will need another variety for pollination. When you purchase a packet of gynoecious seeds, most companies will have included a percentage of seeds from another variety so that pollination will occur.

Cucumbers like rich soil and plenty of moisture, especially when the fruit is being produced. As soon as any of the plants have produced cukes that are large enough to eat or pickle, the fruits must be picked or the vines will cease setting flowers and producing fruit. We never replant cukes during the summer, but we do remove mature fruits every few days. If your plants have ample sun and water, and are disease free, they should produce most of the summer. Eventually, the quality of the fruit will diminish due to lower intensity of the sun, lack of moisture, and cooling temperatures.

The fourth category of cukes include European or greenhouse varieties and they are meant only for indoor cultivation. Don't be tempted to try them in the garden because they are parthenocarpic varieties, that is, they are seedless and self-pollinating. Any insect cross-pollination would cause seeds to form inside the fruits and make them gourdlike and unpalatable. Their culture is quite demanding even in optimum greenhouse conditions.

Since garden cukes have ample time to produce mature fruit even in the shortest seasons, it is quite easy to save your own seeds. Choose any non-hybrid variety and select one or two of your most vigorous plants for seed production. Allow the fruit to stay on the vine until they are large and ripe, which will be evident by their size and color change. Pick off the ripe specimens, scoop out the seeds, and place them in a container of water and allow them to sit for several days. They will begin to ferment, and the mixture should be stirred daily. During fermentation, the mucilaginous layer surrounding the seeds will begin to break down. Over a period of a week, empty seeds and pulp will stay on top of the water and full seeds will tend to sink. Separate the good seeds (full) from the bad (empty), wash and rinse them, and spread them out on a paper or screen to dry.

A dark mulch assures a good production of eggplant in our northern gardens. This slender long fruit is best harvested young.

EGGPLANT

Solanum melongena
var. *esculentum*

SOLANACEAE

THESE EXQUISITELY beautiful vegetables are native to India, so it will come as no surprise to know that they need warmth at all stages of growth to succeed in the garden. With a little extra care, however, we have grown several varieties in our northern gardens. We start all of our plants in the greenhouse where seeds are sown in flats, covered with 1/16 inch of soil or vermiculite, and placed on a heating mat so that soil temperatures are maintained at 75°–85°F. Cover the seed flats with a piece of glass or plastic (a tent is best) during the night until germination, so that temperature and good moisture are maintained. Transplant seedlings and allow to grow on in warm temperatures. Time the seeding of the plants so that your seedlings are ready to be hardened off gently and set out in the field only after soils have warmed and nighttime temperatures are mild. Cool soils, cool temperatures, and harsh winds shock the plants and greatly diminish their vegetative development and fruit set. Eggplants are good candidates for soil warming mulches and some early season protection from cloches or row covers. You should also avoid planting eggplants in soils that have recently had eggplants, peppers, tomatoes, potatoes, or strawberries growing in them, as all of these plants are subject to verticillium wilt and can infect each other. Eggplants need fertile soil with pH close to 7 and ample moisture all during the season. We like to side-dress our plants midseason or feed them with a foliar fish emulsion.

There are a number of varieties of this vegetable. They include fruits that are large and bulbous, cylindrical and slender, egg-shaped, and pear-shaped.

THESE TWO POPULAR MEMBERS of the onion family are usually planted from sets. While both crops may be planted in the spring, fall planting of garlic will yield the largest bulbs. When purchasing garlic for planting, it is important to know that this vegetable is classified into three basic types. First there is the stiff-neck garlic, *Allium sativum* var. *ophioscordon*. Bulbs typically consist of 6–11 cloves in a single circle around a central woody stem. Plants are characterized by their long upright flower stalks that twist into circles at the top of the plants where they produce clusters of tiny bulblets by midsummer. Cut off bulblets as soon as their stalks begin to turn woody and lose their coils. This allows the plant's energy to redirect itself into producing

good-sized cloves. The harvested bulblets are edible and may be used fresh or added to flavor stir-fry dishes.

Soft-neck garlic, *Allium sativum,* is the strongest flavored garlic and the most widely grown commercially. As underground bulbs develop, the top growth remains soft, resembling onion leaves. Bulbs have 12–20 total cloves in layers, smaller on the inside of the bulb and largest around the outside. After harvest, cure this variety for braiding or allow leaves to die back entirely and remove before storage.

The mildest tasting largest garlic is known as elephant garlic, *Allium ampeloprasum.* As its scientific name suggests, this plant is not a true garlic; it is a close relative of garlic and leeks. It is the least hardy of the three types and benefits from a good mulch after

It's hard to bring ourselves to cut off the tops of stiff-neck or rocambole garlic because they are so beautiful in the garden.

planting. Any flowering stalks that are produced during cultivation should be removed for best clove size.

If you are a garlic lover, you should know that there are hundreds of sub-varieties of these types. They vary in hardiness, color, taste, fragrance, and texture. There are some plant catalogues devoted exclusively to garlic.

All garlics like fertile garden soil with ample organic matter, adequate moisture with good drainage, and full sun. To plant, break an entire bulb apart into the individual cloves. Each clove is set into the ground, root end down, 2–3 inches deep, spaced 4–5 inches apart. Elephant garlic should be planted a bit deeper, from 4–6 inches. In our climate, we plant any time from late September until late October. As with so many other fall planted bulbs, root growth takes place until the ground is frozen and continues in the early spring when the first green tops appear. Keep garlic free from weeds. Water during any periods of dryness especially if you have sandy soils. In late summer, when leaves have yellowed, lift the bulbs with a tool so that no cloves are broken or left in the ground. Cure as you would onions.

Garlic should be stored in a cool humid place for use all winter. Soft-neck garlics are the easiest to cultivate and store the longest. Stiff-necks are the most cold hardy and store moderately well when humidity remains above 50 percent. Otherwise they tend to dehydrate. Elephant garlic has the shortest storage time.

Shallots need the same garden conditions as garlic. We always plant our crops in early spring, but they may be fall planted and protected with a good mulch. Break apart the bulbs into individual cloves. Plant cloves by burying them up to their necks (as you would onion sets), spacing each clove 4–5 inches apart. During the growing season, each clove will multiply to produce 5–10 shallots. Production is very much affected by soil fertility and moisture. When leaves yellow and wilt, bulbs are lifted, cured, and stored. We find that our shallots keep best in the refrigerator for winter use.

Fruits range in color from dark purple-black to striped, pinkish and even creamy white. Be certain to choose a variety that will have ample time to mature during warm weather in your area. Watch closely for the developing fruits that are sometimes hidden inside the bushy vegetative growth. Pick fruits when they are just developed, evenly colored, and glossy. We recommend using a sharp knife or small plant shears for harvesting because pulling or twisting the fibrous fruit stems can damage the plants. Watch out for the spines on the calyxes. Eggplant does not store well (as is obvious from the quality of supermarket varieties that need to be peeled and salted before cooking to remove any bitterness). Freshly grown eggplant will be naturally sweet and tender and should be used skin and all.

Saving your own seed is easy with this vegetable. Choose an open-pollinated variety. Flowers are monoecious and since cross-pollination seldom occurs by bees, you need only to separate one variety from another by 20–100 feet or by a tall "divider" crop. Early in the season, choose several of the best and earliest fruits and leave them on the plant to mature fully until they are actually "punky." Cut these off the plants, scoop out the seeds, and leave them in water for a few days until the seed membranes break down. Wash the seeds, dry thoroughly, and store.

GOURDS

CUCURBITACEAE

THESE INEDIBLE members of the squash family are found in the vegetable and/or flower sections of many seed catalogues. They are technically fruits, but are primarily grown for ornamentation or craft projects. They come in a number of species and in a variety of shapes, colors, textures, and sizes, but most commonly, they are divided into large and small types. Growing gourds is great fun for children, and they are very easy to grow from seed sown directly in the garden. See cultural requirements under pumpkins or squashes and follow these for starting seeds, maintaining plants, and saving seeds. Be certain to check the maturity dates for gourds as they need to fully mature on the vines before the first fall frosts. Most gourds have long vines, so trellising will save garden space. It is also important to isolate them from other squashes or pumpkins because cross-pollination by insects is common. (A distance of 500 feet is suggested.) When gourds have fully developed they should be carefully picked, so the fruits are not bruised. Then wash the fruits in soap and water with a mild disinfectant and set them in a warm, dry place for several weeks to cure. During this time the outer skins will become very tough and hard. Some seed companies recommend preserving the gourds with a coat or two of floor wax or clear varnish. We have tried this and have also left them untreated, with good results. If you wish to save your own seeds, isolate specific plants as previously mentioned.

KALE

Brassica oleracea Acephala Group

CRUCIFERAE

KALE IS SO EASY to grow, so tasty and nutritious, that we always have about a dozen plants in our garden, giving us enough to harvest fresh and to freeze for a whole year. A member of the cabbage family, kale has finely curled bluish green leaves, and is attractive enough to be included in an ornamental bed. In fact, even if you think you don't know this vegetable, you have undoubtedly seen it many times as that ubiquitous garnish surrounding thousands of salad bar bowls and supermarket fish trays. Kale is a crop that can be sown directly in the garden from spring to midsummer. To plant outdoors, cover seeds with ½ inch of soil and transplant or thin plants to stand 12–18 inches apart, depending on the variety. We usually start a few plants in the greenhouse and set out transplants in the spring so that we can begin harvest early in the summer. Seeds started indoors germinate in 4–7 days and are ready to set out in 6–8 weeks. Young plants will tolerate late spring frosts and older plants will go on producing until a killing frost. As soon as the plants develop some size

One of the most nutritious garden vegetables, kale can be harvested from early summer until late into the fall.

in the field, harvest by breaking off a few outer leaves from several different plants. Plants continue to set new center growth all season.

Like most of its relatives, kale is a biennial brassica, but it is not difficult to overwinter for saving seed. With a good heavy mulch it will survive our harsh winters and produce seed stalks the second season. Kale is cross-pollinated by insects, so it must be isolated from other flowering brassicas during flowering.

KOHLRABI

Brassica oleracea Gongylodes Group

CRUCIFERAE

KOHLRABI, both white and purple varieties, is quick to mature from seed, and may be sown directly into the garden several times in one season. You can begin seeding in early spring by covering seeds with ½ inch of soil and transplanting or thinning plants to 4–6 inches apart. You can also seed a few peat or paper pots inside, placing 2–3 seeds per pot and transplanting young plants in the garden. Seeds germinate in 4–10 days and the plant is ready to harvest in 7–8 weeks. Kohlrabi, a lesser-known member of the cabbage family, is unusual in appearance. It has an edible swollen stem, often called a bulb, out of which grow long petioles and leaves. It is an undemanding vegetable so long as it has good garden soil, sun, and adequate moisture. When the bulbs are 2–4 inches in diameter they are ready to harvest. Cut the root below the bulb, remove the leaves and stems from the bulbs, and use the vegetable fresh, cooked, or pickled.

Kohlrabi is a biennial that can be saved for seed either by heavily mulching the whole plant in the garden, or by pulling the whole plant with its roots and storing it in cool temperatures (35°–40°F) over the winter. Then the plant is set in the garden the following spring to produce seed stalks. The plant is insect-pollinated and must be isolated from other flowering brassicas for seed purity.

LEEKS

Allium ampeloprasum Porrum Group

AMARYLLIDACEAE

ONE OF OUR FAVORITE members of the onion family, leeks are large, non-bulbing onions with white, slender sheaths of leaves on the lower part of the plant and flat, blue-green upper leaves. They are more tender and milder in flavor than most regular onions, but they are equally easy to grow from seed.

Cultural requirements for leeks are the same as those for onions, and you should refer to that section for planting seeds indoors or directly into the garden. We plant all of our leeks indoors 10–12 weeks before they are to be set out in the garden. Leeks require a rather long growing season, so the early indoor start allows the vegetable ample time to form large flavorful plants which are harvested at the end of the summer. Like onions, leeks are heavy feeders, and need even more continuous moisture to produce sizable plants. Leeks differ from onions in that they benefit from having soil or mulch pulled up around the base of the plants during their growing season. This produces vegetables with long, white edible necks. Some gardeners plant their seedlings in trenches and pull soil around the developing leeks. Others plant at ground level and hill with soil or a straw mulch as the season progresses. We have planted on open ground and mulched leeks with soil and then hay. Our current method is to grow them on raised mulched rows, several plants abreast.

Assuming the soils are adequately fertile and moist, leeks will go on growing vigorously until a killing frost, so the plants are harvested before weather damages their top leaves. Leeks do not store by drying, but we have found ways to keep and use this vegetable year-round. We pull and wash all of our crop and store several dozen leeks, with roots just slightly trimmed, in plastic bags in the refrigerator. They can be kept this way for several weeks. When ready to use, cut off all of the roots, peel off and discard a few outer leaves, and prepare. We store the bulk of our crop by cleaning and chopping the leeks into small sections and sealing a cup or two in plastic bags in the freezer. You might want to double, or even triple bag these vegetables, as their pungent fragrance can leak into the freezer. Frozen leeks are wonderful for soups, stews, stir-fries, and even boiled and mashed with potatoes.

Leeks are biennials and will survive most winters even in our northern garden. If winters are very open, a good protective mulch will help. Seeds are easy to save. Simply leave a few vigorous plants to overwinter and they will produce flowers and seed heads (large beautiful round globes) the second season. Allow the seeds to mature on the plant, pick before they shatter, rub clean, dry, and store. Alternatively, you may want a few seed heads as decoration. If so, pick flowers when fully mature before seeds have formed and hang upside down to dry. Stems are a good 3–5 feet tall, and the flower heads are every bit as beautiful as some of the better-known ornamental alliums.

I T'S NOT AS IF we are wanting for space in which to garden. With nearly two hundred acres of land, our farm has plenty of arable soil. But every garden laid out is another place to be worked, and given our enthusiasm for plants, we are becoming more determined to cultivate no more than we can properly care for. That attitude has led us to look for ways to make existing gardens more productive, easier to maintain, and as beautiful as possible. Our perennial asparagus bed is one example of using space well, but it wasn't always so.

Initially our asparagus was grown as a field crop. The roots were planted in long trenched rows, and the space between the rows was worked annually with machinery or by hand-cultivating. As our gardens expanded at the farm, the asparagus bed grew more and more weedy, until we gave up on an overgrown area and plowed the whole thing back into the ground.

Our second attempt at locating this crop proved more successful. We built and planted a small raised bed with no more than several dozen plants. Furthermore, we located the raised bed right in the center of our display gardens, where any neglect would be all too obvious. For the first couple of years we made certain to weed and fertilize the asparagus, and production was excellent.

But we soon noticed that the bed looked rather bare all through the early spring. Later, as we were

As the asparagus is left to develop, it hides the leaves of the daffodils and shields the early summer spinach from intense sun.

harvesting the newly emerging spears in early summer, we noticed it was still bare. It wasn't until harvest was over and the asparagus was left to develop fully that the garden had any definition or shape—any visual appeal. This gave us the idea of using the space for double, and then triple, planting, so that we were harvesting multiple crops from a single site.

The first idea was to use the perimeter of the raised bed to plant early edible greens. These now include spinach, lettuces, arugula, and escarole. A mesclun mix would also do well. While the plants are young they do not need to compete for light or moisture with the asparagus. When the greens are more mature, they are given some protection from the hot sun and winds by the asparagus plants that have been left to size up. By the time the asparagus is fully leafed out, we have stopped harvesting the early greens and clean them out of the bed.

That was a good solution for the perimeter, but it still left the center of the bed with unused space. Here we have chosen to underplant with several dozen bulbs of fragrant perennial daffodils. Almost as soon as the snows have melted, daffodils have poked their first growth through the earth. By mid-spring the flowers are budding; blossoms begin to open just about the time the first spears of asparagus are ready to be cut for eating. So we are eating and cutting fresh flowers from the same space at about the same time.

Daffodil bulbs should be left to die back naturally in the garden, which is easy to do, because their withering foliage is masked by the developing asparagus stalks.

At the end of the growing season, after asparagus stalks have been frosted and are completely brown, we cut them back to the ground, and as soon as the ground is frozen, we apply liberal amounts of composted horse manure to cover the whole raised bed in preparation for next spring's planting of edible greens. All in all, this small site is now a great producer.

LETTUCE

Lactuca sativa

COMPOSITAE

buttercrunch lettuce

LETTUCE HAS BEEN a widely grown garden vegetable for centuries. It was cultivated by the Greeks, Persians, and Moors, and many of the forms we now know were also grown in Europe prior to the Middle Ages. The cultivated plant is descended from a common weed, a wild lettuce. Its popularity seems to be on the increase in this time of health food consciousness despite the fact that it has little food value. But there are so many varieties with visual, taste, and textural appeal that it is hard to imagine a good kitchen garden without it.

Any vegetable catalogue will offer a number of varieties, but real enthusiasts will find some specialty catalogues with dozens of choices. Lettuce varieties can be broadly classified in the following way. There are loose-leaf, butterhead, romaine or cos, and crisphead types. Each of these types includes plants with either green or reddish leaves. Perhaps the easiest to grow are the loose-leaf varieties. These are non-heading lettuces with varying leaf shapes from plain to crinkled to oak-like and frilly. Loose-leaf types are also among the quickest to grow from seed. The butterhead types are also referred to as Boston lettuces. Many catalogues include the bibbs with this type. These lettuces are characterized by loosely folded heads surrounded by rosettes of leaves. At maturity the heads have creamy interiors. The cos or romaine lettuces have upright cylindrical heads firmly wrapped at maturity. Loose-leaf, butterheads, and cos types are rapid growers, with maturity dates ranging 45–70 days from seed. Crispheads as their name suggests are heading lettuces. Sometimes they are referred to incorrectly as iceberg lettuces; in fact, an iceberg is only one variety of crisphead. They are the slowest of the four types to mature, some varieties taking up

cos lettuce

to 3 months from seed to harvest.

Lettuce is easy to grow from seed so long as you garden in areas where the summers are not too warm and dry. Southern gardeners usually plant lettuce as a winter crop. We start our lettuces both indoors and out. Remember that lettuce seed needs light for germination as well as constant *red sails lettuce* moisture, so wherever you plant it, press the seed into the soil, but do not cover it. Seeds sown in an indoor flat will germinate in 3–4 days and can be transplanted into growing flats when they have the first set of true leaves. They must be transplanted no deeper than they were growing in the seed flat. After transplanting, they will flop over for a few days, but will quickly regain vigor and turgidity. For 3 or 4 days from transplanting, we protect the seedlings from direct sun by placing them under a greenhouse bench or erecting a lath covering over them. Lettuce seedlings will do well in their growing-on period in a cold frame. Indoor transplants are ready to be set out into the field in 6–8 weeks. Never let the seedlings dry out completely during their growing period, and that goes for indoor or outdoor seedlings and developing field plants. Lettuces are more than 95 percent water and they cannot grow properly without ample moisture. Make certain that indoor transplants are hardened off before setting them in the garden. Once hardened off they can withstand light spring frosts. We plant our earliest greenhouse lettuce plants between the small plants of tomatoes, peppers, or potatoes, since the lettuces will mature before there is any harmful competition for light and space. In fact, the developing companion plants help shield maturing lettuces from early summer heat. Lettuce can withstand some light shade as long as moisture is adequate.

As soon as the ground can be worked in the nursery bed, cold frame, or garden, lettuce can be seeded directly, raking it lightly into the soil and keeping the seedbed watered, so it never dries out completely. In a succession of outdoor seeding, midsummer and late summer plantings will benefit from a light lath cover to keep the soil cooler and more moist. If you transplant lettuce seedlings (instead of thinning plants to 12–18 inches apart), it is best to do so at the beginning of a cloudy or rainy spell so that young transplants do not have to struggle with direct sun and wind, both of which may dry out the tender seedlings beyond their ability to recover.

Lettuce does well in a good garden soil with (and we repeat ourselves) continuous moisture. Since it also prefers cool weather, lightly mulch around the plants to lower soil temperatures and retain moisture. Plant several different types of lettuce sequentially since it is a crop that does not store well; too much at any one time will go to waste. Once plants are mature and the weather warms up, heads will bolt readily. They may also turn bitter and bolt if allowed to get too dry. Read catalogue descriptions to find summer varieties that have some ability to hold up during hot weather. A carefully planned planting of several varieties is quite manageable in a small garden and will give you excellent crops from spring to fall. The loose-leaf lettuces can be harvested by picking outer leaves from several plants, or by cutting the whole head. Other varieties are usually cut whole. Mulched lettuce will be much easier to clean because there will be little to no dirt on the leaves.

It is easy to save your own lettuce seed. Flowers are self-pollinating, so different varieties do not have to be isolated at great distances. Choose vigorous specimens of the kinds you wish to preserve from the earliest spring plantings so that there will be ample time for them to complete their bolting, flowering, and seed production. When seeds begin to dry on the stalk, collect them in a paper bag, dry, and store. We have succeeded in saving seeds for every type except the crispheads; they do not have time to mature in our area.

MELONS

Cucumis melo Reticulatus Group, Muskmelon
Cucumis melo Inodorus Group, Honeydew
Citrullus lanatus, Watermelon

CUCURBITACEAE

musk melon

MELONS ARE heat lovers, so varieties for northern gardens have to be carefully chosen. Although southerners may envy us for our lettuces and apples, we in turn covet the delicious vine-ripened fragrant melons that are grown in zones much warmer than our own. Melon seeds can be started only in warm soils, so we sow our seeds indoors in peat or paper pots 4–6 weeks before the last spring frost. Cover seeds with 1 inch of soil, allow them to germinate at temperatures of 70°–80°F and grow on at 70°F. Gently harden off the plants and set them in the garden, 12–18 inches apart, on a heat absorbing mulch. When transplanting melon seedlings, care must be taken not to disturb the roots. Do not try to separate any plants, and water well after setting out. If weather has not completely settled and warmed up, use cloches or row covers to ensure warmth. Melons prefer a rich soil with a pH of 6.5–6.7 and continuous moisture during early growth, flowering, and fruit set. They will not tolerate standing water, so a fertile, well-drained soil (as in a raised bed) is best. Gardeners with long, warm growing seasons can seed their plants directly, but only after soil has reached a temperature of 70°F. Seeds planted in colder soils will rot. Plant seeds where plants are to grow, cover with 1 inch of soil, and thin seedlings to desired spacing. Most melons have a long vining habit, so they are best planted on the perimeter of the garden.

Both muskmelons and honeydews should be allowed to mature on the vine. Ripeness can be judged by the increased netting of the muskmelon, the increased fragrance of the fruit, and the fruit's tendency to "slip" from the vine. To "slip" means that the fruit stem breaks away from the vine with a bit of pressure from the thumb or forefinger. If it is very difficult to pull the fruit from its vine, the melon is not adequately ripe. There are more good varieties of muskmelons for northern gardens than there are honeydews, the latter being types that were grown extensively in the dryer, hotter climates of the West and Southwest. Mature honeydews do not slip from the vine; when the fruits begin to show signs of ripeness by a paling of color in the rind, they must be cut from their stems.

watermelon

Seeds for both types of melons are ready for cleaning and saving when the fruit is ripe for eating, so in this case you can have your cake and . . . Melons will not cross with other cucurbits, but varieties will cross within a genus. For absolute seed purity, varieties must be isolated by a distance of 800 feet. Ripe seeds are scooped out of the seed cavity, put in water, allowed to ferment for a few days, and then rinsed clean, dried, and stored.

The cultural requirements for watermelons are the same as those for the two melons previously described. What we think of as the true watermelons—those great oval giants with their green-gray striped skins—are restricted to gardens with 90–120 days and nights of warm temperatures. Over the past decades there have been some varieties introduced for cooler climates, and several of these are quite reliable, sweet, and flavorful. They are usually referred to as small refrigerator types, and are often round with deep green rind and pinkish red flesh. There are some types with yellow flesh and orange rind, and a few seedless varieties as well. We have grown both bush and vining types with success. Like the melons just described, watermelons should be left to ripen on the vine. One telltale sign can be found by turning the mature-looking fruit over on the plant. The spot that was touching the ground will turn from white to a bright yellow as the fruit ripens. It may take some experimenting and a few disappointing cuts into pale pink flesh before you perfect your abilities to spot and harvest correctly.

To save seed for watermelons, follow the same requirements as for the other melons. Cleaning seed for watermelons is easy because the seed is not entwined in fleshy membranes in the middle of the fruit. In fact, you can eat and save simultaneously, with a well-placed container at your feet. Discard any seeds that are not fully developed. You will notice that the most mature seeds are black and well-formed. You may want to wash the seeds after separating them from the fruit. It's not necessary. Spread out the cleaned seed to dry thoroughly before storing.

OKRA

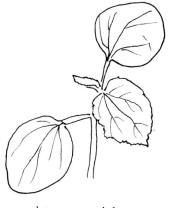

Abelmoschus esculentus

MALVACEAE

THIS VEGETABLE, a native of tropical Africa, made its way into European gardens by the early 13th century, and is now widely grown in tropical and subtropical climates throughout the world. Southern gardeners often refer to the plant by its Spanish name, "gumbo," and young pods of okra are used to flavor and thicken soups of the same name. There are several varieties of okra available for northern gardens. We have had moderate success in growing this crop in our gardens by starting plants indoors about 4 weeks before the ground has warmed up outside. Soak seeds for 24 hours before sowing. Seed 2–3 seeds each in peat pots and cover the seeds lightly. Peat pots are used with this crop because okra is difficult to transplant and the young plants can be set in the garden, peat pot and all, without disturbing plants or roots. Soil temperatures need to be very warm for germination, 75°–85°F, which takes place in about a week. Seedlings are grown on in a warm sunny location, hardened off, and set out into the field only when the weather has settled, and nighttime temperatures are above 55°F. There is no sense in hurrying the process, as okra plants are very sensitive to cold. Soil-warming mulches are pretty much required for northern growers, and cloches or early covers will also help.

Gardeners farther south can seed okra directly into the garden, washing and soaking the seed first, and planting 3 seeds to a hill, at a distance of 12 inches apart, the same distance used to plant the peat pots. Plants will grow from 3–5 feet tall depending on the variety. Okra likes a fertile garden soil with average moisture. Plants have large, lobed, spiny leaves and yellow hibiscus-like blossoms that are blotched with brown. Blossoms grow out from leaf axils and are quickly followed by tapered and ribbed green or burgundy pods.

Harvest the pods every 2–3 days when they are young and tender, no longer than 3 or 4 inches. It is best to cut the pods from the stems with a sharp knife or stem-cutters. Some people are sensitive to the spines on this plant; they should wear protective clothing when harvesting. Okra should be used as soon as it is picked, since the fruit deteriorates quickly. We have used the pods in both soups and stir-fry cooking. The young pods are very mucilaginous when cooked, serving as a natural thickening agent.

If you wish to save your own seeds it is not necessary to isolate the crop because okra flowers are perfect and thus self-pollinating. Choose a few of the most vigorous plants from your garden and allow the pods to mature fully. They will become woody. Before a frost threatens, collect these ripe pods and crack them open; the seeds will come out readily. Dry and store. Some growers use the mature dried okra pods for decorative purposes in everlasting arrangements.

ONIONS

Allium fistulosum, Allium cepa

AMARYLLIDACEAE

ONIONS, NATIVE to the Mediterranean region and Southeast Asia, have been raised for more than four thousand years. They have been used not only for food and flavoring, but also for medicinal purposes and in religious rituals. This vegetable is now cultivated over a large part of the world, in both temperate and tropical climates. Onions were brought to America by the early colonists. Current gardening catalogues offer a great number of varieties for the home gardener. Onions may be raised from divisions, bulblets, or seed, and we will begin our discussion with seed propagation.

Onions are very easy to grow from seed and some experienced gardeners feel that the best quality comes from seed grown varieties. Onions are divided into several categories. These include bunching onions or scallions, types that are bulbless and eaten young when both the lower white flesh and tender green leaves are edible. Bunching onions are usually grown as annuals, but they will self-divide and can be

SEVERAL MEMBERS OF the onion family need to be dried before storage. These include onions, garlic, and shallots. The drying method is simple. Harvest these vegetables when mature and lay the bulbs out to dry in a warm sunny spot. We choose a warm late summer day for harvest, pull the crop and lay it out in rows (perhaps for a day or so) in the garden so that any dirt will easily shake from the roots.

Then we spread the onions on a clean bench in an empty greenhouse and let the bulbs dry for the next 1 or 2 weeks. Drying time is affected by the number of sunny days and the size of the individual bulbs. Notice that the outer skins of the onions will darken in color, and several layers of skin will actually dry and enclose the inner bulb. The neck and slender leaves of the bulbs will also dry.

The amount of time that you allow the onions or garlic to dry is important if you want to be able to braid some of the crop. Watch the harvest and evaluate the degree of curing that is taking place. Here's what to look for. In order to braid onions or garlic (we've never tried to braid shallots, so you're on your own there), each bulb will need an attached neck that is both dry enough not to mold or rot, but strong enough to withstand being braided. Test the bulb necks and determine that time when they are nearly dry to the touch but still attached enough to work with. This probably sounds harder than it is. Use your common sense. When ready, simply choose a selection of the largest, most well-shaped bulbs and braid them together, starting with three and adding as you work up the braid. We usually try to work 15–20 bulbs into one braid. Finish the top of the braid by folding over the final necks and leaves and winding them with a sturdy piece of twine so that the twine can be used for hanging.

We always like to have a braid or two in our kitchen and several to give as gifts. The remaining dried bulbs are stored in a different manner. Once thoroughly dried, the bulbs are cleaned of their dried up necks and leaves and packaged in net bags to be hung in the basement of the farmhouse. Here they will last until early spring. We try to grow a supply that will last into March or April when the bulbs tend naturally to sprout inside the storage bags.

Braided onions never store as long as the bagged ones for us because we keep the braids in a much warmer and drier location in the kitchen. We check the braids from month to month, and when we notice that they are beginning to deteriorate, we either start to use them or resign ourselves to the fact that they will completely dry out but still look acceptably decorative for another few months. Usually beauty wins over function in our house, and we have been known to toss out nearly hollow braids in early summer when one of us tires of cleaning up the continually shedding skins. Food as decoration is powerfully symbolic, so we can really say that we enjoy the crop in a variety of ways.

Wait until the onion leaves fall naturally before pulling the crop for drying. If some few plants don't collapse on their own, simply bend the stems by hand and allow the leaves to dry on the plants for a week or two before pulling.

left in the ground and treated like perennials. We always have a patch of Welsh onions that we treat this way, leaving the lower bulbs in the ground from season to season and harvesting only the tender green tops from early spring throughout the summer. When grown as annuals, bunching onions are a quick crop, and produce edible harvests in 60–75 days.

The next category, referred to as true onions, includes short season summer onions, varieties that have small bulbs and are meant to produce harvests by midsummer. Main season onions come next, and they are divided into short- and long-term storage types. All of the true onions are available in a great range of size, shape, color, flavor, and rate of maturation. Although some of the summer types may reach edible size in 55–60 days, there are storage types needing 80–120 days to develop. It is important to choose onions that are well suited to your own growing areas. There are short-day and long-day bulbing varieties. Short-day onions are grown in southern gardens and long-day onions in the north.

CULTURAL REQUIREMENTS for all of these onions are similar, and seeds can be planted directly in the garden or started indoors. Let's begin our discussion with indoor planting, since that takes place in late winter in our area. For onions that take a long period to mature, we sow seeds in flats or individual cells, 8–10 weeks before plants are to be set out. Seeds are large and easy to handle; if you plan to transplant into pots or directly from the seed flats into the garden, space the seeds 1–2 inches apart in the seed flats and cover them lightly. They need continuous moisture, and although they will germinate under a wide temperature range, optimum germination rates are achieved between 65° and 85°F. At these temperatures, growth will appear in 7–10 days. Young slender green spears poke up through the soil and will release a lovely pungent onion fragrance when brushed. Keep the seedlings well watered and clipped to a height of about 4–5 inches so that growth will be concentrated in the lower root forming part of the plant. A good alternative to sowing in flats is to sow 2–3 seeds in individual cells and thin to the most vigorous plants when ready to set out in the garden. Clip as described earlier. Seedlings can be set in the garden as soon as the ground can be worked.

Soil preparation for growing onions is very important. Soils should be tilled, raked free of stones and weeds, and have good fertility. Work in ample amounts of organic matter, composts, and manures, and amend any very heavy soils so that there will be constant moisture, but no standing water. Having prepared the beds, you are ready either to set out the seedlings or to direct seed into the garden. Seedlings are hardened off and set in the soil to the same depth that they were growing in their containers. They will tolerate light spring frosts. If you choose to purchase bare-rooted onion plants from garden centers or catalogues, they benefit from a good soaking in water before planting.

When planting onions directly into the garden, take the time to prepare the bed as carefully as described earlier for transplants. Seeds are sown into garden rows (we use several rows abreast on a raised mulched bed) at a distance of 1–3 inches apart, depending on the varieties chosen. Cover seeds with about ½ inch of soil. Thin seedlings, according to variety, 2–4 inches apart for good quality harvests. The biggest problem with onions in the garden, either direct seeded or transplanted, will be weed control, unless you seed or transplant into holes made in plastic mulches. If you grow on open ground, pay attention to preparing the bed and keep at the weeds from day to day. Cultivation needs to be shallow to avoid disturbing onion roots. Once weeds get a good start in the onion patch, they will be hard to eradicate and will compete with onions for nourishment and moisture. Your onions are likely to suffer from such a competition. We have used open bed growing and have grown crops successfully on black plastic. You can also use grass or straw mulches to reduce weeds and conserve moisture. During any extremely dry periods, water the onions.

Harvest onions as soon as they have reached edible size. Use the short-storage varieties first and leave the long-storage varieties to get you through the winter. As onions mature, the tops will begin to wither and yellow. At the end of the season, tops that show no signs of yellowing can be bent over at the neck of the bulb so that growth stops. When onions have developed skins, it's time to pull and cure them. We do our curing in the field, or if we have left the harvest until it is very late, we pull and cure in a hot sunny greenhouse.

In either case, allow the harvested onions to dry out or cure for at least a week before bringing them in for storage. During this time the tops and necks will wither further and can be clipped off before putting the onions in netted bags or shallow containers. Onions should be kept for the winter in cool conditions with low humidity. With some of our long storage types, we have cured the onions and left their stems attached for braiding. Braided onions are not only attractive to hang but are convenient to have on hand in the kitchen. Use them as needed by cutting individual fruit from the bottom to the top of the braid.

Bunching onions are almost always seeded directly into the garden, following the same rules for soil preparation as described above. Bunching types can be seeded thicker and allowed to develop until the thinnings are of edible size. You can harvest and use all of these varieties or leave some of the crop in the ground for another year. They may be planted in the spring or late summer for fall and spring use.

We have focused our discussion on onions that are grown from seeds. Growing from seed is the most economical way to produce onions, and a greater number of varieties is available from seed. Onions are also grown from sets and we have had good results from this method as well. Sets are very small onions that were grown in the previous season from seed. They are little onions called "bulblets" that were planted too close together and not allowed to mature. Sets are sold (often by weight) at garden centers and through catalogues. When choosing sets from a garden center, don't be tempted to pick out the largest bulblets. Instead choose the smallest firmest ones. They will produce the best quality onions. Some of the largest sets tend to "double" or even go to seed. Sets are planted in the garden just as you would plant seedlings. Press each set into the soil, leaving just the top of the bulblet poking up through the soil. We plant our sets in holes made in black mulches about 5 plants abreast a 4-foot-wide row. Cultivate and harvest like any other onions. Other important members of the onion family—shallots and garlic—are also grown from bulblets (each individual garlic clove is considered a bulblet) and they are planted and cultivated like true onions. We have found however that we get our best and largest garlic from fall planting.

Saving seeds for true onions requires two seasons because onions are biennials that produce plants the first season and flowers the second. Flowers are pollinated by bees, and seed purity can be obtained by separating varieties by as much as a quarter of a mile. In northern gardens onions are grown as they would be for eating, then harvested; the best bulbs are reserved for seed production. Seed bulbs need to be cured and stored in a cool area. In regions where onions are hardy, they can be left in the ground and allowed to flower and seed naturally the following spring. Stored seed onions are replanted in the spring when they will develop flowers and seeds. Allow seeds to mature on the plants and collect them before they shatter. Dry the seed heads, rub seeds free, and store.

PARSNIPS

Pastinaca sativa

UMBELLIFERAE

WE THINK OF PARSNIPS as old-fashioned vegetables. Many of our elderly neighbors continue to grow them in their gardens but would never plant anything so modern as eggplant or even bell peppers. Parsnips are native to Europe and were used by Greeks and Romans. They are included in many old herbals. The plants made their way to colonial gardens at the beginning of the 17th century. The roots are very high in sugar and even contain some fat.

Parsnips are easy to grow, but they need a long season (100 days or more) to mature. We sow our seeds directly into the garden as soon in the spring as the ground can be prepared. Roots need a soil with good tilth, good fertility, and adequate moisture. Prepare soil as you would for carrots, making certain it is free of rocks. Enrich the site with compost or other organic matter, but avoid using fresh manures. See the section on carrots for a discussion of open ground seeding versus seeding through a dark mulch; either method will apply to parsnips. If you do seed in an open bed, we advise you to use radishes as a marker crop as parsnips are very slow to germinate. Marking the rows will allow you to weed and cultivate even before the parsnips are apparent. Check your catalogues for plant descriptions. Although there are only a few varieties offered, there are some new strains that offer higher germination rates. When young plants have developed, parsnips should be thinned to a distance of 3 inches apart. This is important for good root development. The crop is relatively trouble free, needing only adequate weeding and watering during any extreme dry spells.

Harvest usually begins as the weather turns cold; a few light frosts definitely improve root flavor by converting some of the starches to sugars. New England gardeners traditionally harvest a few parsnips for eating in the fall but leave the bulk of the planting in the ground over the winter for early spring harvest. The roots are a welcome spring treat and can be lifted and enjoyed just as soon as the ground thaws. If you leave plants in the ground, cover with a good mulch in case there is a very cold open winter without protective snow cover. Alternatively, you may harvest all the plants in the fall and store them in a root cellar like the carrots.

Seed saving is very easy. Plants are biennials with perfect flowers that are insect-pollinated. For seed purity, grow only one parsnip variety at a time. Seed plants need 2–3 feet spacing. Either thin the roots that were left in the ground to that spacing or select the best of the stored roots and replant them in the spring, burying them at or just below the crown. Seed stalks will develop into flowers in the summer, and seeds will mature to a light brown. Cut the whole stalk when most seeds are mature and before they begin to shatter. Clean, dry, and store.

A peanut plant pulled and ready to be dried. It takes a longer season than our own to produce large peanuts, but it's still fun to grow, dry, and roast these small nuts.

PEANUTS

Arachis hypogaea

LEGUMINOSAE

THIS SOUTH AMERICAN vegetable has done some considerable traveling to get to North American gardens. Portuguese explorers carried plants to Europe from where they were distributed to India, Africa, and the Far East. Peanuts were introduced to colonists in Virginia by African slaves. These plants have become one of the most important commercial crops in the South. It is interesting to note that these legumes are three times richer in calories by weight than beef.

Peanuts are not difficult to grow from seed if you have a good four months of warm weather for their development. A few catalogues offer varieties for northern growers. We have succeeded in growing peanuts in our Maine gardens, but the harvest was so small that the greatest rewards for our labors were not in the eating but in the experience of watching this plant's interesting life cycle. We still recommend that northern gardeners give them a try. They are especially appealing to children.

Peanuts are of course the seeds themselves. In our area we like to seed our plants indoors for an early start. Sow 2–3 seeds in peat pots or other plantable containers, covering seed with 1 inch of soil. Germinate at 65° to 75°F and allow 4–5 weeks for plants to develop inside before hardening them off for planting in the garden. When the weather has moderated outside, plant seedlings on raised beds at a distance of 12 inches between hills. Northern growers should use dark mulches and early covers for this crop.

In warmer regions with long growing seasons, peanuts can be seeded directly into the ground once the soils have warmed. Plant shelled, whole, unbroken peanuts to a depth of 1 inch, spacing them 12 inches apart. The soil should be very friable, fertile, and moderately moist. Plants have attractive cloverlike leaves. Peanuts grown on open ground benefit from being hilled early in their growth. Small yellow blossoms are self-pollinating, and once fertilized, they turn down toward the soil and produce their fruits underground. (If you have used plastic mulches remember to watch for this stage in plant growth so that you can pull back the mulch, allowing the fertilized blossoms to come in contact with the soil.) Depending on the variety, peanuts will produce pods that contain 2–5 seeds (what we commonly call peanuts). Plants are harvested at the end of the season when they start turning brown. This is done by carefully lifting the whole plant with a spading fork. Then gently shake off the soil so as not to loosen any pods. Hang the whole plant in a dry place to cure (where no mice can get at them). When they are thoroughly dry, remove the pods from the plants, and the peanuts are ready for storing raw or roasting. We like to use raw peanuts in cooking and roast nuts for snacks.

Seed saving is very simple. Select some of the very best and largest unroasted seeds and store them for the following year. They can be stored in their shells, which are removed just before planting.

PEAS

Pisum sativum, Garden Peas
Pisum sativum var. *macrocarpon,*
   Edible Pod Peas

LEGUMINOSAE

GARDEN PEAS ARE native to Eurasia and were cultivated by the Egyptians, Greeks, and Romans. Despite their long history as a food crop, peas were not grown to any large extent by Europeans until the middle of the seventeenth century. This vegetable was brought to colonial America by the first settlers. Although peas are indigenous to warm regions of the world, they thrive in climates with moderate summer temperatures and adequate moisture. Peas are ideal garden crops for Canadian and northern United States gardens. They are so easy to grow and so delicious that young children should be encouraged to grow peas in their first gardens. Our experience has shown that youngsters almost always prefer raw peas to cooked ones.

Plant by the middle of April and you can expect to have a harvest of fresh garden peas for the Fourth of July, still a tradition in this part of the country.

When we talk about garden peas, we are usually referring to the varieties grown for their edible inner seeds. Pea pods are shelled or shucked and the pods are discarded. The peas are then eaten raw or cooked. Like other legumes however peas can be grown primarily for their pods. We call them edible pod or snow peas, and they have long been a popular ingredient in Asian cooking. Some peas are consumed pod and pea together; these types are known as snap peas. They have a more tender pod than regular garden peas and are picked young when they are tender and sweet. All three types of peas are excellent sources of protein and soluble fiber. Cultural requirements are similar for all types.

We like to plant our peas as early as the ground can be worked, and in our area, that often means by mid-to-late April. There is an old tradition that calls for fresh garden peas for the Fourth of July. Early varieties need 55–65 days to develop, so we plant the early crop at least by the beginning of May. Many varieties of peas are offered in catalogues, so read through and be prepared to try several before deciding on your favorites. Varieties differ in vine size, pod size, dates to maturity, and flavor. There are even some varieties that are heat tolerant for summer sowing.

Seeds are sown to a depth of 1–2 inches. The warmer the weather, the deeper the planting, so that moisture is available for germination. We recommend using a bacterial inoculant on the seeds before sowing just as we do for beans. This encourages nitrogen-fixing bacterial growth on the plant roots, which will benefit plant production and garden soils alike. Since seeds are very large and easy to handle, we take the time to space them every 2–3 inches apart so that no thinning is necessary. Thinning is not advisable as a practice because it may disturb the sensitive young roots of adjacent plants. Although pea seeds need ample moisture, they can also be drowned or rotted by cold, heavy, waterlogged soils. Soils should be fertile with a pH above 6 and plenty of potassium and phosphorus. Don't use fresh manures; their nitrogen level is too high. We use raised beds for our peas and since we like to trellis all our varieties, we seed two parallel rows and run the trellis between them. Trellises conserve space, keep the vines off the ground for good air circulation, and make picking much easier. Peas are very susceptible to mildews and molds in warm weather. Good air circulation is the best prevention available to organic growers.

As the young pea vines develop size, it is helpful to carefully hill around the base of the plants. Cultivate with care as roots are close to the surface. If you are growing them on a plastic mulch for weed and moisture control, then it may be useful to cover the dark mulch with a light layer of hay when the weather turns warm, so that soil temperatures are lowered. Alternatively, peas grown on open ground may be mulched with a good hay or straw once plants have sized up and begun to climb their trellises. If a hay mulch is used, don't let it smother the base of the plants and cut off air circulation.

Harvest garden peas just as soon as pods are filled out and seeds are big enough to eat but definitely on the young side. Use peas as soon as they are harvested, when their sugar content is highest. Watch the vines every few days and keep young pods picked for longest production. Peas left on the vines to overripen will cut plant production. Use the same guidelines for edible pods and snap peas.

Seed saving is very easy for any of the peas. The plants have perfect flowers that are self-pollinating, so there is little insect pollination. If you are growing many different varieties that flower at the same time, ensure seed purity by separating pea varieties either by using a tall crop as a buffer or by planting at a distance of 100 feet. For each variety, watch plant production and mark and save seeds from the most vigorous plants that ripen early. Don't be inclined to eat all the best early peas and leave the last peas on the plants for seed production. In so doing, you will be selecting the least vigorous, latest maturing individuals for propagation. Leave seed pods on the chosen plants until the pods fully mature. They will lose their sheen and color and peas will actually rattle inside the pods. Pick, thresh, and dry seeds completely before storing. Since it is difficult to remove all moisture from pea seed, do not store the seeds in an airtight container. Any remaining moisture could turn your collection into a moldy mess. If you are saving several varieties of peas in any given season, be certain to label them carefully.

PEPPERS

Capsicum annuum Grossum Group
Capsicum annuum
   Longum Group

SOLANACEAE

sweet bell pepper

OVER THE PAST DECADE, seed catalogues have expanded their pepper varieties tremendously. Gardeners all over the country can choose from dozens of varieties that are suited to different gardening zones. While peppers are native to the New World tropics, successful cultivation is now possible in northern climates including Canada.

Garden peppers are divided into two basic groups—sweet and hot. Within those two groups there is great diversity of size, shape, color, texture, flavor, and growth rate. Sweet peppers are most commonly represented by the 3- or 4-lobed bell peppers,

HOT PEPPERS
DRIED, DECORATIVE, AND USEFUL

EVERY SEASON, we seem to find yet another variety of pepper to grow. Some are new sweet bell peppers, but most are mildly to seriously hot varieties. These hot types come in countless shapes and sizes, and we have yet to find one that does not preserve well by drying. Here are some tips.

Hot peppers are left on the plants to grow just as long as the fruit continues to mature and turn from its young color (almost always green) to its final hue, which can be a light orange or orange red or bright red or burgundy red. When the peppers are fully mature, they are picked and put into as warm and dry an environment as can be found. Our first choice of drying spots is our drying houses (converted greenhouses) where the temperatures on a sunny summer or fall day can reach as high as 100°–120°F. The peppers are spread out with room around each fruit on a screen table or paper covered table. Time permitting, we prick several small holes in each of the larger fruits to allow inside moisture to escape. Depending on the temperature and fruit size, individual peppers can dry in 2–3 days, or take up to a month to fully desiccate. During this time, we check the harvests routinely to pick out any fruit that may spoil before drying.

Besides using a drying house, we also take advantage of the heat above the kitchen woodstove once the stove is going again early in the fall. We have built wooden frames with screened bottoms and we layer the peppers in these frames and suspend them over the woodstove. We also dry individual fruits on a bread rack placed on the warming shelf of the woodstove.

For gardeners who have neither drying houses nor woodstoves, we recommend another method. Arrange the peppers loosely on a cookie sheet and leave the sheet in a conventional oven set on 100°–120°F for several hours. Check the peppers every few hours so that they do not burn. Keep the oven at very low temperatures or the peppers will not only dry but will lose their bright color and sheen in the process.

Hot peppers, depending on the varieties grown, will mature for drying from midsummer all the way until a first frost. Plants usually have abundant fruit at the time of the fall frost, and when this time arrives, we simply harvest the whole plant, stem and all, and hang the plant from a peg in the drying house until all of the fruits have lost their moisture.

Check each pepper to make certain that it is thoroughly dry before being used in decorative clusters, wreaths, or before being stored in sealed containers for culinary use in the months to come. We always like to make a number of dried hot pepper swags and wreaths for ourselves and as gifts. These peppers can be used in cooking if anyone has the heart to cut the decorative piece. The very best way to store dried fruit for cooking is in a glass container. Dark glass is best. If light jars are used, then store them in a dark place. Fruit properly dried and kept in this manner will be useful for years.

Dried peppers that are used in kitchen swags or wreaths are perfectly useful for cooking. Just check for dust and an occasional cobweb before use.

A good supply of dried peppers is welcome for flavoring winter meals.

but the group also includes some tapered and round cherry types. Although most gardeners grow sweet green bell peppers, this type is also available in yellow, orange, lilac, dark purple, and chocolate brown. Many of the sweet bell peppers, including the green, will mature to red if the seasons are long enough for the fruits to completely mature on the plants.

Hot peppers also are available in a great variety of colors, shapes, flavors, and pungency. Pepper pungency is measured in units called Scovilles. (See the box on page 149 for further information.) In response to our increasing interest in ethnic cooking, American gardeners can find a broad range of hot pepper varieties offered in seed catalogues. Some catalogues are now including information about the pungency of hot peppers to help gardeners make choices based on their eating habits.

Cultural requirements for sweet and hot peppers are similar. We start all of our plants indoors 10–12 weeks before the last frost. Seeds are covered lightly in the seed flats and germination takes place in about 10 days when soil temperatures are kept at 70°–80°F. Transplant into individual pots when seedlings develop their first set of true leaves and set the seedlings into the soil up to the base of the first true leaves. Grow on in a sunny location where temperatures remain above 60°F. Harden off the plants for setting out in the field when the soils have warmed up and night temperatures remain above 58°F. There is no point in rushing the process as many varieties will be shocked and drop their blossoms in cold weather, thus delaying fruit set and overall productivity. If you have timed your indoor seeding a bit early and find that your field transplants are setting first blossoms before you are even ready to harden them off and set them out, remove these early blossoms so that vigor remains in the vegetative production. The result will be more robust plants and greater yields.

Thai hot pepper

Peppers like a moderately fertile soil, good drainage, and a pH of 6 and above. Avoid fresh manures and too much nitrogen. We have also found that we get the best yields by planting our peppers rather close on a wide row, where smaller plants are set two abreast and larger

plants are staggered. When setting plants into the field, bury stems up to the first set of leaves. Pepper production is helped greatly in our area by the use of black mulches and some top protection, such as cloches, slitted row, or floating row, covers early in the season. Selecting a variety of sweet and hot peppers will give you a harvest of fruits over a very long season (50–75 days after setting out). Peppers will continue to set flowers and fruits until a hard frost, and we have noticed that while the plants are very tender in the spring, they are quite cold hardy at the end of the season, much more so than their close relative, the tomato.

Gardeners with limited space (even patio gardeners) can grow a wide variety of peppers as container plants. Follow the same practices for seedlings as for field growing, and when the weather is warm set out individual plants in sufficiently large containers and put them in full sun. Watch soil moisture, but do not overwater. Some of the small hot peppers are excellent both for eating and ornamental use. We like to bring in a few plants to brighten up the winter greenhouse. They are easy to care for but need to be checked for aphids and washed from time to time to remove any infestation.

Sweet peppers may be harvested as soon as they have any size to them. Some of the colored varieties, such as red sweet and chocolate, will start off green and then mature into their color, so these varieties will have to be left on the plants if you want them to turn color, but the fruits can be eaten even when young and green. Similarly many of the hot peppers set green fruits that mature into their final color. Peppers can be carefully twisted from their stems, but there is less stress on the plant if you harvest by cutting with a small pair of stem cutters or garden shears. Be careful when handling hot varieties, which contain high concentrations of the chemical capsaicin, a skin and eye irritant. Use rubber gloves when harvesting, cutting open, and cleaning any hot peppers. We have experienced some real discomfort by handling peppers without protection.

Peppers hold up well on the plants in the field, so pick fruits as you need them. At the end of the season, harvest all plants before a hard frost and store some fruit in the refrigerator where they will hold up well for several weeks. Peppers can also be cut up and frozen for winter cooking. Many hot varieties dry well

AMERICAN GARDENERS now have access to such a variety of pepper seeds that the choices are a bit daunting. Sweet bell peppers come in a profusion of shapes, sizes, colors, and tastes. It is the same with hot peppers. Current flavors are described as mildly hot, hot, very hot, dangerously hot, fiery hot, tangy, and spicy hot. When trying to make sense of these descriptions, it is helpful to know why and how "hotness" is defined in peppers.

The "heat" of a pepper is contained in one of its compounds known as capsaicin, and it is important to note that capsaicin is contained in all parts of the fruit's skin, flesh, and seeds. The level of capsaicin is measured in units called Scoville units, after Wilbur

The look and size of a pepper won't tell you anything about its heat. In the photo above, the tiny Thai hot peppers (middle right-hand frame) and the little orange fruit (middle left) are among the hottest of the lot.

Scoville. We can begin our interpretations by knowing that the familiar green sweet bell pepper has an average of 100 Scoville units. A jalapeño pepper contains 4,000–6,000 units. The Habanero pepper has a Scoville unit count of 200,000–350,000. Many seed companies list the Habanero as the hottest variety available. This small yellow/orange variety is widely grown in the West Indies where it is used in hot sauces. Long before we had any information beyond an adjective to describe its flavor, we grew, tried, and quickly excluded the Habanero from our gardens. It's not a pepper for the timid.

In recent years, a few seed companies have decided to be more helpful by including the Scoville index of

their pepper varieties with other descriptive information. Obviously, this information is very helpful when choosing which seeds or plants to grow.

Whatever hot peppers you do grow, remember to use some type of protective gloves when cutting or cleaning the fruit for cooking, canning, drying, or seed saving. The capsaicin burns the tongue and can also burn the skin and the eyes. When we are making large batches of our hot pepper relish for the farm shop, we wear goggles, a face mask, and gloves. We are not being overly cautious. Large kettles of boiling relish quickly fill an area with irritating vapors. If there were a device called the Scoville alarm, it would certainly go off in our kitchen.

especially if you have a hot dry shed or darkened greenhouse. We also dry some of our cooking and decorative hot types in a slow oven (about 140°F) for a few hours. If you are storing dried peppers for cooking, it is absolutely necessary to remove all the moisture until the fruits are crisp and brittle before putting them in sealed jars.

We have experienced very few problems with insects or diseases with pepper plants beyond the occasional cutworm, a few leaf holes from flea beetles, and some blossom drop during extremes in temperature, or dryness. Since peppers are members of the Solanaceae family (with tomatoes, eggplant, and potatoes), we are careful to practice crop rotation to avoid soilborne diseases. Insects that like nightshade family plants almost always choose to eat our eggplants and potatoes before they eat the peppers.

Saving pepper seed is simple. Flowers are self-pollinating, so there is little cross-pollination. Bees may occasionally travel from one plant to another; seed purity can be ensured by isolating varieties by about 50 feet. Seeds are mature when the fruits are mature, which is when they have reached their mature color. Select the earliest, most vigorous peppers from any variety. Cut open and remove seed (remember to take care with hot peppers), dry seeds, and store.

POTATOES

Solanum tuberosum

SOLANACEAE

IN THE PAST FEW YEARS, we have noticed that a few catalogues offer true seeds for potatoes, but most gardeners continue to use what are called seed potatoes for planting. Seed potatoes are actually very small whole tubers or cut up sections of tubers. If you are planting your first potatoes, purchase seed potatoes, which are available from gardening catalogues or local gardening centers. Purchase tubers certified as virus free, so you won't import diseases into your gardens. There are dozens of varieties available throughout the country; each region has its favorites. Check with other local growers, county extension offices,

and reputable garden centers before making variety choices. It is not advisable for several reasons to buy tubers for planting from your local supermarket. First, market varieties are sometimes sprayed with sprouting inhibitors; second, you have no way of knowing whether the tuber varieties are suited to your gardening climate.

To calculate the amount of seed potatoes for planting, we anticipate a yield of potatoes at least ten times the amount that we plant by weight. If we plant 50 pounds of Kennebec seed potatoes, we hope to harvest at least 500 pounds from that planting. Different varieties, soil, and seasonal conditions will affect yields, so it may take you a bit of experimenting before you can figure out what amounts you want to grow. Your decisions will also be affected by the amount of gardening space you have available and whether you want a crop for eating fresh or for both eating and storing.

Potatoes are very easy to grow and great fun to harvest in the fall. Each hill that is dug yields a different number and assortment of tubers. Digging potatoes is one of our favorite fall chores. But let's start at the beginning. Select your seed potatoes and prepare them either by planting whole tubers if they are very small (no more than 2 inches in diameter) or by cutting the tubers into planting pieces with at least 2 or 3 eyes on each section. Eye is the name for the spot where growth begins on the surface of the tuber. Planting can begin early- to midspring as soon as the ground is well prepared and drained. We plant our crops on raised beds covered with a black plastic mulch. Using a long-handled bulb planter, we make a deep hole every foot down the center of the row and bury one seed potato with 6–8 inches of soil in each hole. We have also planted successfully on open ground by trenching a row and planting one seed potato every foot and covering the seeded piece with several inches of soil. On these open beds we hill the potato plants as soon as they are a few inches tall and then again 1 or 2 times during the season, so that the individual plants are hilled several inches above the garden level by midsummer. This allows the tubers to develop in enough soil so that they are never exposed to the sun, which would cause them to turn green. Hay may also be used to mulch hills of potatoes on open ground. Hilling with soil or hay allows you to control weeds and moisture as well. All of this is simi-

Potatoes are stored by the bushel in our root cellar and usually last us the whole winter.

crop for storage before the beginning of October. Plants will mature, yellow, and wither in the field once the tubers have developed, but it is not necessary to harvest crops until you are ready to use or store the harvest. Tubers can remain in the ground, and we prefer to leave them there until the temperatures in our root cellar are cool. We harvest with a potato digger, a long-handled tool with curved narrow tines. A spading fork will also work; if you have none of these specialized tools, use a shovel. Be very careful to start digging far enough away from the center of the hill so that you do not cut or spear the tubers. Harvest them intact, especially for good storage. Different varieties of potatoes have different growth habits and you will be able to observe this with experience. Some potatoes set their tubers very tightly near the base of the plant and others set tubers very far apart. Some set tubers close to the surface and others go very deep. None of this is complicated, and digging is like a wonderful scavenger hunt. After a quarter of a century of growing potatoes, we still delight in discovering what each hill will yield. If you have grown only a few plants for eating right away, you can rinse off the potatoes and store them in a cool dark place (not the refrigerator). Any tubers that are going to be stored in the fall and winter should be allowed to dry for several hours outdoors so that most of the dirt simply falls off during collection. Store unwashed potatoes in baskets or buckets in a cool root cellar where the temperatures do not fall below freezing. If potatoes remain in storage for a period of time, and especially if the temperatures fall to near freezing, their starches turn to sugars and the potatoes will be sweeter in flavor. We try to store enough for eating all winter and even into late spring. When we have planned just right, we are eating the last potatoes from the root cellar just at the time that we are selecting our own seed stock for planting.

Potatoes are subject to a number of diseases, but the Colorado potato beetle is our main pest. If the problem is light and the planting is small, handpicking may be adequate for control. Once the beetles have had a chance to lay eggs (clusters are bright orange and usually laid on the undersides of the leaves) we use pyrethrum or rotenone for control. You can also use *Bacillus thuringiensis* var. *san diego* or var. *tenebrionis* to control young larvae, the larvae being that stage of insect growth that is least resistant to

larly accomplished by our current method of planting through black plastic, but all three approaches work well.

Potatoes like a soil that is slightly acidic, well drained, and enriched with adequate organic matter containing no fresh manures. Very young plants can endure light spring frosts but will be damaged by a heavy late spring freeze. Potato varieties do not need to be separated in the garden. Flowers are usually self-pollinating, but even if there is some insect cross-pollination, neither the first year's crops nor any ensuing production will be affected, even if you save your own tubers for propagation.

Generally, potatoes mature over a long season, but there is still great variety within the species. You may want to plant both early and late maturing crops so that you can harvest some "new potatoes" in the summer when you can boil them and dress them with dill and garlic fresh from the garden. We start eating from our garden by mid-August but seldom dig the whole insecticides. Young larvae can defoliate a plant very quickly if they are not destroyed. Some potato varieties are more susceptible to disease than others, so check plant descriptions. Crop rotation is very important with potatoes and their family members.

Once you have your first crop of potatoes (assuming you have a place for storage), you also have a supply of seed potatoes for the following season. Eat the biggest tubers and keep the small ones for replanting. Unlike other vegetables, potatoes can be propagated successfully from the smaller fruits. Do not store or use as seed any tubers that are diseased or questionably malformed. Destroy these and do not compost them, as soilborne diseases can easily be transmitted into the garden.

Pumpkins, see under Squashes

RADISHES

Raphanus sativus

CRUCIFERAE

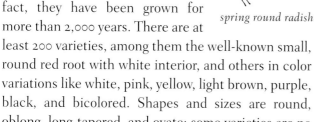

spring round radish

EASY TO GROW and early to harvest, radishes are included in many home gardens; in fact, they have been grown for more than 2,000 years. There are at least 200 varieties, among them the well-known small, round red root with white interior, and others in color variations like white, pink, yellow, light brown, purple, black, and bicolored. Shapes and sizes are round, oblong, long-tapered, and ovate; some varieties are no more than 1 inch in diameter and some weigh a pound and more.

Radishes are classified into two main types—the fast growing annual types sometimes called spring radishes, and the late storage winter types that are biennials. The latter category includes the increasingly popular daikon varieties.

Spring radishes can be sown directly into the garden as soon as the ground can be worked. They like a light friable soil with reliable moisture. Very heavy soils should be amended with composts, sand, or peat and raked into a smooth bed. If the soil is not friable

or lacks adequate moisture, radishes can develop rough, ill-shaped, and woody roots with poor texture and a hot unpleasant flavor. The seed is very easy to handle, so we like to prepare a small raised bed about 3 feet wide, and sow 3 or 4 rows abreast, spacing the seeds ½–1 inch apart. Cover the seeds with ¼–½ inch of soil, tamp the soil lightly, and make certain that the young seed bed doesn't dry out. Germination is

daikon radish

rapid (usually 5–6 days) and some varieties can be harvested as soon as 3 weeks after seeding. Spring radishes can be grown all summer long especially if you carefully choose hybrids that are developed for summer sowing, kinds that are slow bolting in warm weather. Some gardeners prefer the "French breakfast" and "white icicle" types for main season crops as they are less likely to develop the exceedingly hot flavor of some of the round reds when warm temperatures prompt very rapid growth. If you want a continuous crop of spring radishes, make successive plantings. These vegetables do not hold up in the ground nor do they store particularly well. They are best when harvested young; the fine, crisp, flavorful flesh deteriorates after 1 or 2 weeks even when refrigerated.

Spring radishes are also useful as a marker crop, interplanted with other seeds that are either very small or slow to germinate. We have used them in this way when seeding both carrots and parsnips. In so doing, the radish germinates quickly, marking the seeded row. As the radishes mature, they are harvested, making way for the main crop and aerating the soil at the same time. Marking a row in this way allows for early cultivation and weeding even before the main crop is visible. It is also a good space-saving device.

Winter radishes, including the various kinds of daikons and round black Spanish, are slower growing varieties, maturing between 50 and 80 days from seeding. These are best grown during cooler temperatures, so they should be seeded very early in the spring for eating fresh midsummer, or more typically, seeded midsummer for harvesting at the end of the season. Winter radishes are harvested before a heavy frost and stored in moist peat or sand in the root cellar like carrots. These varieties are good for eating fresh, pickling, and cooking. Cultural requirements are the same as for spring radishes except for the spacing dimensions used in the rows. Adjust for the larger root size; for best results, radishes should not be crowded.

Radishes do attract flea beetles, especially early in the season, and as members of the Cruciferae family, they are susceptible to the same diseases. Practice good crop rotation and use the same control methods as you do for other cabbage family plants.

Saving seeds for the annual types is very easy, but in order to collect the very best quality seed, you will need to pay attention to the growth habits of the individual plants. Don't simply save seed from the earliest roots that bolt and flower. In fact, these should be pulled and discarded from the seed bed along with those showing poor form or color. Watch for the earliest and best radishes to mature, and mark them for seed production. Leave them in the garden to go to seed and let the seeds mature fully on the plants. When pods are dry, cut off the stalks. Pods need to be cracked open by hand. Radishes will cross-pollinate with all other Cruciferae root crops, including turnip, rape, mustard, rutabaga, and wild varieties of mustards, as well as Chinese cabbage. Seed so that the plants will be isolated by a quarter of a mile.

Saving seed for the winter or storage radishes is a bit more demanding as these types are usually biennials. See the section on turnips and follow those seed saving techniques.

RHUBARB

Rheum rhabarbarum

POLYGONACEAE

ONE OF OUR FAVORITE old gardening books, *Vegetable Gardening* by Ralph L. Watts, published in 1912, has the following comment on rhubarb: "It belongs to the buckwheat family, Polygonaceae, and is a highly popular herbaceous perennial vegetable, being grown in nearly all home gardens." At first glance, we would not have given a second thought to this comment. Our family and many a neighboring family had well-established patches of rhubarb. It was one of the early spring treats—hot sweet sauces and pies—and we always put up a supply of canned rhubarb sauce for the winter. In fact, we continue to can and freeze rhubarb and never fail to run out of our supply before the next season.

But we think it is safe to say that not only is it not grown in nearly all home gardens but many people have never even tasted this vegetable. We have served rhubarb to many houseguests and watched them politely take a tiny serving and return enthusiastically for a second helping. We are usually asked how to prepare it. It couldn't be more simple. All we do is let the food processor chop fresh rhubarb stalks which we then layer with sugar in a glass or stainless steel (not aluminum) container. The whole kettle of pulp and sugar is then left for a few hours until the sugar draws the juice from the rhubarb so the sauce can be stewed in its own juices without additional water. Occasionally we have used some chopped angelica stalks to reduce the amount of sugar used. Watts's statement at the turn of the century only shows how foods come in and out of fashion. If Americans continue to rediscover gardening as a favorite hobby, perhaps rhubarb will be more commonly grown and enjoyed.

NO VEGETABLE could be easier to grow either from seed or purchased plants. There are several dozen varieties available from plants (commonly referred to as crowns), but catalogues usually offer seed for the variety 'Victoria', which is a heavy commercial producer. Rhubarb can be seeded directly into the ground and grown for a season before being transplanted into a permanent bed. Seed directly into the garden as soon as the ground is prepared in the spring. Cover seed with ½ inch of soil and germination will occur in 2–3 weeks. Thin seedlings about 6 inches apart, cultivate and weed the bed, and allow plants to develop in the nursery until the following spring. We like to prepare a separate bed for rhubarb, just as we do for asparagus. Soils should be rich and able to retain ample moisture. During early spring of the second year, lift and transplant young rhubarb plants, spaced about 3 feet apart. Plants can remain in a well-prepared bed for 5–10 years before needing to be thinned and rejuvenated. Allow the second year plants to develop in the permanent bed, taking care to keep the bed weeded and cultivated. A good summer mulching will help to control weeds and to conserve moisture. In the spring of the third season, light harvesting can begin as soon as the stalks have grown to size. Harvest by twisting off a few outside stalks from several different plants. Even after three or four seasons, do not harvest more than half of the stalks of any one plant at a time to leave some energy for growth. Harvest can continue for several weeks in the spring and early summer. Watch for any sign of flowering stalks and keep them cut from the plants (unless you are saving seeds), as flowering takes energy away from plant production. Very hot weather, dryness, and flowering will all cause production to decrease. This will be marked by the actual number of stalks produced as well as by a change in the taste and texture of the vegetable. When stalks become dry and pithy, harvesting should cease. Rhubarb does best in northern gardens. Plants require winter dormancy and may die where winters are too warm.

Other cultural requirements include maintaining a fertile bed, which we do by top- and side-dressing with manure in late fall when the ground has frozen or very early in the spring before the new shoots begin to emerge. Continue to mulch around the plants each year to conserve moisture. We have experienced no disease or insect problems with our rhubarb.

Rhubarb comes in varieties that differ in sugar content; in color (green to deep red, outer and inner stalks); and in plant size. One variety, 'Colossal', yields stalks so large it takes only one or two to make a pie. Some varieties like 'Victoria' produce a number of seed stalks, but others rarely or never produce seed. Rhubarb is grown for its leaf stalks only; the large leaves should never be eaten as they contain quantities of toxic oxalic acid. Leaves may be cut from stalks and composted or spread around the base of plants for weed control.

When rhubarb is grown from crowns, the crowns are planted in the bed at the same depth as they were grown, and light harvest can begin the second season. Depending on the variety grown and your soil quality, it may be desirable to lift, divide, and replant a bed every 5–10 years. Judge by the quality of stalks from season to season. If production declines in quality or yield, rejuvenation is easily done early in the season. When new growth is first apparent, lift old plants, and

with a sharp shovel or cutting tool, divide old crowns into several new plants, making certain that there is a bud with each root. If the center of the crown is woody, discard it. Replant divisions at the same depth and allow a season of growth before harvest commences again.

Saving rhubarb seed is very easy, but varieties will cross-pollinate because the flowers are insect-pollinated. Choose your most robust plants for seed production, not those that go earliest to seed. Mark the stalks of selected plants. Tall flower stalks will develop masses of tiny white flowers followed by seeds that ripen from light to dark brown. Pick seeds when ripe before they have fallen from the stalk. Dry and store.

Rutabaga, see under Turnip

SPINACH

Spinacia oleracea

CHENOPODIACEAE

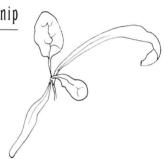

NEW ZEALAND SPINACH

Tetragonia tetragonioides

TETRAGONIACEAE

SPINACH IS ONE of the earliest crops that we harvest from our annual vegetable gardens. It is very easy to grow, and when harvested young, the leaves are tender, flavorful, and very high in nutritional value, including large amounts of vitamins A, C, B complex, and iron. Spinach prefers a cool soil with ample moisture. The climate of the maritime northwest is ideal for spinach production. The crop is sensitive to both day length and warm temperatures. We grow spinach by seeding some plants in peat pots indoors in early March and then transplanting small plants into the garden as soon as the weather has moderated and nighttime temperatures are unlikely to drop much below the freezing point. We seed most of our spinach directly into a well-prepared fertile bed as early in the spring as the ground can be worked. Seeds are easy to handle, should be covered by ¼–½ inch of soil, tamped well and kept moist during germination. Growth will appear in 1–2 weeks and leaves will be ready to harvest 40–50 days from seeding. Spinach likes soil with a neutral pH. Soils should also be fertile, but not overly rich in nitrogen.

Varieties of spinach differ from one another in leaf type (smooth to heavily savoyed), growth rate, and resistance to bolting. We like to mulch our plants with a light organic mulch as soon as they have attained sufficient size. The mulch keeps weeds in check, holds moisture in the soil, reduces soil temperatures, and keeps the leaves cleaner from dirt and rain splatter. Begin harvesting leaves from the outer part of several plants as soon as they are large enough and cut the entire plant for eating when the weather turns warm and before the plants show signs of bolting. Bolting causes both the flavor and the texture of spinach to quickly deteriorate.

Crops can be planted in late summer for fall harvest, an idea we often overlook because we are so busy with other vegetables. We are more inclined to plant a summer substitute for midseason to late fall harvest: New Zealand spinach is a good choice. New Zealand is a true perennial in warm climates and its nutlike seeds germinate as quickly as those of true spinach. Soak the seeds overnight in warm water and direct seed into the garden anytime from spring to midsummer. Plants have cultural requirements similar to spinach, but need more space to develop, so thin seedlings 8–12 inches apart. Plants will tolerate dryer soils, but we still like to mulch for cleaner leaves at harvesttime. Leaves will be ready to harvest in 50–70 days. The tender young leaves are cut from the plants, which go on branching and producing until a heavy frost.

Saving seed for true spinach is easy but requires some attention to plant characteristics if high quality seed is desired. The plants are wind-pollinated, so a single variety should be grown. There will be variety within a single planting, as some plants have male flowers, some female, and some have both. It is important to pull or cut and discard the plants earliest to bolt to discourage early bolting as a characteristic of the seed. Then allow a few vigorous plants to develop flowering stalks and pods. Flowers are difficult to recognize because they lack petals, but when the plants turn yellow, pull them and collect seeds from the stalks.

New Zealand spinach seed saving is more demanding because the plant takes a longer season to produce flowers and seeds. If you do want to save your own seed, start some plants inside early in the season or start some in a cold frame. Transplant hardened off plants in the field after danger of frost has passed. Plants are slow to bolt, but some individuals should have time to flower and produce several pods. Collect pods before they shatter, dry, and store the seeds.

SQUASHES AND PUMPKINS

Cucurbita maxima, Cucurbita mixta,
Cucurbita moschata, Cucurbita pepo

CUCURBITACEAE

SQUASHES AND PUMPKINS ARE wonderfully easy to grow and there are so many different varieties offered that gardeners are certain to find types that are suited to their climates, garden size, and eating tastes. Squashes

acorn squash

are divided into two categories—summer squashes and winter squashes (including pumpkins).

Summer squashes require a short growing time, are eaten either raw or cooked, and are not intended for storage. They include yellow straight-necked and crook-necked squash, zucchini and cocozelle, vegetable marrow, scalloped, and patty pan types. The seeds of all these varieties are large and easy to handle, so plants may be started indoors or seeded directly into the ground after all danger of frost has passed. We usually plant both ways to ensure as early a harvest as possible. Indoor planting takes place about a month before the last frost. Bury 2–3 seeds each ½ inch deep in individual peat pots or other biodegradable containers which can be planted directly into the garden to avoid disturbing the root systems of the squash seedlings. Indoor plants should have true leaves by the time you are ready to set out the plants, but they should not have been stressed into forming flower buds because this will cause the plants to be weak and unproductive. You want to set the seedlings into the garden to develop a sizable vegetative growth before flowering commences. If you have seeded your plants too early, pinch off any flowering parts to stimulate further leaf growth. Space young plants 2–3 feet apart, depending on the variety. Most summer squashes are bush types which require relatively little room in the garden compared to some of the long-vining winter types. All squashes need moisture, full sun, and good fertile soil with ample amounts of organic matter. Sections of your garden that are most fertile are appropriate spots for winter squashes and pumpkins because these are heavy feeders.

Summer squashes are also seeded directly into the garden by burying 2–3 seeds per hill every 2–3 feet when the ground has warmed. There is little to be gained by planting too early as seeds will not germinate in soils that are too cool. Young transplants and seedlings benefit from a soil-warming mulch and protective cloches. Even in northern gardens, there is time for 2–3 plantings for a continuous fruit supply, which we actually do not find necessary because our original plantings produce until the first frost. Notice that the plants set flowers, male first and then female, and fruit begins to swell at the base of the pollinated female flowers. Fruits will be ready to harvest early in the summer, 40–60 days from planting. Summer squash should be enjoyed when it is young and tender. It can be eaten raw, skin and all, at this stage. If you harvest older fruits, you may need to peel and cook them. Young fruits are excellent in stir-fry dishes. If you find that you have more squashes than you can consume (witness the appearance of so many zucchini cookbooks), continue to pick off and compost the developed fruit so that the plants will go on flowering and producing. Squashes left to ripen on the plants will cause the plants to cease production. Plant production can also be curtailed by lack of soil fertility, inadequate moisture, or the presence of disease. If this happens, start a new planting in another section of the garden.

Winter squashes include an even larger number of varieties, most notably the acorns, butternuts, buttercups, hubbard, delicata, spaghetti, pumpkins, and gourds. These varieties require a longer growing season, 70–110 days. When choosing the kinds you want to grow, pay attention to the information in seed catalogues and consult those that specialize in varieties for your area. Winter squashes are available in both bush and vining types, so your garden size will be a factor in choosing seeds. The cultural requirements are similar to those for summer types, but there is little advantage to seeding pots indoors, since you will not hurry along the maturing of fruit in so doing. Winter squash require a long, warm, sunny season and rich soil that retains moisture. In fact, our best plants each year are those that we seed directly into the com-

A close look will show the difference between the male and female summer squash blossoms. The male flower extends out from the plant on a long stem. The female flower is held close to the base of the plant and can be seen still on the end of the developing ovary, or young fruit. This general difference in structure and arrangement is consistent on the various members of the Cucurbitaceae, or squash family.

LEARNING TO PUT FOOD BY requires knowing what method to use for each and every fruit and vegetable. Some things need to be harvested and stored in a cool humid environment. Others need immediate refrigeration. Some vegetables need a period of post-harvest warmth to cure, the process by which they form a protective outer layer that essentially becomes the vegetable's own storage package. Examples of vegetables that need warmth before storage are winter squashes, pumpkins, and gourds, all members of the Cucurbitaceae family.

When these vegetables are first harvested, their skins are easily pierced by a fingernail or bruised by rough handling. For this reason, pick and haul in these crops with care as bruise marks can easily turn into spots that begin to soften and rot during storage. Late summer and early fall, we harvest any squashes or pumpkins individually for eating, but leave the entire crop to mature as long as possible on the vine. Just before a hard frost we pick the vines clean and spread out the vegetables on the benches of our empty greenhouse where they can dry and cure in the warmth of the sun. Greenhouses, enclosed porches, warm windowsills, or any warm dry locations can be used for this purpose. Don't, however, use damp cool garages for the first curing.

Over a period of 2–3 weeks the outer shells thicken and harden. Pack the squashes loosely in boxes or baskets and store where they will last through the winter and early spring. Before packing, look them over for soft spots, cut away around these spots, and use these vegetables first. From week to week during the winter, check the baskets to find any squashes that may have developed a soft spot or mold and remove them from the storage area. We find that the temperature (50°–65°F) and

humidity level of our regular farmhouse basement offer the most convenient place to store this crop. We have left some cured squashes in the farmhouse kitchen, but the temperatures are a bit too high (65°–70°F with the woodstove going) and a bit too dry. The squashes are usable but overly dry in the centers.

Winter squashes also have variable storage times. Our experience has shown us that the hubbards, buttercups, and acorns store the longest, the butternuts next, followed by the delicata and pie pumpkins. It's been so long since we have grown large field pumpkins that we don't recall their storage life. Most never made it past Halloween anyway, and those that did spent their final hours in the pig pen. But we have succeeded in storing fruit from all other varieties until early spring. Squash are such a handy food to have on hand. An entirely satisfactory lunch can be made by halving and baking a delicata or acorn squash stuffed with applesauce, nuts, and raisins. This quick meal is so easy that we tend to overdo it. By the time April arrives, we are ready to abandon winter fare for anything that is fresh, green, and crunchy.

As curing progresses the rinds become thicker and colors deepen.

butternut squash

post pile behind our horse barn. If you have any doubts about the fertility of your garden soil, take the time to enrich the hills beneath each squash planting with a shovel or two of good compost or manure. Side-dressing midseason will also give the plants a boost. Winter squashes and pumpkins that vine are best planted on the outside rows of the garden where they can sprawl without competing with other crops. Some gardeners plant squashes among the hills of corn. We have not found this successful, because it makes it difficult to hill the corn and the vigorous corn stalks rob the squash plants of full sun as well as soil moisture and nutrition.

Late in the summer, a few specimens will ripen from each of the varieties we plant. It is always a treat to bake the first delicata for dinner, but we grow our winter squashes mainly to harvest all at once before a hard frost. Once harvested we set out the fruits in a very warm sunny spot, usually an empty greenhouse bench, where the

delicata squash

squashes are fully ripened and cured for 1 or 2 weeks. During this time, the skins thicken, harden, and dry. Then the squashes and pumpkins are stored in a dry warm spot for the fall and winter. When properly cured, the squashes are clean and delicious and will last well into the following spring. Some of the winter squashes store longer than others; the hubbards, buttercups, butternuts, and pie pumpkins are the most long-lasting. Check your stored fruit every week or so. If you see blemishes forming, cook the fruits and eat them soon or store the fruits, fully cooked and seasoned, in the freezer for eating later.

Although we have treated pumpkins in the section with winter squashes, there is a considerable variation in pumpkins when it comes to using them in the kitchen. You may want large pumpkins for decorative purposes, but they have little to no flavor when compared to the smaller cooking and pie-making varieties. The cooking varieties will have smoother, deeper col-

ored, and sweeter flesh. The mini-varieties are used both for decoration and for eating. It took us several seasons to find our favorite eating varieties of both squashes and pumpkins, so you may want to experiment with these vegetables for several seasons. We have also noticed over the past few decades that seed catalogues are offering more unusual varieties, which we continue to sample.

Both summer and winter squashes are susceptible to the same diseases and predation. Our problems are mainly with the striped cucumber beetles early in the season and squash bugs later. We either hand-pick or use rotenone or pyrethrum if infestations are heavy. Also check the undersides of the leaves from time to time for egg clusters and if you see leaf damage on the plants, remove

hubbard squash

infected leaves. We have had little trouble with predation except when we leave the squashes too long in the late summer garden. Mice find the mature fruits before we do. They will nibble on the skin and flesh and burrow into the middle of the fruit to collect seeds. Slightly damaged fruit can still be harvested, but it should be cleaned, cooked, and either eaten immediately or cooked and frozen for later use.

Saving seeds for your own squashes and pumpkins is just as easy as growing them, but in order to be certain of saving pure seed, you will need to understand the relationships between the members of the genus *Cucurbita*. Squashes and pumpkins will not cross-pollinate with other cucurbits such as cucumbers and melons, but they will cross-pollinate with each other within the same species, and according to some botanists, they will occasionally cross-pollinate across species. So if you plan to save seeds for varieties to come true, you will need to know how both summer and winter squashes are classified.

summer squash

These vegetables are divided into four separate species. *Cucurbita pepo* includes all the summer squashes, most pumpkins, and certain winter squashes, such as acorns, vegetable gourds, spaghetti, and delicata. These squashes are the quickest to mature and have some of the smallest seeds of the group.

Next comes *Cucurbita maxima*, which includes hubbards, buttercups, and delicious squashes. The seeds of these types *zucchini squash* are larger and prefer an even warmer soil for germination; members of this group need 90–100 days to maturation.

Cucurbita moschata includes the butternut squashes, which also require a very long, warm growing season.

The species least familiar to home gardeners, *Cucurbita mixta,* includes the cushaw squashes.

So, for example, you would have little difficulty saving seeds from your garden delicata when grown near the buttercups and the butternuts. But if your garden includes acorns and delicatas in close proximity, you may end up with seed that produces some unusual offspring. We chose those two examples specifically because our compost has sported just such a cross, judging from appearance and taste and previous garden records. The result just luckily turned out to be a delicious, productive type, but there have been other ones in that same compost pile that were watery, unattractive, and useless.

So if you want seed purity, you will need to isolate species from each other by as much as 500 feet to a quarter of a mile. Squash and pumpkin plants are monoecious. The male flowers are usually the first to blossom and have longer stems that hold the flowers away from the plant. Female flowers are set almost stemless and close to the plant. Plants are insect-pollinated and fruits are set only on female flowers. If you are willing and able to isolate species, or to grow only one species, or to go to the trouble of protecting and hand-pollinating individual plants, then it is easy to save your own pumpkin and squash seeds. Fruits are simply allowed to mature as they would normally. With summer squash this means that some fruits would be left on the plant long after they are suitable for eating so that the seeds can mature. Fruit will be large, hard, and almost gourd-like. Mature fruits of all types are harvested and cut open; seeds are then scooped out. We separate and discard as much of the fleshy membrane as possible, washing the pulp away. We spread out the seed to dry thoroughly. When absolutely dry, discard any hollow or misshapen seeds, separate any that are stuck together, and store.

TOMATILLO

Physalis ixocarpa

SOLANACEAE

THE TOMATILLO, a close relative of the tomato, is found in more catalogues, now that our eating habits are influenced by exposure to different ethnic foods. Tomatillos are common to Hispanic cooking. They are a necessary ingredient in salsas, and we also enjoy them in stir-fry cooking and fresh salads. The plants resemble their close relative, *Physalis alkekengi,* the perennial commonly known as Chinese lantern, both in leaf shape and pod formation. Tomatillo pods however produce large, round green fruit that ripens to pale yellow or purple as the husks split open. The plants are harvested as the husks split when the fruits are mature, and still firm. If left too long on the plant, fruits soften, become punky, and the texture and flavor deteriorate.

Tomatillos are grown with the same seeding and transplanting methods used for tomatoes. Refer to that section for complete instructions. When it comes to growing the plant in the field, cultural requirements also follow those for tomatoes, but tomatillos may be staked or allowed to sprawl. We have grown our plants both ways. Smaller varieties (up to 3 feet tall) can sprawl without taking up too much garden space, but larger varieties (up to 5 feet tall) are best staked, both for space and ease of harvest. Unstaked plants tend to ripen fruits a bit earlier because sunlight is more available to the centers of the plants.

Fruits will begin to ripen mid-to-late summer and continue until a heavy frost. Tomatillos are subject to the same insect and disease problems as tomatoes, so similar treatment and crop rotation are recommended.

Tomatillos, either green or purple, are easily grown all over the country. They should be harvested when the husks split to reveal the fruits within.

Seed saving is very easy. A few robust early fruits are left on the plants to mature completely. They will grow very pale in color and soften on the vines. Pick fruit, scoop out the center seed, clean membranes, and soak seed and any remaining pulp in water for several days. Finish cleaning, sorting, and storing as you would for tomatoes.

TOMATOES

Lycopersicon lycopersicum

Lycopersicon lycopersicum var. *cerasiforme.*
   Cherry Tomato

Lycopersicon lycopersicum var. *pyriforme.* Pear Tomato

SOLANACEAE

IT IS THOUGHT that tomatoes are native to Peru and Ecuador, and that they spread northward to Mexico where they were introduced to Europe by Spanish explorers. Tomatoes were accepted more readily by southern Europeans and included in their gardens and cooking well before they caught on in the north. American settlers also showed a reluctance to tomato culture, presumably because they were suspicious of its edibility. They may well have been uncomfortable with one of its early names, "love apple," or "*pomme d'amour.*" After growing tomatoes as ornamental plants in the early part of the nineteenth century, Thomas Jefferson brought them into the kitchen, and by the 1820s and 1830s, this vegetable began to be included more commonly in home gardens.

It is hard to imagine any reluctance to growing tomatoes today. Widely adapted to growing conditions and different soils, tomatoes are a favorite garden plant. There are several hundred varieties offered for sale in both popular and specialty catalogues. There is also broad variation within the varieties—in color, shape, size, flavor, texture, and rate of maturation. Unlike the extensive hybridization of corn, which has produced vegetables with better taste and performance, hybridization work with tomatoes has contributed mainly to the development of fruits that are more disease tolerant and more suitable to mechanical harvesting, long-term storage, and shipping. Seed catalogues offer a number of old open-pollinated tomato seeds along with many new hybrid types. When it comes to taste, some of the old fashioned varieties remain the best. When choosing tomato varieties to grow, steer away from hybrids recommended for storage and shipping. Leave those to the commercial growers and direct your choices toward those varieties known for their vigor and flavor.

Tomatoes come in shades of red, pink, purple, yellow, and orange; solid colors and stripes. The large, late season slicing types usually require up to 90 days of warm weather to mature. There are medium to large pear shaped types with extra meaty interiors making them most suitable for canning and sauces. There are many small and medium slicing types that mature at 50–75 days. Very small tomatoes like cherry and pear types are also offered in a range of size and color. Varieties are generally divided into two types named to describe the plant growth habit, called determinate and indeterminate. Determinate plants are smaller with shorter vines that end in a flower cluster. Once the vine has made moderate growth, it develops flowers and fruits but will not go on setting new growth. Determinate tomatoes can be cherry or slicing types, as the description applies to plant growth, not fruit size or color. Determinate plants are the earliest to mature fruit and are not usually staked or caged in the garden.

Indeterminate plants continue to grow and set flowers and fruit until a frost kills the plants. The indeterminates come in different sizes and are usually ripe by mid- to late summer. These tomatoes are usually best grown by staking, caging, or trellising. Both determinate and indeterminate tomatoes can be grown as container plants, assuming you have appropriate containers.

We seed all of our plants inside in the greenhouse about 6–8 weeks before the weather warms. Cover

We use bushels of Italian paste tomatoes each season to make quarts of marinara sauce for the year. These tomatoes are best because they have so much meat and so little juice, so they cook down quickly to a thick paste.

seeds lightly and germinate at temperatures of 70°–75°F. Seedlings appear in 5–6 days. When they have their first set of true leaves, transplant into flats or individual pots, burying the stems up to their first set of true leaves. Don't rush the season with tomatoes. You want stocky short plants when you are ready to set them out into the field. Plants that have been held too long indoors are inclined to be spindly and weak and their production may be affected. Harden off young plants after all danger of frost has passed and the soil is warm. Tomatoes like a good fertile soil with ample organic matter without too much nitrogen. When our plants begin to set fruit, we usually give them a foliar feeding of fish emulsion or soluble seaweed.

THERE IS NOT a bottled salsa made anywhere that compares to one that you can make at home entirely from fresh ingredients. If you think that this is overstated, let us explain further. There are probably hundreds if not thousands of brands of salsa now on the market. We are told that salsa has even replaced catsup as America's favorite condiment. But salsa in jars has to be cooked and processed to be sold, so it is not the same thing as a freshly made, hand-cut, uncooked salsa. And therein lies all the difference. If you are a salsa fan and have only tasted the very best of the bottled kinds, here's a recipe that you might want to try.

Add some good homemade corn tortillas and cheese and this can become a meal in itself.

12 firm ripe Italian paste tomatoes
4 sweet green bell peppers
5 vine ripened tomatillos
1 vine ripened standard red tomato
1 small hot pepper (jalapeno or chili)
3 cloves of garlic
1/2 cup of cilantro leaves
1 large onion
1 tablespoon vinegar

Pick, wash, dry, and dice into very small pieces the first three ingredients. Place the remaining ingredients into a food processor and chop only until everything is well-cut and blended but not overly pulverized. Alternatively, you may dice, chop, and mince the remaining ingredients, but we find that you will spend enough time handling the first three so that you will enjoy using a processor for the rest. Finally mix all of the chopped and diced ingredients thoroughly by hand in a large mixing bowl. Taste and adjust the hotness of the salsa by adding more hot peppers or the tang by adding a bit more vinegar. If the salsa is too juicy, drain off some of the juice; if it is too dry, chop in another vine-ripened standard red tomato. Finally (if you have the willpower) let the salsa sit out at room temperature for 1–2 hours (or even longer) so that the flavors blend. You will notice that we have not included salt in the recipe simply because we use very little salt in any of our cooking. If you find that the flavor lacks the salt you may want to add a bit to suit your taste.

We try to make a large supply of this recipe to have salsa on hand for a week or so. If you double or triple the recipe you won't necessarily want to double or triple the amount of hot pepper. Experiment and modify this recipe to your own taste. Once made, store any leftover in the refrigerator in a covered glass container. Allow salsa to warm to room temperature for best flavor before eating.

Although we touted the excellence of fresh salsa, we also enjoy having some of our own processed for winter use. We triple or quadruple the same basic recipe above (salt, to taste, is a good addition for the canned salsa), and then heat the salsa to the boiling point in a large stainless steel pot. Once boiling, turn down the heat and continue to stir and boil gently for no longer than 5–10 minutes. The longer you boil the ingredients, the less texture they will have. You don't want to overcook the salsa, but you must make certain that the whole mixture is hot enough to can safely. Have glass canning jars sterilized and ready so that you can pack the jars with hot salsa, seal, and then process a pint or quart jar for about a half hour using the water bath method. Cooks living in different parts of the country or at different elevations should check with their area extension agents for recommended times for processing all canned foods.

We set out all our tomato plants on raised beds with plastic mulch, spacing plants 1½–4 feet apart depending on the varieties. Small determinate plants are allowed to sprawl, but we do stake or trellis all of our indeterminate tomatoes. Tomatoes are greatly assisted by cloches or row covers early in the season. When planting, remember to bury the plants deep into the soil, at least up to the first set of leaves. If you have any leggy plants (we've all had this experience), plant them by laying them on their side, burying the long stem, and supporting the top growth upward with a mound of soil.

We like to set our stakes and trellises when we plant so that there is no injury to plant roots. Use strips of cloth or heavy twine (baling twine is very good) to tie stems to stakes, and be careful that you continue to tie stems as they develop so they don't fall over and break. There is a common practice of training large indeterminate tomato plants to two main stems by pinching all suckers after choosing the growing stems. We don't use this practice, but it means there will be more tying to keep the plants under control. Alternatively, tomato cages are very easy to install and eliminate tying altogether.

Plants that are not grown on a dark mulch will have to be weeded and cultivated, and this should be done carefully to avoid damaging the roots. When working around the plants, it is advisable to bring soil up around the stems a few times early in the season to provide support. Plants on open ground can also be side-dressed midseason with compost or well-rotted manure if soils are not fertile. Otherwise you will not usually need any additional feeding. It is a good idea to mulch tomato plants before the fruits begin to size up, but wait until midseason so that the straw or hay mulch will not cool the soils and slow plant growth. Tomatoes that are allowed to develop and ripen on a mulch are cleaner to pick and less likely to have blemishes or signs of rotting where they touch the soil. Mulch will also keep moisture in the soil, and tomatoes need continuous moisture for good production.

When it comes to harvesting tomatoes, leave the fruit on the plants to ripen. There is nothing to match the flavor of vine ripened fruit. Pick from the garden daily as you are ready to use the fruit, and if you do

Most of our garden tomatoes are open-pollinated varieties from which we are able to save our own seed. Clockwise from the top left, they include Brandywine, a selected strain of Heinz, Yellow Taxi, standard Heinz, Cheerio, Yellow Pear, and Whippersnapper.

need to pick fruit early, leave it at room temperature. Refrigerated tomatoes quickly lose their wonderful texture and flavor. You will be harvesting until a heavy frost, so do whatever freezing and canning you need throughout the late summer. Just before a frost you can harvest both partially ripened and green tomatoes. Spread out partially ripened fruit in a warm place and they will continue to ripen over a period of several weeks. Fruits ripened indoors will not have the flavor of vine-ripened fruit, but by mid- to late October, we welcome the last of the harvest. Thoroughly green tomatoes will not turn color, but may be used in chutneys, pickles, and delicious mock mincemeats.

We have had very little disease or insect problems with tomatoes. Flea beetles do some damage to leaves in the spring, but it is of little consequence. Tomato hornworms can be handpicked. Potato beetles always prefer the potatoes or eggplants. Tomatoes are sub-ject to early and late blight as well as verticillium and fusarium wilt. Where these diseases are a problem, look for resistant varieties, set out only strong, healthy, young plants, and eliminate and destroy any infected plants. Also make certain to rotate tomato crops each season along with all other family members, including potatoes, peppers, eggplants, and tomatillos.

Tomato seeds are very easy to save, and if you have found some delicious old open-pollinated varieties, it would be advisable to do your own saving. Plants have perfect flowers that are seldom insect-pollinated, so even gardeners with small plots can save several varieties in a season. Watch the plants as they develop and note the most vigorous and productive individuals for saving seed. Allow fruits to ripen on the plants as you would for eating and pick when fully ripe. Clean out the seed pulp into a dish, and add a little water. Stir seeds and pulp for several days and the liquid will begin to ferment. The seeds will fall to the bottom of the dish. Top matter can be lifted or poured off. Seed is then washed to remove all pulpy matter. It may be necessary to wash a couple of times and allow another 1 or 2 days of fermentation and cleaning to take place until all pulp is removed from the seeds. Chapter 7 contains a more extensive description of seed cleaning. Spread out seed to dry, separate any seeds that are stuck together, and store.

TURNIP

Brassica rapa Rapifera Group

RUTABAGA

Brassica napus Napobrassica Group

CRUCIFERAE

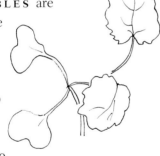

THESE TWO VEGETABLES are being treated in the same section because their cultural requirements are similar, they are close relatives, and we want to clarify the differences between the two. Turnip is the name given to the summer root crop that is rapid-growing, harvested young, and used at the time of harvest. Its greens are also edible. Summer turnip is not suitable for storage. The most popular garden catalogues offer very few varieties, but several dozen are available through specialty catalogues. The roots are all white or white with purple tops and are milder tasting than the winter turnips or rutabagas. Turnips may be seeded directly into the garden anytime that the ground can be prepared from early spring to late summer. Prepare a smooth friable seedbed and cover seeds with ¼–½ inch of soil. Turnips prefer soils with a pH above 6 and they suffer when soils have a boron deficiency.

Boron deficiency can be corrected with an application of agricultural borax. Germination will take place in several days to a week. Plants should be thinned to 6 inches apart and the greens are excellent fresh or steamed. Roots can be harvested as soon as they have any size, but before they are too large, 30–50 days from seeding. Young tender turnips are the most delicious.

Rutabaga, also known as Swede turnip or winter turnip, is the traditional turnip served with Thanksgiving dinner. This vegetable can also be seeded directly into the garden from early spring to early summer, but it needs a much longer growing season to develop (90–100 days). Rutabagas are typically buff-colored with a slight purplish cast at the top of the root, but there are white, green, and purple varieties. While they are hardier than turnips, rutabagas are also less tolerant of hot weather, and so they are grown primarily in northern gardens. Rutabagas are not grown for their greens so the seeding can be done a bit more carefully to avoid having to thin the crop to its final spacing of 6–8 inches between plants. We like to sow both our summer and winter turnips in a wide row, with three or four rows abreast. Rutabagas can be harvested as soon as roots attain edible size, but usually this crop is harvested after the early fall frosts and stored for winter use. Store by cutting off the leafy tops and packing the roots in moist sand as you would carrots. We have also dipped the cleaned roots into paraffin and then stored them in a cool root cellar. Notice that supermarket roots are often waxed to prevent dehydration. Both types of turnips are subject to the same pests and diseases as other members of the cabbage family and should be treated accordingly.

Saving seeds for turnip and rutabagas is not difficult but it is time-consuming, as each of the crops is a biennial. Perhaps the best method of saving seed is to use the root-to-seed method. This means planting either kind so that harvest will be done in the fall. Choose only the best specimens from either type for replanting the following spring. Harvest the roots and cut off the tops, leaving about 1 inch of leaf stubble, then store the roots in moist sand in a near-freezing site, such as a root cellar. The following spring the roots are replanted about 12–18 inches apart with the crowns at ground level. Seed stalks need to be watched so that seed pods are collected before splitting. Since the flowers of these vegetables are insect-pollinated, they will cross easily with each other as well as with radishes, mustards, and Chinese cabbage. A distance of at least 200 feet is recommended between types, and even more if seed purity is desired. When winters are not too severe or when gardeners mulch crops heavily, it is often possible to leave crops in the ground over the winter the first season and the roots will produce seed stalks the second season.

Both turnips and rutabagas have been cultivated for nearly four thousand years. The plants originated in Europe but quickly spread all over the world. Crops have been used as human and animal food. The roots of finer texture have made their way to the dinner table, but large coarser forms are used to feed livestock.

Vegetable Flower Type and Seed Longevity Chart

VEGETABLE COMMON NAME	FLOWER TYPE(S)	DIOECIOUS MONOECIOUS	POLLINATION	ANNUAL BIENNIAL PERENNIAL	AVERAGE SEED LONGEVITY IN YEARS
ASPARAGUS	imperfect	dioecious	cross	P	5–6
BEANS	perfect		self	A	1–5
BEETS	imperfect/perfect	dioecious	cross	B	2–4
BROCCOLI	perfect		cross	A	3–4
BRUSSELS SPROUTS	perfect		cross	B	3–4
CABBAGE	perfect		cross	B	3–5
CABBAGE, CHINESE	perfect		cross	A	3–5
CARROTS	perfect		self or cross	B	2–3
CAULIFLOWER	perfect		cross	B	3–5
CELERY	perfect		self	B	3–5
CHARD, SWISS	imperfect/perfect	dioecious	cross	B	2–4
CORN	perfect	monoecious	cross	A	2–3
CUCUMBER	perfect	monoecious	cross	A	4–5
EGGPLANT	perfect		self	A	2–3
GOURDS	imperfect/perfect	monoecious	cross	A	3–5
KALE	perfect		cross	B	4–6
KOHLRABI	perfect		cross	B	3–5
LEEKS	perfect		self	B	1–2
LETTUCE	perfect		self	A	4–5
MELONS	imperfect/perfect	monoecious	cross	A	4–5
OKRA	perfect		self or cross	A	1–2
ONIONS	perfect		self	B	1–2
PARSNIPS	perfect		self	B	1–2
PEANUTS	perfect		self	A	3–5
PEAS	perfect		self	A	2–4
PEPPERS	perfect		self or cross	A	2–4
POTATOES	perfect		self	A	1
PUMPKIN AND SQUASH	imperfect	monoecious	cross	A	3–5
RADISHES	perfect		cross	A	4–5
RHUBARB	perfect		self	P	2–3
RUTABAGA	perfect		cross	B	4–5
SPINACH AND NEW ZEALAND SPINACH	imperfect/perfect	dioecious	cross	A	1–3
TOMATILLO	perfect		self	A	3–5
TOMATO	perfect		self	A	3–5
TURNIP	perfect		cross	B	4–5

Indoor Vegetable Seeding Chart

COMMON NAME	SCIENTIFIC NAME	FAMILY	SEEDS (M) PER OUNCE (APPROX.)	GERM. TEMP. °F
ASPARAGUS	*Asparagus officinalis*	Liliaceae	7–10	70–75
BROCCOLI	*Brassica oleracea* Botrytis Group	Cruciferae	6	70
BRUSSEL SPROUTS	*Brassica oleracea* Gemmifera Group	Cruciferae	7	70
CABBAGE: COMMON, SAVOY, RED	*Brassica oleracea* Capitata Group	Cruciferae	7	70
CABBAGE: CHINESE, PAK CHOI	*Brassica rapa* Pekinensis or Chinensis Group	Cruciferae	9	70
CAULIFLOWER	*Brassica oleraceae* Botrytis Group	Cruciferae	8	70
CELERY	*Apium graveolens* var. *dulce*	Umbelliferae	10	70–75
CUCUMBER	*Cucumis sativus*	Cucurbitaceae	16–21	70
EGGPLANT	*Solanum melongena* var. *esculentum*	Solanaceae	5.5–7.2	70–85
GOURDS	*Cucurbita* spp.	Cucurbitaceae	.15–.2	65
KALE	*Brassica oleracea* Acephala Group	Cruciferae	6	70
KOHLRABI	*Brassica oleracea* Gongylodes Group	Cruciferae	6	70
LEEKS	*Allium ampeloprasum* Porum Group	Amaryllidaceae	10	70
LETTUCE	*Lactuca sativa*	Compositae	15–30	70
MELON: MUSK, HONEYDEW	*Cucumis melo* Reticulatus Group; Inodorus Group	Cucurbitaceae	.7–1	70–80
MELON, WATER	*Citrullus lanatus*	Cucurbitaceae	.3	70–80
OKRA	*Abelmoschus esculentus*	Malvaceae	.5	70
ONIONS	*Allium cepa*	Amaryllidaceae	9	70
PEANUTS	*Arachis hypogaea*	Leguminosae	.06	70
PEPPER: SWEET, HOT	*Capsicum annuum* Grossum Group; Longum Group	Solanaceae	4–6	70
PUMPKINS AND SQUASHES	*Cucurbita pepo; maxima; moschata; mixta*	Cucurbitaceae	.1–.3	70
TOMATILLO	*Physalis ixocarpa*	Solanaceae	9.5	70–75
TOMATOES, GARDEN; CHERRY; PEAR	*Lycopersicon lycopersicum;* var. *cerasiforme;* var. *pyriforme*	Solanaceae	7–18	70–75

Cover Depth	Germ. Time Days	Growing on °F	Set-Out Time (Weeks)	Distance in a Row	Space between Rows	Width of Plant	Height/ Length of Plant
1/4–1"	7–10	55–70	8–12	12–18"	18–24"	24"	4–6'
1/8"	3–5	55–70	6–8	18"	18"	18"	24"
1/8"	3–7	55–70	6–8	18"	18"	18"	24"
1/8"	3–5	55–70	6	18"	18"	18"	18"
1/8"	3–5	55–70	6	12"	18"	12"	18"
1/8"	3–5	55–70	6	18"	18"	18"	18–24"
top	14–18	65–75	10–12	8–12"	12"	10"	18"
1"	5–8	65–75	3	12"	18–24"	vine	4–8'
1/8"	8–10	65–75	12–14	18"	18–24"	18"	20–24"
1"	7	65–70	3	18"	18–24"	vine	5–6'
1/8"	4–7	55–70	6–8	18"	18"	18"	18–24"
1/8"	4–8	55–70	4–6	4–6"	12"	12"	10"
1/8"	7–10	55–70	8–12	3–4"	3–4"	4"	18–24"
top	3–4	55–70	6–8	10–12"	12"	10–18"	6–18"
1"	7–10	65–75	6–7	12"	24–36"	vine	5–10'
1"	7–10	65–75	6–7	12"	24–36"	vine	5–10'
1/2"	7	65–75	4	12"	12–24"	24"	2–4'
1/8"	7–10	55–70	8–10	3–4"	3–4"	2–3"	18–24"
1"	7–10	65–70	3–4	12"	12"	12–18"	12–18"
1/8"	7–14	65–75	12	12–18"	12–18"	12–18"	6–24"
1"	7–14	65–70	3–4	24–48"	24–48"	vine	2–14'
1/8"	5–7	65–70	6–8	24"	24–36"	36"	4–5'
1/8"	5–6	65–70	6–8	18–24"	24–36"	18–36"	18–60"

Outdoor Vegetable Seeding Chart

Common Name	Scientific Name	Family	Seeds (M) per Ounce (approx.)
Asparagus	*Asparagus officinalis*	Liliaceae	7–10
Beans: Bush Green and Yellow, Fava, Soy, Lima	*Phaseolus spp.,Vicia fava., Glycine max, Phaseolus lunatus*	Leguminosae	.03–.2
Beets	*Beta vulgaris*	Chenopodiaceae	28–40
Broccoli	*Brassica oleracea* Botrytis Group	Cruciferae	6
Brussels Sprouts	*Brassica oleracea* Gemmifera Group	Cruciferae	7
Cabbage: Common, Savoy, Red	*Brassica oleracea* Capitata Group	Cruciferae	7
Cabbage: Chinese, Pak Choi	*Brassica rapa* Pekinensis or Chinensis Group	Cruciferae	9
Carrots	*Daucus carota* var. *sativus*	Umbelliferae	165–600
Cauliflower	*Brassica oleraceae* Botrytis Group	Cruciferae	8
Chard, Swiss	*Beta vulgaris*	Chenopodiaceae	20–40
Corn: Sweet, Ornamental, Pop	*Zea mays* var. *rugosa*; var. *indurata*; var. *praecox*	Gramineae	1.8–4
Cucumber	*Cucumis sativus*	Cucurbitaceae	16–21
Gourds	*Cucurbita spp.*	Cucurbitaceae	.15–.2
Kale	*Brassica oleracea* Acephala Group	Cruciferae	6
Kohlrabi	*Brassica oleracea* Gongylodes Group	Cruciferae	6
Leeks	*Allium ampeloprasum* Porum Group	Amaryllidaceae	10
Lettuce	*Lactuca sativa*	Compositae	15–30
Melon: Musk, Honeydew	*Cucumis melo* Reticulatus Group Inodorus; GroupCucurbitaceae	Cucurbitaceae	.7–1
Melon: Water	*Citrullus lanatus*	Cucurbitaceae	.3
Okra	*Abelmoschus esculentus*	Malvaceae	.5
Onions	*Allium cepa*	Amaryllidaceae	9
Parsnips	*Pastinaca sativa*	Umbelliferae	5
Peanuts	*Arachis hypogaea*	Leguminosae	.06
Peas: Garden, Edible Pod	*Pisum sativum*; var. *macrocarpon*	Leguminosae	2
Pepper: Sweet, Hot	*Capsicum annuum* Grossum Group; Longum Group	Solanaceae	4–6
Potato Sets	*Solanum tuberosum*	Solanaceae	sets
Pumpkins and Squashes	*Cucurbita pepo*; maxima; moschata; mixta	Cucurbitaceae	.1–.3
Radishes	*Raphanus sativus*	Cruciferae	2.5
Rhubarb	*Rheum rhabarbarum*	Polygonaceae	1.7
Rutabaga	*Brassica napus napobrassica*	Cruciferae	10
Spinach: Fall or Spring	*Spinacia oleracea*	Chenopodiaceae	2.5
Spinach: New Zealand	*Tetragonia tetragonioides*	Tetragoniaceae	10
Turnip	*Brassica rapa*	Cruciferae	10

Germ. Temp. °F	Cover Depth	Germ. Time Days	Space in Row	Space between Rows	Width of Plant	Height/Length of Plant
70–75	¼–1"	7–10	12–18"	18–24"	24"	4–6'
65	1–2"	4–5	4–6"	24–36"	18–24"	1½–7'
55–80	⅛"	5–14	3–5"	16"	8–12"	12–18"
60–80	⅛"	7–14	18"	18"	18"	24"
60–80	⅛"	7–20	18"	18"	18"	24"
60–80	⅛"	7–14	18"	18"	18"	18"
55–75	⅛"	7–10	12"	18"	12"	18"
50–80	⅛"	10–20	1–2"	1–2"	2"	12"
60–80	⅛"	7–14	18"	18"	18"	18–24"
50–70	½"	6–10	2–3"	18"	6"	18–24"
65–75	½–½"	6–10	12–18"	18–24"	24"	5–8'
70	1"	5–8	12"	18–24"	vine	4–8'
65	1"	7–10	18"	18–24"	vine	5–6'
60–80	⅛"	4–10	18"	18"	18"	18–24"
60–80	⅛"	4–10	4–6"	12"	12"	10"
50–70	⅛"	10–15	3–4"	3–4"	4"	18–24"
50–75	surface	4–10	10–12"	12"	10–18"	6–18"
70	1"	8–12	12"	24–36"	vine	5–10'
70	1"	8–12	12"	24–36"	vine	5–10'
70–80	½"	7–10	12"	12–24"	24"	2–4'
50–75	⅛"	10–15	3–4"	3–4"	2–3"	18–24"
60–70	⅛"	20–25	3"	3–4"	3"	12–18"
70–80	1"	7–14	12"	12"	12–18"	12–18"
45–65	1"	7–10	1"	12"	vine	4–5'
70–80	⅛"	7–14	12–18"	12–18"	12–18"	6–24"
60–75	6–8"	14–18	6"	24"	18"	18–24"
65–80	1"	7–16	24–48"	24–48"	vine	2–14'
45–70	⅛"	5–10	½–3"	6"	4–6"	6–8"
50–70	½"	14–21	12"	24"	24"	18–36"
60–70	½"	5–10	4–6"	6"	6–12"	10–18"
40–70	½"	7–18	2–6"	6"	4–6"	6"
60–75	½"	3–7	6–12"	12"	8–10"	12–18"
50–70	½"	5–10	4–6"	6"	6"	10–16"

CHAPTER SIX

Herbs

NO AREA OF GARDENING has been more affected by growth in the past decade than herb gardening. Its increase in popularity has probably been the result of several converging factors. Most obviously, gardening is one of America's fastest growing hobbies. In addition, American eating habits have been greatly influenced by information about more healthful diets, prompting many of us to look for alternatives to fats and sugars to make our meals not only more healthful but more flavorful. As interest in new foods has grown, we have also become aware of many ethnic dishes that require the availability of vegetables and herbs new to our gardens. And finally, in response to a nationwide interest in many things "alternative," the small but significant influence of "new age" medicine has prompted many to look to plant-based and often herb-based remedies for a variety of health needs.

It has not taken the plant and seed industry very long to respond to its audience, and in so doing, to further fuel that interest. Until very recently nearly every major seed company offered a respectable but limited number of herbs for the backyard gardener. The commonly known culinary herbs were available, with a variation or two of the most popular. If one wanted unusual culinary herbs or any medicinal herbs, it was necessary to find specialty companies.

Today, even the most modestly stocked garden center offers culi-

FROM LATE SPRING to late fall we make our herbal teas by harvesting handfuls of fresh herbs from our tea gardens. The largest of these gardens (pictured below) measures about 12 by 10 feet and contains a dozen different kinds of tea herbs, all members of the Labiatae family of plants, commonly known as the mint family. These plants are a combination of seed grown herbs including lemon balm (*Melissa officinalis*), anise hyssop (*Agastache foeniculum*), catnip (*Nepeta cataria*), catmint (*Nepeta mussinii*), lemon catnip (*Nepeta cataria* 'Citriodora'), bee balm (*Monarda fistulosa*), and hyssop (*Hyssopus officinalis*). Then there are those mint family herbs that are propagated from cuttings or root division, including spearmint (*Mentha spicata*), peppermint (*Mentha piperita*), orange mint (*Mentha aquatica* var. *citrata*), curly mint (*Mentha aquatica* var. *crispa*), and apple mint (*Mentha suaveolens*).

The raised bed was constructed by using cedar logs on the perimeter and dividing the area into 12 boxes formed by sinking wide cedar boards on end and nailing these boards to the outside and to each other. We compartmentalized the garden in an attempt to keep the 12 mints separated from one another, but over the years some of the more aggressive varieties have managed to invade and overtake their neighbors. Nonetheless, with a little weeding, culling, and replanting, we have managed to use this tea garden successfully for more than a decade.

Herbal teas can be made from several plants, or from a single species such as chamomile (one of the most commonly known), or from a combination of plants. One of our favorite recipes uses lemon balm with lemon catnip and lemon basil.

Teas are made from fresh herbs by simply putting a handful of fresh leaves into a pot of very hot, but not boiling, water. Steep the leaves for 5–15 minutes (to taste) and the tea is ready to drink. During the summer, we make large batches of herbal tea to chill and then to ice. It is a very refreshing hot weather drink. For a winter's supply of tea herbs, we harvest individual varieties of an herb, dry the leaves, and then store them in tightly sealed containers. The dried herb leaves (again of a single variety or in combinations) are steeped in hot water in a tea ball or a strainer.

Other suggestions for herbs that are raised easily from seed for a tea garden include common mint (*Mentha* sp.), sage (*Salvia officinalis*), lemon bee balm (*Monarda citriodora*), mountain star bee balm (*Monarda astromontana*), mountain mints (*Pycnanthemum tenuifolium* or *Pycnanthemum pilosum*), basils (any varieties of *Ocimum*), and fennel (*Foeniculum vulgare*).

A relatively small space can produce an abundance of tea herbs.

nary, ornamental, and medicinal herbs. Seed catalogues that only recently gave us a choice of curly and flat-leaved parsley, now have several named varieties of each. The backyard gardener could devote a whole garden to the cultivation of basils alone or to the growing of Asian medicinal plants. We now have easy access to an abundance of plant material, and one imagines that as long as our enthusiasm for gardening continues, so will the diversity of offerings.

The chapter that follows discusses the horticultural requirements of nearly seven dozen herbs, chosen primarily because they can be started from seeds. Beyond that requirement, we have chosen familiar herbs that we have worked with in our own gardens at Hedgehog Hill. In choosing herbs for our gardens, we are looking for plants that will be useful primarily as culinary or ornamental species. Some of the herbs that we talk about also have interesting histories of medicinal use. We appreciate the role that plants have in the preparation of medicines, but we are not at all qualified to recommend or evaluate the efficacy of herbal medicines. When we write about a plant's medicinal use, we do so from a historical perspective.

We do feel qualified to discuss the horticulture of the herbs in this chapter. They are plants that we have familiarized ourselves with over the past several decades. We have grown, smelled, tasted, harvested, cooked with, designed with, and enjoyed all of the plants that we write about. Our enthusiasm for this area of gardening has also grown rapidly. We expect, along with our readers, to be the beneficiaries of work by plantspeople who will make more and more species and varieties of herbs available.

The herb chapter is arranged alphabetically by common name. Within each section is a general discussion of plant history, cultural requirements, and plant use. At the end of the chapter is a detailed chart giving information that will be useful for seeding each of the herbs discussed. The text is written using a minimum of technical jargon or botanical terminology. When scientific terms are used, we try to explain their meaning.

Many herbs can be started from seed. Just as many are almost always propagated vegetatively. On page 56 there is a list of herbs that need to be acquired initially as plants. These herbs are then propagated either by root or stem cuttings. This list is included to help gardeners understand what herbs are typically available and in what form.

We accent this chapter with special sections on various aspects of herb gardening. These include ideas for cooking, garden design, a few anecdotal items, and design projects. Along with vegetables, herbs are among the most useful plants. They provide not only food and fiber, but materials for dyeing, weaving, and any number of ornamental crafts.

Before delving into the heart of the chapter, we would like to offer a general suggestion about herb gardening. Simply because plants are organized into a category known as herbs, we as gardeners are not required to isolate them in specific gardens. Herbs are too complex, interesting, and diverse to be limited to one place in our cultivated landscape. Rather, we like to regard these plants as candidates for any garden, walkway, container, or natural site that suits them culturally and that suits the designer as well. When planning a garden spot, think initially about all the possibilities for growing things, without the restraints of categories. It will free you to create some very unique plantings.

ANGELICA

Angelica archangelica

UMBELLIFERAE

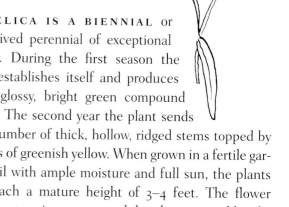

ANGELICA IS A BIENNIAL or short-lived perennial of exceptional beauty. During the first season the plant establishes itself and produces large, glossy, bright green compound leaves. The second year the plant sends up a number of thick, hollow, ridged stems topped by umbels of greenish yellow. When grown in a fertile garden soil with ample moisture and full sun, the plants can reach a mature height of 3–4 feet. The flower heads mature into green, and then brown, seed heads. When the seeds have turned brown, but before they begin to drop, they should be collected and broadcast into an outdoor seed bed and raked lightly into the soil. Seedlings can be left in the seedbed for the fall and

Angelica seed heads will produce hundreds of seeds, which can be collected and sown as soon as they ripen on the plants.

winter and then transplanted into place in the spring of the following year. Angelica plants left unharvested will usually produce their own volunteers.

If you are interested in prolonging the life of the plant (treating it like a short lived perennial), keep the flowering stalks picked before they complete seed formation. The plants will often live for several seasons. We rarely pick either flowers or immature seed heads however, as the fully developed plants are so bold and beautiful that we prefer to let plants complete their two-year cycle, at the end of which we are able to collect fresh seeds to propagate new plants.

All parts of this herb are used for culinary purposes. Seeds and roots are used as flavorings. The leaves and stems can be used fresh, or cooked, and the stems can be crystallized. A few finely chopped stems of angelica can be used to sweeten fruit sauces, cutting down on the need for processed sugars.

This handsome large herb, native to Europe and Asia, is worth the effort to grow, and it can be well incorporated as an accent plant in a perennial border

as well as in the traditional herb garden. Given the choice, we would always prefer to have fresh seeds of angelica for planting. That means, harvest seeds as soon as they are mature on their plants and sow them directly into the ground in late summer. If you cannot plant fresh seeds immediately, store them in slightly moistened peat moss in a sealed bag in the refrigerator until ready to plant. This process of cold storing seeds is referred to as seed stratification. It has been our experience that stored seeds do not show the same high germination rates as fresh ones.

When purchasing seeds, remember that most catalogues are produced and sent out to customers in midwinter; any angelica seeds offered are of necessity ones that are harvested from the previous season. In years past, it was rare to find a seed catalogue that gave any information about how their angelica seed had been handled. We purchased seeds for this herb for a number of years and had no success with germination. In frustration, we finally purchased a plant from which we have continued our seed production.

More recently a number of reputable seed companies have begun to give customers information about the harvesting and treatment of their angelica seeds. Unless you know how the seeds have been treated, purchase a plant from a nursery and then save your own seeds. Angelica can be grown in Zones 3–9. While we have mentioned the difficulties with seed sources, the general cultivation of the plant is very easy after germination.

Another beautiful species of angelica, known as *Angelica gigas,* is worth mentioning. We discovered and purchased a plant of this species from a plant catalogue several years ago. Although this plant is not commonly offered, it is worth finding. Once found you can propagate fresh seed as described above. *Angelica gigas* is slightly smaller than common angelica, growing to a height of 3–4 feet in our gardens. It has stalks and leaves which are blushed with a deep burgundy color. The entire flower head begins as a large umbel of deep burgundy opening to white deeply veined flowers. This plant seems to be a magnet for bees and hornets; they are never absent when *A. gigas* is in full flower. Freshly planted seeds of this species do not have as high a germination rate as *A. archangelica,* but it only takes a few viable seeds to succeed in propagating the variety from season to season.

frost has passed and when the ground has warmed. It does not transplant well and should be thinned to the appropriate spacing. If northern gardeners want to grow a bit of anise, they should start the plants indoors 3–4 weeks before the last frost and plant a few seeds in a cluster in individual peat pots so that the small plants can be set directly into the garden without disturbing the roots. Seedlings grown indoors or out should not be allowed to dry out, and garden plants should be kept free of weeds, as they do not like competition.

The plants have finely serrated leaves and small white flower umbels, typical of members of this family. During the growing season a few leaves can be harvested fresh without affecting seed production. Immediately following flowering, seed pods begin to develop on the plants. When seeds have begun to mature, cut off the heads intact and dry inside. Even those of us who have never grown the plants are usually familiar with anise seeds, as they are commonly used to flavor cakes, curries, baked goods, and candies. The early American colonists carried seed to North America where the Shakers grew the plants and included them in their medicinal crops. Anise oil is not only used in medicine but also in perfumery, toiletries, and beverages. Anise, native to the Mediterranean region, is now cultivated in many warm regions of the world.

ANISE

Pimpinella anisum

UMBELLIFERAE

YOU CAN GROW this annual herb in colder zones, but best results are obtained in the warmer climates of this country because the plant needs about four warm months of growing time to produce a crop of mature seeds. While tender young anise leaves can be used to flavor salads, the seeds are the most commonly used portion of the herb. Anise is best grown when it is seeded directly into the garden plot after the danger of

ANISE HYSSOP

Agastache foeniculum

LABIATAE

THIS PERENNIAL, not a hyssop at all, albeit in the same family, is easy to grow from seed. It germinates readily and grows vigorously to a harvestable size in one season, during which time it also produces flowers and seeds. Anise hyssop is a tall sturdy plant with leaves that are good in teas. Unlike so many other members of the mint family, anise hyssop does not spread from underground roots, but has instead a neat upright habit. However, the plant does

S OME HERBS HAVE fragrances with moth-repelling properties. So many of these are easily grown from seed that we recommend including a few in your gardens so that you can eschew the foul-smelling mothballs and create instead your own recipes for herbal sachets. Many of the herbs in this category are perennials even in our gardening region. They include lavender (*Lavandula angustifolia*), tansy (*Tanacetum vulgare*), wormwood and mugwort (*Artemisia absinthium* and *Artemisia vulgare*), santolina (*Santolina chamaecyparissus*) and rosemary (*Rosmarinus officinalis*). Leaves from several eucalyptus species are also recommended, such as *Eucalyptus cinerea* and *Eucalyptus citriodora*. The annual herbs pennyroyal (*Mentha pulegium*) and camphor basil (*Ocimum kilimandscharicum*) are also suitable.

Dried herbs are crushed and used to make moth-repelling sachets.

To prepare the moth-repelling ingredients, harvest the plants, tie the stems together into small bundles, and hang them to dry in a very warm location with good air circulation but no sun. When the plants are thoroughly dry, remove the leaves and flowers from the stems. We use a wooden-sided tray with a mesh bottom and rub the stems on the mesh. The leaves and flowers that fall through the mesh will be partly broken down. Store the dried material in tightly sealed labeled containers.

When you are ready to make a moth-repelling potpourri, choose one of the dried herbs or mix several species to create an interesting fragrance. Experiment with mixtures that are pleasing to you. Reduce the size of the leaves and flowers by hand-rubbing the pieces until they are small and uniform for mixing. If you wish to increase the intensity of the fragrance, try adding bits of cinnamon bark and nutmeg or whole cloves. To "fix" or preserve the fragrance of the herbal blend, we use a small amount of ground orrisroot, a natural plant fixative made from the roots of the florentine iris (*Iris germanica florentina*). Mix about a tablespoon of orris powder into every quart of dried herbs and blend thoroughly.

The moth-repelling potpourri is now ready to be tied into cheesecloth bags or more decorative cotton bags with ribbons. Tuck these sachets into bureau drawers or attach to hangers in closets. The fragrance will last at least a year in the cloth containers; the herb supply originally stored in airtight containers should be useful for several years.

produce a number of volunteers if the mature flower heads are not cut.

The flower spikes are large, showy, mauve blossoms, appearing on the plants in late summer when color is especially welcome in the herb or perennial garden. Both the leaves and the flowers have an appealingly pungent anise scent, which is very attractive to bees. Flowers are good for cutting fresh, for drying, and for use in making potpourri. There are so many seeds in each flower spike that you will be able to harvest flowers freely, leaving only a few of the most vigorous plants for seed production.

Once you have this perennial in the garden, chances are you will never need to purchase plants or seeds again. Just transplant young volunteers into place each season. This plant's habit of producing volunteers also tells us that mature seeds can be collected in the fall and seeded directly into place for the following spring. Alternatively, they may be seeded into a nursery bed and then transplanted into place as seedlings the following year. Because this herb is both useful and attractive we include it in our tea gardens and in a perennial border where the late summer flowers are welcome color. Anise hyssop is native to North America and can be grown successfully in Zones 3–9. The genus name, *Agastache* is from the Greek words *agan*, meaning "very much," and *stachys*, meaning "spike," in reference to its free flowering habit.

Fortunately, in the past few years, the genus *Agastache* has received much attention from plantspeople and seed companies. The result is more species being made available for the home gardener, either in the form of seeds or plants. Members of this genus are usually easy to propagate from seed, from cuttings, or from division. Some of the species that we have enjoyed from seed in our herb gardens include *Agastache rugosa*, known as Korean mint, and *Agastache cana* 'Heather Queen'. The latter variety is more refined in shape and size with typical upright flower spikes that are covered in warm rosy pink flowers. Not all of the newly offered members of this genus are hardy in our gardens, but since they are such rapid growers, they can be enjoyed as hardy annuals.

ARTEMISIA

Artemisia annua. Annual Artemisia, Sweet Annie, Sweet Wormwood
Artemisia absinthium. Wormwood
Artemisia dracunculus. Russian Tarragon
Artemisia dracunculus var. *sativa.* French Tarragon
Artemisia stelleriana. Beach Wormwood, Dusty Miller
Artemisia vulgaris. Mugwort

COMPOSITAE

Artemisia annua

THERE ARE ABOUT 200 species of artemisias. The few we have chosen to discuss are commonly available species and ones (with one exception) that can be grown from seed (unlike so many plants in this genus). Since there is cultural information specific to each of the species, we will discuss them separately, starting with *Artemisia annua*, a popular annual commonly known as Sweet Annie.

Artemisia annua is easily grown from seed and a ready volunteer in the garden if mature plants are left unharvested. When seeding indoors, air circulation is important especially during the growing period. If seedlings are crowded, leaves are quite susceptible to disease, yellowing, and stunting. Plants seeded directly outdoors show fewer signs of stress, but should be thinned or

Artemisia absinthium

transplanted on a cloudy day and protected from direct sun and wind for a few days thereafter. Annual artemisia is a very graceful, sweetly aromatic plant that is lovely to use fresh and dry. It can be made into everlasting arrangements and wreaths that will retain their fragrance, if not their color, for several years. Sweet Annie's long lasting fragrance makes it an excellent ingredient in potpourri. The plant has inconspicuous small yellow flowers that turn brownish when mature. For decorative uses, harvest the whole plant just as flowers have set and before they begin to discolor. If you want to collect your own seeds, leave a few plants to mature fully in the field. Unharvested

THIS BEAUTIFUL SILVER garden is made up entirely of plants from the genus *Artemisia*. The design was created to group related plants that would be visually appealing as well as interesting and informative. It is one of many teaching gardens that we have at the farm.

Plants of this genus were named for the Greek goddess Artemis, twin sister of Apollo, and goddess of the hunt, of the moon, and of women. Her Roman counterpart was called Diana, after whom many plants are also named. Plant names have frequently sent us back to our dog-eared copies of Hamilton or Bulfinch.

The dominant artemisia in this garden is *Artemisia absinthium*, three plants of which reach a height of 3–4 feet in the center of the planting. *Absinthium*, meaning "without sweetness," is one of the most bitter herbs. A powerful extract made from the roots of the plant was the basis for the French liquor of the same name. The drink, both addictive and poisonous, was supposedly responsible for the deaths of such famous people as Verlaine and Toulouse-Lautrec. Absinthe was made illegal in the early part of this century. The plant's common name, "wormwood," reveals some of its historical use as a vermifuge, a strewing herb, and a moth and insect repellent.

Growing in a semicircle next to *Artemisia absinthium* are some plants of *Artemisia ludoviciana*, commonly called Silver King artemisia. This plant is one of the most important crops for drying and wreathmaking. The species name is derived from Louisiana, this species being a true American plant.

Three plants of *Artemisia abrotanum* complete the circle around the wormwood. Native to southern Europe, its common old English name is southern-

Shades of gray and green in a garden made up exclusively of plants from the genus Artemisia.

wood. The green-gray finely divided leaves of this species persist on the plant until well into the fall. Southernwood has a pleasing lemony fragrance and a history of use as a strewing herb.

Artemisia pontica, or Roman wormwood, has a genus name meaning Pontus, indicating its place of origin. Artemisia stelleriana is named for its discoverer, Georg Wilhelm Steller (1709–1746). The plant's common English name is beach wormwood, perhaps in reference to its preference for sandy dry locations. We first saw this herb growing naturally among the sand dunes of coastal Maine. Both of these low growing perennials occupy a couple of the garden's front corners.

One of the opposite corners is planted with Artemisia dracunculus var. sativa, the one plant in the group that is prized not as an ornamental, but for its culinary use. This herb is the well-known French tarragon. Dracunculus means dragon, and both the words dragon and tarragon have the same derivation. It was once thought that the plant was effective in curing the bites of venomous beasts and rabid dogs.

The fourth corner of the garden is planted with either Artemisia schmidtiana, a commemorative name, or Artemisia annua, the species name an indication that this has to be planted each spring. Artemisia annua has become a very popular plant in the past couple of decades, owing to its pleasingly intense sweet fragrance and usefulness for potpourri and wreathmaking. Most gardeners refer to this herb by its descriptive nickname, Sweet Annie.

So in addition to its beauty and usefulness, this artemisia garden is valued for what it has prompted us to study. It has a selection of plants with names that commemorate goddesses from Greek and Roman mythology, names that describe places of origin around the world, names that are indicative of plant behavior, and names that identify botanists or plant explorers. There are names that make reference to economic botany and give us a glimpse into the rich folklore that surrounds the history of horticulture.

plants will produce volunteers the following spring, or you may collect, dry, and store seeds to reseed indoors or out from year to year. Annual artemisia is not only a useful annual herb, it is pleasing in the garden when used as a background plant, its greenery serving as a backdrop for other brightly colored flowers. Annua is native to Asia and eastern Europe, but has become naturalized in many parts of this continent.

Artemisia absinthium is also easy to grow from seed and may be seeded indoors using the guidelines shown on the chart at the end of the chapter. It may also be seeded outdoors and then thinned or transplanted into place. We have had equal success with each technique. First year wormwood will develop only its basal leaves, which are finely divided and silvery gray. They make good garden accents. From the second season onward, the plants produce flowering spikes 3–4 feet tall of small inconspicuous flowers that ripen from silvery gray to a dull yellow-brown. Flower stalks can be cut back at any time, but only stalks left to mature will produce seeds for collecting or seeds that will surely produce volunteers the following spring. If you allow the seeds to mature, you will rarely need to purchase new plants or seeds. It will be important to save some new young plants from time to time as the original plants tend to become woody and less satisfactory after several seasons. Wormwood leaves and flower stalks are fragrant and pungently bitter to smell, and most certainly to taste. Although you should not use the plant internally, get a sample of its flavor by touching your lips after handling this herb. Wormwood was once used in the manufacture of absinthe, the infamous French liquor, now outlawed. It was also used in worm medicines, hence its popular name. We use the leaves and flowers of this hardy perennial as dried material for herbal wreaths and as an ingredient in herbal moth repellents. A. absinthium is native to Europe and now is naturalized in the United States and Canada.

Artemisia stelleriana is often found naturalized in sandy dune soil, attesting to the fact that this and many of the artemisias will do well in dry soils. This plant is not difficult to grow from seed, but we find

Artemisia vulgaris

that very few seeds are found in each of the flowering stalks, and very few seed catalogues offer seed for sale. Beach wormwood has handsome, broadly scalloped, hairy silver foliage that grows low to the ground on prostrate stems. By midsummer the plant sends up 1-foot flowering stalks with small inconspicuous flowers. The flowers mature from silver to light yellow to brown. We do not find volunteers from this species in our gardens, but the naturalized colonies suggest that this plant does reseed under the right conditions. When growing seedlings indoors, it is important to give the small plants ample room and good air circulation. Beach wormwood can also be propagated from rooted cuttings and by plant divisions in the early spring. This perennial is native to northeast Asia and is now naturalized both in eastern North America and Europe.

Artemisia dracunculus has been included in this section simply because we want to extend a caveat to all growers, lest they purchase seed for what some catalogues call tarragon. The true French tarragon, *Artemisia dracunculus* var. *sativa,* cannot be grown from seed and needs to be purchased as plants that are made generally from rooted cuttings or produced by means of root division. Tarragon grown from seed is what horticulturists refer to as Russian tarragon and the plants are very disappointing. They are easy to grow from seed, and in fact resemble the true French tarragon in appearance, but they totally lack the unique fragrance and flavor of the culinary tarragon. Several years ago, some seed catalogues were rather careless about making a distinction between the two tarragons, but we have noticed that recently the major companies are more careful in describing exactly what they are offering. All you need to remember is not to buy seed for tarragon if it is the cooking herb you are after.

Artemisia vulgaris, the perennial species known commonly as mugwort, can readily be grown from seed. It can also be seen growing naturally along roadsides, in pastures, and in urban parking lots all over the country. We grew this plant for several years before we recognized its ubiquitous and invasive nature. Mugwort does have an interesting history of practical and medicinal uses, and seed is readily available to gardeners. Although we have chosen to exclude it from our gardens, we will include it in this chapter. Seeds may be sown inside or directly into the garden and thinned to space. Plants grow rapidly, producing flowering stalks and seeds the first year. Mature plants reach a height of 3–5 feet tall; leaves are dull green on the top and whitish on the underside. As you may have concluded from the introduction, plants left unharvested in the garden will produce abundant volunteers. Seed can also be collected late in the summer for fall or spring sowing. Mugwort is native to Europe and Asia. One of its best known medicinal uses is in the Chinese practice of moxibustion. The dried leaves (moxa) are made into small cones that are heated and used on the skin to give a deep penetrating heat to soothe ailments such as rheumatism. When we grew this artemisia to any extent, we harvested the fragrant leaves and dried them for use in herbal wreaths and moth repelling mixtures.

Other important artemisias (all perennials) are used in the ornamental border or grown for use in herbal wreath making and flower arranging. These include *Artemisia ludoviciana* var. *albula,* or Silver King artemisia, *Artemisia schmidtiana* or Silver Mound, *Artemisia pontica,* Roman wormwood, and *Artemisia abrotanum,* southernwood. Purchase each of these species as plants, as they are not commonly grown from seed.

BAPTISIA

Baptisia australis

LEGUMINOSAE

ONE OF THE SHOWIEST of the perennial ornamental herbs, baptisia, is native to the eastern part of the United States. It is reliably hardy in our gardens, where it is grown in a fertile well-drained soil in full sun. The seeds of this herb are very large and easily sown in seed flats in early spring. A few seed catalogues recommend scarifying the seeds before sowing, but we don't do this. Seeds germinate well but over a long period of time (see the box on page 49).

The small seedlings of baptisia have characteristic pea-like leaves, and for the first two years, this herb puts on a modest amount of growth. During the third

or fourth season, the plants begin to develop to their full size and start to blossom in midsummer. The beautiful tall spikes are a rich indigo blue. They resemble lupine flowers in form and scale. Flowers last for weeks on the plants and are excellent for cutting fresh. When flowers fade the foliage continues to grow. After a few seasons, one plant will produce several arching stems tightly grouped at the base. A mature baptisia resembles a small shrub, reaching a height of 3–5 feet. When not in bloom, the plant is still attractive because of its luxuriant growth of soft green compound three-lobed leaves.

To save your own baptisia seeds, watch for the small charcoal seed pods that are produced on old flowering stalks. They appear in late summer and are sometimes hidden under the leaves. Allow the pods to develop fully on the plants but pick them before they begin to split. We have seldom seen volunteers from this herb in our gardens, but the collected seeds show good viability for seeding indoors in seed flats or directly in the garden when the soil can be worked in the spring.

The name baptisia comes from the Greek word *bapto*, meaning "to dye." The herb is commonly referred to as false indigo or wild indigo, in reference to its use as a dye plant.

BASIL

Ocimum basilicum

LABIATAE

cinnamon basil

As INTEREST IN culinary herbs increases so do the varieties of basil offered by seed catalogues and garden centers. Until very recently most gardeners had to content themselves with the sweet green Italian basil, still perhaps the most popular. Now some specialized seed companies offer more than two dozen varieties, many of these basils belonging to the species *Ocimum basilicum* and cultivars of that species. We have grown, handled, and cooked with a number of varieties and found that their culture is not at all demanding. As long as you have a good warm sunny garden spot and reasonably fertile soil,

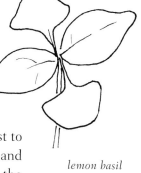
lemon basil

basils can be grown throughout the United States. Basils will also do well in containers located in full sun.

In northern gardens, we recommend starting seeds indoors. Basils like warm temperatures, and it is best to have small plants hardened off and ready to go into the garden when the nighttime temperatures are above 50°F. It is possible to direct seed basil even in our climate, but it is necessary to wait until the soils have warmed. Crops that are direct seeded will not be as productive as transplants. In warmer parts of the country, the seed may be sown directly into the garden when the soils have warmed, and plants can then be thinned or transplanted into place.

sweet green Italian basil

Basils transplant easily. Basil seeds display a gelatinous cover when they have been wetted, which remains until the seeds germinate. Seeds should not be covered with soil but sprinkled on the surface of the seed flat or soil and kept uniformly moist during the germinating period. Once seeds have germinated, grow seedlings at slightly cooler temperatures, 65°–70°F. The green sweet Italian basils grown for their abundant crops of large leaves for using fresh, drying, or making pesto are usually sold as Sweet Green Italian basil, *O. basilicum*, or Lettuce Leaved basil, *O. crispum*. Small-leaved basil, sometimes called piccolo basil, or bush basil is also an excellent culinary type and is sold as *O. basilicum* 'Minimum'. A recent arrival on catalogue pages is called Spicy Globe basil, *O. basilicum* 'Spicy Globe', and it is sold as an ornamental basil to be used at the front of the border or in containers. This small-leaved green type can also be used in cooking. The purple-leaved basils are called purple or opal basils or purple ruffled basil, *O. basilicum* 'Purpurascens', and these are grown as ornamentals but can be used for culinary purposes. They make an attractive wine-colored herbal vinegar. Lemon basil, *O. basilicum* 'Citriodorum', has leaves the size of the bush basils with a distinct lemon fra-

TRY THIS VARIATION of tempura cooking during the summer, when you have access to a variety of fresh herbs. The flavors of batter-fried herbs are superb. If you include a few vegetables in the mix and perhaps some fresh shrimp, this tempura becomes a full meal in itself. Herb tempura alone makes a good appetizer.

BATTER

> 1 egg yolk
> 1 cup ice cold water
> 1 cup flour

In a mixing bowl, whisk the egg yolk and ice water until just mixed. Then add the flour a bit at a time and stir lightly until nearly mixed. Batter will resemble a thin pancake mixture. If bits of flour are floating on top, don't be concerned. It's preferable to undermix rather than overbeat the batter.

SUGGESTED HERBS

Basil (Large Leaved is excellent, as well as Sweet Green Italian, purple varieties, and lemon), chives or garlic chives (small clusters of leaves or individual young flowers), parsley, sage, cilantro, young mint leaves, dill, fennel, young lovage leaves, clusters of tender summer savory, marjoram, Greek oregano (or very young stems of wild oregano), perilla.

Basil, sage, dill, cilantro, bunching onions, and carrots ready for dipping and eating.

DIPPING SAUCE

> 1 cup dashi (a basic soup stock made by boiling 2 tablespoons of bonita flakes in a cup of water for several minutes and then straining the mixture)
> 2–3 tablespoons soy sauce
> 1 tablespoon rice wine or mirin
> 2 teaspoons sugar

Combine all the ingredients and serve in individual small bowls. Freshly grated ginger (to taste) may be added to each bowl.

PICK GARDEN FRESH HERBS (or young vegetables) right before making the tempura so that they will be tender and most flavorful. Use young leaves and the newest growth of stemmy herbs such as marjoram or Greek oregano. That way the leaves and stems can be used completely. We don't wash the herbs since we don't use sprays in the garden and our plants are mulched.

Heat a good vegetable oil to about 350° in a wok. Dip separate leaves or small stem clusters in the batter, turning herbs to coat all sides, and drop a few herbs into the hot oil. Chopsticks (the long cooking type) are the best tools to use for this. Fry herbs briefly on each side until the batter is lightly browned. Remove immediately from the oil and drain on a wok drainer or paper towels. Eat as soon as the cooked herb is cool enough to be handled. Once again, chopsticks or fingers are recommended.

Try the different flavors of the individual herbs first without the dipping sauce so that you can evaluate their flavors. The dipping sauce only makes a good flavor better.

This is an appetizer or meal to be enjoyed family-style with participants sitting around the wok, dipping, frying, eating, and talking all together. It's a meal that we like to have on the open porch adjacent to the kitchen. That way we don't concern ourselves with the messiness and don't have to live with the smell of hot cooking oil in the house.

grance and flavor. This variety is the most finicky of all basils to grow from seed because of its susceptibility to damping-off. Good air circulation is important for these small seedlings. A recently introduced variety of lemon basil, 'Sweet Dani', is a more vigorous and larger-leaved type. Cinnamon

opal basil

basil, *O. basilicum* 'Cinnamon', is an attractive large-leaved basil with deeper green foliage than that of the sweet green. Cinnamon basil flowers are burgundy and white. The whole plant has a spicy fragrance and flavor and is excellent for using fresh and for making herbal vinegars. We also use this variety to flavor our marinara sauces. Holy basil, *O. sanctum,* and camphor basil, *O. kilimandscharicum,* are basils with unique earthy fragrances. These plants have a history of use in Eastern cuisine and perfumery. This list of basils is only an introduction to those varieties that are now available. Seed catalogues offer new choices every season. Many of the new offerings are named cultivars of the species described above.

If you are growing basil for the first time and want the herb primarily for using fresh and cooking, we recommend Sweet Green Italian and Lettuce Leaved. These varieties are the easiest to grow and size-up quickly. They also have the most familiar sweet basil flavor and just two or three plants of either variety will produce enough leaves to use fresh all summer and to harvest for winter use.

All varieties of basils produce longer if the blossoms are continuously removed from the plants. This encourages the plants to set side branches and produce more leaves. Once a plant goes to blossom, it spends its energy flowering and maturing seed. The leaf quality and quantity decline. Basils are very frost sensitive, so harvest their leaves before any threat of frost and dry or store them in oil for winter use. Basils can be used as an ingredient in herbal teas, potpourris, herbal honeys, and herbal vinegars. The plants are also attractive for use in the border and in patio containers.

Basils are native to the warm, temperate, and tropical regions of the Old World; they get their genus name from the Greek *okimon,* a name for an aromatic herb. If you wish to save your own basil seed, select a few vigorous individuals from a given species and

A small garden designed with a variety of basils, including green, opal, ruffled, lemon, cinnamon, and holy basil.

allow the plants to grow uninterrupted to flowering and seed formation. Watch the flowers and seed pods carefully so that you harvest the seeds for drying before they fall to the ground.

BAY LAUREL

Laurus nobilis

LAURACEAE

BAY, ALSO KNOWN AS laurel and sweet bay, is the perennial herb from which we harvest culinary bay leaves. In our climate we must grow bay as a container plant. In regions where temperatures stay above freezing, these elegant large shrubs can be grown in the ground and allowed to reach their mature height of 25 feet and up. Bay leaves are oval, tapered, shiny dark green on the top, and olive colored on the undersides. Plants are upright in habit with many side branches. Stems are dark chocolate brown. Bays may be allowed to grow into their natural forms or they can be pruned into specific shapes.

Our first bay plants were started from cuttings that are made from partially woody stems rooted in a moist rooting medium. See the section on taking cuttings on pages 56–7 for a more detailed discussion. Bay plants are usually offered as small plants but occasionally a seed catalogue will offer seeds.

Bay seeds are produced on mature plants over a period of two years. Buds are set in the fall for spring flowering. Once pollinated, female flowers produce seeds that take up to a year to mature into harvestable dark brown–black shiny berries. Each berry is a single seed. Seeds must be planted fresh or stratified if they are to be stored before planting. We have had very mixed success with germinating bay from seed, either purchased or gathered from our own plants at the farm. One purchased seed lot of healthy appearing seeds gave us nearly 100 percent germination. The following year stratified seed from the same source germinated only about 15 percent of the seed. Seeds collected from our own bay plants were treated in two ways. We planted a portion of the seeds fresh from harvest and stratified an equal number before sowing. There was about a 15 percent success rate with germination in either case.

Home gardeners may want to start with a small, well-rooted bay plant. Although plants appear to be a bit "pricey," it is important to note that cuttings can take months to root. Once bay is germinated as a young seedling or successfully rooted, the plants are very easy to grow.

For the first two to three years, plants grow rather slowly, but once established, they develop into large specimens in a few more years. As container plants, bays should be grown outdoors for as long a season as the climate permits. Keep them well-watered all during the spring, summer, and fall, and grow them in an area where they have excellent light, but not constant direct sun. Our tubs are placed at the outer edge of a garden with overhanging mature oak, ash, and maple

HERB PLANTS ARE ideally suited for gardeners with small sites and for gardeners who want to limit their growing to containers. It is possible to have a small culinary herb garden with several species of herbs growing successfully in a single planter. Some perennial herbs can also be grown in containers. Containers limit the size of the planting and tend to limit the growth of the plants, but herbs can be transplanted from small pots to larger pots and moved from one site to another throughout the year.

We start most of our herbs from seeds or cuttings in the greenhouses at the farm. For the first growing season, as a rule, we field-grow the herbs, planting them directly into the garden where they develop good root systems and top growth. Then we dig and pot healthy specimens to be brought in for the winter. In the case of plants like rosemary, bay, myrtle, and lemon verbena, we are obliged to winter these plants inside. On occasion we locate herb plants immediately in containers. They may be placed in individual pots or grouped into pleasing combinations in large patio planters. One of the herbs that we grow routinely as a container plant is pineapple sage, *Salvia elegans*. Its beautiful and fragrant leaves are lovely all summer long, and as the weather cools, the plant begins to set hundreds of clear red strikingly beautiful blossoms. We enjoy this sage inside all winter and even cut from the large plants for winter bouquets. Scented geraniums make excellent container plants outdoors and in.

Over the years we have designed herbal planters for use on patios, to be placed in conservatories, and for use in cooking. Basil, marjoram, parsley, chives, and Greek oregano share a large pot well, as do bay, rosemary, and myrtle when small. When growing herbs in containers, pay attention to plant nutritional needs and use a soil mix that will retain moisture and allow proper drainage.

We nearly always fill the bottom third of the container with a well-composted manure and the remainder of the pot with a friable potting mixture of peat, vermiculite, perlite, and sterilized garden soil. Plants are then "firmed" into the top mixture and watered well; over time their roots develop, nourished by the rich compost.

Container plants, even in the best planting mediums, can dry out relatively quickly not only during warm weather but also while growing inside heated buildings. It is important to keep the containers well watered. "Well watered" doesn't mean watering superficially and often; it means watering when the topsoil is dry to the touch and doing so thoroughly, so the water penetrates all the way to the bottom of the pot.

An additional suggestion may be helpful especially to those who can't resist growing plants in handsome clay containers. Although these "real" pots are prettier than anything plastic, the soil tends to dry out more quickly than in plastic pots. We address this problem by lining our large clay pots with a heavy piece of plastic that reaches just below the soil line (where it can not be seen). We make several holes in the bottom of the plastic liner to correspond to the hole(s) in the clay container, thus ensuring good drainage. Wooden tubs can also be lined with plastic in the same manner so that the wood doesn't rob the soil of its moisture.

Planting a patio container with herbs that can be enjoyed and harvested throughout the growing season.

trees. The light there is gently filtered. When it is necessary to repot the plants into larger containers, be certain that the new container is adequately large to accommodate growth. Fill the bottom third of the new container with composted organic matter and then repot with good potting soil. The new roots should be able to extend down into the compost for food until a larger pot is needed.

In the fall, when nighttime temperatures approach the freezing mark, we bring the bays inside. Plants will withstand light frosts, but cold temperatures and freezing winds will almost inevitably damage some of the leaves. Once inside, bay plants appreciate a sunny winter window, consistent thorough watering (when the top of the soils dry out), and cool temperatures.

Leaves of these plants may be harvested fresh anytime, preferably as you use them in cooking. The fragrance and flavor of the leaves deteriorate after a short time. Bay is commonly sold as dull dried olive leaves with only a faint resemblance to fresh harvests.

Bay is native to the Mediterranean region. Its botanical name is derived from the Latin *laurus* meaning "laurel," and *nobilis* meaning "renowned." Bay leaf motifs are associated with honor and excellence. The plants are used symbolically in architectural motifs, and leaves are woven into commemorative garlands. The word *laureate,* as in *poet laureate* or *baccalaureate,* means "crowned with laurels."

BEE BALM

Monarda didyma, Bee Balm,
    Bergamot, Oswego Tea
Monarda fistulosa,
    Wild Bergamot
Monarda astromontana,
    Mountain Star Bee Balm
Monarda citriodora, Lemon Bergamot

LABIATAE

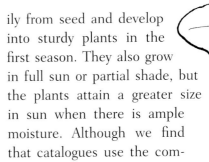

Monarda fistulosa

ALL FOUR OF THESE species of *Monarda* are easily grown from seed throughout Zones 4–9. The first three are perennials and the last one is a hardy annual in our gardens. The annual species could most likely be grown in zones even colder. Plants germinate readily from seed and develop into sturdy plants in the first season. They also grow in full sun or partial shade, but the plants attain a greater size in sun when there is ample moisture. Although we find that catalogues use the common names and species names rather interchangeably for *M. didyma* and *M. fistulosa,* the two species are distinct. *Monarda didyma* is the botanical name for a wide variety of plants, ranging in color from white to pink to rose, lavender, orange red and deep red. Specific colors are often named varieties and are available by purchasing plants. The seeds of *M. didyma* are usually sold in lots of mixed colors. Occasionally a seed company will offer seed packages of the popular red bee balm exclusively.

Monarda didyma

Monarda fistulosa is the botanical name for wild bergamot, the flowers of which are usually bright lavender. Both *M. fistulosa* and *M. didyma* are leafy bushy perennial plants with the characteristic shaggy whorled flower clusters (technically termed *verticillasters*), one growing out of the next as they extend upward along the stems. Both of these varieties produce some volunteers in our gardens, but the scarlet species seems to yield many fewer seeds. The perennial bee balms spread in mintlike fashion by underground roots and they are easily divided when new plants are needed.

A recent introduction to our gardens, *Monarda astromontana,* or mountain star bee balm, is a very lovely refined version of the common types. This hardy perennial reaches a mature height of 1–2 feet, grows in a neat, small, bushy clump, and produces many rosy pink flower spikes the first season from seed. This very fragrant plant is hardy in our climate unless winters are extremely harsh or open. Second-year plants are simply larger clumps, not as widely spreading as the common bee balms.

The annual bee balm, *Monarda citriodora,* is a lemon scented bushy plant with very delicately shaded whorled flowers of green and mauve.

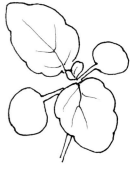

Monarda citriodora

Mountain star bee balm, Monarda astromontana, *is handsome enough to be included in any perennial border.*

We start seeds indoors for earliest production, and plants are vigorous growers in full sun. This species is one of the showiest plants in our annual gardens.

Seeds are collected for bee balms when the flower heads have dried on the plants and nearly lost their color, but before they begin to shatter. Pick off the whole head which may be stored intact until seeds are wanted for sowing, or pulverize the heads to dislodge seeds from the calyces and separate seeds from the chaff. Bee balm flowers are excellent for cutting fresh and for drying. All of these plants are fragrant and their leaves can be used fresh or dried for teas or potpourri. During the time of the Boston Tea Party, the leaves of bee balm were used as a substitute for tea when the black teas were not available. The name Oswego tea originated from that time as the plant was found in abundance in upstate New York, where it was collected and used routinely by the Oswego Indi-

ans of that region. In addition to its usefulness as an ornamental and culinary herb, bee balm also attracts hummingbirds as well as bees to the garden. *Monardas* are native to North America and are named after Nicholas Monardes, a 16th-century Spanish physician and botanist who wrote an herbal on American flora.

Monarda astromontana

BORAGE

Borago officinalis

BORAGINACEAE

BORAGE, AN ANNUAL HERB, may be started indoors, seeded directly into the garden when the soil has warmed, or even fall seeded for spring germination. Seeds are large enough to handle with ease and they may be spaced with some precision in a seed flat or in the garden. If borage is seeded indoors, it should be grown on at cooler temperatures, about 60°F, as it seems to be stressed by hot greenhouse conditions. Plants that are seeded outdoors will germinate as the ground warms and they may be thinned or lifted and transplanted with ease. The young, slightly gray-green leaves are used as salad herbs and they have a refreshing cucumber-like taste. The flowers, blossoming pink or blue on the same plant (a characteristic of many plants in the Boraginaceae family), are also edible and may be used to garnish food or be crystallized for decorating baked goods. See the special box on page 223 showing how to crystallize flowers.

Over the years, we have found that we use this herb less and less for culinary purposes, but the plant is so appealing that we continue to include it in our gardens. Some gardeners will find that their borage volunteers very freely and they will only need to lift and relocate new young plants from year to year. If you wish to save your own seed, watch the maturing flowers carefully. Each flower will produce a small tan fruit containing a few seeds. When the fruit is almost completely dry, but before it drops its contents, harvest, clean, and dry the seeds for fall seeding or storage. This herb is native to the Mediterranean region and it can be grown in American gardens from Zones 3–9.

BURNET

Poterium sanguisorba

ROSACEAE

BURNET MAY BE seeded directly in the garden as soon as the soil is warm, but since it can be slow to germinate, we prefer to start our plants indoors and then grow them at cooler temperatures until they are ready to go into the garden. Seeds germinate well and the small herbs can be grown in Zones 3–9. These perennial herbs are grown primarily for their small, finely toothed leaves that are picked during the first part of each season and used to flavor salads, soups, and sauces. The taste of the fresh leaves can be likened to a nutty cucumber flavor. Burnet, also called salad burnet, grows most vigorously during the first summer months and once the plant has produced its small rather inconspicuous green and red flowers, the leaves become a bit too fibrous for eating fresh. The plant's vigor and harvest period can be prolonged by trimming back the flowering stalks. This will encourage tender new growth from the crown. The perennial will live for many years in a good garden soil that is not too heavy or moist, as those conditions can cause crown rot. Burnet is native to Europe and western Asia. The name *Poterium* is from the Greek *poterion,* "drinking cup," alluding to the herb's use as a flavoring for beverages. Some seed companies still refer to this herb by an older name, *Sanguisorba minor.*

CARAWAY

Carum carvi

UMBELLIFERAE

CARAWAY GERMINATES readily, transplants easily when young, and self-sows freely in the garden if its seed heads are not removed. True to its biennial status, caraway develops its ferny, graceful light-green foliage only during the first season and sends up flowering stalks topped by lacy white flowers that develop into the familiar caraway seeds during the second season. All parts of the plant are edible. The young leaves can be picked and used in salads. Seeds should be left on the plant until they begin to turn brown and then the whole seed head is cut and brought inside to dry. The seeds are used fresh in flavoring and in baked goods. After the seeds have been collected, the plant's roots can be dug and cooked. One year, longer ago than I can accurately recall, we set out about 1–2 dozen caraway plants from which we harvested enough seeds to last us a couple of years. All around this area in the garden we have lifted and reset volunteers from that time onward.

Borage flowers are excellent for decorating fresh salads and for crystallizing.

That area acts as an ongoing nursery for this particular herb. By now the volunteers number in the hundreds and we enjoy cutting some of the flowers for bouquets in the early summer. They look very much like Queen Anne's lace. This herb can be grown in Zones 3–9, but it does not do well in hot and humid conditions in some of the warmer zones. Caraway seeds that are harvested for culinary purposes may be used as well to seed new plants.

A few years ago, several catalogues offered seeds for an annual caraway, which we tried in our garden. The plants did manage to flower and seed at the end of the first season. We treated the plants as we do common caraway, but at the end of the summer, we harvested only half of the crop. The remaining plants produced volunteers in the garden, and we have continued the same partial harvest in this area ever since. The annual variety perpetuates itself regularly. When the area becomes too heavily planted, we lift and relocate small new plants early in the season. Caraway is native to Europe and its name comes from the Greek *karum*.

When catmint is in full flower it attracts more bees than cats to its fragrant blossoms and leaves.

and dry soils, but a second blooming period can be achieved if the whole plant is cut back after the first flowers are spent. Catmint, grown in Zones 3–9, is gently aromatic and makes a good tea herb. It will grow in light shade, but may have fewer flowers under those conditions. Plants can easily be lifted and relocated in the garden in the spring. Seeds are saved by harvesting dried flower heads before they shatter on the plants. Store heads whole, or clean seeds and separate from chaff. Catmint is native to the Caucasus and Iran and the genus name comes from Nepet, a town in Tuscany.

CATMINT

Nepeta mussinii

LABIATAE

CATMINT IS a graceful small perennial herb that works beautifully as a border plant and does not seem to attract as much attention from felines as its close relative, catnip. Catmint is easy to grow from seed and transplants readily. The small gray green leaves form rather neat mounds the first season and the plant comes quickly into bloom the second spring, when light blue lavender blossoms cover the entire plant. This perennial does not like intense heat

CATNIP

Nepeta cataria

LABIATAE

CATNIP IS EASY to start from seed and germinates readily as long as the seed has not been stored too long. This perennial herb can be started indoors or seeded in the late fall or early spring directly into a prepared seedbed and then transplanted into place. If you have cats, or if your neighbors have cats, you should start your seeds indoors as the tender young plants may not survive the chomping and romping the aromas of seedlings inevitably stimulate. We have customers every season looking for the largest field-grown catnip plants we have to offer, explaining that every plan they have devised to fool their cats had failed until their young plants had developed some size. Our own farm cats have long since lost interest, perhaps because they have free access to hundreds of catnip plants (which we grow in large quantity to harvest for our herbal teas).

Plants started indoors should be grown on at cooler temperatures, and mature plants should be harvested by no more than half their full size and no later than August. A too-severe harvest can disable the plant's ability to survive the winter. As with most herbs, catnip should be harvested before it blossoms. Some northern growers treat catnip like an annual herb and harvest it twice in a growing season without concern about the plants living over another year. Plants that are left unharvested to blossom and set seed in the garden will produce numerous volunteers the following season. Unless you are intent on having a specific number of plants from season to season, you may simply want to lift and relocate volunteers in the spring. If you do wish to save seed, it is very easy. Allow a few vigorous plants to mature, but keep a close check on their development so that you are certain to collect seeds before they drop and scatter. Catnip is a rather large, not particularly handsome plant, with gray green leaves and off-white mintlike blossoms. It can be grown in Zones 3–9.

CHAMOMILE

Matricaria recutita,
   German Chamomile
Chamaemelum nobile,
   Roman Chamomile

COMPOSITAE

German chamomile

GERMAN CHAMOMILE, an
annual herb, is easily grown from seed, and we like to sow the very fine seed directly into plugs or peat pots, sprinkling about a dozen seeds to a container. That allows us to grow the plants on in their original con-

tainers and set them out in the garden without separating the tiny plants and damaging the fine root systems. The species can also be sown directly into the garden bed as long as you have a spot that is well prepared where the young seedlings do not have to compete with weeds. This annual herb germinates and develops rapidly. The delicate, small, ferny foliage is bright green and the blossoms are white with yellow centers. As the blossoms mature,

Roman chamomile

petals fall off and the yellow seed head enlarges. At this point the blossoms are ready to be harvested and used fresh or dried for tea. Chamomile tea is used medicinally in various countries of the world. The herb is attractive and the flowers and leaves are sweetly scented, making it an excellent bedding or container plant. Plants that are not harvested will most likely produce a number of volunteers the following spring. For saving seeds, a few plants must be left in the garden to mature fully. The flowers will shed their petals and enlarge into seed heads. Pick when the heads look as if they are beginning to dry but before they start to break apart. This maturation can happen in a matter of days. German chamomile will do well in gardens from Zone 3–9. This annual herb was found originally in Europe and Western Asia.

Roman chamomile is a perennial herb, rather like a much smaller version of the annual. Its low-growing spreading habit makes it well suited as a groundcover, but it has similar uses to the annual herb. For tea production, we prefer the larger German type.

CHERVIL

Anthriscus cerefolium

UMBELLIFERAE

CHERVIL MAY BE
seeded inside or directly
into the garden early in the season. For starting inside, we recommend scattering a few seeds onto

the surface of soil-filled plugs or peat pots where the plants will germinate. We place the containers, once sown, in a dark place, or cover them with a piece of dark plastic until the seeds begin to germinate. We immediately remove the cover or relocate the seeding container in the light where the plants are to be grown on. Like many members of the Umbelliferae family, young seedlings prefer to be grown on at lower temperatures. Chervil, a relative of parsley, has parsleylike foliage that is lighter green and very delicate. Its flavor is a mild anise flavor so favored by the French that it is included in the *fines herbes*. Unlike parsley however, chervil is best used fresh or added to soups and other dishes at the very last stages of preparation, since cooking the herb destroys its flavor.

By midsummer in our gardens, chervil will begin to set small white blossoms that develop quickly into seedheads. When this happens, the leafy part of the plant declines in vigor. Some gardeners like to sow several plantings of this herb for successive harvests of the tender leaves. We find that we can harvest from the original plants for most of the summer as long as we keep the flowering stalks cut before they have a chance to develop.

If you are saving seeds, or if you want to leave some mature seed stalks to produce volunteers for the following season, allow a few plants to develop to maturity. Chervil prefers a cool soil and moisture throughout the summer, so a light mulch or gentle shading from neighboring plants will be advantageous. The herb can be grown in Zones 3–9 as long as it has protection from extreme sun, heat, and dryness. The plant is native to southeastern Europe and western Asia.

CHIVES

Allium schoenoprasum. Chives
Allium tuberosum. Garlic Chives

AMARYLLIDACEAE

CHIVES ARE the perfect herbs for beginning gardeners. These perennial herbs are extremely easy to grow from seed or purchased plants. Plants that

chives

are allowed to mature in the garden produce many volunteers, and individual plants multiply so rapidly that they can be lifted and divided every few years. We have clumps of chives that we planted more than twenty years ago in gardens long since abandoned. Although the leaves of these survivors are rather small in comparison to our well-tended plants, the old chive plants faithfully send up their little onion-flavored spears each spring. Furthermore, old plants can easily be rejuvenated by lifting, dividing, and replanting in newly enriched soils.

garlic chives

We grow from seed new plants of both kinds of chives by clustering a few seeds in individual plugs or peat pots and letting the plants germinate and develop

Garlic chives in full bloom.

in the greenhouses before setting them out into the gardens. You can easily seed directly into a garden spot, but the young seedlings look so much like grass that weeding could be a problem. It is easier to produce the seedlings inside and set them out into a well-prepared site.

The cultural requirements for chives and garlic chives are similar, but there are a few differences in the appearance and flavor of the two species. The leaves of chives are rounded hollow tubes; garlic chives have flattened leaves. Both varieties begin to flower in their second year from seed. Chives blossom very early in the spring. The fragrant blossoms are lovely round deep pink flower clusters held on upright solitary stems in the center of the edible leaves. Garlic chives flower in late summer. Fragrant flower clusters are bright white and more flattened atop rigid stems. Chive leaves have a mild onion flavor; garlic chives definitely taste like garlic. The flowers of both species are edible and are an attractive and spicy addition to fresh salads. We also dry the blossoms of both species for winter arrangements.

The flavor of the leaves is best before the plants go to flower. That means that chives must be harvested very early in the spring. Once bud production begins, we cease harvesting, allow the flowers to develop, collect flower heads early for ornamental use, and leave a few to mature seeds. When flowering is over, we cut the entire plant back to the ground and within a matter of days, new growth emerges. This new growth can be used for culinary purposes for the remainder of the summer. Garlic chives are harvested only during the early part of the spring and summer before flowers have developed. Once the flowering stalks have set buds, the flavor and texture of the edible leaves is diminished. And since the flowers are produced late in the summer, there is no time in our climate to cut back the plant for any second growth. That also means that there is a longer early season of harvest for garlic chives, and we take advantage of this time to enjoy the plants fresh and to harvest extra leaves for freezing and drying. Both chives can be grown in Zones 3–9. The name *Allium* comes from the Celtic *all* meaning "hot" or "pungent."

SWEET CICELY

Myrrhis odorata

UMBELLIFERAE

SWEET CICELY IS difficult to grow from seed unless the seed is fresh, or it has been harvested fresh and then placed in cold storage. (See the section on angelica for a complete explanation of cold storing.) For this reason, some gardeners prefer to start by purchasing a plant and then collecting seeds as soon as they are ready to drop naturally from the plant. Fresh seeds are best planted directly into a well-prepared garden site in the fall. Growth will begin the following spring. If you purchase stratified or fresh seeds, you may seed them either indoors or outside. Plant seeds inside in individual plugs or peat containers so that transplanting can be done carefully. Like so many other members of the Umbelliferae family, this herb can be difficult to transplant. Inside, grow seedlings on at cooler temperatures, 55°–60°F, until they are ready to be set outside in the garden. Seeds germinated in an outside bed should be transplanted carefully when the plants are small and protected from direct sun and wind for several days until the shock of transplanting has passed.

Sweet cicely prefers a cool partially shaded location and a soil that has plenty of humus. Some gardeners like to incorporate these plants into lightly shaded woodland sites. Despite the difficulties that it takes, this herb is a lovely addition to the garden for its delicate ferny foliage and characteristic white umbels. Sweet cicely is sometimes referred to as giant chervil because of the similar anise flavor of the leaves that can be used to flavor salads and other dishes. Leaves can also be chopped and cooked with acidic fruits and berries to sweeten the sauces without using too much sugar. The green seeds are used raw to flavor salads and food. Sweet cicely is grown in Zones 4–9, but with more difficulty in the warmest areas because it needs cold weather to complete its cycle.

We have attempted to grow these herbs in a num-

DRYING CULINARY HERBS

WHEN HERBS AND VEGETABLES can be picked fresh from the garden, cooking is easy and even the simplest foods have exquisite flavor. With so short a growing season, however, we are very dependent on harvested stored herbs to make winter foods as appealing as possible.

There are a few simple tricks for drying culinary herbs to ensure that their flavor, fragrance, and color are truly well preserved. The process begins by choosing the right harvesttime. Most herbs should be picked when they have well-developed vegetative growth, but before they have started to flower. Harvest in the early part of a sunny dry day. Cut stems and tie herbs in small bunches if you have a good hot drying shed or attic.

The more quickly herbs are dried, the more flavorful they will be. We convert one of our greenhouses into a drying house by covering the inside walls with black plastic to shut out all sunlight. On a sunny day in July or August, the months when most of the harvesting is done, temperatures reach as high as 120°F inside. The small harvested herb bunches are hung along pegged boards on the ceiling of the greenhouses. It takes only a day or two for them to dry completely. They are then removed from the drying house, crumbled only slightly, stems are removed, and leaves are put into airtight containers and sealed. Dried herbs are then stored in a dark closet.

We also use the heat from our kitchen woodstove for drying herbs that are harvested in late summer and early fall. A small wooden framed tray with wire-mesh bottom is suspended over the woodstove. Leaves such as parsley, fennel, and marjoram are spread in a thin layer in the bottom of the tray. It takes only a few hours of hanging over a hot stove for the herbs to become crispy dry. Conventional ovens can also be used to dry small quantities of herbs. Place a thin layer of leaves on a cookie sheet. Place the sheet on the top shelf of a preheated oven set at a temperature no higher than 120°F and check the herbs often so that they are removed when totally dry but not browned in any way.

Always store dried herbs in sealed containers and out of sunlight. If you like having bottles of herbs on open shelves in the cooking area, dark colored or opaque glass will work best in preserving color and flavor. We have all seen photographs depicting lovely old colonial farmhouses with herbs hanging from wooden beams and pegs. These pictures convey the notion that the cook simply reaches up to pinch off a sprig of this or that during food preparation. We assure you that culinary herbs stored this way are valuable only as decoration. Beautiful as they may be, their leaves will be flavorless, colorless, and dusty.

The kitchen woodstove serves double duty when the weather turns chilly.

ber of sites where they survived irregularly until we found the perfect conditions in our region. Now we have vigorous seven-year-old plants that are located in a cool semi-shaded corner of a perennial garden on the northwest side of the farmhouse. The garden contains a number of hostas, iris, ligularia, and hemerocallis. The sweet cicely plants grow to a height of 2–3 feet each summer, flower profusely, and mature hundreds of glossy dark brown seeds. We harvest most of the seeds for production, but some that we miss inevitably find a spot to produce volunteers in the spring. Volunteers are relocated easily, but mature plants should not be moved. This herb is native to Europe.

COMFREY

Symphytum officinale

BORAGINACEAE

ONCE YOU HAVE comfrey in your gardens, you will have plants forever. We were given several roots of comfrey about twenty years ago as a gift. Not knowing how vigorous a plant this was, we set them out in several sites. Unfortunately one of those sites was directly in the center of a production garden. It took about a dozen years of plowing, tilling, and weeding to rid the area of plants. Locate your plants wisely.

Comfrey is a large rangy but not unattractive perennial. Its gray-green hairy leaves are pleasing to the touch and its stems are topped in late summer with very small pink tubular flowers. For many years there was controversy about the medicinal use of comfrey. The current position of even the most enthusiastic herbalists seems to be to restrict comfrey for use as an external medicine, because of the toxic properties of the alkaloids that are present in its leaves and roots. Some growers recommend using comfrey as a green manure, a fodder crop, or for leaves to enrich the compost pile. We grow it simply for its ornamental value and because of its interesting history.

Comfrey seeds can be sown directly into a well-prepared bed in fall or early spring. We seed our plants indoors in early spring to be transplanted and set out after danger of frost has passed. Seed coats of comfrey are very hard. Better germination may be obtained by soaking the seeds in warm water for a day or by scarification of the seed before sowing. See a complete discussion of scarification on page 25.

Plants prefer a good garden soil in full sun to partial shade. Once established, they may be lifted and divided for propagation from year to year. We have not focused our attention on gathering any substantial amount of seed from our plants, because we do all of our propagation vegetatively.

CORIANDER

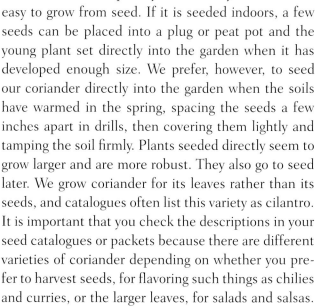

Coriandrum sativum

UMBELLIFERAE

CORIANDER IS ALSO CALLED cilantro or Chinese parsley and it is very easy to grow from seed. If it is seeded indoors, a few seeds can be placed into a plug or peat pot and the young plant set directly into the garden when it has developed enough size. We prefer, however, to seed our coriander directly into the garden when the soils have warmed in the spring, spacing the seeds a few inches apart in drills, then covering them lightly and tamping the soil firmly. Plants seeded directly seem to grow larger and are more robust. They also go to seed later. We grow coriander for its leaves rather than its seeds, and catalogues often list this variety as cilantro. It is important that you check the descriptions in your seed catalogues or packets because there are different varieties of coriander depending on whether you prefer to harvest seeds, for flavoring such things as chilies and curries, or the larger leaves, for salads and salsas.

Mature plants of coriander are tall and large leaved with loose white to lavender umbels that produce the small round beige seeds. If you are most interested in leaf production, keep the flowering stalks cut off; if you want to collect seeds, allow them to ripen on the plant, cut them off, and dry inside. All parts of the plant have a pungent, rather earthy aroma which appeals to some and repels others. Coriander can be grown in Zones 3–10, but (like many of its relatives) with difficulty in the hot, more humid areas. This herb is native to southern Europe and it gets its name from the Greek name *koriandron,* which in turn comes from the Greek word *koris,* meaning "bug."

CUMIN

Cuminum cyminum

UMBELLIFERAE

CUMIN IS NOT OFTEN SEEN in northern gardens because the plants require three to four months of warm summer weather to mature. It is generally found in Zones 5–10, but if northern gardeners want to have a few plants, the seeds can be started indoors. Scatter a few seeds into a plug or peat pot and press them into the soil. When seeding outdoors, the small seeds are broadcast carefully over a small well-prepared bed and the soil must be kept from drying out throughout the growing cycle. Plants can be grown close together so that the rather limp stems with their feathery foliage support each other. Cumin has small white to rose blossoms that mature to yellowish brown seeds. The seeds of this plant are very important in the foods of Southeast Asia, India, and Latin America. They are used in flavoring chili powders and curry mixtures. Cumin is native to the Mediterranean region.

DILL

Anethum graveolens

UMBELLIFERAE

DILL MAY BE SOWN indoors or out. We usually sow a few plugs or peat pots indoors for earliest harvests, but the plants produced from this early seeding never match in size or longevity those that are seeded directly into the garden. This is a characteristic of so many of the Umbelliferae herbs, which seem to prefer being seeded and grown in one spot without the interruption of transplanting. Dill may be seeded outdoors when the soils have warmed and if you want young fresh dill until the fall, you may want to have several seedings. Early outdoor seedings mature midsummer.

We grow large numbers of dill plants for leaf production. For these plants, we carefully prepare a seed bed to be planted in June. The bed is seeded in long double or triple rows, the seeding being done carefully enough so that no thinning is required. Germination takes place quickly in the warm summer soils and the dill rows need only one or two quick weedings before the plants have reached enough size to crowd out any serious competition. Dill grown for seed production could be handled in the same manner, but should be seeded somewhat earlier so that seed heads have time to mature by midsummer when most pickling is done. Dill is familiar to most of us as a pickling herb, but its feathery green leaves are excellent when used fresh in salads or cooked into soups and fish dishes. Seeds are available for several named varieties of dill, some varieties being grown for seed production and others mainly for leafy growth. There are also a few dwarf varieties available for small gardens and container growing. Read the descriptions of the various kinds to match the variety to your needs.

This aromatic herb produces tall flowering stalks topped by yellow green umbels that mature into seeds. The seed heads can be picked green for flavoring herbal vinegars and pickles and the brown mature seeds can be dried and used for flavoring all winter. Leaves may also be picked fresh, dried, and crumpled into an airtight container. Dried dill retains its color and flavor for months, especially when stored in a dark place. If dill plants are left unharvested in the garden you will almost certainly have volunteers the following spring, which tells us that the plants could be seeded in the fall as well as in the spring. Very young volunteers can be lifted with lots of soil intact and relocated successfully. Dill is native to Europe.

ELECAMPANE

Inula helenium

COMPOSITAE

GARDENERS CHOOSE TO GROW plants for any number of reasons, some of them so

WHEN WE GREW our first eucalyptus plants from seed about fifteen years ago, we could find only a handful of American seed catalogues offering seeds for no more than two to three species. We were so intrigued by the enormous variability of the genus (there are 400–500 species of eucalypts) that we wrote to several Australian seed companies that specialized in these plants. It was our introduction to some of the most beautiful, useful, and easily grown plants of our gardens. We treat eucalypts as annuals in our zone, but many American gardeners will be able to grow selected species as the perennial shrubs and trees that they naturally are.

Eucalyptus cinerea

We sow eucalyptus seeds in flats of our regular seeding medium, pressing the seeds lightly into the medium in the case of small seeds, and lightly covering larger ones. Here's a partial list of species we have grown: *E. cinerea, E. globulus, E. citriodora, E. nitida, E. moorei nana, E. ficifolia, E. risdonii, E. bridgesiana, E. camphora,* and *E. gunnii.* Each of these varieties germinates in 1–2 weeks when seed flats are maintained at temperatures of 65°–75°F. Once germinated, plants develop a couple of sets of true leaves in a matter of weeks. Seedlings are then ready to be transplanted into plugs or small pots for growing on. We set out small plants in the garden after danger of frost has passed and field-grow the plants for the first season. Depending on the varieties grown, we can expect a plant to reach 1–3 feet even in our short growing season.

In late summer (before a heavy frost), we either harvest the entire plant to dry the foliage for decorative use or we pot field-grown plants to be brought inside. Many eucalypts make beautiful houseplants. They are easy to care for and can be pruned to shape or to keep size in check. After the first season of growth, we usually return eucalypts to the summer garden in pots. Pots may be sunk into a bed or border, or used as patio or accent plants. Gardeners in warmer climates of the country will have no trouble finding species of eucalyptus that will be hardy outdoor plants. These gardeners should make note of plant descriptions because many of the plants of this genus will grow into sizable shrubs and even into very large trees. We gave visiting friends a small pot of *Eucalyptus cinerea* to take home to their Florida garden. Once planted, this rapid grower took no time developing into an impressive tree.

Even in our Maine gardens, we have replanted second- and third-year plants directly in the garden for summer growth. Our experi-

Eucalyptus citriodora

Its form and the fragrance of the leaves makes Eucalyptus citriodora *one of our favorite species.*

ence has shown us however that the plants put on so much size that it is somewhat difficult to lift the whole root system after the first year. Extensive root damage in transplanting may result in plant loss. We also discovered that growing eucalypts in containers in our climate allows us to check the rapid growth of the plants so that we can continue to enjoy them indoors and out for many seasons. It has been interesting to observe that many of our mature eucalypts, plants 2–3 years old, have flowered in our winter greenhouses. They also exhibit their characteristic exfoliating bark. Rather than dropping leaves in the winter, as our deciduous trees do, the eucalyptus bark splits, curls, and falls off irregularly along the trunk.

Eucalyptus nitida

Our method of selecting eucalypts to grow at the farm has been totally arbitrary. Other than choosing the commonly known *E. cinerea* (used widely in the floral industry of this country), we try varieties after reading names and descriptions of leaf shape, color, fragrance, overall plant morphology, and any other intriguing history of plant use. Rarely have we been disappointed in watching the species develop, and we encourage other gardeners to experiment. It has been gratifying to watch American seed catalogues increase the number of eucalyptus seeds for the past several years. We expect that its popularity will continue to increase, given the plants' ease of cultivation, beauty, and usefulness.

Eucalyptus risdonii

Eucalyptus moorei nana

idiosyncratic that they are amusing to relate. Here's our confession about why elecampane continues to grow in our gardens. We purchased a couple of volumes of *Good's Family Flora* published in 1845 and illustrated liberally with lovely colored engravings. The engravings take considerable liberty in interpreting some of the plants contained within. The illustration for elecampane distorts the size and color of the flower, turning the plant into something resembling an exotic tropical. That engraving prompted us to purchase seed for elecampane, and once grown, it's very hard to abandon a vigorous plant.

Elecampane is vigorous. Mature plants stand 4–6 feet tall. They have large, coarsely toothed, pointed leaves that are over a foot long, gray green on the top and downy gray on the undersides. In late summer the stems are topped by modest daisylike yellow flowers. Many herb growers end up looking into the history of their plants; elecampane has a rich history of associations (with Helen of Troy, as the species name would imply) as well as culinary and medicinal uses. Homely plants are a little like homely pets. Once they come into your life, they ingratiate themselves and are probably there to stay. Catalogues often recommend that plants like elecampane be located at the back of the border.

This herb is very easy to grow in Zones 3–9. It is best propagated by seeds. Seeds can be saved once the flowers have finished blooming and matured their seeds in the heads. Pick heads when they begin to dry and before they shatter.

Elecampane is thought to be native to central Asia, but it is now naturalized throughout the world.

FENNEL

Foeniculum vulgare var. *dulce*,
    Green Fennel
Foeniculum vulgare var. *dulce* 'Rubrum',
    Bronze Fennel

UMBELLIFERAE

OF ALL THE UMBELLIFERAE we have started from seed indoors, we have had the best results with both green and bronze fennel. The herb

This fennel plant was grown for its edible bulb as opposed to its feathery leaves. Bulbs are harvested at this size for eating fresh or for cooking.

may be seeded in plugs or peat pots, using a few seeds to a container. Seeds germinate readily and young plants can be set into the garden after the last frost. Like dill, fennel may also be seeded directly into a well-prepared garden row and thinned to the proper spacing. Plants grow rapidly and they are very handsome all season long, meaning that they could be incorporated into an ornamental mixed border. Both fennel varieties have finely cut feathery leaves, either green or coppery bronze. By midsummer the herbs begin to develop yellow to green umbels which mature into seed heads.

We use the fresh leaves in salads, soups, and herbal tea. Some growers choose specific varieties of fennel, referred to as Florence fennel or Finocchio, for the large succulent bulbous rootstock which is eaten raw or cooked. If you are growing fennel primarily for the bulb, thin the plants, so that they are not crowded. If you wish to save both your own dill and fennel seed for next year's crops, the herbs should be planted away from one another as they can cross-pollinate. In our gardens, we have noticed that the bronze fennel is slower to go to seed than the green, but sometimes our bronze fennel winters over and produces seed during

Tall fennel plants are grown close together for leaf harvest.

the second season. Fennels are classified as perennials, but northern growers treat them as annual herbs. Fennel is one of the oldest known cultivated herbs and it is native to southern Europe.

FENUGREEK

Trigonella foenum-graecum

LEGUMINOSAE

FENUGREEK DOES NOT like to be transplanted, so in the north it is best to start the seeds 2 or 3 to a plug or peat pot and grow them in a sunny warm spot until the plants are ready to be set out into the garden after all danger of frost has passed. In areas where the summers are long, the seeds may be sown directly into the garden when the soils have warmed. If soils are too cold or wet, seeds are likely to rot in the ground. It takes fenugreek about 4 months to mature. The herb has attractive small oval leaves in groups of 3 along the stem and then tiny fragrant off-white blossoms. The blossoms mature into characteristic legume pods along the stems. Fenugreek is grown primarily for its seeds which smell a little like maple syrup with a hint of celery. The seeds are used in curries and chutneys and can also be sprouted. The whole plants are harvested once the pods brown but before they open and the seeds are allowed to dry before storage. In the Mediterranean region the plant is used as a forage crop. It is native to southeastern Europe and Asia.

GARLIC, FRAGRANT FLOWERING

Allium ramosum

AMARYLLIDACEAE

THIS UNCOMMON HERB CAN be grown in Zones 3–8 and is attractive enough to hold its own even in a perennial border. Start plants indoors or seed them directly into the garden. Indoors it is best to plant into plugs or peat pots as the young seedlings are thin grasslike spears that are difficult to transplant. If seeding directly into the garden, prepare and weed the bed so that you will recognize the emerging herb seedlings. Whether planting indoors or outside, cluster a few seeds and cover them lightly with soil. During the first season the small plant clump will develop in size and in the second year it will begin to flower. The flowers are fragrant, handsome, slightly flattened white blossoms on the tops of sturdy stems. The flowers mature into seed heads that are good to dry for winter arrangements. If you are collecting seeds, harvest the heads just as they begin to split, and before they start losing the seeds. Although we grow this herb as an ornamental, the leaves can be used in cooking. From the third season onward, fragrant flowering garlic plants can be propagated by lifting and dividing the clumps in the early spring, just as you do with chives or garlic chives. *Allium ramosum* is sometimes confused with *Allium tuberosum*, but if you see the plants in close proximity, you'll see that fragrant flowering garlic is larger in leaf and flower size, has a thicker flower stem, and blooms earlier than garlic chives. This herb is originally from central Asia.

GERMANDER

Teucrium chamaedrys

LABIATAE

IT IS BEST to start germander indoors in a regular seed flat as the herb needs warmth and high humidity to germinate. Young seedlings are easy to transplant into small pots and the plants are grown on inside until the weather warms. Germander can be started outdoors, but you will find that germination is slow and sporadic, and the small seedlings have to compete with weeds and changing weather. The small herbs have delicate dark-green glossy leaves on plants with a spreading habit. They are slow growers and do not bloom for us until the end of the first season or the beginning of the second. Blossoms are a rosy pink. Germander is grown in

ICK A BREEZY MILD summer day. Put on your oldest gardening clothes. Clean out one of your wheelbarrows and choose a couple of hoes. Then gather a few simple ingredients and you will be ready to fashion a collection of rustic homemade plant containers, known as hypertufa planters. We first saw them described in an issue of *Herb Companion* and subsequently in several other gardening books and magazines. We read the instructions, taught ourselves to make them, and then offered several workshops on the subject. These workshops have always been among our favorite activities on the farm. They are enjoyed by adults and children, men and women, equally. Hypertufa planters are not only easy to construct, they are relatively lightweight, durable, and lend themselves to much creative interpretation by their makers.

To start you will need a supply of peat moss (finely milled), vermiculite, portland cement, fibermesh (available at any company that carries masonry supplies), and water. We use the following proportions for the mixture: 6 quarts peat moss, 6 quarts vermiculite, 4 quarts cement, about a half cup of fibermesh, and enough water to make the cement into something resembling a wet dough.

Begin by measuring out the dry ingredients (use an old plastic quart container), making 1–3 batches at a time in a wheelbarrow or mason's trough. Thoroughly mix all the ingredients before adding water. Make

Shaping a plant pot around a plastic-covered form.

certain that you break apart the clumps of fibermesh (wear rubber gloves for this operation) before adding it to the mixture so that the mesh is evenly distributed throughout. Then add water slowly (a quart at a time), mixing between each addition until the consistency is right. The mixture should be moist enough to stick together and dry enough to avoid being too watery when handled.

Next, choose a form for the pot. An old plastic plant pot will do, as will a plastic food colander, a heavy-duty corrugated box, a large plastic tub, or even a large disposable aluminum baking pan. Once you begin to make these pots, you will become quite inventive when trying to find forms. Cover the form you are using with a thin piece of plastic. This allows the removal of the inner form more easily once the pot has been made and dried. Place the form topside down on a sturdy work surface.

Wear rubber gloves for the rest of the work. Start to shape the planter by scooping up the mixture and packing it against the form. Begin at the sides of the form and cover it from bottom to top with a thick layer of the moist mixture. Try to cover the form evenly so that the planter is at least 1½–2 inches thick. Pay closest attention to corners so they are as thick as the sides. A good tip here is to have a few toothpicks or thin twigs on hand to test the thickness all over the pot. Thin spots will be weak places in the finished pots. Also make certain that you shape the top (which will in effect be

Mixing the mortar for making hypertufa planters.

the bottom) so that it is flat and smooth. When it comes time to turn the planter rightside up, you will want it to sit solidly and evenly. When shaping is done, make several drainage holes in the base of the planter.

Once the form is well covered and smoothed (lots of patting and pushing will be needed), the basic container is done. You may embellish a plain container by drawing in lines or designs and embedding pebbles, shells, or other matter for visual effect. The planter is now ready to be dried and cured. We use our greenhouses for curing but any warm dry location will do. It takes 2–7 days (depending on weather and container size) for a pot to dry thoroughly.

When the container feels totally dry to the touch, turn it over and carefully pull out the inner form. Finishing steps include "roughing up" the top lip (the part on which the work-in-progress was resting). It will be flat and almost without texture because the cement mixture will have drained down during the drying process. We correct this rather unappealing appearance by wetting the top lip and roughing it up with a wire brush, to make the top texture resemble the texture of the sides. If there are any fibermesh pieces sticking out from the sides of the pot, quickly burn off these pieces with a small propane torch or leave them to wear off naturally. After several years of making pots according

Several homemade planters, naturally colored and with dyed mortar, ready to go outdoors for the summer.

to the official recipe, we wondered if we could alter the color of the mixture by using regular cement dyes. The results were quite successful. We tried red, brown, and black dyes. Dyes are mixed with the dried ingredients and amended after seeing the resulting colors when water is added. Remember that the color of any dyed mixture will lighten considerably when dried. Once you experience this color change, you can adjust the amounts of dye in subsequent mixtures.

Admittedly, hypertufa containers don't have the elegance of the scrolled terra cottas, but they have a pleasing rustic quality to them and are very affordable. Their natural appearance makes them especially appropriate for small herb plantings.

The handmade planter is ready to be dried. Once dried, it is turned upright, the inner form is removed, and the pot is ready for finishing.

Zones 5–9 primarily as an ornamental herb, and it benefits from a mulch in zones and locations where it is exposed to harsh winters. In the spring, young plants may be lifted and divided as they spread through underground roots. If you are collecting your own seeds from these plants, let the flowers develop into small spikes and collect the browned little cones, each of which contains about 2–4 small seeds. Seeds remain viable for only a year or two. Germander is used as a border or edging herb and has also been one of the traditional knot-garden plants. It is native to Europe and southwest Asia.

A less common species of germander, *Teucrium fruticans,* is commonly known as Tree Germander. It differs greatly from the plants described above. The latter species is a large shrubby perennial with light silver leaves and very soft lavender blue flowers. It is a beautiful tender perennial in our gardens, so we prefer to grow it as a large container plant. Its growth is so vigorous that we need to trim plants to scale every other year. We have not observed any seeds produced nor found a source of seed, but plants can be propagated easily from stem cuttings.

HOREHOUND

Marrubium vulgare

LABIATAE

HOREHOUND IS NOT difficult to grow from seed, but seed does not retain its viability for more than 2–3 years. Old seed may not perform well. Horehound also germinates erratically over a long period of time, meaning that a seed flat could show some growth in only 10 days, but continue to germinate new seedlings when the first little plants have their true leaves and are ready for transplanting. When this happens, we prick out the developed seedlings and replant them in their new growing containers and very gently replace the tiny germinating seeds in a seed flat where they can continue to

develop. If you try this method, be certain to water the seed flat generously to compensate for the disturbances you have caused. Results are typically very good. The thinning out of the larger seedlings allows more light and air to get at the slowest seeds, and there will be less likelihood that the slower plants will have damping-off problems.

Horehound is an attractive herb with wrinkled gray green hoary leaves. Flowers are inconspicuous small white blossoms held in rings around the leaf nodes, arranged in the manner so typical of members of the Labiatae or Mint family. Seeds of this herb are collected after the flower pods turn brown, but be aware that the calyces of horehound are prickly.

This herb is grown in Zones 3–9, and it is perhaps best known for its medicinal uses. Horehound cough drops are an old-fashioned medicine that can easily be made at home. Horehound is native to the Mediterranean region, Europe, and Asia, and its name comes from the Hebrew *maroob* meaning "bitter juice."

HYSSOP

Hyssopus officinalis

LABIATAE

HYSSOP GROWS READILY from seed. This perennial herb begins as a very small seedling, but during the first summer it will develop fairly quickly into a sizable evergreen shrubby specimen. During the second season, hyssop will begin to blossom midsummer. A plant can have pink, purple, or white blossoms. We have never seen hyssop seed sold for specific flower colors. Each seed packet will produce a mixture of colors.

Hyssop is grown in Zones 3–8; in the coldest zones there will most likely be some winter die-back. When this happens, wait until new green growth appears in the spring and then trim the plant back to the point of new growth. The plants will branch out and regain their size in a matter of weeks.

Hyssop is a good tea herb, but leaves should be

harvested for tea before the plants begin to flower. Once flowering commences, the leaves develop a very bitter taste. Hyssop is such an attractive plant with its nearly evergreen glossy leaves and flowers that we use it in a number of our perennial borders. Bees are attracted to its blossoms. When the blossoms are spent and the seed heads turn brown, seeds can be collected easily. Hyssop that is left unharvested will produce volunteers readily and these new plants can be lifted in the spring and transplanted into place. Plants can also be propagated by layering. Hyssop is native to southern and eastern Europe.

Pink flowering hyssop shares garden space with a perennial blue salvia (Salvia nemorosa) *and pink mallow* (Malva moschata).

LAVENDER

Lavandula angustifolia

LABIATAE

THERE ARE MANY different species of lavender. The one discussed here is commonly referred to as English lavender, the species usually available from seed and reliably hardy even in our northern gardens. Generally speaking, catalogues offer what they call English lavender and this is a plant about 12–18 inches tall with narrow fragrant gray-green leaves and highly scented flower spikes. If the seed package does not specify anything more than the general species, the seeds will typically produce plants with flower colors ranging from light to medium lavender. If you wish to germinate specific varieties of this herb, there are a number of good choices and you should read the catalogue or seed package descriptions. Several of the most common offerings include 'Hidcote', a compact plant with purple flowers; 'Jean Davis', a variety with pale pink flowers; 'Munstead', with lavender blue blossoms, bluer than most; 'Rosea', with light pink flowers; and 'Lavender Lady', a recent introduction that produces lavender flowers the first year from seed.

Lavender is not difficult to germinate, but the percentage of seeds to germinate is lower than that of many other plants, and germination takes place over a long period of time. Lavender seeds need constant humidity and high temperatures to begin germinating, but once the seeds have sprouted, the plants can usually be handled successfully. When the young seedlings have true leaves, they should be transplanted to their proper spacing either in flats or in individual containers. From that point on, given good light, warmth, and moisture, the plants will begin to branch out and put on size.

It is enjoyable to transplant even the smallest plants because your work area will be filled with that familiar and delightful aroma. Lavender can be grown in Zones 4–10. In Zone 4 we have found that it will survive even the coldest winters provided that it is

DIEGO WAS TAUGHT to make them by his grandmother in Argentina. While a member of the staff at the farm, he taught us. In turn, we teach visitors to the farm, and so it continues. Lavender bottles are one of those old-fashioned handicrafts performed by gardeners throughout the world. It's easy to understand why the custom of wrapping fresh lavender in ribbons has persisted over the years. The work is visually pleasing, and the fragrance of lavender lingers on the hands for hours.

The lavender must be in full flower for best results. Pick stems fresh right before starting. Each stem should be at least a foot long. Remove lower leaves from the stems, leaving only the flowers. A lavender "bottle" is made by clustering an uneven number of stems with a very narrow ribbon first tied at the base of the flowers. We use about 15–17 stems for best effect. Ribbons are cut to a length of 42 inches for this scale. Tie the ribbon tight, leaving a foot of ribbon to hang until the end, and use the remaining length for weaving.

Once tied, turn the lavender stems upside down, and very gently and carefully bend the stems back over the blossoms. Then starting with the long ribbon, weave in and out around the stems, enclosing the blossoms as the rows of woven ribbon increase. Try to

Hand-crafted bottles or wands are made from fresh lavender.

weave so that the stems are evenly spaced around the bottle. When you have come to the end of the bottle (the tips of the flowers) pick up the 1-foot length of ribbon that was carried down through the middle of the flowers and tie it tightly to the weaver ribbon. Make a bow or simple knot.

Trim the stems of the lavender and with a small length of ribbon, tie them together at the base of the bottle. The lavender bottle, also referred to as a lavender wand, should be dried in an airy place for a day or two, out of direct sun, and then it is ready to be used. Place one in a drawer with linens or clothing. They keep their fragrance for several years.

grown in well-drained soil and given some winter protection. Some reference materials caution that lavender is a short-lived perennial. That has not been the case in our gardens. We have plants in 15-year-old beds that continue to thrive, even though their lower stems have become rather woody.

Young lavender plants may produce some flowers the first season, but during the second summer and henceforth, plants will be even more floriferous.

While both leaves and flowers are fragrant, it is the fully developed flowers that produce the strongest fragrance. Flowers can be collected for drying and used in winter arrangements or in potpourris and sachets. One of our favorite uses for lavender blossoms is in the preparation of lavender wands or bottles (see the box above for details).

If you wish to save your own seeds, collect them from the plants after the flowers and stems have turned brown. There are not many seeds to a stem and only some of the seeds will be viable. Lavender is native to Spain and the eastern Pyrenees. Its botanical name comes from the Latin *lavo* meaning "to wash," in reference to the use of lavender as an herb to scent soaps.

LEMON BALM

Melissa officinalis

LABIATAE

ALTHOUGH SEEDS can be sown directly into the garden in the fall or spring, we like to start our plants indoors where we can monitor the soil moisture and temperature. Seeds germinate readily if they are not old, and the young seedlings are handsome bright-green plants. The strongly veined oval leaves give off their pungent lemon fragrance when handled. Seedlings set out in the garden in May will develop into vigorous plants by midsummer when we harvest at least half of the top growth to dry for teas. This early harvest causes the plant to set out new growth instead of flowers, and we are able to harvest a second time in late summer. Lemon balm leaves, used fresh or dried, make a very pleasing herbal tea.

The plants do best where there is ample moisture and good drainage. We have had lemon balm in several locations, and although it will survive in a variety of conditions, we have found that the combination of dry soils and intense sun causes leaves to yellow and fragrance and flavor to become harsh. This herb can be grown in Zones 4–9, but in the hottest and most humid areas it will not do well because it needs a cold period to complete its growing cycle.

Conversely, if winters are harsh or open (without a protective snow cover), lemon balm does not winter over consistently unless measures have been taken to provide the plants with a heavy protective mulch. Due to the irregular performance of this perennial, we have chosen to treat it as an annual in our production gardens as we must rely on a steady harvest from one season to another.

The flowers of this plant are small inconspicuous white to blue blossoms, borne in clusters along the stems, as is characteristic of Labiatae members. If you wish to collect seed, allow some plants to complete the flowering cycle and then collect after the flowers have turned brown. Seeds are very small. Unharvested plants often produce volunteers the following spring. *Melissa* is from the Greek word for "honeybee," and bees are indeed attracted to its flowers. The herb is native to southern Europe.

LOVAGE

Levisticum officinale

UMBELLIFERAE

THIS PERENNIAL HERB deserves to be much better known, both for its beauty in the garden and its many uses as a culinary and decorative herb. Lovage is not difficult to grow, but it does germinate slowly over a period of time, so the seed flat needs to be watched. Once the seeds have germinated, lovage should be transplanted when small and placed into a container where its tap root will have room to develop before the plant is set out into the garden.

Lovage will develop some size in the first summer, and during that season, side leaves and stems can be

Fragrant lemon balm leaves are large enough to be harvested. They make very refreshing herbal teas, served hot or iced.

picked sparingly and used either fresh or cooked as a celery substitute. Its flavor is a pungent variation of celery. During the second season the plant will grow to its full height and dramatic form, producing tall hollow flowering stems with pale yellow-green umbels followed by brown seed heads. All parts of the plant are edible and very flavorful. Since lovage is one of the earliest spring herbs to develop, we value the tender young leaves and stems as spring salad greens. Furthermore, the plants are so attractive that they can be incorporated as good accent plants in a perennial border as well as in a traditional herb garden.

We gather the seed heads just before they are mature and dry them for winter arrangements. If you want to collect seeds for cooking or propagating, seeds should to be allowed to mature on the plant and then cut off before they start to disperse. Once the seed heads have been removed, the whole plant can be cut back to the ground and there will be new young succulent leaf growth available for use in late summer and early fall. If plants are left unharvested, lovage may produce volunteers in the garden. Although we have listed its soil requirements as average, lovage will suffer during any extended dry periods. This herb is grown throughout the country, but with some difficulty in the hottest climates because of its need for a cool period to complete its cycle. Lovage is native to southern Europe and has become naturalized in the United States.

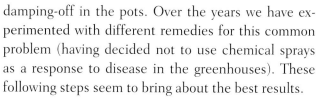

MARJORAM

Origanum majorana

LABIATAE

GROWING SWEET MARJORAM from seed has always been problematic. It is very easy to germinate, and the seed flats are always filled initially with promising-looking healthy seedlings. We transplant the seedlings into individual containers where the plants develop their small round leaves and begin to branch out. It is sometime during this period and the time when we are waiting to set the plants out in the garden that we begin to see signs of disease and damping-off in the pots. Over the years we have experimented with different remedies for this common problem (having decided not to use chemical sprays as a response to disease in the greenhouses). These following steps seem to bring about the best results.

Once marjoram has been transplanted, find a growing-on place that is warm with excellent air circulation. We locate our plants very close to the heat in the greenhouses, we use circulating fans to blow air over the leaves, and we don't water the plants on cloudy days. In addition, watering from the bottom of a tray is helpful. The plants need moisture but should be on the dry side between watering. When the plants are ready to go outdoors, we plant them on raised beds where there is good air circulation and full sun. Once plants are established in the gardens, we rarely have any problems. Sweet marjoram is worth the effort that it takes to grow as its sweetly pungent leaves are a unique flavoring for a variety of salads, dressings, and cooked dishes.

If you wish to avoid the difficulties of indoor seeding, sweet marjoram can be seeded directly into the garden once the soil has warmed. The seed is extremely small; it is advisable to have a very well prepared seed bed, where there will be minimal competition from weeds. As with all plants seeded directly, watch soil moisture as seeds begin to develop and don't let the soils dry out. Once germinated and thinned or transplanted into place, sweet marjoram is a rather sprawling small herb with tiny white blossoms. For continuous leaf production, it is best to keep the flowers picked off.

If you want to collect your own seed, let some plants produce flowers and the seeds will mature in the small seed pods after the flowers are spent. Despite all the difficulties we have experienced with growing this herb, we find that sweet marjoram is one of the easiest plants to lift, pot, and bring inside for the winter (see a further explanation on herbs for the winter windowsill on page 213).

When purchasing seed for sweet marjoram, be certain that you are choosing *Origanum majorana,* an annual, and not *Origanum vulgare,* a perennial. The latter is sometimes called wild marjoram, but it is a very different plant, and we refer to it as wild oregano. It is discussed below. Sweet marjoram is native to northwest Africa and southeast Asia.

MINT, COMMON

Mentha spicata

LABIATAE

LET'S CLARIFY THE CONFUSION about growing mints from seed by stating at the outset that seed-propagated mint is not any specific variety of the species. It is only correct to call it a common mint, or as some packages do, a menthol mint. That is not to say that common mint is an inferior plant. Its leaves are fragrant and flavorful and may be used for a number of culinary purposes. It will not, however, be the specific fragrance or flavor of a true spearmint, peppermint, orange mint, pineapple mint, or any number of the dozens of named varieties that are propagated by some form of plant division. Many seed companies (but not all) have corrected their information in the past decade.

The seed for common mint (from here on referred to only as mint) is very fine, so care must be taken not to seed the flats too densely. This herb also needs constant moisture while it is germinating. Young seedlings are very small, but as soon as they have true leaves, they can be transplanted. Even in young seedlings, the roots of healthy mint plants will be quite developed and you will see the first evidence of the plant's habit of spreading through underground roots. While this herb could be seeded outdoors in a prepared seedbed in spring or fall, the seeds and seedlings are so small that the effort to keep the area weeded and uniformly moist might make direct seeding unwise.

Once mint is set into the garden it will develop rapidly, and by the end of the first summer, if plants are spaced a foot apart, there will be little visible ground between them. Mint, like so many of the named varieties, is a very invasive perennial and it should be located where it can spread without taking over any other valued plantings. Some gardeners grow mint in containers to keep its growth in check. The herb can grow in partial shade, but the best flavor is found in plants that are grown in full sun and in soils with ample moisture.

Mint is grown for its leaves which can be used fresh or dried. It is a common ingredient in herbal teas, sauces, and jellies, and its leaves are used in a number of Middle Eastern dishes. Leaves are best when harvested before the plants flower. Mint can also be propagated by root and stem cuttings. Seeds can be collected, but this mint will cross with other mints in its vicinity so there is no guarantee of seed purity. This popular perennial is hardy to Zone 4 and although its origin is not known, it is cultivated and has become naturalized throughout the world.

OREGANO

Origanum vulgare.
  Wild or Common Oregano
Origanum heracleoticum.
  Greek Oregano

LABIATAE

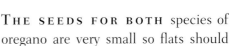

wild oregano

THE SEEDS FOR BOTH species of oregano are very small so flats should be seeded carefully. These plants are easy to germinate and grow, having few of the problems we described with their close relative, *Origanum majorana*. We do however pay close attention to watering these plants so that there is not too much water on the surface of the soil or on the rather hairy small leaves, especially on cloudy days.

It will be hard to distinguish between wild and Greek oregano when the plants are small seedlings. These differences become more apparent after the plants have grown for a season in the garden. Once planted outside, wild oregano will develop into a rather tall, very rapidly spreading plant with pink to mauve to burgundy flowers atop the stems. Leaves have a pungent, slightly peppery fragrance and flavor, and can be used to flavor salads, dressings, and cooked dishes. Wild oregano is not nearly as valuable for culinary use as Greek oregano. We use wild oregano principally as an ornamental herb. Flowers are beautiful for cutting fresh and they also dry very well for use in winter bouquets and herbal wreaths.

By comparison, Greek oregano is a much smaller plant. The leaves are similar in size but the plants only reach about a foot in height. Greek oregano leaves have a truly pungent flavor, one that we associate with Greek, Italian, and Middle Eastern cuisines. Flowers of this smaller plant are white and of little use ornamentally. Both plants spread through underground roots. Plants can be propagated readily by lifting and dividing mature clumps early in the spring. In our gardens, Greek oregano is a tender perennial, meaning that it does not winter over unless it has some protection. Early snow cover or heavily applied mulches have proved successful. Both of these oreganos come originally from southeast Europe.

Greek oregano

Saving seeds for wild oregano will probably not be necessary as the plant is so invasive that once you have an established bed, more likely than not you will be removing extra plants. Any flowers that are left unharvested will produce seeds for many volunteers at the same time that the original plants continue to spread out through underground roots. Volunteers are easy to lift and relocate. If you do wish to save seed, simply allow the flowers to mature until they are nearly dried out, and pick before they begin to shatter.

There are many beautiful species and varieties of oregano, beyond those discussed here, available from nurseries and plant catalogues, but they must be propagated vegetatively. Other named oreganos are variably hardy but usually easy to grow. More tender plants can be brought inside for the winter, or new plants can be started by making cuttings. Some of the named varieties are used for culinary purposes; many however are of interest primarily as ornamental herbs.

PARSLEY

Petroselinum crispum var. *crispum,* Curly Parsley
Petroselinum crispum var. *neapolitanum,* Italian Parsley

UMBELLIFERAE

PARSLEY CAN BE seeded directly into the garden, but it will take a long time to show growth, and all the time you will be battling weeds and moisture in a seed bed. For this reason, we start all of our plants indoors.

This herb is easy to grow from seed. Once the seedlings have true leaves, the young plants may be transplanted and grown on until they are large enough to set out in the garden.

The basic difference in the two varieties listed above is in the shape of their leaves. Curly parsley is perhaps the more familiar of the two and the most commonly grown. Its leaves are finely cut and curled, with toothed margins. Italian parsley has a flat cut leaf and slightly thinner stems. Both varieties are used fresh and for cooking and they can be dried or frozen for winter use. Parsley plants are hardy enough to withstand very cool late

curly parsley

summer and fall evenings. They can endure light frosts and even colder temperatures with some protection. We like to cover our late summer plants with mulch or fabric when nighttime temperatures fall below freezing, removing the cover during the daytime. That allows us to harvest leaves until well into October. It is during late harvests that we particularly appreciate the flat-leaved parsleys. Their leaves remain more tender and flavorful for fresh use than the curly types. During the summer, we use either variety interchangeably.

Parsleys are raised as annuals but they are really biennials. Occasionally a few plants will winter over in our climate, and early in the second year the plant will send up a flowering stalk, produce greenish white umbels, and the flowers will produce seeds. Once the plants go to flower, the leaf production declines and the leaves become rather fibrous. If you want to collect your own seeds, mulch a few plants to bring them through the winter. For culinary purposes however the plants are best grown as annuals.

Italian parsley

Parsley is one of the annual herbs that will do well in a container as long as the container is deep enough for the plant's deep taproot to form. Parsley is grown in Zones 3–10. It will grow in an average garden soil, but the most luxuriant plants develop where the soil

E VERY TIME WE GIVE a class or lecture on growing herbs, we are met with the same questions, which can be summed up in one. "What herbs will I really use in my kitchen?" Catalogues now offer such a large assortment of species, and varieties within the species, that it can be overwhelming for a first-time herb gardener to know where to start. Here are some thoughts, and admittedly these thoughts will be met by challenges and exceptions from experienced growers, but a good defense could be made for choosing what we will call the essential dozen.

We'll start with six herbs easily grown from seed as annuals. Pick at least one variety of sweet green Italian basil (*Ocimum basilicum*). It's easy and will give you fresh material for salads, cooking, freezing, or drying. Parsley, curly or flat leaf (*Petroselinum crispum*), should be grown for the same reasons. We recommend a variety of leafy coriander (*Coriandrum sativum*), also called cilantro, because we find more use for its leaves in Mexican dishes and salads than for its seeds. Sweet marjoram (*Origanum majorana*) is essential for cooking soups and stews; plants can easily be potted at the end of the summer and brought inside. This means that you don't need to bother with drying a winter's supply. You will want 1 or 2 plantings of dill (*Anethum graveolens*) for eating fresh, for pickling, and for drying. Summer savory (*Satureja hortensis*) has lots of uses in salads, cheese and herb spreads, and cooking. It dries wonderfully. All these plants can be started indoors for an early harvest, but we have successfully direct seeded each one except for parsley (which requires a longer growing season).

The list of essential perennials includes chives (*Allium schoenoprasum*), Greek oregano (*Origanum* sp.), rosemary (*Rosmarinus officinalis*), garden sage (*Salvia officinalis*), English thyme (*Thymus vulgaris*), and French tarragon (*Artemisia dracunculus* var. *sativa*). Tarragon is propagated only from cuttings or root division; all the others can be grown from seed. Once started, a patch of chives will increase over the years, giving you early leaves to use fresh and a supply to freeze or dry. Greek oregano can be left in the garden, or slipped and potted for inside use during the winter months. It is excellent for salads, pizzas, sauces, and herbal cooking mixtures. Rosemary should be grown not only for its culinary purposes but for its beauty and fragrance. We use sage and thyme fresh and dried throughout the year, and these plants can be brought inside successfully. Tarragon does best if left in the garden to go dormant, but a couple of plants will produce enough leaves for cooking all summer as well as a supply for harvesting at summer's end for drying. The dried leaves hold their flavor and fragrance for a couple of years if dried and stored with care.

Curly parsley is near the top of the list of essential culinary herbs.

has ample organic matter and moisture. It is native to Europe and western Asia. *Petroselinum* comes from the Greek words *petros,* meaning "rock," and *selion,* meaning "parsley."

PATCHOULI

Pogostemon cablin

LABIATAE

ANYONE WHO IS old enough to remember the sixties will recognize the fra-

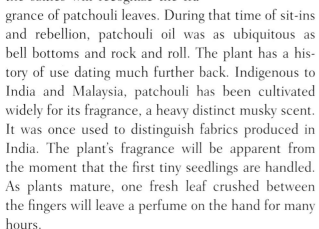

grance of patchouli leaves. During that time of sit-ins and rebellion, patchouli oil was as ubiquitous as bell bottoms and rock and roll. The plant has a history of use dating much further back. Indigenous to India and Malaysia, patchouli has been cultivated widely for its fragrance, a heavy distinct musky scent. It was once used to distinguish fabrics produced in India. The plant's fragrance will be apparent from the moment that the first tiny seedlings are handled. As plants mature, one fresh leaf crushed between the fingers will leave a perfume on the hand for many hours.

This tender perennial is easy to germinate from seed. Seeds are very small and should be carefully distributed over the seed flat to avoid crowding. Once transplanted, seedlings need warmth and good light, but not intense sun, for growing on. In northern zones, it is best to grow patchouli as a container herb. It needs warmth, filtered sun, and adequate moisture. By the end of the first summer, plants will reach a height of 1–2 feet and have numerous side branches.

Long before the nights turn cold, plants should be brought inside and placed in a sunny winter location. Despite the best of care, we find that our plants begin to look ratty and leggy by the middle of the winter. They benefit from being cut back so that new growth can start in early spring. Cuttings root easily. Two- and three-year-old plants will produce flowers by the end of the summer. Flowers are very small whitish lavender, resembling in form and size many other flowers of the Labiatae family.

The plant's name comes from the Greek word *pogon* meaning "beard," and *stemon* for "stamen," in reference to the bearded filaments.

PENNYROYAL

Mentha pulegium

LABIATAE

PENNYROYAL SEEDS germiate readily and seedlings grow rapidly after being transplanted. This member of the mint family has a low spreading habit and it will send down roots wherever the leaf nodes come into contact with soil. Therefore it is best to transplant the young seedlings into individual pots and allow spacing between the pots. Several plants in one flat or pots closely arranged will allow plants to become so intertwined that it can become difficult to separate them without damaging the roots. Pennyroyal likes to be grown on at slightly cooler temperatures.

Once the plants are in the garden, they continue to spread, making an attractive ground cover in sunny or partially sunny locations. By mid- to late summer, the plants send up some short flowering stems that have small but pleasing lavender blossoms. This herb is also a good candidate for container growing. It will spill attractively over the side of its pot and it can be harvested easily, causing it to branch out and become even more full in appearance. We have used it in combination with other herbs in patio planters that were grown outside all summer and then brought in for the winter. Pennyroyal continues to grow inside and can be pruned back or slipped for new plants in early spring.

Seeds may be collected by gathering the entire mature spikes. When you wish to seed new plants, simply crush and sprinkle the spikes on the tops of seeding containers. In zones warmer than ours, pennyroyal will perform as a perennial, but our garden plants winter over only occasionally. We do find a few volunteers next to the rows where plants have been left unharvested.

Pennyroyal has a long history of medicinal uses, but it also has many caveats in that history. The leaves

EVERY FALL, there are countless magazine and newspaper articles giving advice on how to grow culinary herbs inside during the winter months. These articles usually appear with attractive photographs of lush parsley plants, pots of full-bodied chives, containers with vigorous basils ready for snipping, and other misleading suggestions. For the most part, these articles overstate the ease of winter gardening (gardening indoors), and they nearly always encourage the cultivation of plants that don't do well indoors in northern regions of the country.

This is not to say that home gardeners can't have considerable success with herb plants on the kitchen windowsill or warm window bench in front of a south facing bay window, but the kinds of plants selected are critical. After years of experimenting, we have made a list of herbs that really do well inside from early fall (before hard frosts) until late spring (when they can be relocated outdoors). The list includes most of the thyme varieties, sages (both the perennials and annuals like pineapple sage), low-growing oreganos (Greek and golden), sweet marjoram, bay, and rosemary. "Grown successfully" means thriving inside, being harvested for use all winter long, and—perhaps most important—maintaining flavor all year round.

The thymes and oreganos (including sweet marjoram) continue to produce tender shoots and leaves all winter; the hardy sages maintain their summer growth and set new leaves as the days lengthen in late winter; pineapple sage puts out new growth all winter; the bays and rosemaries grow slowly during the fall and early winter, and then respond to the longer days of March and April with new growth and bud set.

Eucalyptus, scented geraniums, myrtle, and rosemary share a window space with pots of anemones and freesias.

Clipping these plants simply encourages them to branch out.

The tender annual culinary herbs respond very differently when grown inside during the diminished daylight of winter. Basils may grow but they tend to be leggy, and their leaves are rather anemic with a flavor decidedly inferior to field-grown summer plants. Culinary herbs such as parsley and chervil can be kept in a pot if you will be satisfied by an occasional new central stem with a few leaves to garnish a recipe every few weeks. Perennial herbs like chives and tarragon really need to be left to die back in the garden, go dormant for a period of time, and then sponsor new growth when the weather warms. When grown inside as potted plants, their production and taste are quite inferior.

Some garden writers have suggested that winter windowsill gardens can be equipped with grow-lights. These lights do extend the perceived growing time, but they cannot substitute for real sunlight, which stimulates production of the essential oils that give edible herbs their rich flavors.

have an appealing spicy fragrance, but we avoid the herb for culinary purposes. We use it instead as an ornamental or for making insect repelling mixtures. We have found that we can at least discourage black flies and mosquitoes by rubbing fresh leaves over our faces and arms. We have also made a strong infusion for bathing our cats to help relieve them of fleas. Some pet owners dry the leaves and stuff them into pillows for their animals to sleep on. Pennyroyal can be grown in Zones 3–10. It is native to Europe and western Asia.

ROSEMARY

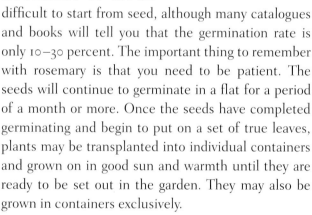

Rosmarinus officinalis

LABIATAE

ROSEMARY IS not too difficult to start from seed, although many catalogues and books will tell you that the germination rate is only 10–30 percent. The important thing to remember with rosemary is that you need to be patient. The seeds will continue to germinate in a flat for a period of a month or more. Once the seeds have completed germinating and begin to put on a set of true leaves, plants may be transplanted into individual containers and grown on in good sun and warmth until they are ready to be set out in the garden. They may also be grown in containers exclusively.

The spacing dimensions for planting (given at the end of the chapter) apply when growing this herb in the garden as an annual in northern zones. Here the herbs must be brought inside before a hard frost and grown on in the winter as a pot plant. In the warmest zones of this country, Zones 8–10, gardeners can treat this plant like the shrub that it is and have the pleasure of incorporating rosemary into the perennial border where it will grow to luxurious proportions. Whatever the choice, it is best to take advantage of the full sun and humidity of an outdoor site for the summer. If you are growing rosemary as a container plant, be certain to give it an adequately large pot and ample organic matter and moisture so that the plant has time to develop as much growth as possible from season to season.

We transplant most of our rosemary seedlings into the ground for their first summer. These first-year field-grown plants are easily 12–18 inches tall by the end of September when they are potted and brought inside. The plants will stand some of the first light fall frosts, but the real trick to bringing them inside successfully is to put them through a reverse hardening-off period. Just as plants need to be readied to go from the greenhouse into the garden in the spring, so do field-grown plants need to be prepared to come out of the garden and go into the rather dry air and reduced light of our homes.

Pot rosemary plants, taking care to lift and include all the roots, into a container with good organically enriched soil. Bring the plants onto the porch or into the house for a few hours of each day and gradually lengthen the time that they are inside. For a more complete discussion of reverse hardening off, see the box on pages 60–1. Never try to place rosemary near a woodstove, fireplace, or heating registers; the dryness will cause the leaves to wither and die.

First-year garden-grown plants like full sun. Once plants have been placed in containers, rosemaries should be summer grown outside in locations where there is morning sun and filtered sun for the second half of the day. Full scalding sun, even in our location, is too harsh for container plants that are more than a year old. Inside light and temperature requirements for the remainder of the year are somewhat different.

Rosemary likes the best southern light it can have during the winter months and enjoys being misted often or grown over a tray of pebbles and water so that the evaporating moisture reaches the plant continuously. It does not need or particularly appreciate winter heat. We keep all our mature plants in a growing area that gets as cold as 35°F some winter nights. We never allow the plants to freeze, but the temperatures fluctuate widely in this greenhouse. A cool room in the house would be preferable to one that is warm and dry. Try various locations in your own home or greenhouse to find the most suitable spot for your plants.

If you are willing to make this effort, you should have good luck in getting some beautiful old specimens that you can shift from indoors to outdoors for years on end, repotting the plant in ever larger pots or wooden containers. We have plants that have been here for more than a decade and their trunks are

ROSEMARY
TO SEED OR NOT TO SEED

THERE ARE GOOD BOOKS on herbs that offer discouraging words about growing rosemary from seed. Our advice: don't listen. Be aware that the seeds may be slow and erratic to germinate, but with the proper conditions (see details on pages 214 and 217), there is no reason to rule out growing your own plants. Seed catalogues refer to seed-propagated rosemary plants as standard rosemary. This only means that the exact form of the plant, flower color, and leaf size cannot be defined precisely. We have seen considerable variability in our seed-grown plants. As a general rule, however, we can say that the plants have a growing habit that is bushy and upright. The leaves are small, but not extremely needle-like. The flowers range in color from very light to medium light blue. When it comes to culinary use, fragrance, and vigor, the seeded rosemaries are every bit as desirable as named cultivars.

But then again, having one variety never rules out wanting others. There are a number of beautiful choices. Each of the following rosemaries is produced from stem cuttings or layering so that the offspring are true to type. We will talk about them in groupings, according to general plant morphology and flower color.

Low growing, creeping, sprawling, or trailing plants are generally referred to as prostrate rosemaries. They are especially beautiful container plants. One of our favorites is *R. officinalis* 'Mrs. Howard's Creeping', a plant that grows vigorously, has medium sized leaves and blue flowers. 'Lockwood de Forest' is another well-known prostrate with blue flowers; 'Santa Barbara' resembles 'Lockwood' but has lighter blue blooms; 'Severn Sea' also has lighter blue flowers and its leaves are larger than those of 'Lockwood'.

Plants that are decidedly upright in their growth habit include 'Tuscan Blue', with wide leaves (by rosemary standards) and deep blue flowers. The cultivar 'Majorca' is also upright, but with a hint of trailing, making its branches bend and twist into interesting shapes. It has soft pink flowers. There are upright plants with white flowers, named *R. officinalis* 'Albus'.

Two of the hardier named cultivars are recommended for gardeners in Zones 6 or 7 and warmer. These are *R. officinalis* 'Arp' and 'Hill Hardy'. We've been tempted to try these in a very protected spot with generous mulching.

The list of named cultivars is much more extensive than the few mentioned above, and plant hybridizers are adding to the list yearly. Where growers have the luxury of leaving their rosemary plants in the ground year round, it would be hard to imagine not having several types. We are limited somewhat by the size of our winter greenhouse and the strength of our backs. The great old standard potted rosemary plant shown below now weighs about 200 pounds. Every October we steel ourselves for the task of lifting and hauling this plant inside. It measures 5 feet in height and spreads out to about 7 feet. For much of the late fall, winter, and early spring, it is covered with soft blue flowers. Its dark chocolate-gray trunk is exquisitely twisted and gnarled. We started this plant from seed 20 years ago.

One of our old seeded rosemary plants shares summer space in a wooden barrel with a low-growing impatiens.

To DATE WE HAVE found three seed-propagated aromatic grasses to include in our herb gardens. We categorize these as herbal grasses because of their multiple-use histories. Two are quite unappealing visually, one handsome enough to be included in a border garden.

The first two are referred to as sweet grasses. *Hierochloe odorata,* or sweet grass, is indigenous to the United States and Eastern Europe. Native Americans used the dried leaves to scent hair and clothing, weave baskets, and as a ceremonial incense. We have read that the dried leaves were used in parts of Europe to flavor vodka, much as dried sweet woodruff is used to flavor May wine. *Hierochloe* is a hardy perennial in our gardens. We started our plants from seed sown indoors in flats. When transplanting small grasses, we don't always try to separate each individual plant; rather, we pinch a small clump of plants and then transplant it into a plug. Once plants are sized-up, we harden them off and locate them in a permanent garden spot.

Vanilla grass, *Anthoxanthum odoratum,* is also known as sweet vernal grass. When dried, it has a lovely sweet vanilla fragrance, which lasts for several years. Its fragrance comes from an aromatic hydrocarbon known as coumarin. Cultural requirements for this hardy perennial are the same as those for *Hierochloe.* Both of these perennial sweet grasses grow to a height of 12–18 inches and once established in the garden can be lifted and divided from year to year to increase plantings. You are advised to carefully mark these plants in the garden because they are easily confused with any number of common grasses that you might be inclined to eliminate when weeding.

We use dried *Hierochloe* and *Anthoxanthum* as sachets. They do not need to be processed at all. Simply harvest the grasses, tie in small bunches to dry, and then place the clusters directly into linen closets or drawers.

The third herbal grass, *Cymbopogon flexuosus* or lemon grass, needs to be grown as an annual in our gardens or lifted and brought inside for the winter. This grass is significantly larger than the first two species discussed, so after seeds have been germinated, plants can be transplanted as individuals or by placing no more than 2–3 to a plug for growing

on. Once set out in the garden, in a warm sunny location with good soil and adequate moisture, our late summer plants stand 3–5 feet tall. Size variation depends in large part on the warmth and moisture of the season. Leaves resemble tall slender iris leaves. At summer's end we either cut down the crop and hang bunches to dry, or cut back the top growth to within a couple of inches of the ground and lift and pot plants to be wintered inside. Plants brought inside our greenhouses show little new growth until late winter when the daylight increases. Lemon grass is the source of lemon grass oil used to flavor teas and other food products. It is also used in the perfume industry. We fashion the leaves into decorative culinary wreaths or use them in making potpourri.

Lemon grass, Cymbopogon flexuosus, *is grown as an annual in our gardens, but it can be cut back and wintered inside in a cool greenhouse.*

beautifully aged and gnarled. They also bloom pro-fusely all winter with blossoms of light blue.

There are many varieties of rosemary that vary in their overall plant shapes and flower colors, but all these varieties have the characteristic needle-like leathery leaves and wonderful earthy fragrance. When rosemary is grown from seed, it is typically referred to as standard rosemary, with a bushy upright habit. We have grown hundreds of plants from seed and have seen only slight variation in flower colors, almost imperceptible differences in shades of light to medium blue.

There are a number of named rosemary varieties produced not from seed but from cuttings. For more information about some of our favorites, see the special section on page 215. Regardless of whether you grow standard rosemary from seed or a named variety from a purchased plant, you will find that their cultural requirements are quite similar. Furthermore, all of the rosemaries that we are familiar with are used both as ornamental and culinary herbs.

Rosemary is an excellent culinary herb, and you will be able to snip your plants year-round whether they are in the garden or in your homes. For those of you with rosemary as shrubs, the plant can be allowed to develop into natural forms or sculpted into hedges and topiary. Container plants may likewise be allowed to branch out at will or pruned to special shapes. Rosemary can also be propagated by layering the branches and by rooting some cuttings. We have had modest success collecting seeds from a few of our mature standard plants. On occasion we have seen tiny volunteers in the soil beneath a potted rosemary. When this happens, it is very easy to lift and repot the tiny plants. This herb is native to the Mediterranean region. Its name comes from two Latin words, *ros* meaning "dew," and *marinus* meaning "of the sea."

RUE

Ruta graveolens

RUTACEAE

RUE GERMINATES READILY over a period of time and the young seedlings are

Rue is beautiful in and out of flower, but some people must take care not to touch the plant, especially during the blooming period.

very attractive little blue-green plants with their unique, round-lobed small leaves. Once seedlings have been transplanted, the young plants like to be grown on in a cool location. The only word of caution about growing rue pertains not to any difficulty in the horticulture of the plant but to the fact that some people have a strong reaction to the plant's oils and can develop a rash that resembles that caused by poison ivy. This seems especially true when the plant is in flower and is handled on a hot humid day. We have never had a reaction to the plant while seeding it or setting out young plants into the garden, but some on our staff have had allergic reactions when the plants were being harvested, usually when the mature plants were in flower. We strongly recommend that you wear long-sleeved shirts and gloves when handling the mature plants.

Rue has a history of use in medicines, but it is now

grown primarily for its ornamental value. It is an exceptionally beautiful perennial, successfully grown in Zones 4–9. Rue has graceful scalloped blue-green leaves and clean yellow blossoms that are good to cut fresh. The flowers produce tan pods that almost look as if they were carved out of wood. The pods are used in dried arrangements.

Rue pods that are left unharvested in the garden may provide you with many volunteers the following spring. These small seedlings can be lifted and relocated easily. Chances are you will never have to start this herb more than once from seed sown indoors. In early spring, you may notice that mature plants suffer some winter dieback. Wait until new growth appears and prune plants back to active growth. Plants regain their size and proportions very rapidly. All parts of the plant have a unique musky fragrance and seem to be insect free. Rue is native to southern Europe.

SAGE

Salvia officinalis

LABIATAE

SAGE IS NOT DIFFICULT to grow from seed. The seeds germinate readily over a period of 1–2 weeks. Once seedlings have been transplanted, the young plants prefer to be grown on in a cool place and it is important not to overwater as this can cause the stems to rot. Sage plants should be allowed to be a bit dry between waterings. This herb can be grown in Zones 3–9. It has handsome gray-green pebbled foliage and from the second season onward it will flower with soft, white to lilac flowers. Garden sage is attractive both in and out of flower and can be successfully incorporated in the perennial border. The whole plant has the sharp aroma we have come to associate with the traditional poultry dressing of which sage is an important element.

In the colder zones there is some winter dieback and plants need to be trimmed once new growth appears in the spring. Sage is a rather short-lived perennial in our area. Plants tend to get woody after a few years, but we have noticed that they survive the

longest where the soil has good drainage. In order to ensure the plant's winter survival, sage should be harvested by no more than a third of its growth in one season and the harvest should be done no later than the middle of August.

Sage is important as a culinary herb, but its leaves are also excellent dried material for making everlasting wreaths. In addition to the common garden sage, there are a number of other varieties and species, most of which are propagated by cuttings and are hardy only in zones warmer than our own. Some of these named varieties have purple leaves, variegated leaves, and leaves with a lovely pineapple fragrance.

Salvia is a large genus of ornamental and culinary plants and we have enjoyed growing many ornamental sages. Once you have purchased a plant, it is usually very easy to propagate new ones from stem cuttings. Sages can be grown successfully as container plants inside during the winter months.

Salvia is from the Latin *salvos* meaning "safe," referring to the use of this herb in medicines. Sage is native from north and central Spain west to the Balkan Peninsula and Asia Minor.

SANTOLINA

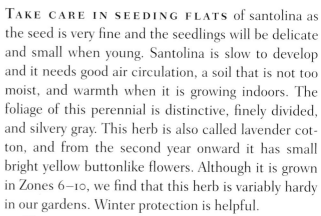

Santolina chamaecyparissus

COMPOSITAE

TAKE CARE IN SEEDING FLATS of santolina as the seed is very fine and the seedlings will be delicate and small when young. Santolina is slow to develop and it needs good air circulation, a soil that is not too moist, and warmth when it is growing indoors. The foliage of this perennial is distinctive, finely divided, and silvery gray. This herb is also called lavender cotton, and from the second year onward it has small bright yellow buttonlike flowers. Although it is grown in Zones 6–10, we find that this herb is variably hardy in our gardens. Winter protection is helpful.

Plants are very attractive in an ornamental garden for they have a neat mounded habit of growth. They are often seen in traditional knot gardens. Santolina is a good container herb, and will winter over inside easily. When grown inside in the winter, the plants bene-

CULINARY HERBS FOR DECORATION

I T IS NECESSARY TO process and store our culinary herbs carefully if we want them for cooking. That usually means putting them totally out of sight once the harvest is in. But we always reserve some of the crops to be used exclusively for decoration, knowing full well that we are sacrificing their culinary potential for the sake of using them more symbolically. There are several culinary herbs that hold their color, form, and fragrance best for handcrafting. They include bay leaves, rosemary, sage, wild oregano, lemon verbena, lemon grass, marjoram, garden thyme, lavender, chive blossoms, and fragrant flowering garlic pods.

Swags can be made from combinations of these herbs simply by choosing forms that are pleasing and tying a group together with twine or raffia. Dried red peppers are good for highlights. Swags can be made entirely from dried red peppers. Attach a piece of twine or yarn to each pepper stem and then braid the peppers together, adding more and more pieces of yarn and peppers as you work up the braid.

Culinary wreaths are the most enjoyable to fashion.

There are no rules about what to use as long as the herbs are dry enough to hold their shape once the project is done. If you tie a wreath of fresh herbs, the bulk and the shape of the wreath will be very different as the materials wilt, diminish in size, and then stiffen again once dry.

We tie all our wreaths on a crimped wire ring. Rings may also be made from a bound circle of willow, alder, or any supple branch or vine. Start the wreath by making a fan-shaped cluster of herbs and attach the cluster to the ring with thin wire or twine. Continue to make clusters of herbs, one kind or several kinds to a fan, and attach one right next to another until the circle is complete. Final details may be added, such as dried peppers, dried pods, cones, or grasses. Some of our culinary wreaths are made from bearded wheat or winter rye with accents of bay leaves and tiny dried peppers.

Any of these culinary objects could be snipped for cooking if they were used right after being made. Somehow we never have the heart to unravel the handiwork. Instead they decorate the kitchen.

They are all edible, but most will probably be hung for decoration only.

THEY ARE NOT usually grown from seed, but it is hard to write about herbs without talking however briefly about scented geraniums. Like their relative, the garden or house geranium, their common name is misleading as they are not members of the genus *Geranium* at all. Scented geraniums are from the genus *Pelargonium*. There are relatively few natural species of scented *Pelargonium*, but there are hundreds of varieties that are the result of hybridization between species and between species and hybrids.

Scented geraniums are best known for their fragrances, but we appreciate them for the beauty of their leaf form and color as well. The fragrances are produced in oil glands located at the base of tiny leaf hairs. When leaves are brushed or handled, the fragrances are easily released into the air and onto the hands. There are rose, lemon, orange, mint, peppermint, nutmeg, coconut, lime, and lemon-rose scents of varying intensities and interpretations, just to name a few.

Leaves can be a solid color or variegated, smooth or very hairy, shallow lobed or deeply incised, large as a small hand or small as a fingertip. Colors vary from deep green to light green to green gray with variegation ranging from white to yellow to light shades of green.

Scented geraniums are not known for their flowers which are decidedly smaller than the bedding *Pelargonium*, but we have come to prefer the beauty of the scented flowers because they have a pleasing proportion to the overall plant. Flower colors range from white to pink, to lavender, to red and deep magenta.

Scented geraniums are good house plants and excellent outdoor plants as well, either grown in the ground or in containers. Given a fertile soil with ample moisture and at least a half day of full sun, our garden *Pelargonium* often double or triple in size in just three months. At the end of the summer, we either slip cuttings for rooting or lift and repot plants. If plants have become

Beautiful fragrant foliage and appealing small blossoms of a variety of scented geraniums.

very large, it is best to trim back some top growth after repotting. Cuttings taken from late fall to late winter root in 5–6 weeks in moist sand or vermiculite.

Scented geraniums are almost entirely insect free in the open garden and they have no predators in our climate. Once inside, however, they need to be watched closely for whiteflies primarily, but occasionally for aphids. Always turn plants on their sides and check the undersides of the leaves. Either of these insect problems can usually be managed if caught early by taking the plants outside when temperatures permit and using a soapy spray or an insecticidal soap.

When grown inside during the winter months, *Pelargonium* does best in a warm south facing window. If they do not have adequate light they tend to get leggy very fast. It's simple enough to correct this by frequently pruning for shape. We use the clippings of these plants along with other herb cuttings to bring as dinner gifts when visiting friends. Arrange a few different plant cuttings in a simple old mug or pitcher, and the gift resembles a living potpourri. Recipients can use the culinary herbs in the kitchen, or root each plant for their own gardens. It's an easy gift to assemble and always seems to be very well received.

fit from being cut back in early spring, prompting new bushy growth.

Seeds can be collected after the flower heads have dried out and it is easiest to seed directly with these flower heads by simply crushing them and sprinkling them over the surface of the soil. Santolina is a fragrant herb and can be used in potpourris and in moth-repelling mixtures. Its foliage can also be woven into herbal wreaths. There is a green species, *Santolina virens,* which is usually propagated by cuttings. Santolina is native to Spain and northern Africa. Its name is derived from two Latin words, *santum* meaning "holy," and *linum* meaning "flax."

herb is a small, bushy, slightly upright plant with tiny green leaves and light lilac flowers. It resembles English thyme in appearance. Winter savory is an attractive border perennial. Its seeds are very fine and do not retain their viability for more than a couple of years. We prefer to start winter savory indoors. Once the seeds have germinated, plants should be transplanted into individual containers and grown on in a cool location. This perennial herb is found in gardens from Zones 5–9. Both herbs are native to the Mediterranean region.

winter savory

SAVORY

Satureja hortensis, Summer Savory
Satureja montana, Winter Savory

LABIATAE

summer savory

SUMMER SAVORY IS an excellent annual culinary herb easily grown from seed. We seed this plant by sprinkling a few seeds in a plug or container and letting 3 or 4 plants develop in one spot. The plants grow rapidly and have a rather sprawling habit. Summer savory will be ready to harden off and set into the garden about 5 weeks after seeding. Alternatively, you could seed this annual directly into a row after all danger of frost has passed. Bury the seeds very lightly and tamp down the soil. Seeds of this herb are large enough to handle with some precision, so that sowing can be done carefully enough to eliminate any need to thin young seedlings. During germination, make certain that the soils are kept moist.

The plants have small spicy peppery leaves that are good in salads, dressings, and in cooked dishes. Once summer savory begins to flower, leaf production will decline. You may keep the plants from setting seed by pinching them back, but if you want to collect seed, let the flowers mature.

Winter savory has a similar flavor to its annual relative, but the plant has an altogether different appearance, and the leaves are more fibrous. The perennial

SESAME

Sesamum indicum

PEDALIACEAE

THIS ANNUAL HERB is best suited to gardens in the warmer Zones, 7–10, as it needs about four months of hot weather to mature. In these zones, sesame may be seeded directly outside as soon as the nights are warm. Seeds should be covered lightly and the soil firmed over the row. For those northern gardeners who want to experiment with the herb, it will be necessary to seed the plants inside. Peat pots are best for this purpose as sesame has a long delicate tap root and does not transplant well. Put 2 or 3 seeds into one pot. They will germinate quickly and young plants should not be allowed to dry out as it will check their growth. Set peat pots in the garden after all danger of frost has passed. Dark mulches will benefit these plants.

Sesame has whitish trumpetlike flowers that will develop into square seed pods. Since the plants are grown primarily for their seeds, the whole stalk should be harvested before the lower pods mature to the point of bursting open and dispersing their seeds. The stalks are brought inside to dry. The flavor of the seeds is enhanced when they are toasted or baked. Sesame is native to the Tropics.

SORREL

Rumex acetosa,
 Garden Sorrel
Rumex scutatus, French Sorrel

POLYGONACEAE

garden sorrel

SORREL IS EASY to grow from seed as long as the seed has not been stored for more than three or four years. There is much confusion about what species of *Rumex* is the true French sorrel as both *Rumex acetosa* and *Rumex scutatus* have been referred to as French and garden sorrel. According to *Hortus Third, Rumex scutatus* is the French sorrel, but in most of the seed catalogues you will be offered seed of *R. acetosa.* The latter species has fairly large elongated leaves, which are harvestable the first year from seed, and then early on in the season for many years hence. The quality and quantity of the harvest make this our favored culinary sorrel. *R. scutatus* is a much smaller plant which is variably hardy in our gardens. The flavor is excellent, but so many plants would be needed to make soups, sauces, and greens for salads, that we abandoned it in favor of its larger relative.

Whichever species you choose to grow, their seeds germinate readily. When sown indoors and transplanted, young plants should be grown on at a slightly cooler temperature. Garden sorrel will have good-sized leaves when the plants are set out in the garden, and plants develop into sizable clumps by the middle of their first season. At this point you can begin to harvest these tart greens as salad or cooking herbs. Leaves can be gathered even after early frosts turn them a reddish color. Very early in the spring of its second year, garden sorrel will be one of the first edible plants in the garden, coming at a time when fresh greens are most welcome. By early summer of the second year, this herb will put up tall flowering stalks. Flowers are shaggy plumes of greenish beige, turning to a light and then rusty brown as they develop into seeds.

French sorrel

We gather the young seed stalks for drying as they are excellent in everlasting arrangements. If stalks are left on the plants they will produce volunteers, or you can gather and save your own seeds. Flowering causes the plants to produce fewer leaves for culinary use, so if you want to continue harvesting tender edible greens, either keep the flowers cut off or cut the whole plant back after it finishes flowering. If old garden sorrel plants start to become woody and less productive, they can be lifted and divided in the early spring, or new seedlings can be started. Sorrel may be seeded directly into the garden in the fall or early spring. The plant is grown in Zones 3–9 and will grow in ordinary garden soil, but it prefers a rich moist soil and will decline during hot weather if the soil is dry. Garden sorrel is native to Europe and Asia and is naturalized in North America.

STRAWBERRY, ALPINE

Fragaria vesca

ROSACEAE

THESE SMALL everbearing strawberries are not difficult to grow from seed, and once the seeds have germinated and put on a set of true leaves, the plants may be transplanted into flats or pots and grown at cooler temperatures, about 60°–65°F. When transplanting strawberries into pots or into their permanent positions outdoors, care must be taken to set the plants into the soil at just the proper depth. The best way to evaluate this at the seedling stage is to examine the position of the plant's cotyledons and make certain that you do not bury them or have them planted much above the level of the soil. As the young plants develop size you will be able to recognize the crown of the plant and in setting the young plants into the field, make certain that the crown is planted at the same depth as it was growing naturally in its container. Burying the crown can cause crown rot, and planting the crown not deep enough can cause improper root formation.

Alpine strawberries are attractive plants with their

WE DID EVERYTHING possible to interest our young child in plants. We used the Latin names as a point of departure to talk about mythological tales. Our early gardens were full of yarrow, or *Achillea,* and the story of Achilles and the Trojan War was one of his favorites. Whenever we took trips away from home, we carried along several field guides to identify interesting plants. He was fascinated by the uses for wild plants—chicory roots to make a coffee substitute, the residue from the leaves of *Saponaria* to make a soapy water, the use of the down from common cattails to stuff pillows. But there was one project that really captured his imagination: crystallizing edible flowers.

The first flowers we tried were tiny young spring violets. Later in the summer we worked with borage blossoms and then with the flowers of wax begonias. By the end of the summer we had several tins of beautifully candied flowers that we used to decorate his birthday cake in October. This is a perfect children's project for a rainy summer day.

Pick any number of fresh young blossoms of small edible flowers. The ones already mentioned work well because they are simple and single petaled. Remove any stem and green calyx and gently pat the flowers dry. Whip until frothy a small mixture of powdered egg whites and water. Use only powdered egg whites for safety's sake, as they will not be heated before eating. Then with a very small clean paint brush, cover both sides of every petal and the center of the flower with a light coating of the whipped egg

white. If the mixture loses its frothiness during the project, rewhip so that you are painting with a light airy mixture.

After each flower is covered, dip both sides of the flower into a dish of fine granulated sugar or spoon sugar over the petals, making certain that you are coating all of the surfaces. Sugar may be plain or tinted with food coloring to match the color of the flowers. Place each sugared flower on a piece of waxed paper and allow to dry for several hours or a day until totally dry. Alternatively, place sugared flowers on a piece of brown paper on a cookie sheet and put in a very slow oven to dry. Once dried, flowers are stored in a tin container that can be tightly sealed. Line the bottom of the tin with waxed paper and place a piece of paper between each layer of flowers.

Of course, we always tested for taste as we worked.

Leaves from mints and scented geraniums accompany geranium flowers. Leaves and flowers are preserved using the technique described on this page.

characteristic strawberry leaves and small white blossoms. The basic difference between these and regular strawberry plants is that the alpines do not set runners and their smaller berries are produced all season, including the first summer that you set out the plants. Production is modest, but plants produce fruit from mid-to-late summer; the berries are ½–1 inch in length, tender and sweet. We use these small perennials in an ornamental border, but they can also be grown in containers as long as they are given ample sun and water. These plants are native to Europe, Asia, and North America. The genus name comes from Latin and refers to the fragrance of the fruit.

TANSY

Tanacetum vulgare

COMPOSITAE

TANSY IS EASY to grow from seed, and chances are once you have introduced a few plants into your gardens, you will not need to start any new plants from indoor seeding. Young tansy seedlings are a pleasure to transplant because they give off their characteristic musky fragrance when handled. They grow rapidly and by the end of the first season they reach almost full size in our gardens, sometimes blooming that summer, but certainly by the second. Foliage is feathery and fern-like and blossoms are bright yellow button clusters.

Once established in the garden, tansy spreads through underground roots, and if the flowers are not picked off, they will produce many volunteers. This habit tells us that seed may be started outdoors in the fall or spring. Seed is collected when the flowers have turned brown and before they begin to shatter. The seeds are located at the base of each of the small buttons and can be collected easily. There are several varieties of tansy, all of which are attractive perennials, albeit rather invasive. Although we grow tansy in our fertile garden soil, we have seen very large colonies of this plant in abandoned waste sites where there appeared to be more gravel than soil.

Tansy has some history of use as a culinary herb,

but its bitter taste and toxic properties make it both unpalatable and unsafe for eating. It is however a good herb for making moth-repelling potpourris and the flowers are excellent for use as fresh and dried material. The genus name for this herb comes from the medieval Latin *tanazita,* which is thought to come from the Greek *athanasia,* referring to the immortality of the flowers, as they do dry without withering. Tansy is native to Europe and Asia and is now naturalized in North America. It is hardy throughout this country.

TEASEL

Dipsacus fullonum

DIPSACEAE

TEASEL GERMINATES readily and grows rapidly. The first season teasel looks quite attractive and unobtrusive; it develops only its large basal leaves that grow in neat compact mounds. The second season however the plants begin to send up their dramatic tall flowering stalks. The flowers are stunning and unique. The spindle shaped heads, about 2 inches thick and 3–5 inches long, start out green and then the soft lavender flowers form in a circle around the middle of the flower head. As they develop, they appear as rings of lavender blossoms maturing toward the ends of the spindles.

All parts of the plant have sharp thorny features: leaves, stems, and curved sharp bracts at the base of the flower heads. Teasel is beautiful in the garden, lovely as material in fresh arrangements, and the seed pods are prized for use in dried arrangements. A few plants however will produce a number of flowers and pods. More than a decade ago, we unwittingly planted our first teasel plants—in fact, a whole garden row of some 300 plants. We were delighted by their performance, but overwhelmed by the number of stems we should have harvested at the end of the season. Wearing welders' gloves and using heavy loppers, we ran out of time, interest, and patience after collecting several hundred stems—at least a ten-year supply of dried material. We left the rest of the seed pods in the garden for bird food or compost. Ever since that year, we have had more teasel volunteers than we care to count, and

Teasel, during its second season, is an impressively tall, sharply thorned plant. It would make an excellent protective hedge if planted around a small garden.

THYME

Thymus vulgaris. English Thyme
Thymus praecox. Creeping Thyme

LABIATAE

THESE TWO VARIETIES of thyme are not difficult to grow from seed, but they produce very small seedlings and are slow to develop size. As soon as the plants have true leaves and can be handled, they are ready to be transplanted into flats or individual pots. Their root systems should be of good size in proportion to the top growth. In a few weeks, the plants will begin to branch out.

English thyme

There are some differences between these two varieties. As a young plant, English thyme has small leaves that are green on the top and burgundy purple underneath. In one season, English thyme will grow into a plant that reaches about 8–12 inches across. The plant likes full sun and good drainage. Its leaves, used fresh or dried, are excellent for flavoring salad dressings and cooked dishes. The flowers of English thyme are small white to pink blossoms and the whole plant is attractive as an ornamental border plant.

Creeping thyme has slightly larger, rounded green leaves and pink to light-rose flowers that cover the plant starting in the summer of its second season. It is grown more for its ornamental use than as a culinary herb and will perform well in sun or partial shade in a soil with ample moisture but good drainage. Creeping thyme is an excellent rock garden, border, and walkway plant. We have it growing between the stones of many pathways around our herb and everlasting shop, and it rarely succumbs to foot traffic. It is an excellent ground cover for small areas. Both thymes are rated to grow in Zones 4–9, but we find that English thyme is not reliably hardy in our Zone 5 gardens, while creeping thyme lives on through many different kinds of winters. Both plants attract bees when in flower and both plants can also be propagated by layering or stem cuttings.

creeping thyme

the plant has persisted as one of our most obnoxious weeds. We offer this as a warning to other gardeners.

If the numbers are controlled, this herb is well worth including, for its drama, beauty, and usefulness, but be prepared to collect all the seed heads before they take over your property. Seeds from unharvested plants will volunteer, and seeds may easily be shaken out of dried heads and directly seeded into the garden in the fall. Seeds are so large that they can be handled with accuracy. Alternatively, seeds may be planted in a nursery bed in the fall or spring and then lifted and relocated. Teasel does perform as a biennial.

Its name comes from the Greek *dipsa* meaning "thirst," referring to the characteristic way that the leaf axils collect and hold water. The herb is native to Europe and Asia, and is now naturalized in North America. It can be grown in Zones 3–9.

MAKING YOUR OWN herbal vinegars is one of the easiest projects if you have an herb garden. These vinegars are flavorful and fragrant. They have a bouquet that greatly improves even the most simple salad dressing. First you must purchase enough cider or wine vinegar to be used separately or in combination. If we are using only one herb to flavor a vinegar, we like to mix two kinds of vinegar for flavor and color. If we are using a broad assortment of herbs and vegetables, and some of the ingredients will lend color to the vinegar, we may use only cider vinegar as a base. Experiment with different combinations and you will find ones that suit your taste.

Begin by heating up the vinegar in a large stainless steel pan until the liquid is hot, but not boiling. Turn the heat off. While the vinegar is heating, prepare the fresh herbs, vegetables, and bottles. If herbal vinegars are homemade, you have your choice of bottles—old, used, new, plain or fancy. If you plan to sell any of the vinegars, check with your state licensing agent for packaging and labeling requirements. We are required to have a food production license and must use only new glass.

Wash and sterilize all containers, screw caps, and corks. Pick fresh young herbs from the garden, wash off any dust, and shake off the moisture. Place an herb sprig or combinations of herbs into each bottle. We use a sterilized wooden chopstick for this. Then fill the bottle to the brim with hot vinegar. The liquid will settle somewhat from the top as it cools and tiny air bubbles rise. Seal each bottle well. It is good to label and date bottles and store them for at least a week to a month before using. This allows the flavors to develop.

When choosing what to use for flavoring the vinegar, consider the compatibility of herbs with an acidic base. Chives and garlic chives work well, as do lovage, rosemary, dill, savory, and basils. Also note that some herbs give off a pleasing tint to the vinegars, especially chive blossoms and purple basils. Experiment with combinations of herbs, hot red peppers, and cloves of garlic, bay and dill. One of our favorite herbal vinegars contains eight herbs, two kinds of hot peppers, and garlic. The bouquet of this vinegar is so appealing that we use it to make all of our salad dressings by mixing it with a very fine olive oil, two parts vinegar to one part oil.

Decorative bottles are used for vinegars that will be given as gifts.

Lemon thyme, in flower in the foreground, is not propagated by seed, but creeping thyme, in the background, grows readily from seed and will have equally attractive flowers later in the summer.

Seeds can be easily collected after flowers have dried on the stems. Our creeping thymes send up many volunteers which can be lifted and transplanted in the spring or summer as long as the transplants are watered well for several days after being moved. English thyme is native to the western Mediterranean region and creeping thyme is native to northern Europe.

There are a great number of other varieties of thyme, but most of them are grown from divisions or cuttings as opposed to seed. We have incorporated a number of these varieties in our gardens. They include Lemon Thyme (*T. x citriodorus*), Variegated Lemon Thyme (*T. x citriodorus* 'Aureus'), Silver Variegated Thyme (*T. x citriodorus argenteus*), Woolly Thyme (*T. pseudolanuginosus*), Caraway Thyme (*T. herba barona*), and Nutmeg Thyme (*T. praecox articus*). Each of these plants is characteristically small, low growing, and fragrant. Of the varieties named, only Lemon and Woolly are reliably hardy here, but it is easy to winter over the other varieties in a protected cold frame or cool winter greenhouse. Most thymes are good herbs for containers.

VALERIAN

Valeriana officinalis

VALERIANACEAE

VALERIAN IS a tall, showy perennial herb that is found naturalized throughout parts of Canada and the northern United States, although the plants came to us originally from Europe and western Asia. Our wild plants undoubtedly were "escapees" from colonial gardens, where they were grown for their medicinal properties. One of the older botanical names for this herb is *Valeriana phu;* there is speculation that our sound for expressing displeasure at a given scent came from this species name. Dried valerian roots, used medicinally, are often described as smelling like stale perspiration or dirty sneakers.

The herb is easy to grow from seeds that can be

A COMBINATION OF ornamental and culinary herbs can be fashioned into a fragrant decorative wreath. There are a few perennial herbs that are commonly used for this purpose. They include the leaves of artemisias, particularly *Artemisia ludoviciana*, and garden sage. Color, fragrance, and accents are added by using the blossoms of chives, tansy, lavender, and wild oregano. Herbs are dried before the crafting begins.

The fans are attached to a circular wire frame.

Artemisia and sage are made into a fan-shaped cluster.

All of our wreaths are fashioned on a crimped wire circle. These may be purchased at craft stores or improvised out of wire or old coat hangers. It is also possible to make a circle out of a thin supple branch from grapevine, bittersweet vine, or shrubs with similar growth and texture.

Start working with the leafy dried background herbs, by making a fan-shaped cluster out of the herbs.

The finished wreath is ready to be hung and enjoyed. It was made entirely from home-grown herbs.

Colorful accents of chives, tansy, oregano, lavender, teasel, and fragrant flowering garlic are added.

Use enough stems to make a full graceful fan. With a very thin piece of wire, at least 12–18 inches long, wrap the base of the fan-shaped cluster to the circle. Continue to make leafy fans and wire them to the circle until you have formed the entire background of the wreath. Make certain that the fans are wired very tightly to the circle. Also keep the fans uniform in shape, length, and fullness so that the wreath is evenly formed.

Decorate the background with clusters of herb flowers by inserting the flowers on their own stems, catching the stems securely within the background. You may also use small wooden floral picks to wire the accents into clusters and work into the background. Try to arrange the accents so that they flow around the wreath gracefully rather than placing them symmetrically.

Ornamental wreaths can be accented with a few pieces of color or decorated heavily to build up a rich blend of colors, textures, and fragrance. Pods from rue, teasel, fragrant flowering garlic, and woad work well, as do herb flowers from bee balm, *Agastache*, and Welsh onion. Seed heads of dill, caraway, lovage, and angelica are very graceful, and will hold their shape if picked young.

sown directly into the garden in late summer or early spring, or in seed flats inside in early spring. Young plants show considerable growth their first year from seed. During the second year plants attain their full size of 4–5 feet tall. Foliage is spare but attractively paired along the stems. Flowers resemble umbels and range in color from off-white to whitish pink. They are very fragrant, not sweet exactly, but sweetly earthy. One of the common names for this herb is garden heliotrope.

Flowers are good for cutting fresh. The herb is attractive enough to be incorporated in a perennial border. Valerian plants may be lifted and divided every three or four years. Seed is easily saved from the flower heads that are allowed to mature on the plant. Watch the maturing heads closely as they will disperse their seeds shortly after the flowers go by. If mature flowers are unharvested, they will likely produce a number of volunteers. The name valerian comes from the Latin *valere*, "to be in good health."

WELSH ONION

Allium fistulosum

AMARYLLIDACEAE

AS WITH MANY OF the other small allium plants, we seed Welsh onion in plugs or peat pots, using 6–12 seeds to a pot. The young seedlings resemble thin spears of grass. As the plants are growing indoors, you can encourage the tiny underground bulbs to put on size by cutting back some of the top green growth. This is done by taking a pair of scissors and trimming an inch or so off the tops of the plant clusters, giving these plants what we refer to as a haircut. We do this once or twice before the plants are hardened off and set out in the garden.

During the first summer, Welsh onions grow to their full size and the individual stems become rather thick hollow green tubes. Beginning in the early spring of the second year, we start to snip and enjoy these bunching onions, coming as they do at a time when we are all hungering for fresh garden produce. In fact, Welsh onions can be selectively harvested and

The whimsical blossoms of Welsh onions are good for drying. The leaves, picked in early summer, are an excellent salad ingredient.

used fresh or in cooking all summer and into early fall. During the summer of their second season and henceforth, these onions will blossom with large rounded white flowers. The blossoms of Welsh onions can be dried for use in winter bouquets. Unharvested flowers will mature on the plants to produce seeds that can be collected.

The plants are attractive enough to be included in the ornamental garden, and they are actually very useful when planted among perennials that are particularly susceptible to aphid infestations. We have used Welsh onions for years planted between our lupines and these lupine plantings remain insect free, whereas other plantings of lupines are almost always infected.

The only cultural problem we encounter with Welsh onions is our need to compete with deer early in the season, as they seem as hungry for green onions as we. If we don't cover the new green growth, we are sure to find young plants chewed to the ground. Many plants will survive nonetheless and send up new growth. Welsh onions will grow in Zones 3–9 in average garden soils, but the most vigorous plants are found in soils that have plenty of organic matter and ample moisture.

WOAD

Isatis tinctoria

CRUCIFERAE

THE LARGE BROWN seed pods of woad make this a very easy herb to harvest and handle. Seeds need to be cleaned from their pods for best germination. Most purchased seeds will be cleaned, but if they are not, or if you are saving your own, here is how we prepare our seed before sowing. A few pods are placed in a small blender, spun for several seconds, and broken apart. The broken pods are then winnowed by hand to extract seeds that are still sizable

The biennial woad blossoms early in the spring of its second year. Flowers are succeeded by large shiny brown pods.

enough to be seen and handled. Cleaned woad seed will germinate readily as long as the seed is not old. The young seedlings have the plant's characteristic blue-green leaf color. Woad is classified as a biennial.

During the first year the plant develops only its leafy base. Then very early in the spring of the second year, each plant sends up a tall flowering stalk that produces a large complex head of many small delicate yellow blossoms. Woad flowers at the same time as chives and catmint, and the three plants in combination are an early treat, coming into color on the heels of the spring bulbs.

Woad flowers mature into showy pendulous shiny brown seed pods which we always collect as dried material or seed stock. If seeds are wanted for ornamental use, they must be picked when they have just turned brown, but before they are mature. If seeds are collected for propagation, the seed pods should be left to mature on the plants until they are just about to scatter themselves naturally. By harvesting the flower heads early, we undoubtedly stimulate some plants to live longer than the usual 2-year cycle. If you leave the seeds on the plant, woad will self-seed and produce numerous volunteers.

This herb has a history of use as a dye plant and was a principal source of blue dye throughout Europe until the introduction of indigo. Woad has a similar dye in its leaves, but in much smaller concentrations than indigo. Woad is still used by spinners and weavers for dyeing. The plant is hardy and easy to cultivate. It can be grown in gardens from Zones 3–9 and is native to Europe.

Herb Flower Type and Seed Longevity Chart

Herb	Flower Type(s)	Dioecious Monoecious	Pollination	Annual Biennial Perennial	Average Seed Longevity in Years	
						201
Angelica	perfect		self	B	1	
Anise	perfect		self	A	2–3	*3–9*
Anise Hyssop	perfect		self	P	2–3	*3–9*
Artemisias: absinthium, vulgaris	perfect		self	P	1–3	
Artemisia annua	perfect		self	A	1–2	
Artemisia dracunculus sativa	veg. propog.			P	n/a	
Artemisia stelleriana	perfect		self	P	1–2	
Baptisia	perfect		self	P	5–8	
Basil	perfect		self	A	3–4	
Bay Laurel	imperfect/perfect	dioecious	self or cross	P	1	
Bee Balm: fistulosa, didima, astrom.	perfect		self	P	3–4	
Bee Balm: citriodora	perfect		self	A	3–5	*4–9*
Borage	perfect		self	A	2–3	*3–9*
Burnet	perfect		self	P	1–3	*3–9*
Caraway	perfect		self	A	2–3	*3–9*
Catmint	perfect		self	P	1–2	*3–9*
Catnip	perfect		self	P	2–3	*3–9*
Chamomile, German	perfect		self	A	4–5	*3–9*
Chamomile, Roman	perfect		self	P	1–2	*3–9*
Chervil	perfect		self	A	2–4	*3–9*
Chives	perfect		self	P	1–2	*3–9*
Chives, Garlic	perfect		self	P	1–2	*3–9*
Cicely, Sweet	perfect		self	P	1	*4–9*
Comfrey	perfect		self	P	1–2	
Coriander, Cilantro	perfect		self	A	2–4	*3–10*
Cumin	perfect		self	A	1–2	*5–10*
Dill	perfect		self	A	2–4	
Elecampane	perfect		self	P	2–3	*3–9*

HERB	FLOWER TYPE(S)	DIOECIOUS MONOECIOUS	POLLINATION	ANNUAL BIENNIAL PERENNIAL	AVERAGE SEED LONGEVITY IN YEARS	ZONE
FENNEL	perfect		self	A	3–4	3-9
FENUGREEK	perfect		self	A	1–2	
GARLIC, FRAGRANT FLOWERING	perfect		self	P	2–3	3-8
GERMANDER	perfect		self	P	1–2	5-9
HOREHOUND	perfect		self	P	1–2	3-9
HYSSOP	perfect		self	P	2–4	3-8
LAVENDER	perfect		self	P	2–3	4-10
LEMON BALM	perfect		self	P	2–3	4-9
LOVAGE	perfect		self	P	2–3	
MARJORAM	perfect		self	A	4–5	
MINT, COMMON	perfect		self or cross	P	2–3	4
OREGANO	perfect		self	P	2–3	
PARSLEY	perfect		self	B	3–4	3-10
PATCHOULI	perfect		self	A	1–2	
PENNYROYAL	perfect		self	B	1–2	3-10
ROSEMARY	perfect		self	P	2–3	8-10
RUE	perfect		self	P	2–3	4-9
SAGE	perfect		self	P	3–4	5-9
SANTOLINA	perfect		self	P	1–2	3-9
SAVORY, SUMMER	perfect		self	A	3–4	6-10
SAVORY, WINTER	perfect		self	P	1–2	5-9
SESAME	perfect		self	A	2–3	7-10
SORREL	perfect		self	P	3–4	3-9
STRAWBERRY, ALPINE	perfect		self	P	1–2	
TANSY	perfect		self	P	4–5	
TEASEL	perfect		self	P	4–5	3-9
THYME	perfect		self	P	1–2	4-9
VALERIAN	perfect		self	P	2–3	
WELSH ONION	perfect		self	P	3–4	3-9
WOAD	perfect		self	B	2–3	3-9

*Zones Not Marked = All Zone Friendly

Indoor Herb Seeding Chart

Common Name/ Hardiness Zone	Scientific Name	Family	Seeds (M) per Oz. (Approx)	Stratify	Germ Temp
Angelica (B, 3–9)	Angelica archangelica	Umbelliferae	5.5	stratify	45–65
Anise (A)	Pimpinella anisum	Umbelliferae	7–15		65–75
Anise Hyssop (P, 3–9)	Agastache foeniculum	Labiatae	60		55–70
Baptisia (P, 3–8)	Baptisia australis	Leguminosae	1.7		60–70
Basil, Sweet Italian (A)	Ocimum basilicum	Labiatae	16–25		70–80
Bay Laurel (Gh, 8–10)	Laurus nobilis	Lauraceae	28	stratify	65–75
Bee Balm, Wild (P, 4–9)	Monarda fistulosa	Labiatae	56		65–75
Bee Balm, Lemon (A)	Monarda citriodora	Labiatae	56		65–75
Bee Balm, Mountain Star (P, 4–9)	Monarda astromontana	Labiatae	56		65–70
Borage (A)	Borago officinalis	Boraginaceae	1.5		55–60
Burnet, Salad (P, 3–9)	Poterium sanguisorba	Rosaceae	3.7		60–70
Caraway (B, 3–9)	Carum carvi	Umbelliferae	10		60–70
Catmint (P, 3–9)	Nepeta mussinii	Labiatae	60		65–75
Catnip (P, 3–9)	Nepeta cataria	Labiatae	48		60–70
Chamomile, German (A)	Matricaria recutita	Compositae	300		60–70
Chamomile, Roman (P, 3–9)	Chamaemelum nobile	Compositae	180		60–70
Chervil (A)	Anthriscus cerefolium	Umbelliferae	10–16		50–70
Chives (P, 3–9)	Allium schoenoprasum	Amaryllidaceae	10–25		60–70
Cicely, Sweet (P, 4–8)	Myrrhis odorata	Umbelliferae	2.5	stratify	50–65
Comfrey (P, 3–8)	Symphytum officinale	Boraginaceae	2–2.8		65–70
Coriander, Cilantro (A)	Coriandrum sativum	Umbelliferae	5		55–65
Cumin (A)	Cuminum cyminum	Umbelliferae	10–15		70–75
Dill (A)	Anethum graveolens	Umbelliferae	14–21		55–65
Fennel (A) var.	Foeniculum vulgare var. dulce	Umbelliferae	5–7		65–70
Fenugreek (A)	Trigonella foenum-graecum	Leguminosae	2.2		70–75
Garlic, Fragrant Flowering (P, 3–8)	Allium ramosum	Amaryllidaceae	10–25		60–70
Germander, Common (P, 3–8)	Teucrium chamaedrys	Labiatae	25–27		65–75
Horehound (P, 4–8)	Marrubium vulgare	Labiatae	20–23		65–70
Hyssop (P, 3–8)	Hyssopus officinalis	Labiatae	40		65–70
Lavender, English (P, 4–10)	Lavandula angustifolia	Labiatae	25		70–75
Lemon Balm (P, 4–9)	Melissa officinalis	Labiatae	40–50		65–70
Lovage (P, 4–9)	Levisticum officinale	Labiatae	8–9		65–70
Marjoram, Sweet (A)	Origanum majorana	Labiatae	280		70–75
Mint, Common (P, 3–9)	Mentha spicata var.	Labiatae	200–300		65–70
Mugwort (P, 3–9)	Artemisia vulgare	Compositae	200		65–70
Oregano, Wild (P, 3–9)	Origanum vulgare	Labiatae	120–140		70–75

Germ. Days	Growing on °F	Seed Cover	Germ. Light Needs	Set-Out Time	Handle: Direct/ Transplant	Best Light	Width	Height
14–30	55–65	lightly	light	6–8 weeks	T	S/PS	24"	4–5'
7–14	65–75	lightly	light	4 weeks	D	S	3–6"	1–2'
6–8	55–70	no		10–12 weeks	T	S/PS	12–18"	3–4'
15–45	55–60	¼"		10–12 weeks	T	S/PS	2–3'	3–4'
3–7	65–75	no	light	8–10 weeks	T	S	8–18"	24–36"
10–180	60–75	½"		n/a	T	S/PS	2–4"	6–12"
4–8	60–70	no		8–10 weeks	T	S/PS	12–18"	2–4'
4–8	60–70	no		8–10 weeks	T	S	12–18"	18–14"
4–8	60–70	no		10–August	T	S	10–12"	18–24"
6–10	55–65	press	light	3–4 weeks	D	S	18–36"	18–36"
6–8	60–70	lightly		8–12 weeks	T	S	6–10"	12–18"
6–14	55–65	no	light	4–5 weeks	T	S	6–18"	3–4"
6–8	60–70	no		10–12 weeks	T	S/PS	6–10"	6–10"
3–7	55–70	no		10–12 weeks	T	S/PS	18–24"	3–5'
4–7	55–60	no	light	5–6 weeks	T	S	6–8"	12–18"
4–7	55–60	no	light	5–6 weeks	T	S/PS	4–6"	4–6"
7–10	55–65	no	dark	4–5 weeks	T	S	6–8"	8–10"
6–12	55–60	⅛"		6–8 weeks	T	S/PS	6–8"	12–18"
30–45	55–65	lightly		6–8 weeks	T	PS/SH	18–24"	2–3'
7–14	55–65	⅛"		6–8 weeks	T	S/PS	24–26"	3–4'
7–10	55–65	press	light	4–6 weeks	D	S	12"	2–3'
5–7	65–70	press	light	5–6 weeks	T	S	4–6"	4–6'
7–10	60–70	press		5–7 weeks	T	S	10"	2–3'
7–10	65–75	press		6–7 weeks	T	S	18–24"	4–5'
2–5	60–70	¼"		3–4 weeks	D	S	4"	1–2'
5–7	55–65	⅛"		8–10 weeks	D	S	8–10"	2–3'
7–10	65–70	press		10–12 weeks	Transplant	S	10–12"	8"
7–10	65–70	press		12–14 weeks	T	S	12–18"	2'
7–10	55–70	press		8–10 weeks	T	S	18–24"	18–24"
10–60	65–75	press	light	14–20 weeks	T	S	12–18"	12–18"
5–8	55–70	no	light	14–18 weeks	T	S	18–24"	18–36"
9–14	55–70	lightly	light	12–14 weeks	T	S	18–14"	4–6'
7–10	55–65	no		12–14 weeks	T	S	12"	12"
7–10	55–70	no	light	14–16 weeks	T	S	12–48"	2–3'
7–10	55–65	no		8–10 weeks	T	S/PS	24–36"	3–6'
7–10	55–65	no		10–12 weeks	T	S	12–18"	8–24"

Herbs

Common Name/ Hardiness Zone	Scientific Name	Family	Seeds (M) per Oz. (Approx)	Stratify	Germ. Temp.
Oregano, Greek (P, 4–9)	*Origanum heracleoticum*	Labiatae	120–160		70–7
Parsley (B, 3–9)	*Petroselinum crispum*	Labiatae	15–18		70–7
Patchouli (A, Gh)	*Pogostemon cablin*	Labiatae	40–50		65–7
Pennyroyal (P, 5–9)	*Mentha pulegium*	Labiatae	100–200		60–7
Rosemary (P, 8–10)	*Rosemarinus officinalis*	Labiatae	25		70–7
Rue (P, 4–9)	*Ruta graveolens*	Rutaceae	29		60–7
Sage (P, 3–9)	*Salvia officinalis*	Labiatae	3–4		65–7
Santolina (P, 5–9)	*Santolina chamaecyparissus*	Compositae	50		65–7
Savory, Summer (A)	*Satureja hortensis*	Labiatae	40		60–7
Savory, Winter (P, 4–9)	*Satureja montana*	Labiatae	50		65–7
Sesame (A)	*Sesamum indicum*	Pedaliaceae	10–15		65–75
Sorrel (P, 3–9)	*Rumex acetosa*	Polygonaceae	25–35		65–7
Strawberry, Alpine (P, 3–9)	*Fragaria vesca*	Rosaceae	30		65–7
Sweet Annie (A)	*Artemisia annua*	Compositae	270		65–7
Tansy (P, 3–9)	*Tanacetum vulgare*	Compositae	240		65–7
Teasel (B, 3–9)	*Dipsacus fullonum*	Dipsacaceae	8		65–7
Thyme, Creeping (P, 3–9)	*Thymus praecox*	Labiatae	110		65–7
Thyme, English (P, 4–8)	*Thymus vulgaris*	Labiatae	80		65–7
Valerian (P, 3–9)	*Valeriana officinalis*	Valerianaceae	30–38		65–7
Welsh Onion (P, 3–9)	*Allium fistulosum*	Amaryllidaceae	10–25		65–7
Woad (B, 3–9)	*Isatis tinctoria*	Cruciferae	5.6		65–7
Wormwood (P, 3–9)	*Artemisia absinthium*	Compositae	270		55–65

🫖 *Key*

Stratify	Moisten and refrigerate until futher use
Germ. Temp. °F	Preferrable germinating temperature in degrees Fahrenheit
Germ. Days.	Days until seeds begin to show germination
Seed Cover	Lightly = less than 1/8" with fine vermiculite No = sprinkle on the surface Press = press the seeds into the surface without covering
Light Needs	Light = need light to germinate Dark = cover with black plastic until germination is evident
Set-Out Time	Time from seeding to planting in the garden
Handling: Direct/Transplant	D = direct seeded in the field or greenhouse T = transplant after seeding
Growing Conditions: Best Light	S = sun PS = partial sun SH = shade

GERM. DAYS	GROWING ON °F	SEED COVER	GERM. LIGHT NEEDS	SET-OUT TIME	HANDLE: DIRECT/ TRANSPLANT	BEST LIGHT	WIDTH	HEIGHT
7–10	60–70	no		10–12 weeks	T	S	12–18"	4–12"
14–18	60–70	press	light	12–15 weeks	T	S	12"	8"
10–21	65–75	no		12–15 weeks	T	PS/SH	12–18"	12–18"
10–12	55–65	no		10–12 weeks	T	S	12–18"	3–5"
10–40	60–70	press	light	14–18 weeks	T	S	4–8' (pot)	4–5'
10–30	60–70	no		8–10 weeks	T	S/PS	12–18"	18–24"
4–7	60–70	press		8–10 weeks	T	S	12–18"	18–24"
5–8	65–70	no		12–14 weeks	T	S	12–18"	12–18"
6–9	55–65	no		4–12 weeks	T	S	6–10"	12–18"
6–9	60–70	no		8–16 weeks	T	S	12"	6–10"
7–10	65–75	lightly		5–8 weeks	T	S	6"	12–18"
5–7	55–70	lightly		8–10 weeks	T	S	12"	12–36"
8–10	60–70	no		8–12 weeks	T	S	10–12"	8–12"
4–12	55–70	no		8–10 weeks	D/T	S	24"	5–6'
7–14	55–70	no		8–10 weeks	T	S	24"	3–5'
7–10	55–70	lightly		8–10 weeks	T	S	18–24"	3–6'
4–7	55–70	no	light	12–16 weeks	T	S	10–12"	4–8'
7–10	60–70	no		8–12 weeks	T	S	6–12"	6–12"
7–10	55–70	lightly		8–12 weeks	T	S	12–18"	3–5'
6–7	55–70	lightly		8–12 weeks	T	S	6"	18–24"
7–10	60–70	lightly		8–10 weeks	T	S	12–18"	2–3'
4–8	55–70	no		8–10 weeks	T	S	24"	3–5'

Outdoor Herb Seeding Chart

COMMON NAME HARDINESS/ZONE	SCIENTIFIC NAME	FAMILY	SEEDS (M) PER OZ. (APPROX.)	SOW DIRECTLY FALL/SPRING
ANGELICA (B, 3–9)	Angelica archangelica	Umbelliferae	5.5	fall
ANISE (A)	Pimpinella anisum	Umbelliferae	7–15	spring
ANISE HYSSOP (P, 3–9)	Agastache foeniculum	Labiatae	60	fall/spring
BAPTISIA (P, 3–8)	Baptisia australis	Leguminosae	1.7	fall/spring
BASIL, SWEET ITALIAN (A)	Ocimum basilicum	Labiatae	16–25	spring
BEE BALM, WILD (P, 4–9)	Monarda fistulosa	Labiatae	56	fall/spring
BEE BALM, LEMON (A)	Monarda citriodora	Labiatae	56	spring
BEE BALM, MOUNTAIN STAR (P, 4–9)	Monarda astromontana	Labiatae	56	fall/spring
BORAGE (A)	Borago officinalis	Boraginaceae	1.5	fall/spring
CARAWAY (B, 3–9)	Carum carvi	Umbelliferae	10	fall/spring
CATMINT (P, 3–9)	Nepeta mussinii	Labiatae	60	spring
CATNIP (P, 3–9)	Nepeta cataria	Labiatae	48	fall/spring
CHAMOMILE, GERMAN (A)	Matricaria recutita	Compositae	300	spring
CHAMOMILE, ROMAN (P, 3–9)	Chamaemelum nobile	Compositae	180	fall/spring
CHERVIL (A)	Anthriscus cerefolium	Umbelliferae	10–16	spring
CHIVES (P, 3–9)	Allium schoenoprasum	Amaryllidaceae	10–25	fall/spring
CICELY, SWEET (P, 4–8)	Myrrhis odorata	Umbelliferae	2.5	fall
COMFREY (P, 3–8)	Symphytum officinale	Boraginaceae	2–2.8	fall/spring
CORIANDER, CILANTRO (A)	Coriandrum sativum	Umbelliferae	5	spring
DILL (A)	Anethum graveolens	Umbelliferae	14–21	fall/spring
FENNEL (A)	Foeniculum vulgare var. dulce	Umbelliferae	5–7	spring
FENUGREEK (A)	Trigonella foenum-graecum	Leguminosae	2.2	spring
GARLIC, FRAGRANT FLOWERING (P, 3–8)	Allium ramosum	Amaryllidaceae	10–25	fall/spring
HOREHOUND (P, 4–8)	Marrubium vulgare	Labiatae	20–23	fall/spring
HYSSOP (P, 3–8)	Hyssopus officinalis	Labiatae	40	fall/spring
LEMON BALM (P, 4–9)	Melissa officinalis	Labiatae	40–50	fall/spring
LOVAGE (P, 4–9)	Levisticum officinale	Umbelliferae	8–9	fall/spring
MINT, COMMON (P, 3–9)	Mentha spicata	Labiatae	200–300	spring
MUGWORT (P, 3–9)	Artemisia vulgaris	Compositae	200	fall/spring
OREGANO, WILD (P, 3–9)	Origanum vulgare	Labiatae	120–140	fall/spring
PARSLEY (B, 3–9)	Petroselinum crispum	Umbelliferae	15–18	spring
PENNYROYAL (P, 5–9)	Mentha pulegium	Labiatae	100–200	spring
RUE (P, 4–9)	Ruta graveolens	Rutaceae	29	fall/spring
SAVORY, SUMMER (A)	Satureja hortensis	Labiatae	40	spring
SORREL, GARDEN (P, 3–9)	Rumex acetosa	Polygonaceae	25–35	fall/spring
SWEET ANNIE (A)	Artemisia annua	Compositae	270	fall/spring

Good Germ. Temp °F	Germ. Days	Seed Cover	Germ. Light Needs	Best Light	Width	Height
45–65	21–35	rake	light	S	3'	5–6'
65–75	7–14	lightly	light	S	3–6"	1–2'
55–70	10–15	rake		S/PS	12–18"	3–4'
60–70	25–45	1/4"		S/PS	2–3'	3–4'
65–80	5–10	rake	light	S	8–18"	24–36"
55–75	10–15	rake		S/PS	12–18"	2–4'
65–70	6–10	rake		S	12–18"	18–14"
60–75	6–10	rake		S	10–12"	18–24"
55–60	6–10	press	light	S	18–36"	18–36"
55–70	8–15	rake	light	S	6–18"	3–4'
60–70	8–14	no		S/PS	6–10"	6–10"
60–70	6–10	no		S/PS	18–24"	3–5'
60–70	5–10	no		S	6–8"	12–18"
50–70	7–10	no		S/PS	4–6"	4–6"
50–70	7–10	lightly	dark	S	6–8"	8–10"
50–70	10–14	1/8"		S/PS	6–8"	12–18"
50–70	21–30	1/2"		PS/SH	18–24"	2–3'
65–70	14–21	1/8"		S/PS	24–26"	3–4'
55–60	8–14	rake	light	S	12"	2–3'
55–75	7–14	rake		S	10"	2–3'
65–75	10–14	rake		S	18–24"	4–5'
65–75	2–5	1/4"		S	4"	1–2'
50–70	10–21	1/2"		S	8–10"	2–3'
65–70	7–10	press		S	12–18"	2'
55–70	10–14	rake		S	18–24"	18–24"
65–70	5–8	no	light	S	18–24"	18–36"
65–75	14–21	rake		S/PS	18–14"	4–6'
65–70	7–10	no	light	S	12–48"	2–3'
55–70	14–21	rake		S/PS	24–36"	3–6'
55–70	14–21	no		S	12–18"	8–24"
60–75	30–45	rake	light	S	12"	8"
60–70	10–12	no		S	12–18"	3–5"
60–70	14–21	rake		S/PS	12–18"	18–24"
65–75	8–10	rake		S	12–18"	18–24"
55–70	10–21	rake		S	12"	12–36"
50–70	10–21	no		S	24"	5–6'

Common Name Hardiness/Zone	Scientific Name	Family	Seeds (M) per Oz. (Approx.)	Sow Directly Fall/Spring
Tansy (P, 3–9)	*Tanacetum Vulgare*	Compositae	240	fall/spring
Teasel (B, 3–9)	*Dipsacus fullonum*	Dipsacaceae	8	fall/spring
Thyme, Creeping (P, 3–9)	*Thymus praecox*	Labiatae	110	fall/spring
Valerian (P, 3–9)	*Valeriana officinalis*	Valerianaceae	30–38	fall/spring
Welsh Onion (P, 3–9)	*Allium fistulosum*	Amaryllidaceae	10–25	fall/spring
Woad (B, 3–9)	*Isatis tinctoria*	Cruciferae	5.6	fall/spring
Wormwood (P, 3–9)	*Artemisia absinthium*	Compositae	270	fall/spring

❧ Key

Germ. Days.	Days until seeds begin to show germination
Germ. Temp. °F	Preferrable germinating temperature in degrees Fahrenheit
Lightly	Less than $1/8"$ with fine vermiculite
No	Sprinke on surface
Rake	Take the top of the soil to spread the seed smoothly and evenly over the surface
Press	Press the seeds into the surface without covering
Light Needs	Light = need light to germinate Dark = cover with black plastic until germination is evident
Growing Conditions: BestLight	S = sun PS = partial sun SH = shade

Good Germ. Temp °F	Germ. Days	Seed Cover	Germ. Light Needs	Best Light	Width	Height
55–70	10–21	no		S/PS	24"	3–5'
55–70	10–21	lightly		S	18–24"	3–6'
55–70	7–21	no		S/PS	12"	6–10"
55–70	10–21	lightly		S	12–18"	3–5'
55–70	10–21	lightly		S	6"	18–24"
55–70	10–14	lightly		S	12–18"	2–3'
50–70	10–15	no		S	2'	3–5'

CHAPTER SEVEN

Saving Seeds

OUR FARM IS LOCATED in a rural community, most of which was once made up of working farms. At the early part of this century, much of the land was cleared for agriculture. Families cobbled together a living from raising livestock, growing row crops, harvesting orchards, and working in the woods. There were small canning factories for the crops of corn, peas, beans, and the making of pickles. Milk was produced on farms for family use but also for sale to a broader public. Small manufacturing plants produced wooden products including barrels, tool handles, sleds, and skis. Railroad lines, one running along a border of our property, were used daily to deliver fresh produce to small cities as close as 20 miles away and large urban centers as far as 150 miles away.

Even our recent ancestors took seed saving very seriously. The task was as much a part of the year's work as was putting food by, getting in a winter supply of dry wood, and stocking a pantry with enough staples to last through the months when roads were impassable. Very few of us now pay attention to raising even a small portion of our own food, much less to taking responsibility for propagating varieties of plants. We go to the local markets not just for staples but to purchase food fully prepared for the table. We no longer eat foods only in season; we take for granted the availability of every kind of food at any time of year. We have shifted our work away from meeting the needs of the household in real terms to earning enough money to purchase those goods.

Today in our small community there are only three working farms. The railroad beds have been abandoned and are now used primarily by people on their snowmobiles and all-terrain vehicles. Livestock are now mostly pleasure horses. Farmland has reverted to woodland with the old stone walls running through them as reminders of past activities. Those of us who raise food do so not as farmers but as backyard gardeners. We no longer raise food out of necessity, yet most of our neighbors have gardens. The history of our little rural community is fairly reflective of changes and attitudes all over this country. As a population, we have left the farm to find our work and pleasures in other areas. And as a population we are turning in increasing numbers to gardening, which now ranks as one of America's leading hobbies.

We can't make any overarching statements about what this means about the national psyche. But we can examine our own experiences with growing plants and know that what drives and intrigues us are often the same things that speak to many others. If you begin to grow plants, even in a modest way, and if the work captures your imagination, chances are you will continue—tilling more soil, tasting more varieties of vegetables, and waiting for spring to arrive so that you can get back into the garden.

Saving Our Own Seeds

THERE ARE MANY REASONS that we began to save our own seeds. The biggest motivation at first was economic. As our gardens increased in size, and as we began to sell produce and then plants, we were spending more money purchasing seeds. The increase was so significant that in a matter of one decade the outlay of money rose from less than a hundred dollars a season to more than a thousand dollars. That became a rather compelling factor in prompting us to look at what was growing in the garden and understanding what we could harvest in a much broader sense.

Some of the first seeds that we saved were for Italian paste tomatoes, a crop that we grew in large amounts, and a crop with obvious differences in performance from one plant to another. We ventured out from here to saving seeds for perennial flowers, probably because they were so easy to collect and the pur-

chase price of seeds seemed out of proportion to the ease of saving them. And because the quality of our seeds was decidedly better than the seeds we had been buying, the benefits of saving were extending beyond the economic issue.

The evolution of our interest in saving seeds was also fed in great part by the real pleasure that it gave us in knowing that we could rely on our own work to supply ourselves with seeds for the future. The movement toward self-reliance very much fed our decision to step

Seeds of arugula are ready to be collected, fully dried, and stored.

out of the mainstream during the seventies, so it is not surprising that yet another way of "doing it for ourselves" had such intrinsic appeal. The issue of self-reliance was made very real when we began to notice that we could not rely on seed companies to ensure the availability of certain kinds of plants from one season to the next. We might come to appreciate a particular variety of vegetable only to see the seed for it disappear from the market. In some cases, if we did not save our own seeds, we were not able to grow the crop.

The task of saving seeds also made us look at plants more thoughtfully. The work generated many questions. Why do plants flower? Why do they flower at different times? How are flowers different from one another? Why are some plants self-pollinating, as opposed to insect- or wind-pollinated? Why don't all plants set seeds? Why are some seeds fertile and some sterile? We read more, observed more closely, and began to remember and apply the terms and lessons of earlier botany classes. Our education as gardeners is ongoing, but we are constantly fed by the

THE FLOWERS OF a plant are produced specifically for reproductive purposes. They contain the male and female reproductive organs of the plant, but depending on the species, there are still some basic differences in flower morphology. In order to understand these differences, it is helpful to know a few names for parts of flowers. A typical flower of an angiosperm is composed of petals, sepals, stamens, and pistils.

Petals are usually the most conspicuous parts of flowers, their colors and shapes visibly pleasing to gardeners. But more important, the petals attract insects that are essential for pollination. Sepals are the outer layer of the flower bud before it opens and the green whorl directly beneath the petals after the bud opens.

The stamens are the male pollen-bearing organs of flowers. A stamen consists of the anther or pollen-bearing part, and the filament or stalk. The female organ of a flower is called the pistil, which consists of the stigma, or top, and the style, or the part through which the pollen travels, and the ovary containing the ovules. Once pollinated, the ovules develop into seeds. A seed is therefore a ripened ovule.

Flowers that have all four parts (petals, sepals, stamens, and pistils) are called complete flowers. Incomplete flowers lack any one of these four parts. A further distinction is made based on the presence of the reproductive organs. Flowers that contain both stamens and pistils are called perfect flowers. A flower that is unisexual, that is, having only male or female reproductive parts, is called imperfect. They are either staminate (male) or pistillate (female) flowers.

If we extend this understanding of flowers to their presence on plants, we add a few more essential words to our gardening vocabulary. Some plants have only perfect flowers; these are beans, peppers, basil, and lavender. Some plants have separate male and female flowers on the same individual; these plants are referred to as monoecious. Examples of monoecious plants are corn and summer squashes. With corn, the top tassel is the male flower and the female flower is located farther down along the stem in the ears or cobs. With summer squashes, both flowers are located at the base of the plant and have the same shape and color, but the male flower extends out from the plant on a more extended stem.

If a species of plant has only male or female flowers on separate individuals, then the plant is referred to as dioecious. Examples include asparagus and spinach. The differences are clearly visible in asparagus. Only the female plants produce the red seed berries in the fall.

Petals, stamens, and pistils are all clearly visible in the flowers of this scented geranium.

WHILE WE ARE working in our gardens we are able to watch considerable pollination taking place in the activity of insects moving from plant to plant and from flower to flower. In fact insects are responsible for pollinating most of our fruits and many of our vegetables, herbs, and flowers. They include bees, beetles, butterflies, moths, and other insects.

Pollination is also carried out by birds, bats, and even non-flying mammals for some species. Insects and animals are attracted to flowers because of their color and fragrance. It is interesting to watch the activity of insects in our gardens, and if we took careful notes we might be able to draw up a kind of preference menu based on what plants attract what insects in the greatest numbers. At any given time during the growing season, there are typically a hundred different species of plants in bloom. But when members of the mint family are in flower, they seem to attract an inordinate percentage of the pollinating population. Flowers of creeping thyme, lavender, and salvias are constantly humming with insect life.

Wind and water are also important pollinators, transferring pollen from one plant to another both in close proximity and sometimes at long distances.

When a flower has both male and female reproductive parts it may be self-pollinating, as in the case of

Bees are some of the most commonly recognized pollinators in our gardens.

beans whose flowers usually finish pollinating even before the buds open. But fertilization may also take place from one flower to another and would therefore be termed cross-pollination. When flowers are unisexual, they are of necessity always cross-pollinated. Any one of the pollinators mentioned above may be responsible for transferring pollen from the male to the female flowers.

Whenever you can, take the opportunity to watch pollinators at work in your gardens. Some are large enough to observe with the naked eye. Others require a small hand-held magnifying lens. The movements are not only fascinating but unique to the types and shapes of flowers being pollinated.

need to learn more in order to understand the place we work each day. And we can say without hesitation that it is the pleasure of learning that fuels our interest in gardening, and more specifically in saving our own seeds.

One additional reason for saving our own seed is not about money or commitment. Saving seeds is just

plain fun. Compared to all the other work of the field, it's not very taxing. While collecting seeds, we are free to wander the gardens, look at the plants and insects there and appreciate the beauty of the place. Collecting is usually done on pleasant quiet days, and it's a task that needs to involve only one person. It is a time to be quietly absorbed in work that speaks mainly of the future. It's gentle work and yet productive. What could be more satisfying?

If you are at all intrigued by the notion, prompted by economics, self-reliance, or sheer curiosity, here is some basic information to help you get started. If you want more technical terminology and lengthy explanations about the physiology of plants or the stages of reproduction, we refer you back to your old botany textbooks. In gardeners' words, here are some guidelines for saving your own seeds.

Open-Pollinated Versus Hybrids

OPEN-POLLINATED PLANTS are those that produce seeds for plants that will resemble the parents. They are sometimes referred to in catalogues as standard varieties, or, occasionally, as heirloom varieties, but the latter term is still not clearly defined (see the box on page 250). Some plant catalogues offer only open-pollinated varieties of plants, others offer very few. The overall trend in the plant industry has been away from the production of open-pollinated plants because large scale agriculture rarely makes use of these varieties. In response, many seed savers, as individuals and groups, have become more active over the past twenty years. If you are interested in saving your own seeds, and you are trying to propagate specific varieties of plants, you should begin with seeds or plants that are open-pollinated.

Hybrids are plants that result from crossing species or varieties of plants by means of cross-fertilization. Plants are hybridized for a number of reasons, but generally to produce offspring with improved characteristics. These improvements have to do with larger fruit, different colors, better taste, resistance to disease, earlier ripening, and other factors. Hybrid seeds may produce plants with seeds that are either viable or sterile. But even if seeds are viable, they can not be counted on to reproduce the characteristics of the plant from which they came. Seeds, if viable, may have some of the characteristics of the first generation parent or characteristics of some of their more distant relatives. The disadvantage of hybrid plants is that one has no control over their reproduction by saving seeds. Seed and plant catalogues refer to their hybrid plants with the word "hybrid" or the code "F1" after the name.

Evaluating Plants

WHEN WE DECIDE to save our own seeds, we are trying to reproduce the same varieties of plants that we grew originally. We are not doing any fancy hybridizing or plant development. Nonetheless, in a planting of a dozen or so plants of one variety, there are bound to be some differences in performance. In any population of individuals we refer to this as *diversity*. In a stand of tomato plants, not all the plants will be identical. As seed savers, we exercise some critical choices among the individuals in the garden.

In order to save seed from open-pollinated plants, it is necessary to choose individuals and assign those individuals to seed production. The selection of individuals from a group of identical vegetables or herbs is influenced by a number of factors. In a general sense, we are looking for the most desirable characteristics of a given plant. That usually means that we watch the vigor of the plants from the time that we start them from seed. During the growing season in the garden, we continue to watch plants. When we see noticeable differences in performance, we pick out the strongest individuals and monitor their development so that we can save their seeds. This explanation will be easier to understand if we look at different plants and talk specifically about what it is we want in their performance.

Some of our garden vegetables are grown primarily for their edible foliage. These include greens such as spinach, lettuce, and arugula. The best producers are those plants with abundant leaf production, good color, good texture and flavor, and the ability to produce over as long a period as possible before going to seed. Individual plants that exhibit the greatest number of these attributes would be the plants we would want to use for seed collection. If late bolting is a desirable characteristic, we would deliberately not save seeds from the first individuals of these plants that went to flower, because in so doing, we would be selecting for the very behavior that we don't want to promote. Instead we would choose seeds from the plants latest to flower and seed.

We grow some vegetables for their fruit, such as tomatoes, cucumbers, eggplant, and peppers. In evaluating the characteristics of these plant types, we look

WHILE WE HAVE ADVISED you to save seeds from open-pollinated plants, we also recognize that it is interesting to play with seeds from hybrid plants, if for no other reason than to see what results. Our own work with a hybrid hot pepper over several years has been well worth pursuing. It began with purchased seeds for an F1 hybrid of Thai hot peppers, described in the catalogue as "short 8"–10" plants bearing small 1" upward facing peppers that matured from green to red."

At the end of the first growing year, we harvested peppers for drying and repotted a few plants for the indoor winter windowsill. These small plants can easily be grown inside and harvested whenever peppers are wanted for cooking. If the mature fruit are consistently removed, the plants will set new buds and continue fruit production year-round.

The following spring we planted seeds from three dozen peppers collected from two different plants. The seedlings and later the garden plants exhibited a great variability, first in the foliage, then in the overall proportions of the plants, and finally in the variety of fruits set. Some peppers resembled the parent plants. Others were 3"–4" long. Some were downward facing. Some fruits were short and stubby, with a portion of these facing upward and the remainder facing downward. We collected the various types, saved seeds, and labeled them descriptively.

The following year we again planted the seeds from the peppers that most closely resembled the hybrid fruit, and for another season collected and saved seeds from the fruit most resembling the original. Each year of the continuous plantings, we increase the percentage of small one inch upward facing fruit, but are able to select some unusual individuals. Some of these individuals have turned out to be excellent for decorative use.

We have not seen the original hybrid in catalogues for the past several years, but through selection and replanting, we have been able to reproduce the plants with seeds only distantly related to their parents.

Planting seeds from the Thai hot pepper plants, shown in the upper right-hand corner, resulted in all the varieties of fruit pictured above.

for overall vigor, color, taste, productivity, and in northern climates, the ability of a plant to ripen the greatest number of fruits in a growing season. In a planting of a dozen or so tomato plants of a single variety, we would save the seeds from any one plant that excelled in these characteristics. In this case, we would be selecting in part for the earliness of flower, fruit, and seed production. If we had a planting of one variety of sweet bell peppers and one plant produced a number of fruits some of which ripened quickly to red, we might want to select this individual for seed saving.

In the case of many vegetables, we are eating the root of the plant, and will have to examine its development to save seed. When working with carrots, parsnips, beets, and turnips, we look for a combination of size, color, flavor, and texture.

Many of our vegetables are grown for the edible seeds themselves, like beans, peas, and peanuts. We are harvesting and eating the crop at the same time that we are isolating some plants to mature seed. If we are looking for earliness of production, we would mark those plants and not harvest them for eating, and wait instead for the next most early ones for table use. It would not be advisable to harvest and eat the earliest and save the last and least vigorous individuals for seeds.

When we are evaluating herbs for seed selection, we select for overall vigor, fragrance, hardiness, leaf production (in some cases), and perhaps the colors of the flowers. Herbs that we are growing for culinary purposes would be evaluated differently from herbs that are to be used ornamentally or for making potpourri.

In addition to the list of criteria mentioned, we avoid collecting seeds from plants that are the weakest of the group, any plants that show signs of disease, or ones that appear susceptible to insect predation in a group. Diseases and insects are often drawn to the least vigorous individuals. Criteria that we apply

as gardeners may also arise from personal preferences. These could include the hotness of a pepper, the uniqueness of a flower color, or the height of an individual. One cannot be assured that the seeds from each plant will reproduce all the characteristics that you are observing, but evaluating plants will give you the best opportunity to make wise choices in a general sense.

Having pointed out all the possible differences in performance, we know that you will not always see

The largest, most well-developed carrots will be chosen to replant for seed production.

appreciable differences between individuals in the garden. If none is apparent, you may simply mark any individual to use for seed saving. If however you are saving for certain characteristics, note your choices as early in the season as possible, and label whatever plants you want for seed saving so that they are not inadvertently harvested. We usually tie several bright ribbons in conspicuous places on the plant to alert anyone working in the garden to the selection. In your own backyard, choose a method understood by all, and one that you remember yourself. Early traits that motivated you to select plants may well be masked by later growth so that you will not recognize your original choices.

PLANT CATALOGUES, magazine articles, and gardening columnists have all contributed to the trendiness of heirloom plants. Each season there are more offerings of seeds and plants that have not been commonly available. But when we try to understand what makes a plant an heirloom, the definition is somewhat vague. The only thing that we are certain is meant is that the plant is open-pollinated, or a non-hybrid. The reverse is not true; there are non-hybrid plants that are not considered heirlooms.

"Heirloom" is also meant to imply that the plant is very old, but "old" can mean that the plant was originally cultivated in the nineteenth century or that it made its appearance during the middle part of the twentieth. The heritage of the plant may or may not be American. Brandywine tomatoes were named in the late nineteenth century by Johnson & Stokes, a seed company in Philadelphia. Zinnias were introduced to this country from Mexico nearly two hundred years ago. We are indebted to English breeders for many of our sweet peas.

Reading through back issues of garden catalogues does not shed much light on the specific meaning of *heirloom*. It is interesting to note that some open-pollinated species are suddenly labeled "heirloom" one year after having been described in an ordinary manner. This series of claims of "old," "older," "oldest" will no doubt sort itself out over the next decade, but for now, be aware that heirloom seems to be as much a term conveying status as a specific definition of age.

In trying to sort out other gardening terminology, we also notice that catalogues have a number of ways of informing us if plants are hybrids or non-hybrids.

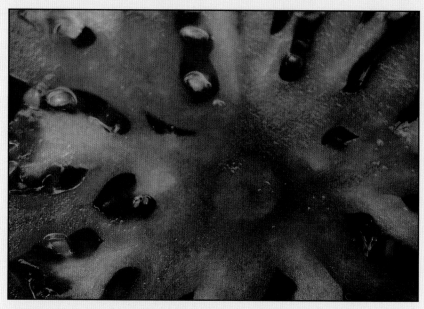

Brandywine tomatoes, widely recognized as heirloom plants, have large, flavorful, and meaty fruit.

Some descriptions always include the notation "F1" after the name, meaning that the plant is a first generation cross or hybrid. Some catalogues refer to the plants as hybrids included with the name. Others explain that the plant is a hybrid somewhere in the descriptive material.

Although we know that heirloom plants are open-pollinated, it is interesting that the word *standard* is occasionally used to mean the same thing. And finally, if a catalogue doesn't use any of the words *heirloom, standard, open-pollinated, F1,* or *hybrid,* we are left to assume that the plant is a non-hybrid.

Despite the imprecise use of words to describe older plants, it is pleasing to see a renewed interest in vegetables and flowers from the past. Many unusual varieties of plants were disappearing from common view. We hope that this new attention to preserving old species will be taken seriously by the general gardening public, so that what is now only a trend may become a long-standing commitment.

SEED SAVERS ALL

OUR FIRST GARDEN MENTORS were seed savers. They collected and dried varieties of vegetables that performed well, tasted good, and were easy to store. They also did it because it meant that they didn't have to spend any more money than was absolutely necessary to continue truck farming from year to year.

Seed saving was a common practice on thousands of family farms all across America in the earlier part of the twentieth century. Much has changed, most visibly the number of small independent family farms still in existence. We have, as a culture, moved off the farm and into the cities and suburbs. Farming in America has become an activity now conducted on a scale much larger than the sum of many households.

In response to these changes, the focus of plant research conducted at the university and corporate level has also switched from addressing the needs of small-scale farmers to research promoting plant hybrids that perform optimally on large-scale mechanized operations. In the process, maintaining production of many old species of plants has been abandoned. With fewer individuals saving seeds and a reduction in the number of varieties offered by seed companies, we have lost many varieties of plants that were once commonly available. The loss is felt most significantly in the area of old open-pollinated plants—varieties that are now often referred to as "heirloom" plants.

Out of concern for this loss of genetic diversity, individuals and groups, across this country and across the world, have started saving and exchanging home-grown seeds and plants. Some people have made this concern a lifetime commitment, most notably Diane and Kent Whealy. In 1975 they founded Seed Saver Exchange in Decorah, Iowa. Their work was honored recently when they became the recipients of a MacArthur Fellowship for their outstanding achievements in saving seed varieties. Another well-known group, Seeds of Diversity Canada, has also done much to identify and preserve endangered plants.

If you are interested in learning more about seed-savers' work and exchanges, we suggest you search the Internet, which has available an impressive amount of information. It is in areas of endeavor such as this that the Internet serves to link individuals and groups, nationally and internationally.

Bean seeds are very easy to save. These wax beans were allowed to mature enough pods for sowing next season's crop.

When to Begin Harvesting Seeds

THE ANSWER SOUNDS simplistic. We begin harvesting seeds when they are ripe on the plants. Depending on the plant, seeds can be ready as early as June for some spring greens, chives, and certainly for many ornamental plants that we don't discuss in this book. We start harvesting seeds then and continue the process all through the summer and into late fall. Seeds are not ready to be picked at one time because flowers are not produced on plants at the same time. All the vegetables and herbs that we are discussing are classified as angiosperms, meaning that they are plants producing flowers and reproducing by seeds enclosed within the female parts of those flowers. We can witness from watching our gardens that flowers appear on plants at various times in a year. The act of flowering is brought on by a number of factors, including heat, light, length of day, temperature, the age of plants, and stress.

We already know some of the basic differences in flowering plants. Annuals, for the most part, flower over a long period of time, during which they may set seed and continue to flower until cold weather kills the plant. Annuals must be started from seed another year. Perennials, on the other hand, usually flower for a specific period of time during the summer, often for no longer than a month, and then they may produce seeds. The plants of true perennials will die down during the cold months but begin new growth the following year when the weather warms up. In addition, perennials that have set seed may reproduce themselves by volunteers in the garden. Depending on the time of flowering, the seeds dropped by perennials into the garden may begin growing the same summer or wait until the following spring to germinate. Biennials are plants that typically develop vegetative growth the first season, go dormant during the winter, and then flower, produce seed, and die the second year. Their long-term

survival relies on their production of seeds to generate new plants.

The vegetables and herbs that we cultivate are found in each of the categories that we describe earlier. Tomatoes act like annuals, as do basils, eggplant, and cucumbers. They set flowers and fruit continuously during the summer. Biennials include parsley, woad, cabbage, beets, and angelica. These plants need two seasons to flower and produce seeds. Asparagus, rhubarb, lavender, and sweet cicely are all perennials. They flower during a specific time of the summer and mature their seeds, very early in the case of rhubarb, very late in the case of asparagus.

If you are interested in saving seeds, it will not take long to learn when different plants flower. You will see them in the gardens and watch the formation of the flowers and the maturation of flowers into fruit and seed. Annual herbs and vegetables produce seeds that are easy to save because they mature their seeds in one growing season. Biennials are somewhat more demanding if the plants are not hardy in your gardening site. If you want to collect seeds from certain biennial vegetables such as celery or cabbage, you must make special storage arrangements to winter over the plants for a second season. See the individual plants in Chapters 5 and 6 for specific instructions. On the other hand, biennials that are hardy, such as leeks and woad, are very easy to grow for seed, as these plants

Ripe red berries on the female asparagus plants provide seeds that germinate readily.

W E SAVE MANY OF our own seeds because we have found that they germinate in very high percentages. Although purchased seeds for most vegetables and annuals have high germination rates, that is not always true for some of the lesser known perennials that we grow on the farm. When working with our own seed, we have no way of knowing ahead of seeding what to expect in terms of production unless we first perform a simple germination test. You may want to test some of your own home-saved seeds or even purchased seeds that you have stored for a few years. Here is how to go about it.

A germination test for these cucumber seeds shows a high percentage of viability.

Take a sample of seeds from their storage container. The number you choose is based on the amount of seed available, but make certain that the sample is large enough so that you can draw some conclusion from the results. If possible, test at least two dozen seeds of a given variety. If the seeds are extremely dry or have been stored in a desiccant, allow them to rehydrate to normal room humidity for several hours before beginning the test. Line the bottom of a shallow pan with several layers of very moist paper towels, blotter paper, or cotton, and arrange the seeds on the top of the layers. Then cover the seeds with the same material that has been similarly moistened. You want the environment to be reliably moist but not soggy.

Place the container in a warm location with temperatures between 65° and 75°F. Every day, check the moisture of the germinating tray and briefly lift the cover to allow air into the center. Mist the paper or cotton if necessary. Look up the anticipated germination time for the seeds you are testing and allow an additional week beyond that time before you count the results.

As seeds germinate, they may be removed from the tray, but keep count of them so that you can calculate the results. When testing time has elapsed, count the number of germinated seeds and compute the percentage against the number originally counted out. If 80 percent or more of the seeds showed signs of growth, you have a very good reading. If 70 percent grew, that is an acceptable number. If the percentage is below 50 percent, still consider collecting or purchasing that variety again. You can use seeds with poor germination rates but sow them more densely.

will winter over without much attention. Hardy perennials like creeping thyme, lavender, and asparagus are very easy to grow for production and seed. We routinely save seeds for most of the open-pollinated perennials at the farm.

Recognizing Ripe Seeds

THERE IS ESTABLISHED botanical terminology for the containers that hold the ripened seeds, something that we gardeners refer to casually as seed pods or seed heads. We will not be strictly scientific in describing how to look for seeds, but we think it may be interesting to understand some general terminology for seed production. It begins with the use of the word *fruit*. Botanically speaking a fruit is the mature ovary and its associated parts. It is the organ containing the seeds. There are fleshy fruits such as eggplant, peppers, tomatoes, cucumbers, gourds, and squashes. Dry fruits include peas and beans and corn, and the parts of broccoli, cauliflower, radishes, carrots, and

bee balm that hold the seeds. We might be willing to call peas and beans *fruit,* but when it comes to the rest of the dried fruit in the list, gardeners would probably quickly revert to *seed pods* or some such common terminology for what is technically still fruit. When we say we are collecting seeds, we are actually collecting the fruit of the plants, from which we extract the seeds. With some plants we harvest the whole fruit and clean out the seeds. With others, we obtain the seeds by shaking them out of the fruit. For our instructions about seed collecting, we will be less scientific. We will refer to seeds in the "fruit" when obvious and seeds in their "pods" when they are gathered along with plant material that we do not readily refer to as fruit.

Collecting Seed from Fleshy Fruit

FLESHY FRUIT DISCUSSED in the vegetable chapter include tomatoes, tomatillos, eggplant, cucumbers, melons, squashes, and gourds. Each of these fruits should be left on the plants to mature as

GUARD THE SPECIAL SEEDS

IF YOU GET INVOLVED in seed saving in any significant way, you are likely to accumulate a collection of seeds that have value. Some may represent seasons of saving the best individuals from a favored vegetable. Some may have come into your possession from a neighbor or through involvement in a seed-savers' exchange. If you are planting and propagating varieties of plants that can easily be replaced from ordinary seed catalogues, then you can be rather cavalier about seeding out all your supply.

On the other hand, if you have a limited number of seeds for some special plants, be cautious about planting every last seed. Even under the best of conditions, strange things can happen in our gardens. A sudden late freeze, uncommon insect predation, an especially hungry herd of deer can wipe out a whole crop without notice. If your seeds are special, reserve a few of each kind as insurance against the unforeseen.

An elderly neighbor presented us with some of his prized seeds for an antique variety of shell beans.

The fruits of three open-pollinated tomatoes include (from left to right) *Brandywine, Nepal, and Heinz. These tomatoes are cut open to collect the seed for processing.*

long as possible until the fruits are very ripe but not to the point of spoiling. The fruits are picked and the seeds are scooped out of their cavities. Some seeds come out of their fruit attached to the pulp. The process of cleaning and preparing the seeds for storage involves separating the seeds completely from the pulp and drying them.

Once the seeds have been removed from their cavities, mash the pulp and seed gently to remove the pulp that clearly does not contain seed. Then place the whole mass into a container with at least enough water to equal the amount of pulp. Label each container immediately; you will have no other way of identifying the seed, especially when saving several kinds of one variety.

Set the containers aside for several days; the pulp

Seeds are scooped out of the tomato and mixed with water to ferment.

will begin to break down and ferment. Don't let the containers dry out during this time and keep them at room temperature. Add a little water if necessary to keep the contents moist. After some fermentation has occurred, start to clean the seeds from their pulp. We place the whole mash into a sieve and run lukewarm water through the sieve, rubbing and stirring gently to separate and wash away any broken down debris. Watch that the sieve is the right size to keep seeds from washing through. If all the debris does not pass through the sieve the first washing (and it generally does not), return the seeds and pulp to a clean container with warm water and repeat the process until rinsing removes all the decomposed pulp. The final rinsing is done with warm water; the seeds are now free of pulp and ready to be dried.

Labeled containers of tomato seeds that will be fermented, washed, dried, and stored.

Place the cleaned wet seeds between several layers of paper towel and pat them as dry as possible. Place the partially dried seeds on new dry paper towels, separate them so they are not all in a clump, and set the cleaned seeds in a spot where they can dry thoroughly. Be absolutely certain that you attach the identifying labels to the seed lot or write the information on the paper towel itself. We use our darkened greenhouses for the drying process, which takes place in a matter of days. Find a dry spot in your own environment, perhaps near a register or woodstove. Some people place a light bulb near the drying seeds to lower the humidity. You are trying to dry the seeds quickly and completely. If it helps to stir them or place them on fresh dry paper towels, do so, and check them from day to day. When they are absolutely dry to the touch they are ready to be removed and placed in a storage container. We discuss storage containers later in the chapter.

If you are saving strawberry seeds, use the same method. Technically, strawberries are not called fleshy fruit, perhaps because the seeds are attached to the outside of the placenta as opposed to being contained within. The difference here really is academic as the cleaning and storing methods are the same for both.

Anytime that you are collecting in the garden, be aware when you are gathering up vegetative matter that a drowsy bee may be concealed beneath some leaves. Bees and hornets are rarely interested in us when we are in the gardens, but if one is accidentally pinched, it can respond quickly. Some of us have no reaction other than feeling a mild prick, but there are others who have sudden allergic reactions. If you are stung and begin to swell, pay attention to the sting and use appropriate medication immediately. Allergic reactions can appear any time in a lifetime, even in individuals who have previously shown none.

When collecting fleshy fruits, the weather is not a terribly important consideration. If it's overcast or windy, the task may not be as pleasant, but increased humidity and breezes will not adversely affect the collection. The seeds are securely within the moist fruit you will be handling.

Choosing times to collect the next categories of seeds is much more important. The partially dry seeds should be picked when they are as dry as possible. Wait for a sunny day, and late enough in the day, so that any morning dew has dried from the plants. Collect on a calm day so that wind gusts won't interfere with the work. Some of the seeds will be easy to lose when transferring them to the collection bags.

Seeds from Dry Fruits

WE ARE NOW TALKING about most of the remaining vegetables and herbs discussed in the book. The seeds for these plants are located in different places on the plants, but in every case, the seeds are already partially dried when they are collected. The same general rule applies to collecting the seed however. Wait until the seeds have ripened as much as possible on the plants but watch the ripening so that you gather the seeds before the plant disperses them.

Plants rely on a number of mechanisms for distributing their own seeds and thus ensuring reproduction. When we collect seeds we are contributing to that process, but in the general scheme of things, gardeners are not counted on to spread seeds intentionally. When we harvest for the sake of cultivating, we are simply being resourceful. When we, like other animals, come in contact with plants and inadvertently cause them to release seeds, we become participants in seed dispersal. The shape of seeds and their placement on the plants has much to do with the distribution process. For a further look at seed dispersal, see the box on page 257.

It is interesting to examine some of the common ways that seeds are located within their fruit and how the fruit functions in the seed collection process. The annual members of the Cruciferae family—the mustard plants such as broccoli, greens, radishes, and Chinese cabbage—contain their seeds in similarly shaped fruits that resemble small slender pods arranged along tall flower stalks. Young seed pods are fleshy and green and as they mature and ripen they turn beige. The beige pods continue to mature and become even lighter in color, and if left unharvested, they split open and expel their seeds into the garden. The pods should be harvested just before they begin to split, but not too much before or the seeds held within will not be ripe. Watch and test. Pick a pod that looks ripe and try to open it. If it will not split easily and the seed inside is still very fleshy and light in color, the seeds are not ready to be harvested. When this type of seed is ready for gathering, we either carefully strip off the pods and put them into a gathering bag in the field, or cut the whole stem and put it in a large gathering bag to be cleaned once we are out of the field. When gathering, bring permanent ink markers and labels. If we are using paper bags, we write on the bag. If we are using plastic just to haul materials inside, we write on a piece of paper and put it in the bag.

Many herbs are members of the Labiatae family. The flowers and hence the seeds of this family of plants are located along the stems of the plants. Nei-

PLANTS UTILIZE a number of mechanisms to disperse their own seeds. If we examine the ways that seeds are released from their fruit, we can better evaluate when to gather seeds. We want to leave them on the plants as long as possible, but harvest them before natural release takes place.

Some plants produce fruit that split open with sudden force, expelling the seeds some distance from the parents. The mustard family is an example. Another plant, often enjoyed by children, is the spotted touch-me-not, *Impatiens capensis*. This wildflower grows by the wayside in profusion. It has small bright orange flowers followed by a green tightly curled fruit. When ripe fruit is touched, it springs open, throwing out its seeds in all directions.

The wind is probably the greatest single disseminator of seed. It picks up the mature seeds of lettuce, dandelions, and milkweed and carries them for long distances with the aid of the small group of fine hairs, called pappus, attached to one end of the seed. Look at each of these examples and see the exquisite design that coordinates the size of the pappus to the size and weight of the seeds that it must carry through the air. Wind also catches the winglike fruit of trees such as maple and ash.

Some animals are responsible for relocating plant seeds as they gather and store fruit for the winter. We have all watched the work of chipmunks and squirrels in the late summer and fall, gathering the fruit of a number of trees. Mice and other small rodents are seed carriers as well. Their activities are increasingly visible in late summer when they begin to eat into the garden vegetables.

From August until very cold weather, our fields are filled with foraging birds. They land on the tall sturdy stems of *Dipsacus*, *Valeriana*, and any trellising still in the garden. Birds are present when the seeds of amaranth ripen. Their presence indicates the maturity of a number of cultivated plants. Birds ingest many fruits that pass through their digestive systems before the seeds drop to the ground and germinate far from where they grew.

Some seeds are equipped with sharp barbs, little curved spines, or rough coats that resemble a natural Velcro. When these seeds are brushed by passing animals, ourselves included, the seeds stick to hair and clothing and are carried off to a distant location. Burdock is the best known example. Annual artemisia has very sticky fruit that adheres to any rough dry surface. Sticky seeds are commonly picked up by the feet of passing animals and birds.

Some insects (especially ants) transport seeds from place to place. As seed gatherers, we are in the company of many other members of the animal kingdom. Our efforts as gardeners are simply more intentional, like our desire to keep the plants growing in our own backyards.

Lettuce seeds are distributed by the wind.

These mature hyssop stems are stripped of their seeds by carefully pulling a hand along the stems and emptying fruit into a paper bag.

ther the seeds nor the fruits are as visible or as easy to evaluate as the fruits of the mustard family. It is necessary to wait until the plants have set flowers and the seeds have had ample time to ripen on the plants. Seeds from this family of plants are collected during the summer and into early fall. It is necessary to examine the plants carefully. When seed pods are brown and fairly dry, we strip the stems of their seeds and place them into labeled paper bags. The paper bags are left open in a warm dry place for several days so that the contents can dry.

The time it takes between gathering the seeds and drying them depends on the temperature, the humidity of the drying space, the amount of seeds in a harvest, and the amount of fruit included with the seeds during the collection process. If there is any chaff that will dry along with the seeds, spread out the collection on an open clean surface or fine mesh screen to hasten the process. We use both methods successfully.

Plants belonging to the Umbelliferae family may be annuals, biennials, or perennials, but they re-semble one another in their flowering and seed formation. Think of the flowers of dill or caraway. If you look closely, the flower is actually an assemblage of many tiny flowers each on its own stem but arranged in such a way as to appear to be one flower. The fact that the "flower" is really many individual flowers is more apparent when we examine seed production because each fertilized flower produces a seed. The seeds are arranged in the same pattern in a gently rounded cluster on the tops of the flower stalk. When seeds are first formed they are green, and as they mature, they turn to beige and then to various shades of brown, almost to black, depending on the species. Caraway has a medium gray brown color. Dill is similar. Sweet cicely is black-to-brown when fully ripe. Despite the differences in color, time of ripening, and size of seeds, harvest should take place when the seeds have ripened as long as possible on the plants, but before they start to shatter and fall to the ground.

The discussion of plant families can be used as a guide for collecting seeds of other varieties. The essential rules are to watch the plants for flowering and seed production, allow the seeds to ripen as long as possible on the plants, and remove the seeds by whatever method is most efficient to get the seeds inside, cleaned, and dried. For specific instructions on individual plants, we refer you to the full discussion of each vegetable and herb in the earlier chapters of the book.

Seeds That Should Be Stratified

THERE ARE A FEW plants whose seeds should be planted as soon as they ripen on the plants. These include angelica and sweet cicely. If this is not possible, as is the case with commercially harvested seeds because the time of harvest doesn't correspond with the time that most customers buy their seeds, then the seeds are collected and placed into cold storage. The process is called cold stratification.

Let's start with our first recommendation to backyard gardeners who can plant their own seeds as they ripen. Prepare a good nursery bed, use a cold frame, or site where you want the plants to grow. Harvest the ripened seeds and cover them lightly with soil. Press the soil firmly, water, and make certain that the seed bed doesn't dry out. Depending on your location and time of planting, you will see growth begin in the fall or spring. Young seedlings may be lifted early in the season and relocated or left to develop in place.

If you cannot or do not want to plant at the end of the season, collect seeds to be stratified and place them immediately in a plastic bag with slightly moistened peat moss to protect them from drying out. Place the bag in a refrigerator or freezer for the winter and sow seed either indoors early in the spring or directly in the ground when the soil can be worked.

Final Cleaning and Storage

THE SEEDS OF FLESHY FRUITS are cleaned for storage once the pulp has been removed and the seeds are dried. Partially dried seeds from the remain-

Fully developed heads from chamomile are filled with very small seeds.

Wait until the seeds of caraway turn brown and dry partially on the stems before collecting. Seeds that fall to the ground naturally will produce volunteers in the garden.

ing plants may be gathered as clean or in need of cleaning after they are brought inside. As a general rule, the more chaff you can remove from seeds before storage, the less likelihood there is for humidity to remain in the storage container. The cleaning process also allows you to eliminate insects and insect eggs that may be hidden in the chaff. At the same time, home gardeners are not expected to clean each and every seed to the standard of commercial seeds, and in many cases would not want to spend the time doing so.

When seeds and their chaff are completely dry, we hand clean and remove large extraneous pods, leaves, and stems from such plants as dill, caraway, peas, beans, and any other relatively large seeds that can be easily and obviously separated. Once the seeds are cleaned, they should be allowed to dry for some additional time as their pods could have slowed the drying process.

Very small seeds like those of the mint family are cleaned with sieves of several sizes. Starting with the largest mesh, you can quickly eliminate the biggest pieces of leaf and stem by rubbing the contents care-

fully through the mesh and discarding the chaff. Work the sifted materials through several sieves, graduating each time to a smaller mesh, until you have been able to remove most of the chaff.

Some members of the Compositae family have very small seeds contained in tight heads and these heads are cleaned of extraneous matter and left intact until you are ready to plant. Examples include chamomile and tansy.

Extremely fine seed such as that of *Artemisia annua* and *Artemisia absinthium* is dried thoroughly in the seed heads and further broken down only when it is time for planting in the spring. See the photograph on page 262, which shows a small processor and various sieves we find helpful in separating and cleaning small seed heads.

As your experience with collecting increases, you will evaluate how much you want to process the seeds in the fall before storing, but whatever techniques you come upon, the most important rule is always be certain that the seeds, including any surrounding material, are as dry as possible before packaging.

Packaging

ONCE SEEDS ARE DRIED, they need to be packaged, labeled, and stored until you are ready to use them, perhaps as soon as the following spring, but maybe not for several years. It is instructive to look at the way that the seed industry packages its seeds to evaluate some of our own packaging options. Most garden seeds are sold in small paper envelopes. Some of the envelopes are more complex in their design and have an inner layer of coated paper, a middle layer that acts as a moisture barrier, and an outer layer for sealing. Any of these paper envelopes protects the seeds in an obvious sense, but paper packaging can absorb moisture if the packages are left in a humid location. That's not to say that paper bags or envelopes are not good holders. We use paper for many of our small dry seeds, but once the seeds are packaged in paper, we store the bags inside larger closed plastic bags or inside containers in a dark dry location where temperatures remain cool all during the year.

Plastic containers and glass containers may also be used to store seeds. Each of these has the advantage of protecting the seeds from insects and rodents. But if used, it is absolutely essential that the seeds are as dry as possible when they are packaged because plastic and glass will not allow moisture out or in.

The seed stalks of garden sorrel are as decorative as they are useful.

Bay fruits need to be left on the plant until they are fully blackened before harvesting. If mature seeds are not planted immediately, they are usually stratified by seed companies until shipment.

Trapped moisture in the containers could allow fungus to develop and completely spoil the contents. Plastic and glass may work for the seeds of dried fruit, but we would not recommend them for large fleshy fruit seeds such as peas and beans. Even though these seeds must be dried before storage, there is a greater risk of spoilage if they are kept in airtight containers.

Whatever packaging you use, make certain that each container is well labeled and dated. If you are collecting a variety of seeds, sort packages into categories such as vegetables, herbs, annuals, perennials, and the like, and group packages in larger storage containers such as coolers, closed boxes, or large tin containers with tightly fitting covers.

Storage Locations and Longevity

SEED LONGEVITY IS the ability of seed to maintain its viability over a period of time. Even under the best of conditions, seeds deteriorate differently. Some species have great longevity, as evidenced by the fact that seeds excavated from ancient tombs were germinated after hundreds of years of dormancy. Some species of plants produce seeds that are not viable after a year, regardless of how well they were processed and stored. The vegetables and herbs discussed in this book are less extremely variable than those two examples and the charts on pages 167 and 232–3 will list each of their predictable storage times for our purposes as home gardeners. If we were equipped with special chambers where we could measure and control the level of drying, the humidity of the storage area, and the temperatures for different species, we could store many seeds for longer periods than the chart would indicate. But most of us will make an effort to collect, dry, and store with the tools and conditions of our own homes, and these charts are prepared for those circumstances.

Once the seeds are packaged, find a storage area that is dark and as dry as possible, where temperatures stay as cool as possible year-round without going below freezing. Some seeds may be stored by keeping them in the freezer, but we don't recommend this because it requires a specific moisture content for the seeds, which most of us cannot measure at home. Remember that animals, especially rodents, eat seeds, so use closed containers to protect them. Some seed savers use desiccants in their large containers, or even in individual seed packages, to remove even more humidity from the storage environment. We don't feel the need for this in our location, but would certainly consider using them if we gardened near the coast or in a warmer more humid part of the country. Desiccants are usually made up of silica gel, ground into various sizes.

If you are new to seed collecting, you may want to check your stored seeds from time to time for the first

A small food processor and a variety of sieves are used to beat and clean small seeds from their chaff.

Several varieties of potatoes that will be saved for seeding. Unlike many other crops, even the small potatoes can be planted for vigorous crops.

year or two. Make certain that the location is dry enough so that any paper bags or envelopes are still completely dry to the touch. If you are using sealed plastic and glass containers, look inside to see if the contents are as you packaged them (dry, insect free, and fungus free). This process of evaluating will allow you to adapt your drying and packaging techniques to the types of seeds you are saving. You will learn to refine your practices.

Simply because a seed is listed as having an aver-

age period of longevity, don't assume that you cannot use seeds stored beyond that time. We frequently screen our collection of seeds and before disposing of any, we perform a simple germination test to measure viability (see sidebar on page 253). As we mentioned early in the chapter, our own garden seeds often demonstrate good longevity and garden vigor. You will come to count on your own work for the same kind of performance.

Bibliography

Barton, Barbara J. *Gardening by Mail*. Boston: Houghton Mifflin, 1997.

Bailey, L. H. *How Plants Get Their Names*. New York: Dover, 1963.

Becker, Jim, and Faye Brawner. *Scented Geraniums*. Loveland, Colo.: Interweave Press, 1996.

Bown, Deni, ed. *Encyclopedia of Herbs*. New York: Dorling Kindersley, 1995.

Bremness, Lesley. *The Complete Book of Herbs*. New York: Viking, 1988.

Brickell, Christopher, ed. *Encyclopedia of Gardening*. New York: Dorling Kindersley, 1993.

Bubel, Nancy. *The New Seed Starter's Handbook*. Emmaus, Pa.: Rodale Press, 1988.

Bush-Brown, James, and Louise Bush-Brown. *America's Garden Book*. New York: Scribners, 1965.

Carr, Anna. *Color Handbook of Garden Insects*. Emmaus, Pa.: Rodale Press, 1979.

Coombes, Allen J. *Dictionary of Plant Names*. Portland, Ore.: Timber Press, 1985.

Copeland, L. O., and M. B. McDonald. *Principles of Seed Science and Technology*. New York: Macmillan, 1985.

Cravens, Richard H. *Pests and Diseases*. Alexandria, Va.: Time Life Books, 1976.

Crockett, James U. *Herbs*. New York: Time Life, 1977.

Davies, Dilys. *Alliums*. Portland, Ore.: Timber Press, 1992.

Deno, Norman C. *Seed Germination Theory and Practice*. 2d ed. State College, Pa.: self-published, 1993.

Encyclopedia of Organic Gardening. Emmaus, Pa.: Rodale Press, 1978.

Foster, Gertrude B. *Herbs for Every Garden*. New York: E. P. Dutton, 1973.

Foster, Gertrude B., and Rosemary F. Louder. *Park's Success with Herbs*. Greenwood, S.C.: Park Seed Co., 1980.

Foster, Steven, and James A. Duke. *Medicinal Plants: A Field Guide*. Boston: Houghton Mifflin, 1990.

Haring, Elda. *The Complete Book of Growing Plants from Seed*. New York: Hawthorn Books, 1967.

Heffernan, Maureen. *Burpee Seed Starter*. New York: Macmillan, 1996.

Hill, Albert F. *Economic Botany*. New York: McGraw-Hill, 1952.

Hortus Third. New York: Macmillan, 1976.

Jabs, Carolyn. *The Heirloom Gardener*. San Francisco: Sierra Club, 1984.

Johnson, Judith B. *The Heritage of Our Maine Wildflowers*. Rockland, Maine: Courier of Maine Books, 1978.

Johnston, Rob. *Growing Garden Seeds*. Albion, Maine: Johnnys Selected Seeds, 1976.

Justice, Oren L., and Louis N. Bass. *Principles and Practices of Seed Storage* (USDA Handbook 506). Washington, D.C.: USDA, 1978.

Nau, Jim. *Ball Culture Guide*. West Chicago, Ill.: Ball Seed, 1989.

Phillips, Roger, and Nicki Foy. *Herbs*. New York: Random House, 1990.

Rickett, Harold William. *Botany for Gardeners*. New York: Macmillan, 1957.

Rogers, Marc. *Growing and Saving Vegetable Seeds*. Pownal, Vt.: Garden Way, 1978.

Smith, Leona. *The Forgotten Art of Flower Cookery*. New York: Harper and Row, 1973.

Smith, Miranda, and Anna Carr. *Garden Insect, Disease and Weed Identification Guide*. Emmaus, Pa.: Rodale Press, 1979.

Solomon, Steve. *Growing Vegetables West of the Cascades*. Seattle, Wash.: Sasquatch Books, 1989.

Stern, William T. *Botanical Latin*. London: David and Charles, 1983.

Sugden, Andrew Longman. *Illustrated Dictionary of Botany*. Harlow, Essex: Longman York Press, 1984.

Taylor's Guide to Vegetables & Herbs. Boston: Houghton Mifflin, 1987.

Westcott, Cynthia. *The Gardener's Bug Book*. New York: Doubleday, 1973.

Whealy, Kent. *Garden Seed Inventory*. 2d ed. Decorah, Iowa: Seed Saver Publications, 1988.

Index

Page numbers in *italics* refer to illustrations.

266

A Note About the Authors

Mark Silber and Terry Silber are gardeners, experts on everlastings, designers, writers, and co-founders of Hedgehog Hill Farm in Sumner, Maine. Mark has his A.B. in biology from Harvard and his Ph.D. from Boston University in medical anthropology. Mark is the author of *Rural Maine* and *Racing Stock,* and editor of *Family Album* and *Thoreau Country.* Terry Silber has her B.A. in French from the University of New Hampshire. She has been on the staffs of the Smithsonian Astrophysical Observatory and *Harvard Magazine.* From 1970 to 1978, she was art director for the *Atlantic Monthly.* She is the author of *A Small Farm in Maine.* Together, the Silbers authored *The Complete Book of Everlastings.*

A Note on the Type

This book was set in Fairfield, the first typeface from the hand of the distinguished American artist and engraver Rudolph Ruzicka (1883–1978). In its structure Fairfield displays the sober and sane qualities of the master craftsman whose talent has long been dedicated to clarity. It is this trait that accounts for the trim grace and vigor, the spirited design and sensitive balance, of this original typeface.

Rudolph Ruzicka was born in Bohemia and came to America in 1894. He designed and illustrated many books, and was the creator of a considerable list of individual prints—wood engravings, line engravings on copper, and aquatints.

Composed by North Market Street Graphics,
Lancaster, Pennsylvania

Printed and bound by R. R. Donnelley & Sons,
Roanoke, Virginia

Designed by Cassandra J. Pappas